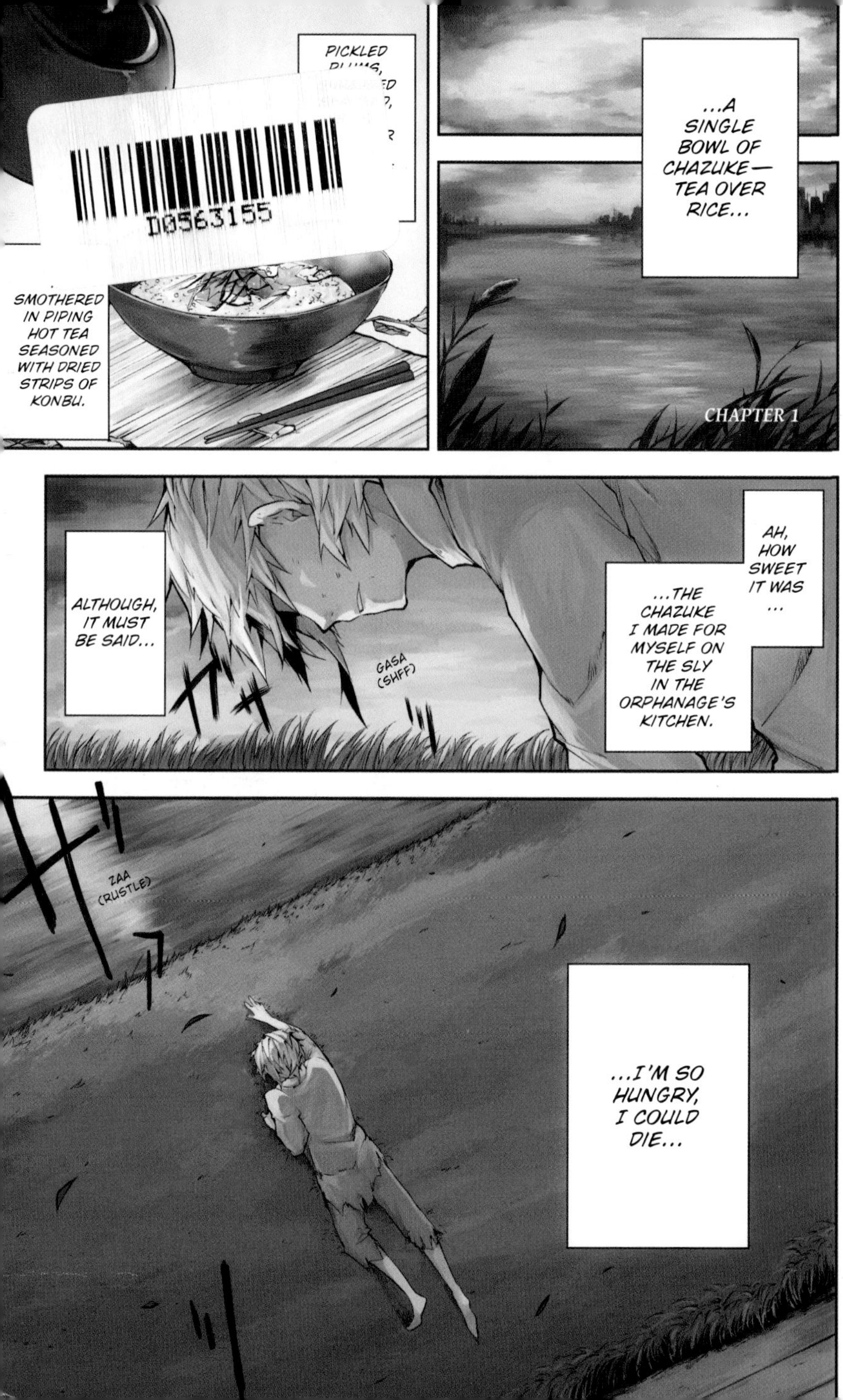

...A SINGLE BOWL OF CHAZUKE— TEA OVER RICE...
CHAPTER 1
PICKLED
SMOTHERED IN PIPING HOT TEA SEASONED WITH DRIED STRIPS OF KONBU.
AH, HOW SWEET IT WAS...
...THE CHAZUKE I MADE FOR MYSELF ON THE SLY IN THE ORPHANAGE'S KITCHEN.
GASA (SHFF)
ALTHOUGH, IT MUST BE SAID...
...I'M SO HUNGRY, I COULD DIE...
ZAA (RUSTLE)

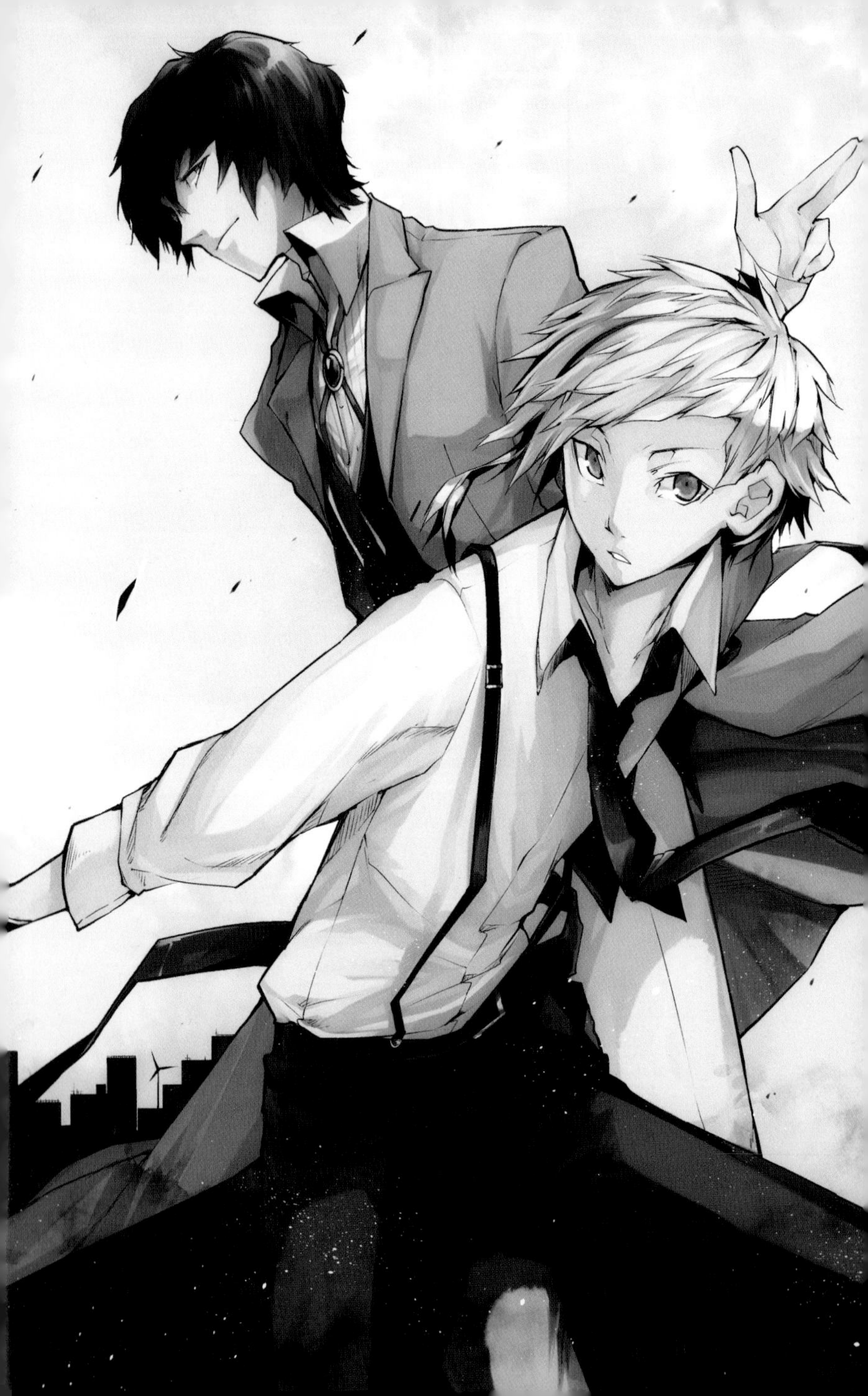

BUNGO STRAY DOGS

Story by KAFKA ASAGIRI Art by SANGO HARUKAWA

CHAPTER 1 *Looking the Gift Tiger in the Mouth*

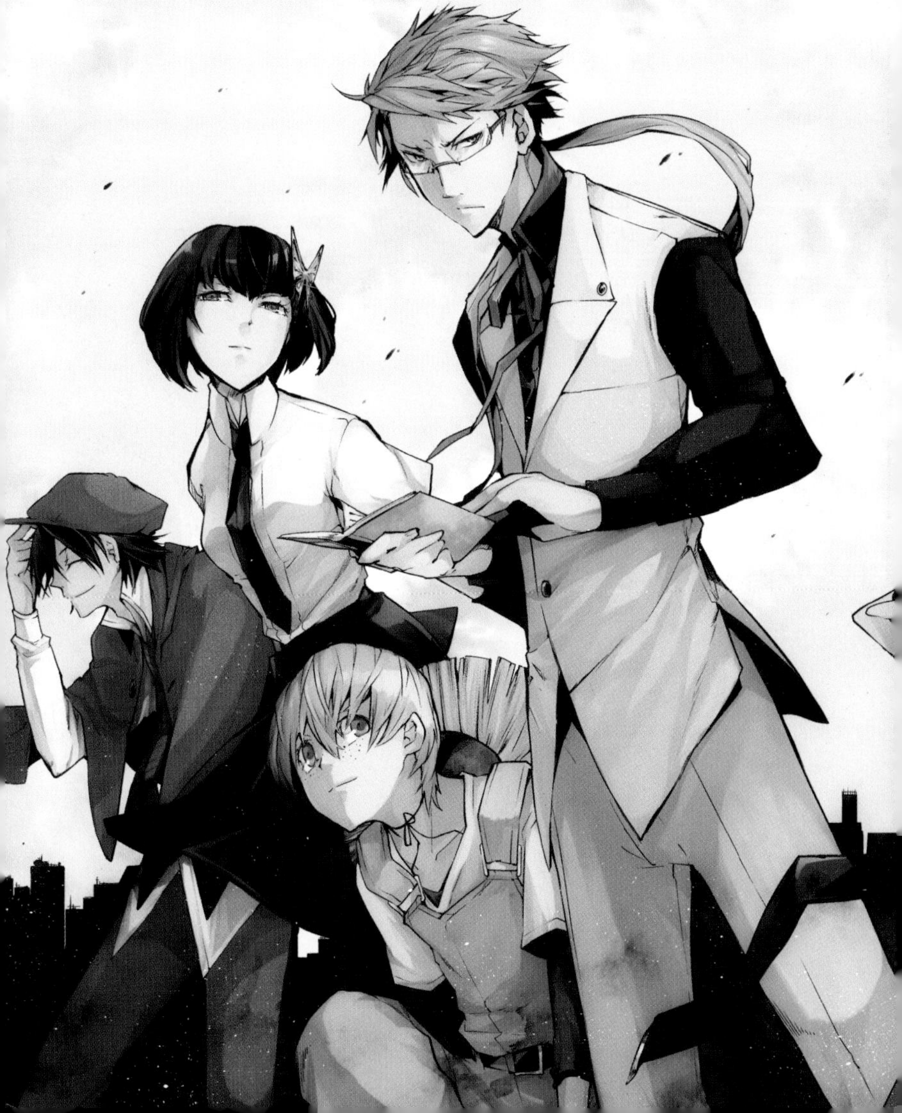

TABLE of CONTENTS

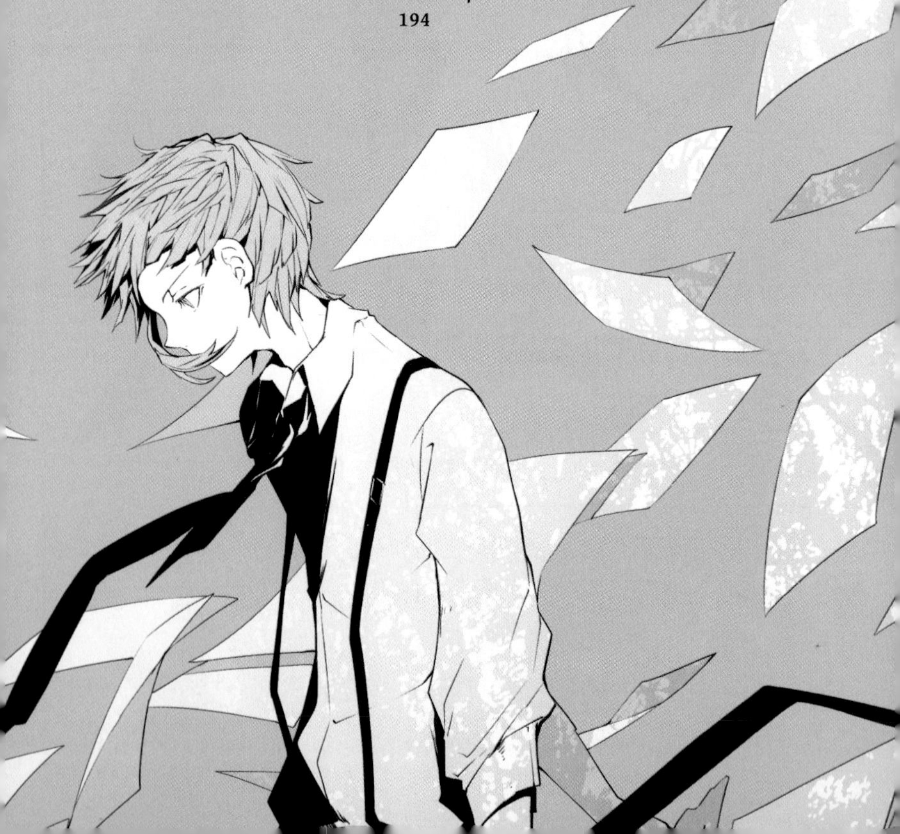

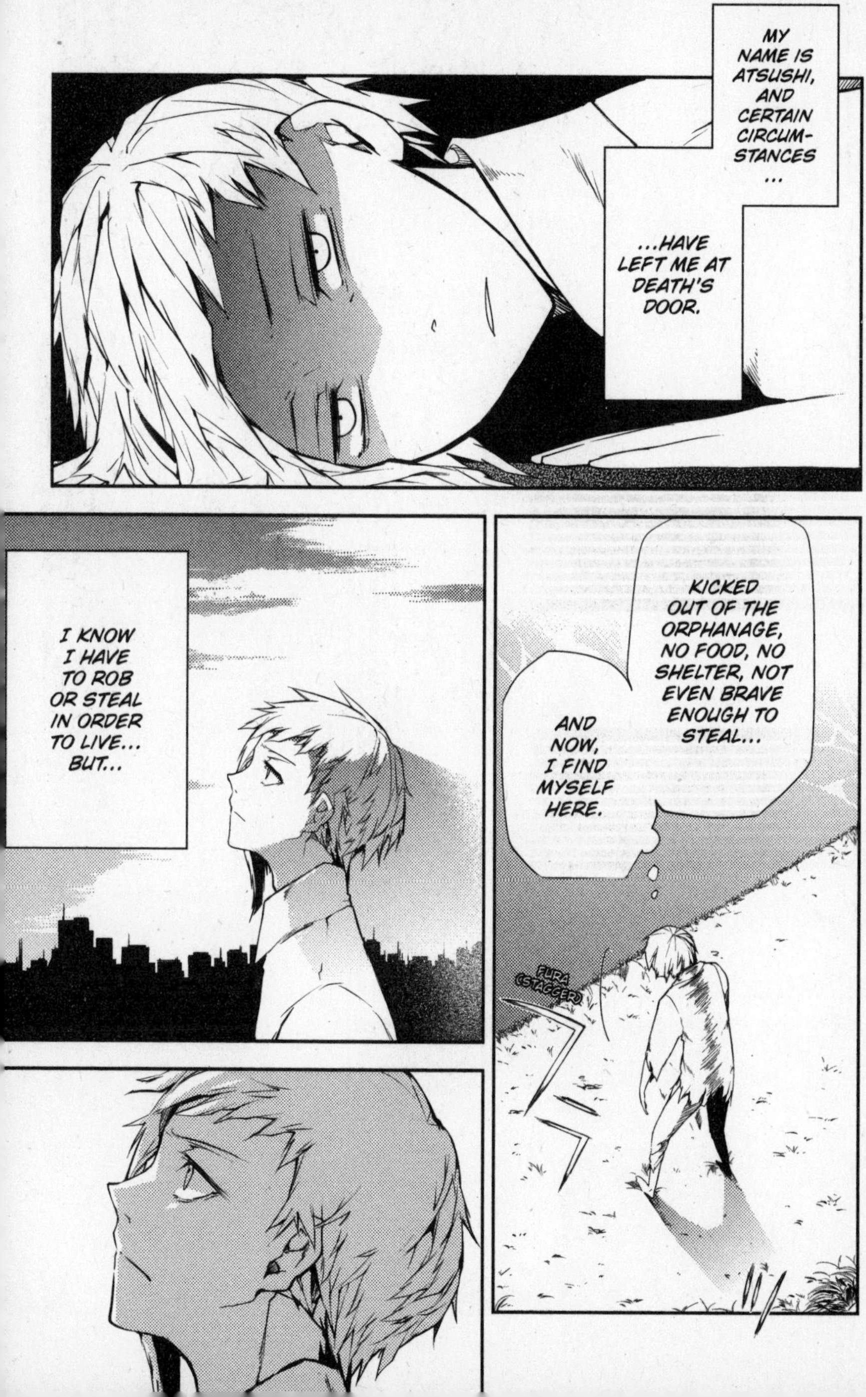
MY NAME IS ATSUSHI, AND CERTAIN CIRCUM-STANCES...
...HAVE LEFT ME AT DEATH'S DOOR.
KICKED OUT OF THE ORPHANAGE, NO FOOD, NO SHELTER, NOT EVEN BRAVE ENOUGH TO STEAL...
AND NOW, I FIND MYSELF HERE.
FURA (STAGGER)
I KNOW I HAVE TO ROB OR STEAL IN ORDER TO LIVE... BUT...

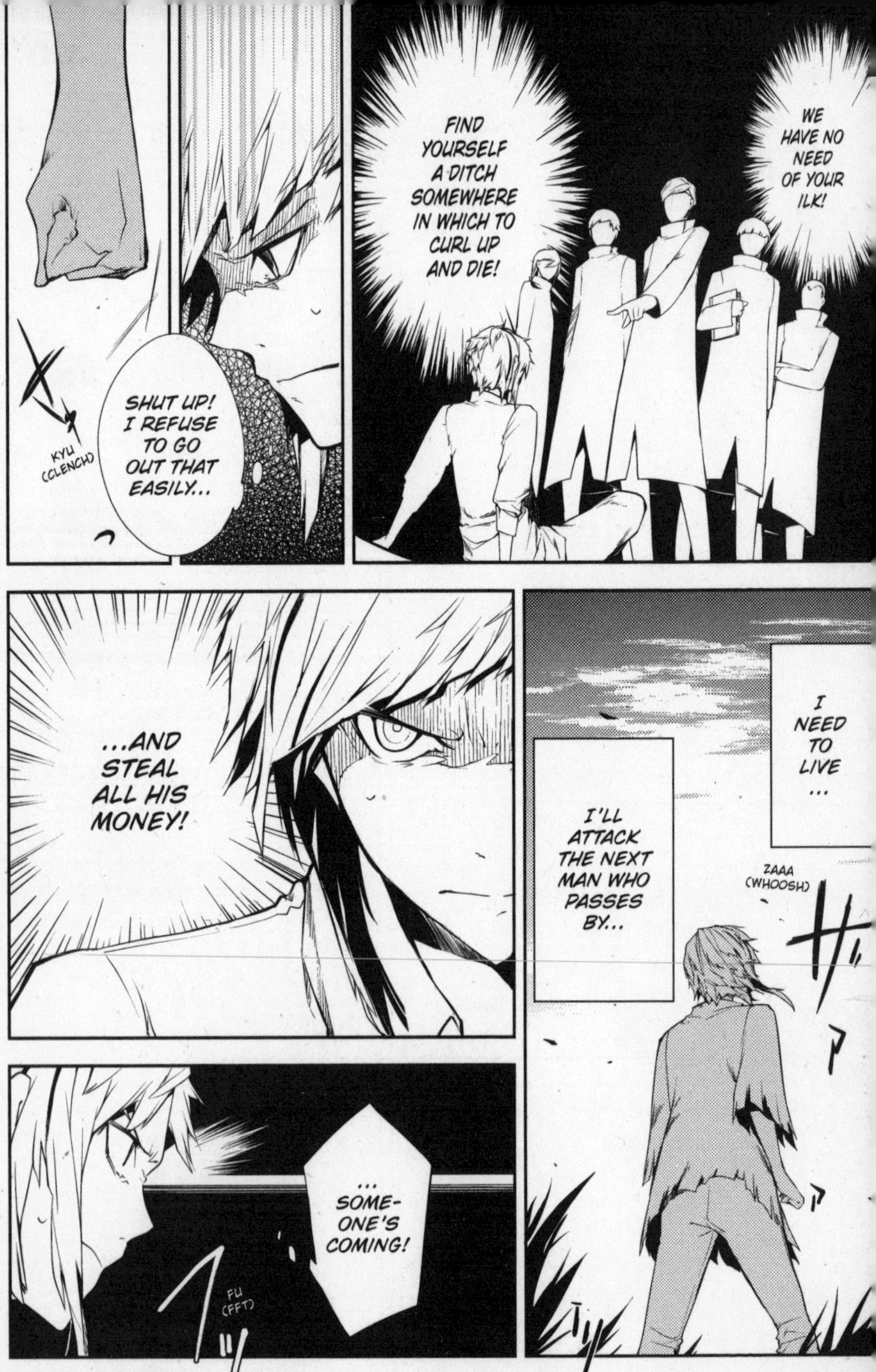
WE HAVE NO NEED OF YOUR ILK!
FIND YOURSELF A DITCH SOMEWHERE IN WHICH TO CURL UP AND DIE!
SHUT UP! I REFUSE TO GO OUT THAT EASILY...
KYU (CLENCH)
I NEED TO LIVE...
I'LL ATTACK THE NEXT MAN WHO PASSES BY...
ZAAA (WHOOSH)
...AND STEAL ALL HIS MONEY!
...SOME-ONE'S COMING!
FU (FFT)

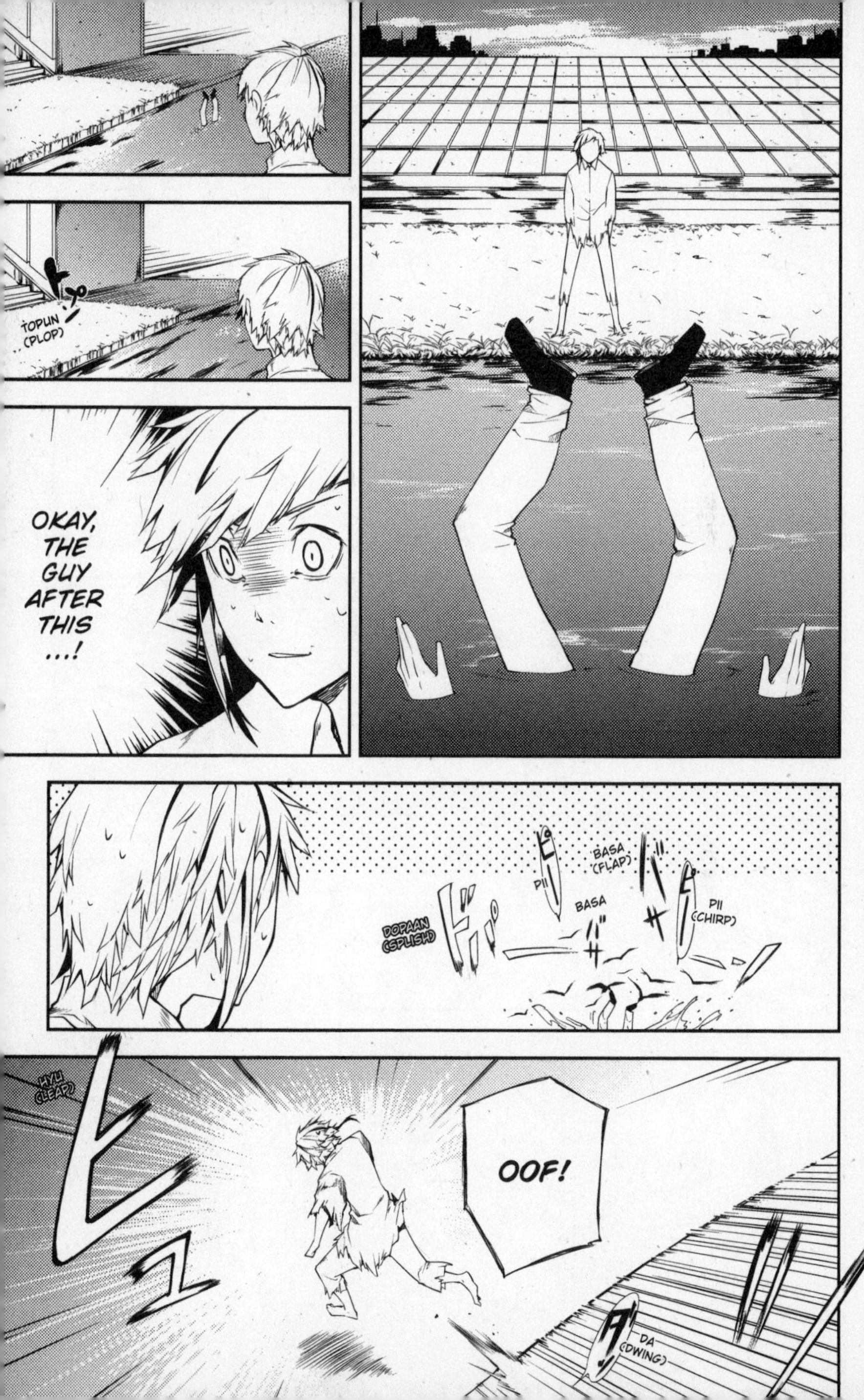
TOPUN (PLOP)
OKAY, THE GUY AFTER THIS ...!
PII (CHIRP)
BASA (FLAP)
PII
BASA
DOPAAN (SPLISH)
OOF!
HYU (LEAP)
DA (DWING)

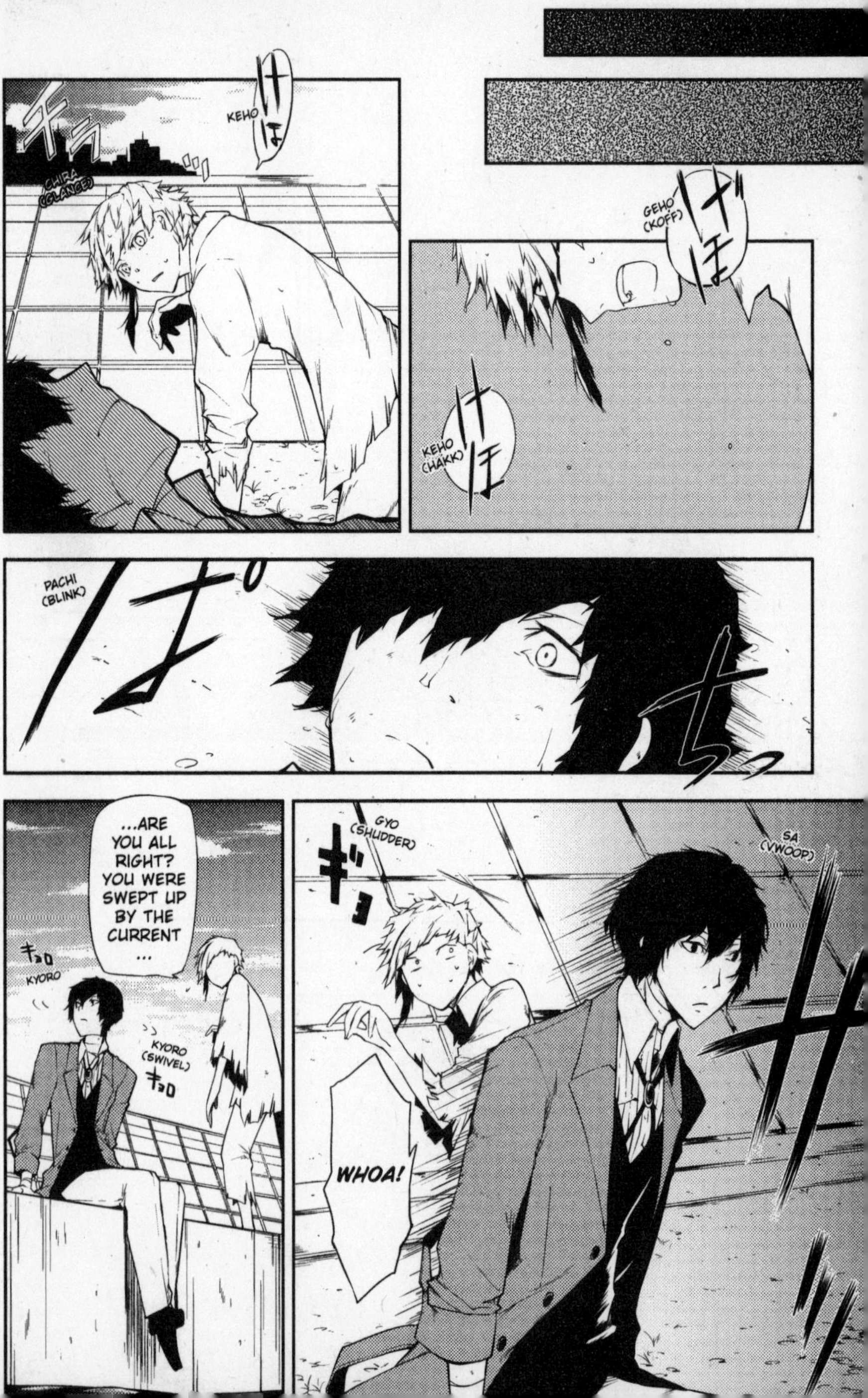

げほ
GEHO (KOFF)
けほ
KEHO (HAKK)
けほ
KEHO
CHIRA (GLANCE)
PACHI (BLINK)
SA (VWOOP)
GYO (SHUDDER)
WHOA!
...ARE YOU ALL RIGHT? YOU WERE SWEPT UP BY THE CURRENT ...
KYORO
KYORO (SWIVEL)

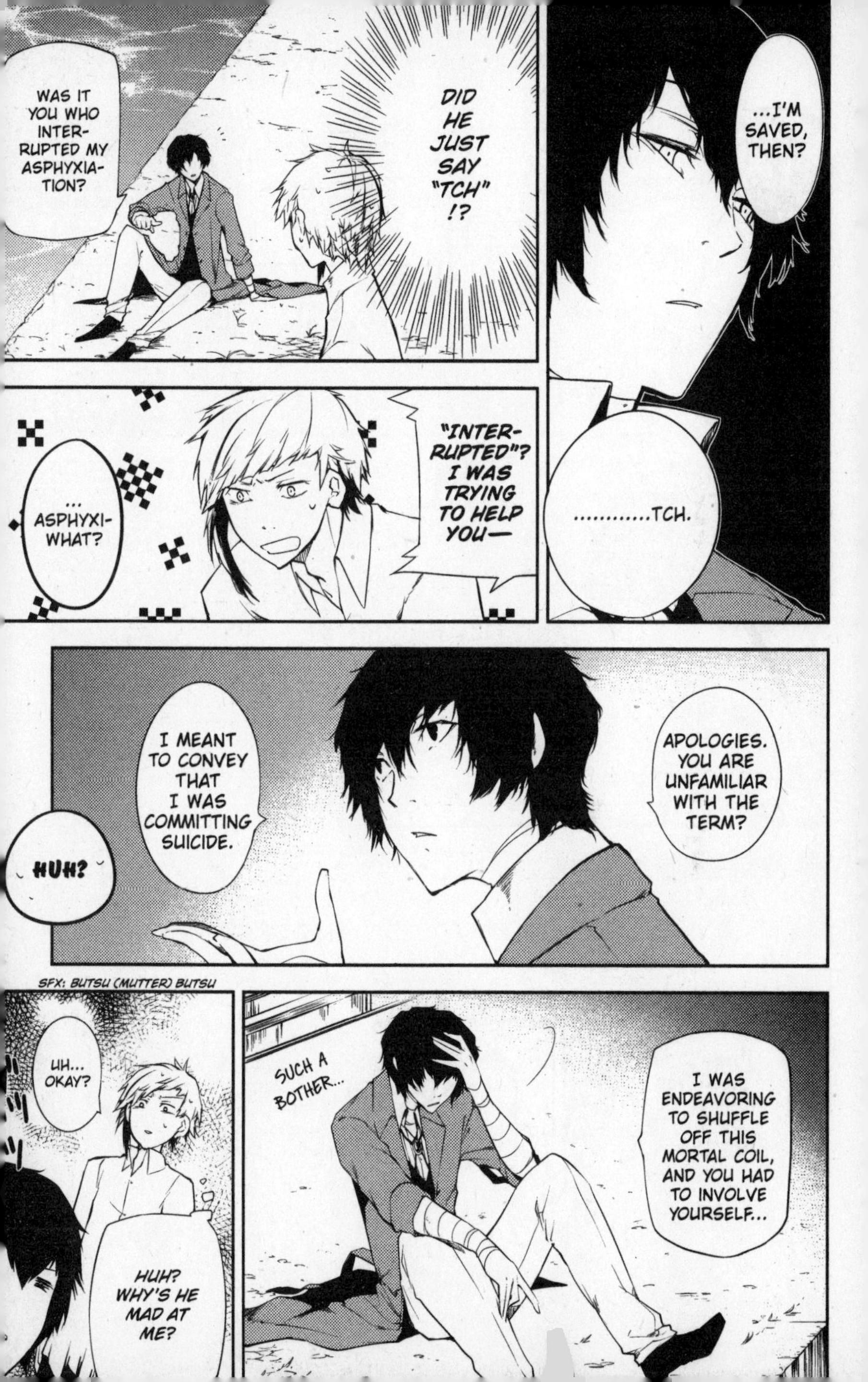
...I'M SAVED, THEN?
............TCH.
DID HE JUST SAY "TCH" !?
WAS IT YOU WHO INTER-RUPTED MY ASPHYXIA-TION?
"INTER-RUPTED"? I WAS TRYING TO HELP YOU—
... ASPHYXI-WHAT?
APOLOGIES. YOU ARE UNFAMILIAR WITH THE TERM?
I MEANT TO CONVEY THAT I WAS COMMITTING SUICIDE.
HUH?
SFX: BUTSU (MUTTER) BUTSU
I WAS ENDEAVORING TO SHUFFLE OFF THIS MORTAL COIL, AND YOU HAD TO INVOLVE YOURSELF...
SUCH A BOTHER...
UH... OKAY?
HUH? WHY'S HE MAD AT ME?

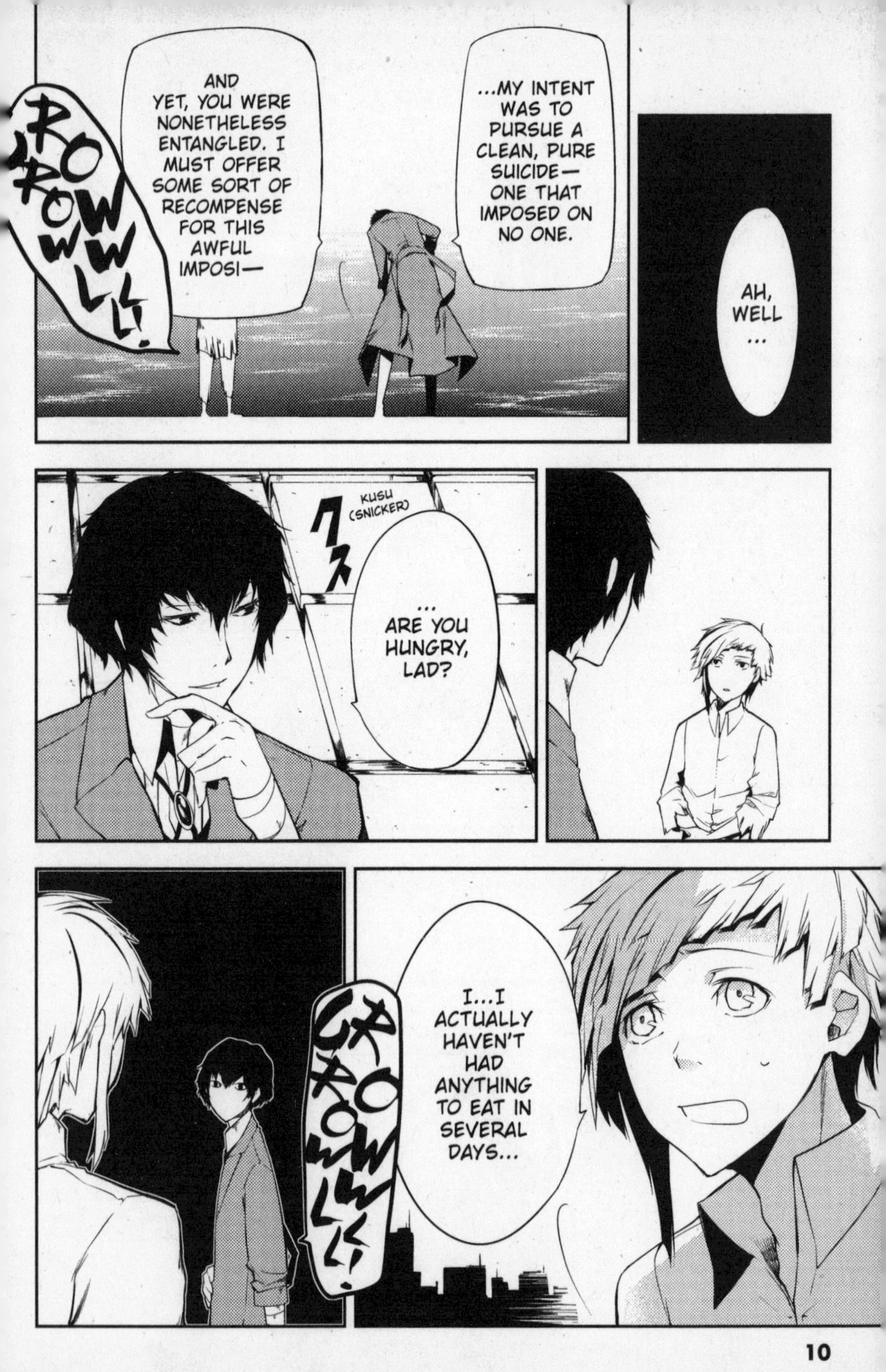
AH, WELL...
...MY INTENT WAS TO PURSUE A CLEAN, PURE SUICIDE—ONE THAT IMPOSED ON NO ONE.
AND YET, YOU WERE NONETHELESS ENTANGLED. I MUST OFFER SOME SORT OF RECOMPENSE FOR THIS AWFUL IMPOSI—
GROWWLL!
クス
KUSU (SNICKER)
...ARE YOU HUNGRY, LAD?
I...I ACTUALLY HAVEN'T HAD ANYTHING TO EAT IN SEVERAL DAYS...
GROWWLLL!

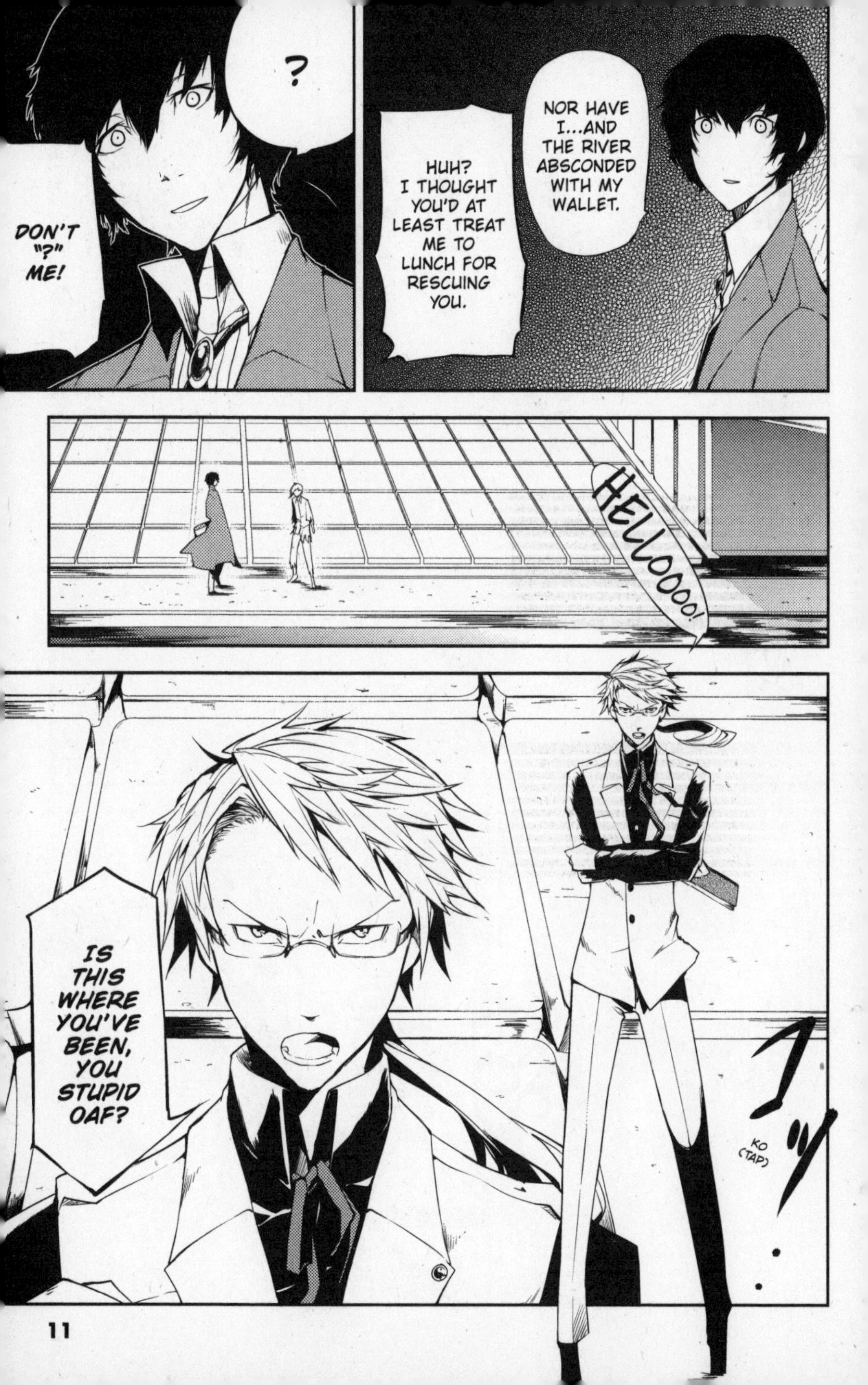
HUH? I THOUGHT YOU'D AT LEAST TREAT ME TO LUNCH FOR RESCUING YOU.
NOR HAVE I...AND THE RIVER ABSCONDED WITH MY WALLET.
?
DON'T "?" ME!
HELLOOOO!
KO (TAP)
IS THIS WHERE YOU'VE BEEN, YOU STUPID OAF?

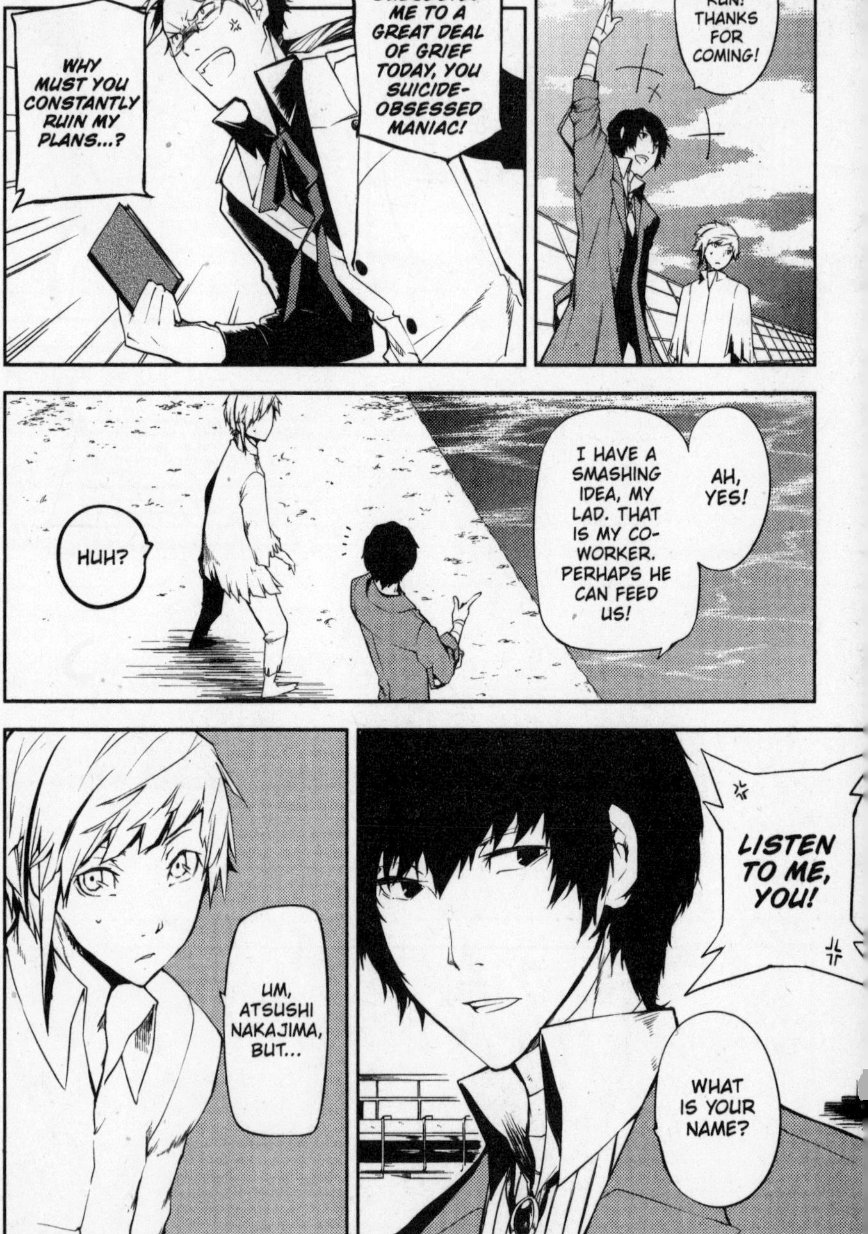
OH! KUNIKIDA-KUN! THANKS FOR COMING!
YOU HAVE SUBJECTED ME TO A GREAT DEAL OF GRIEF TODAY, YOU SUICIDE-OBSESSED MANIAC!
WHY MUST YOU CONSTANTLY RUIN MY PLANS...?
AH, YES!
I HAVE A SMASHING IDEA, MY LAD. THAT IS MY CO-WORKER. PERHAPS HE CAN FEED US!
HUH?
LISTEN TO ME, YOU!
WHAT IS YOUR NAME?
UM, ATSUSHI NAKAJIMA, BUT...

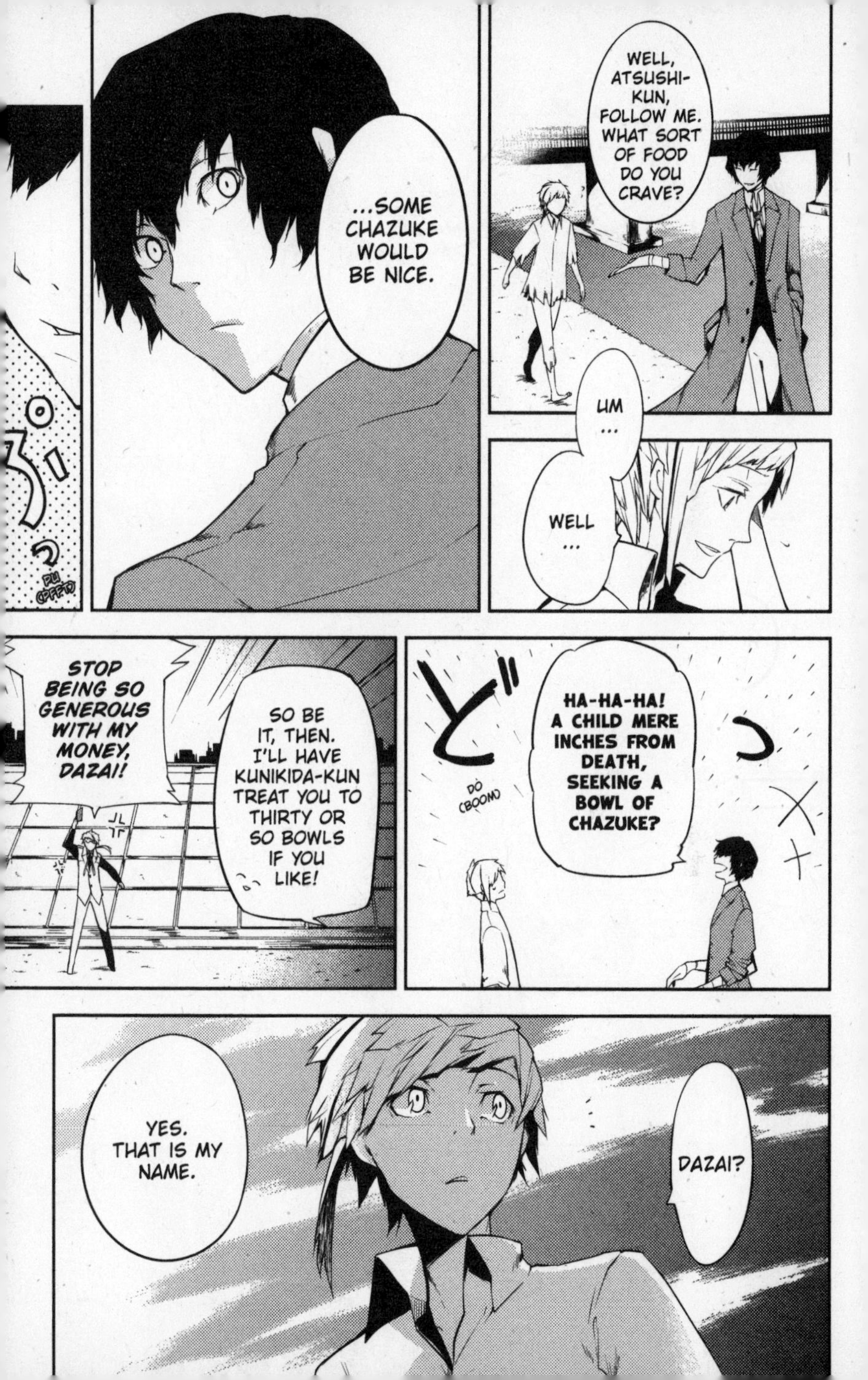
WELL, ATSUSHI-KUN, FOLLOW ME. WHAT SORT OF FOOD DO YOU CRAVE?
UM ...
WELL ...
...SOME CHAZUKE WOULD BE NICE.
PU (PFFT)
DO (BOOM)
HA-HA-HA! A CHILD MERE INCHES FROM DEATH, SEEKING A BOWL OF CHAZUKE?
SO BE IT, THEN. I'LL HAVE KUNIKIDA-KUN TREAT YOU TO THIRTY OR SO BOWLS IF YOU LIKE!
STOP BEING SO GENEROUS WITH MY MONEY, DAZAI!
DAZAI?
YES. THAT IS MY NAME.

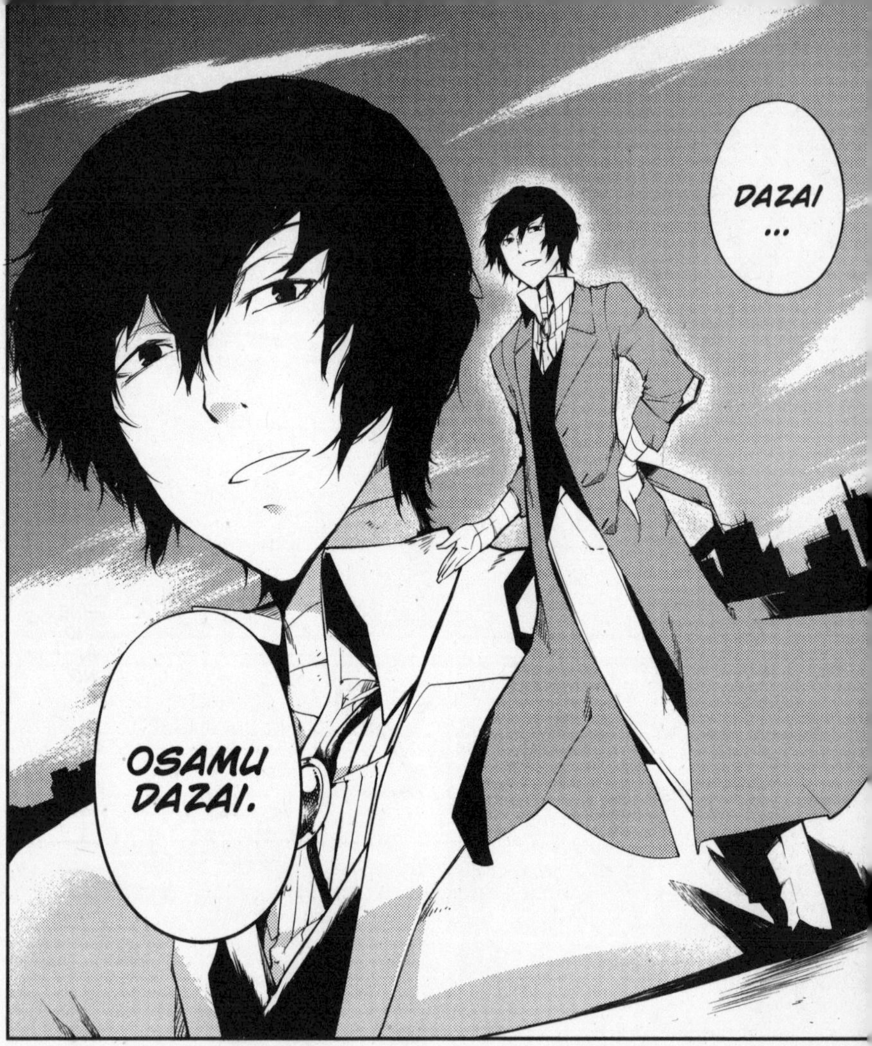
DAZAI ...
OSAMU DAZAI.
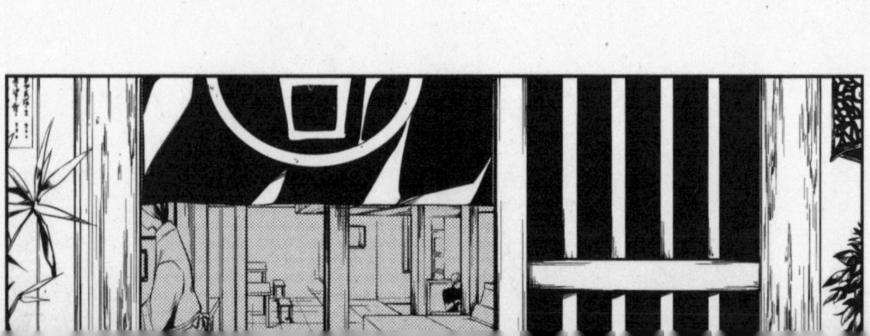

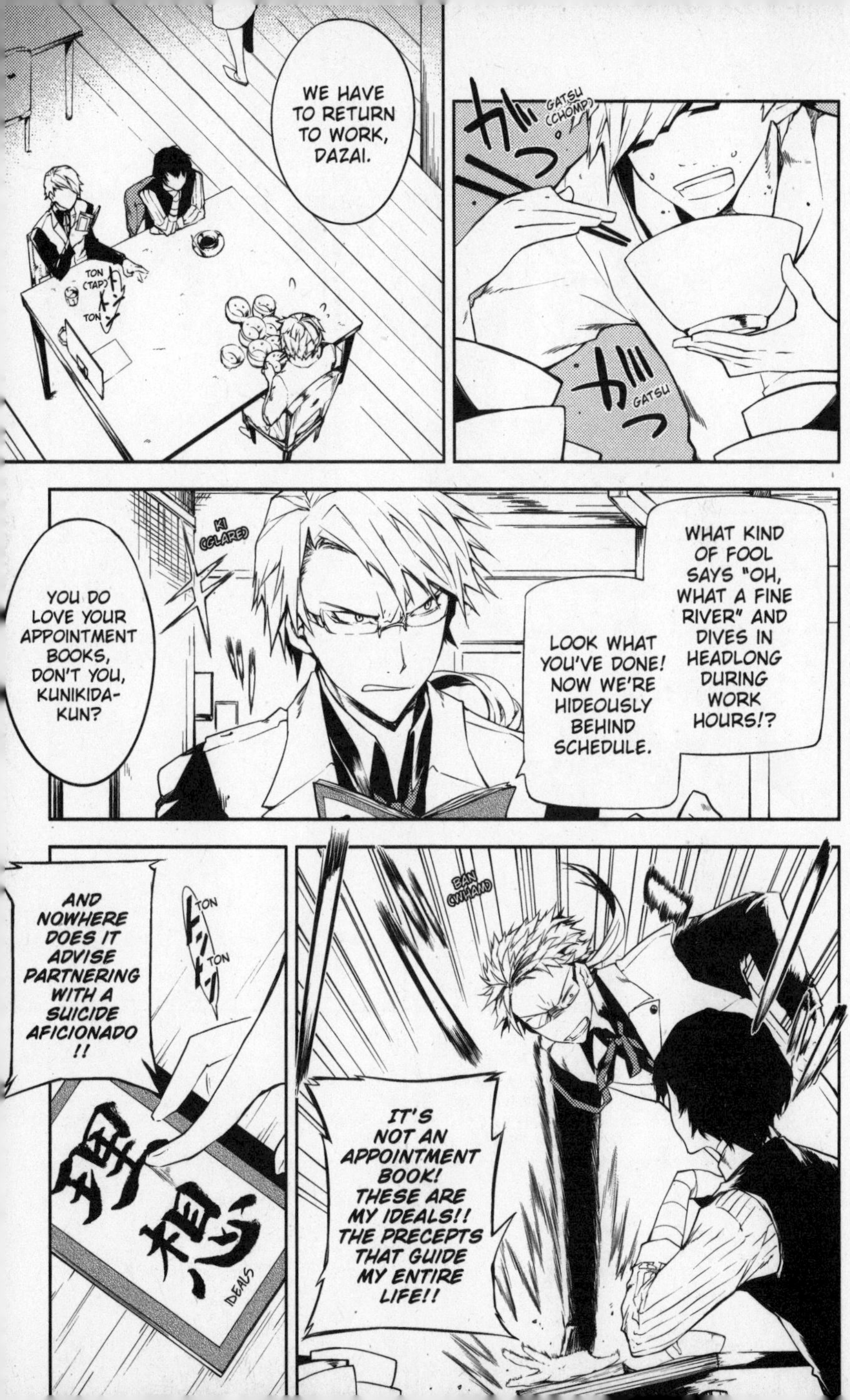
GATSU (CHOMP)
GATSU
WE HAVE TO RETURN TO WORK, DAZAI.
TON (TAP)
TON
WHAT KIND OF FOOL SAYS "OH, WHAT A FINE RIVER" AND DIVES IN HEADLONG DURING WORK HOURS!?
LOOK WHAT YOU'VE DONE! NOW WE'RE HIDEOUSLY BEHIND SCHEDULE.
KI (GLARE)
YOU DO LOVE YOUR APPOINTMENT BOOKS, DON'T YOU, KUNIKIDA-KUN?
BAN (WHAM)
IT'S NOT AN APPOINTMENT BOOK! THESE ARE MY IDEALS!! THE PRECEPTS THAT GUIDE MY ENTIRE LIFE!!
AND NOWHERE DOES IT ADVISE PARTNERING WITH A SUICIDE AFICIONADO!!
TON
TON
IDEALS

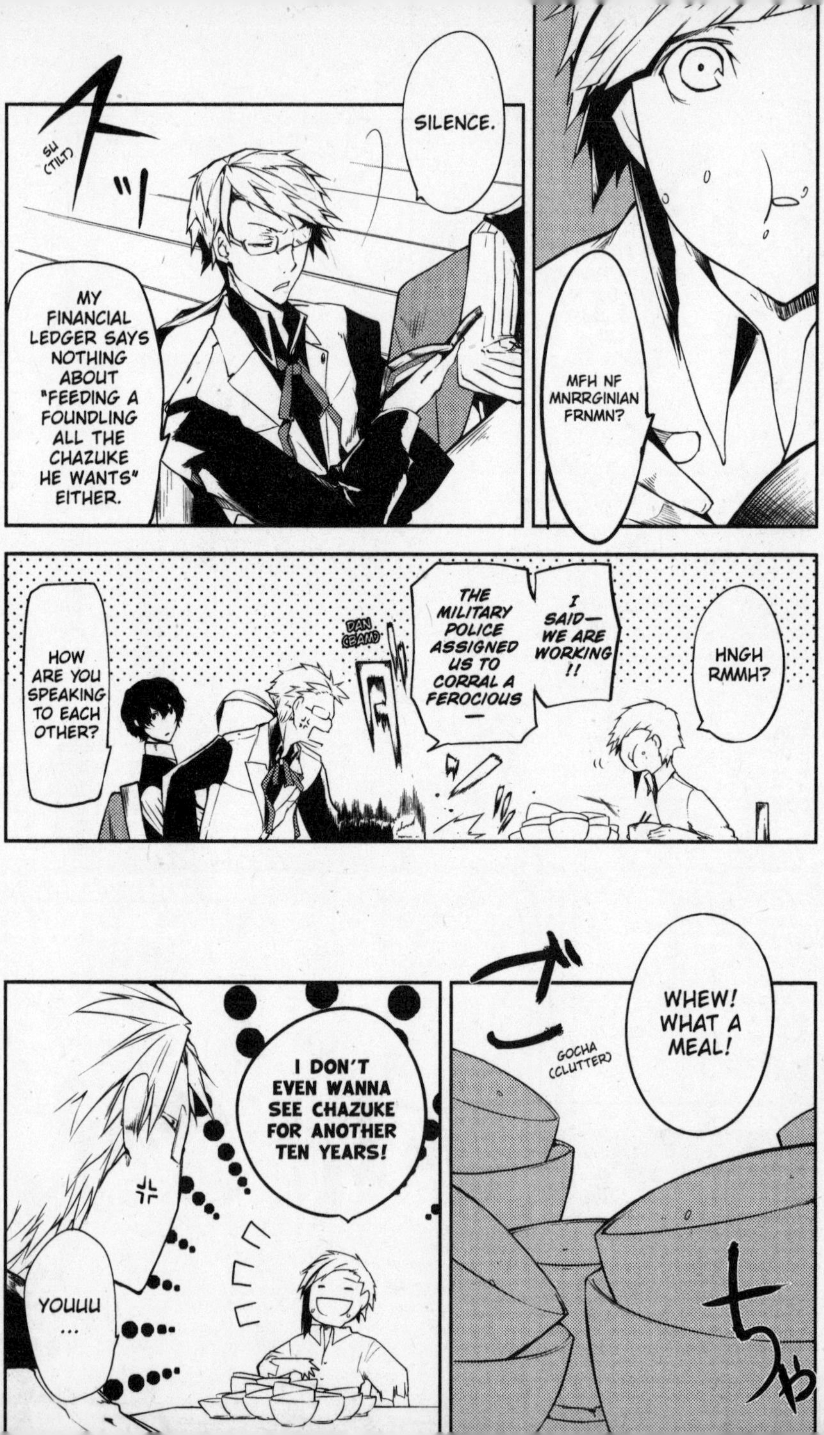
MFH NF MNRRGINIAN FRNMN?
SILENCE.
SU (TILT)
MY FINANCIAL LEDGER SAYS NOTHING ABOUT "FEEDING A FOUNDLING ALL THE CHAZUKE HE WANTS" EITHER.
HNGH RMMH?
I SAID— WE ARE WORKING!!
THE MILITARY POLICE ASSIGNED US TO CORRAL A FEROCIOUS—
DAN (BAM)
HOW ARE YOU SPEAKING TO EACH OTHER?
WHEW! WHAT A MEAL!
GOCHA (CLUTTER)
I DON'T EVEN WANNA SEE CHAZUKE FOR ANOTHER TEN YEARS!
YOUUU...

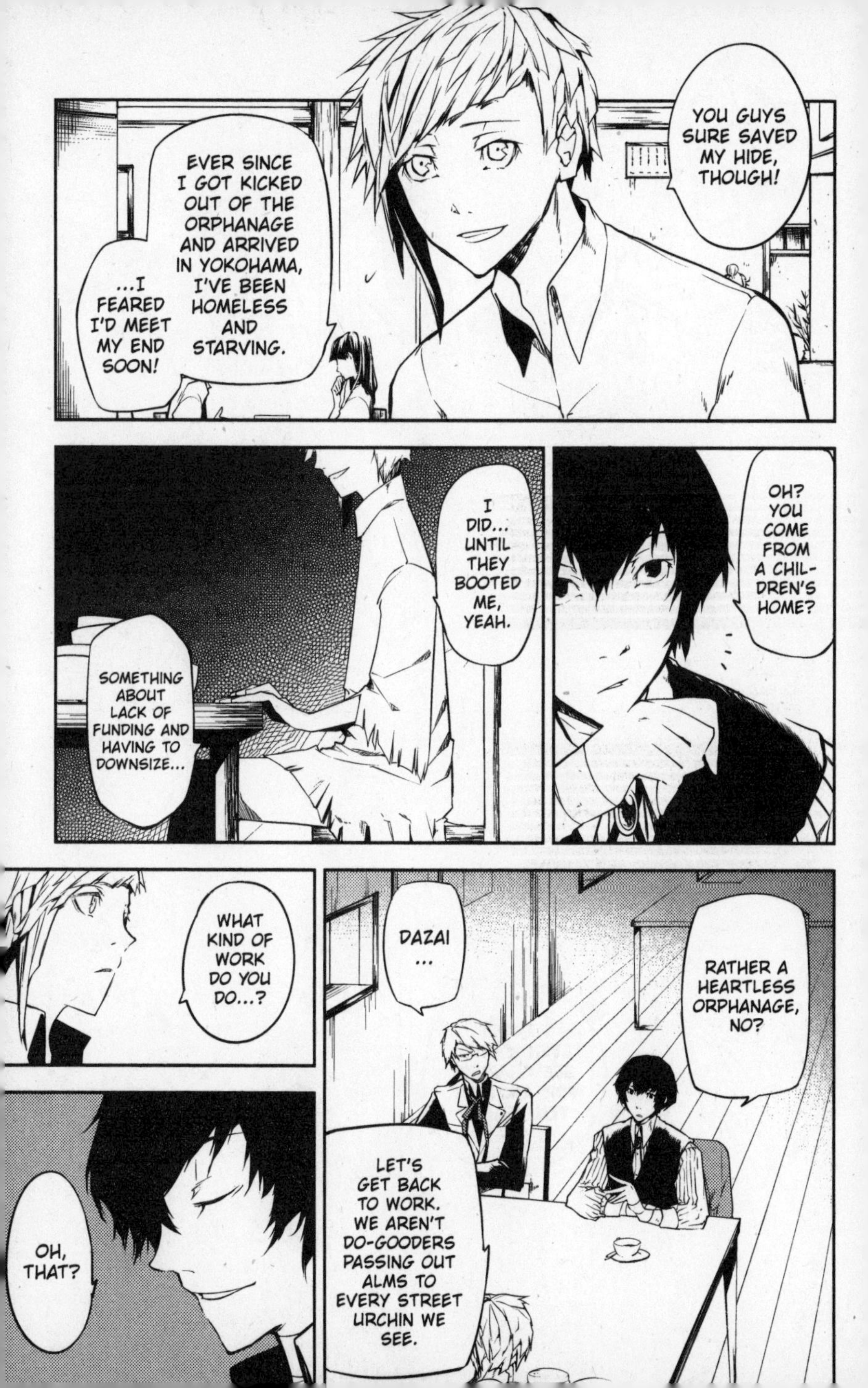

YOU GUYS SURE SAVED MY HIDE, THOUGH!
EVER SINCE I GOT KICKED OUT OF THE ORPHANAGE AND ARRIVED IN YOKOHAMA, I'VE BEEN HOMELESS AND STARVING.
...I FEARED I'D MEET MY END SOON!
OH? YOU COME FROM A CHIL-DREN'S HOME?
I DID... UNTIL THEY BOOTED ME, YEAH.
SOMETHING ABOUT LACK OF FUNDING AND HAVING TO DOWNSIZE...
RATHER A HEARTLESS ORPHANAGE, NO?
DAZAI...
LET'S GET BACK TO WORK. WE AREN'T DO-GOODERS PASSING OUT ALMS TO EVERY STREET URCHIN WE SEE.
WHAT KIND OF WORK DO YOU DO...?
OH, THAT?

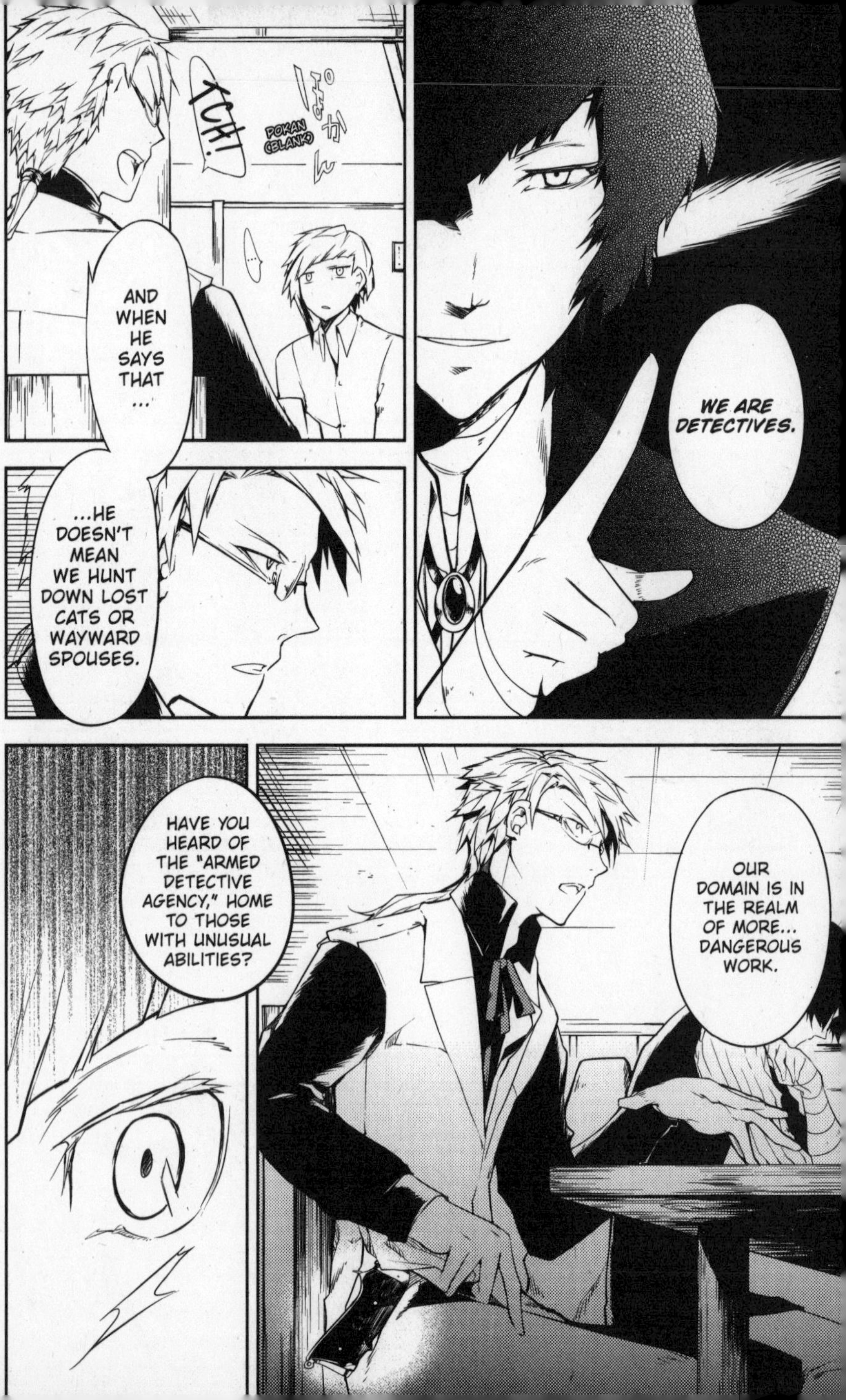
WE ARE DETECTIVES.
TCH!
ぽかん
POKAN (BLANK)
...
AND WHEN HE SAYS THAT...
...HE DOESN'T MEAN WE HUNT DOWN LOST CATS OR WAYWARD SPOUSES.
OUR DOMAIN IS IN THE REALM OF MORE... DANGEROUS WORK.
HAVE YOU HEARD OF THE "ARMED DETECTIVE AGENCY," HOME TO THOSE WITH UNUSUAL ABILITIES?

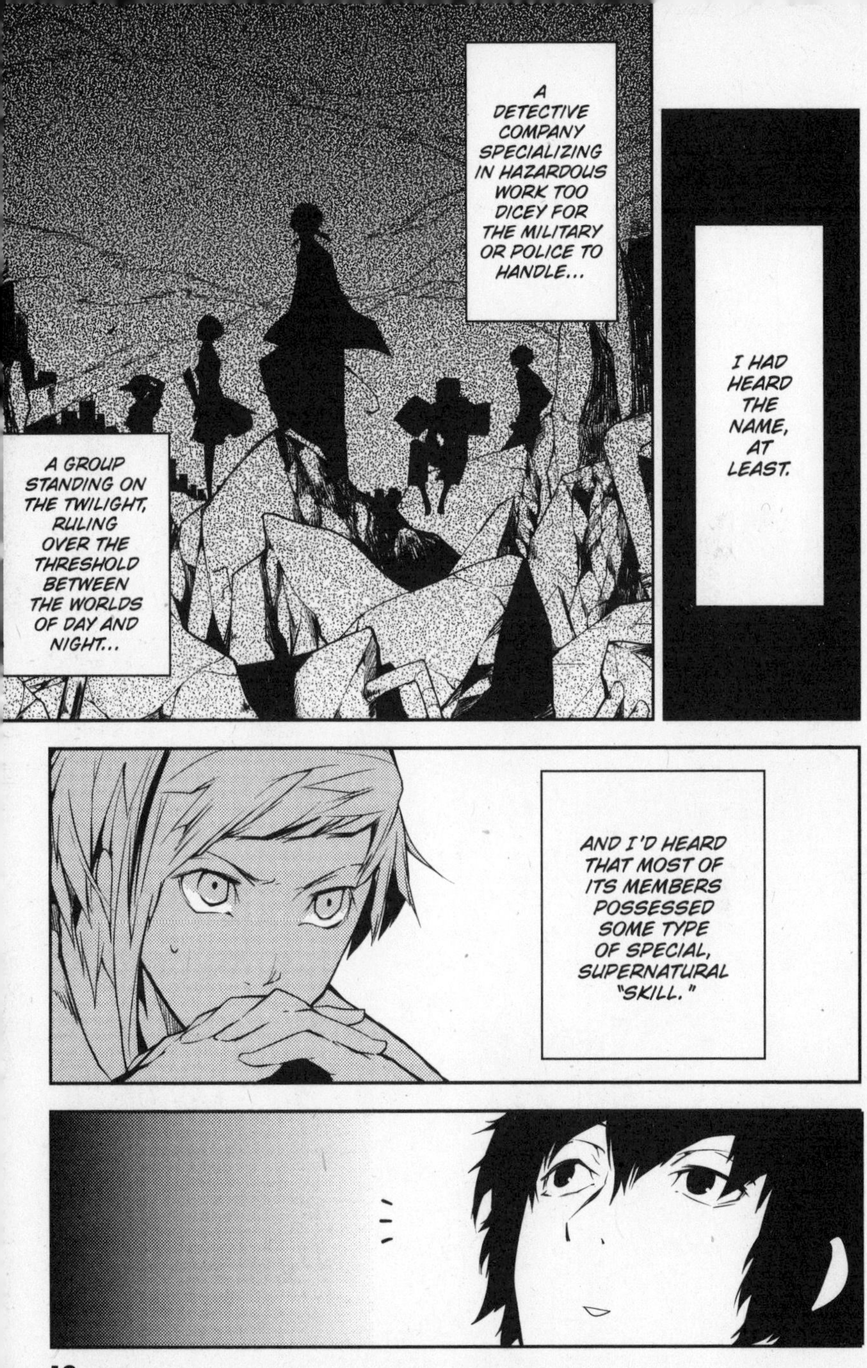
I HAD HEARD THE NAME, AT LEAST.
A DETECTIVE COMPANY SPECIALIZING IN HAZARDOUS WORK TOO DICEY FOR THE MILITARY OR POLICE TO HANDLE...
A GROUP STANDING ON THE TWILIGHT, RULING OVER THE THRESHOLD BETWEEN THE WORLDS OF DAY AND NIGHT...
AND I'D HEARD THAT MOST OF ITS MEMBERS POSSESSED SOME TYPE OF SPECIAL, SUPERNATURAL "SKILL."

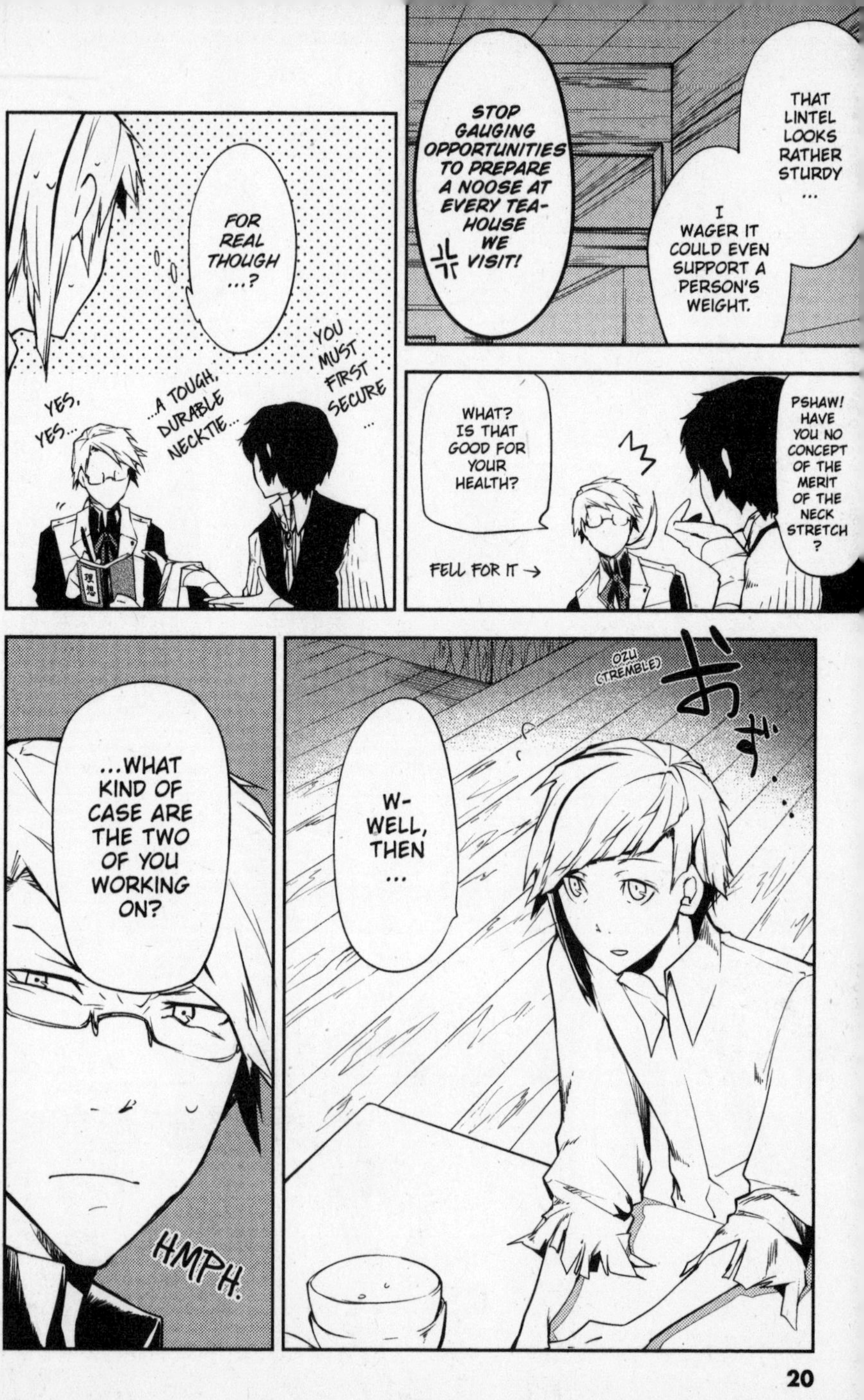
THAT LINTEL LOOKS RATHER STURDY ...
I WAGER IT COULD EVEN SUPPORT A PERSON'S WEIGHT.
STOP GAUGING OPPORTUNITIES TO PREPARE A NOOSE AT EVERY TEA-HOUSE WE VISIT!
PSHAW! HAVE YOU NO CONCEPT OF THE MERIT OF THE NECK STRETCH?
WHAT? IS THAT GOOD FOR YOUR HEALTH?
FELL FOR IT →
FOR REAL THOUGH ...?
YOU MUST FIRST SECURE ...
...A TOUGH, DURABLE NECKTIE...
YES, YES...
理想
おず...
OZU (TREMBLE)
W-WELL, THEN ...
...WHAT KIND OF CASE ARE THE TWO OF YOU WORKING ON?
HMPH.

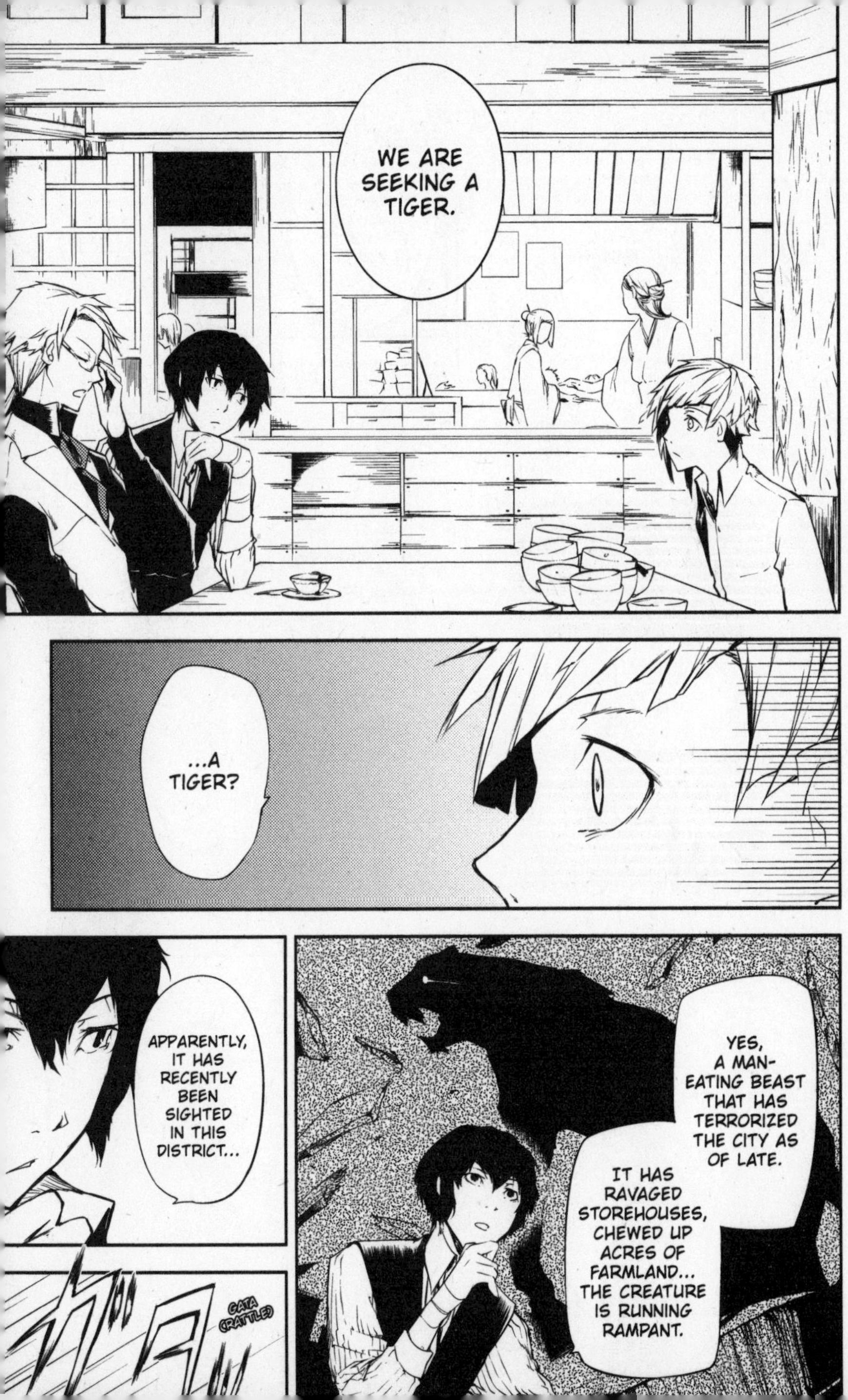
WE ARE SEEKING A TIGER.
...A TIGER?
YES, A MAN-EATING BEAST THAT HAS TERRORIZED THE CITY AS OF LATE.
IT HAS RAVAGED STOREHOUSES, CHEWED UP ACRES OF FARMLAND... THE CREATURE IS RUNNING RAMPANT.
APPARENTLY, IT HAS RECENTLY BEEN SIGHTED IN THIS DISTRICT...
GATA (RATTLE)

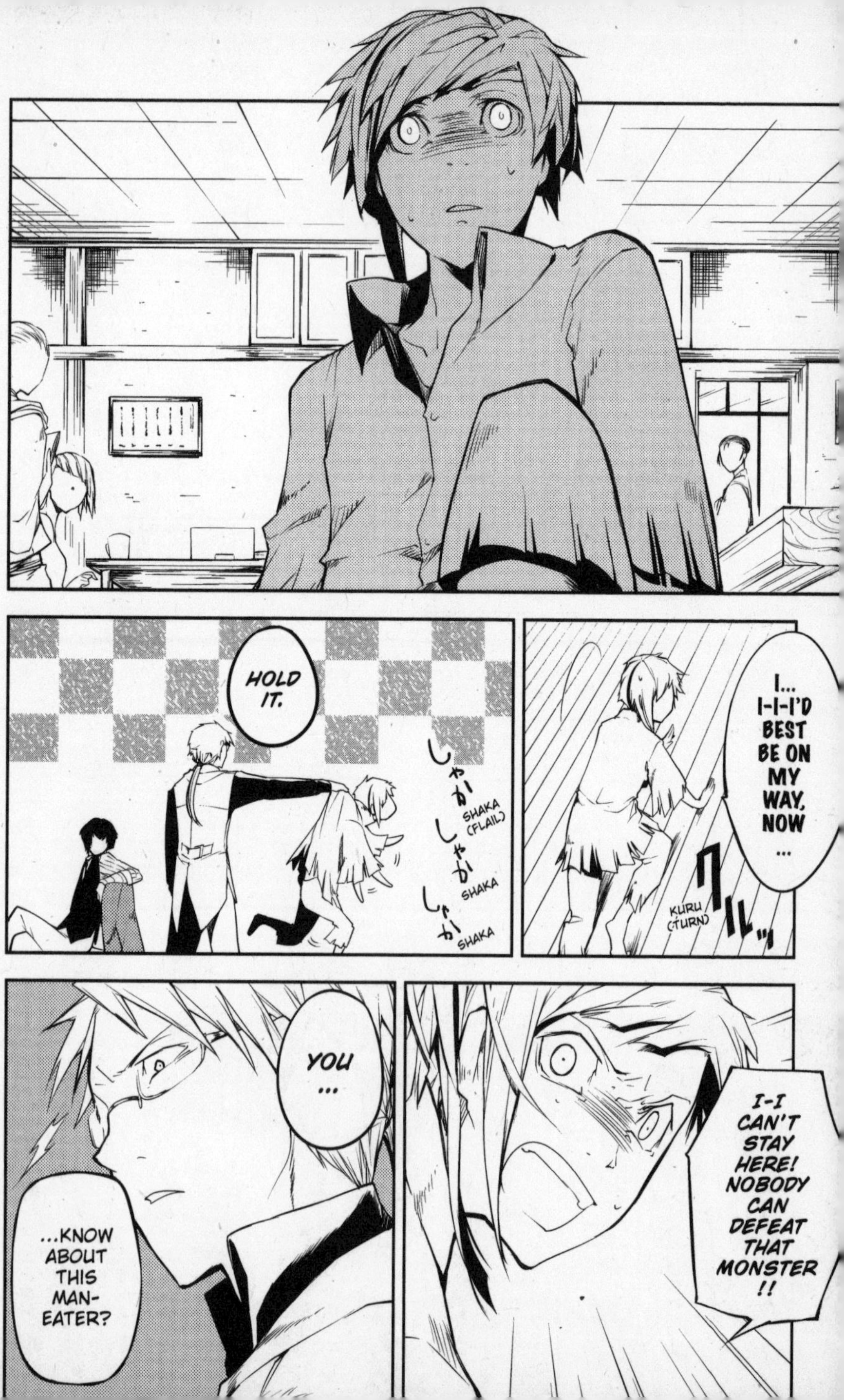
I... I-I-I'D BEST BE ON MY WAY, NOW ...
クルッ
KURU (TURN)
HOLD IT.
しゃか しゃか しゃか
SHAKA (FLAIL)
SHAKA
SHAKA
I-I CAN'T STAY HERE! NOBODY CAN DEFEAT THAT MONSTER!!
YOU ...
...KNOW ABOUT THIS MAN-EATER?

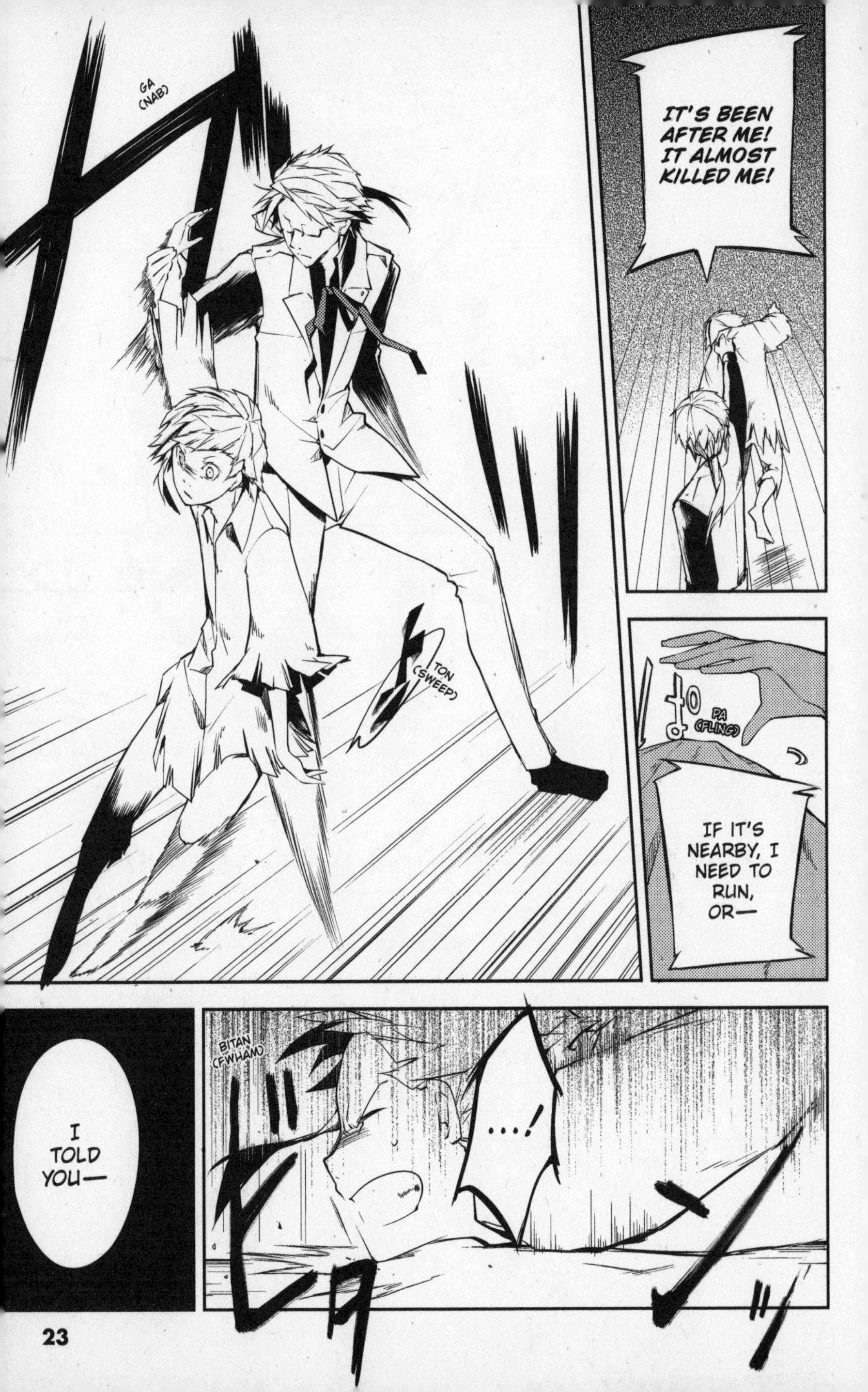

IT'S BEEN AFTER ME! IT ALMOST KILLED ME!
PA (FLING)
IF IT'S NEARBY, I NEED TO RUN, OR—
GA (NAB)
TON (SWEEP)
BITAN (FWHAM)
...!
I TOLD YOU—

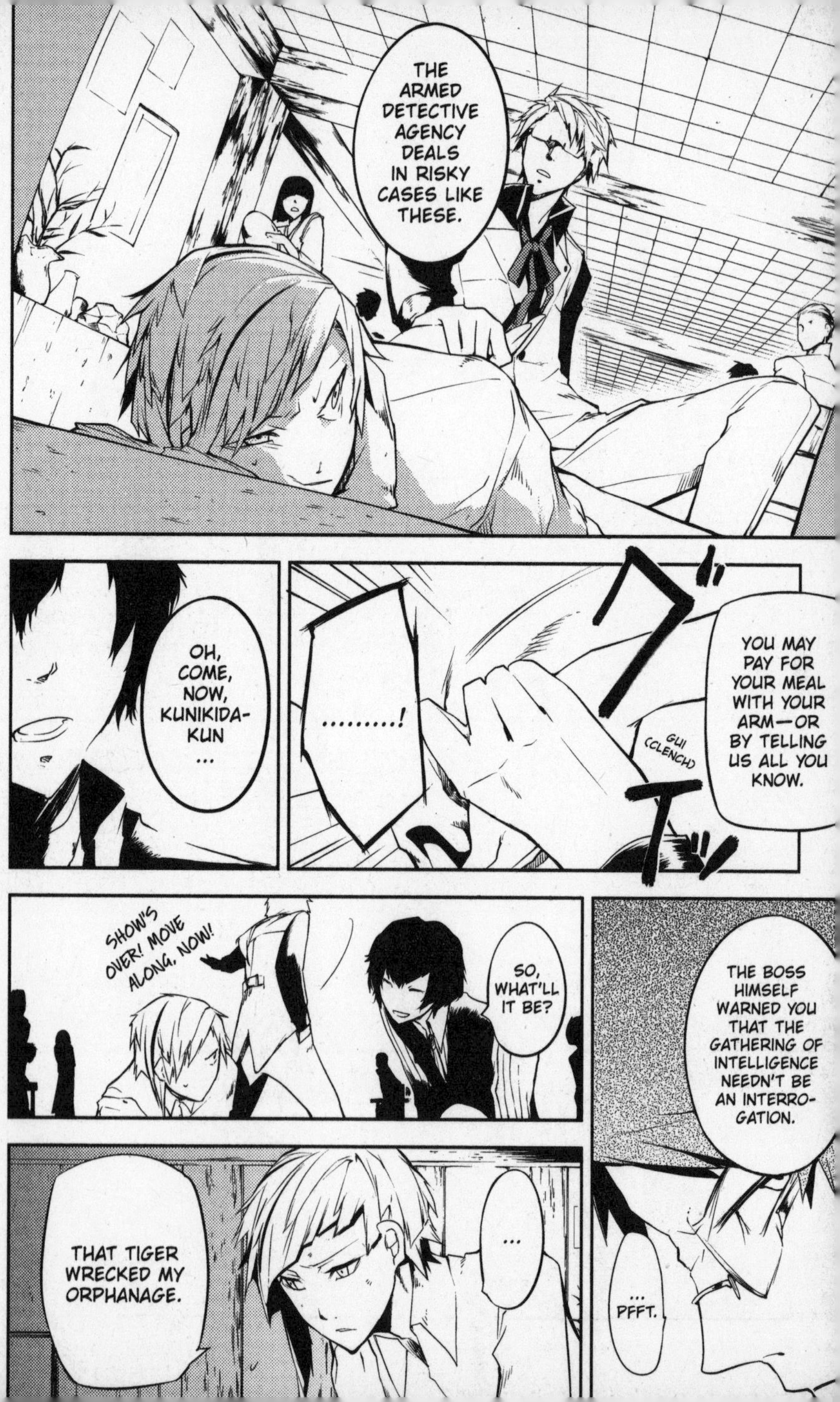
THE ARMED DETECTIVE AGENCY DEALS IN RISKY CASES LIKE THESE.
YOU MAY PAY FOR YOUR MEAL WITH YOUR ARM—OR BY TELLING US ALL YOU KNOW.
GUI (CLENCH)
..........!
OH, COME, NOW, KUNIKIDA-KUN ...
THE BOSS HIMSELF WARNED YOU THAT THE GATHERING OF INTELLIGENCE NEEDN'T BE AN INTERRO-GATION.
... PFFT.
SO, WHAT'LL IT BE?
SHOW'S OVER! MOVE ALONG, NOW!
...
THAT TIGER WRECKED MY ORPHANAGE.

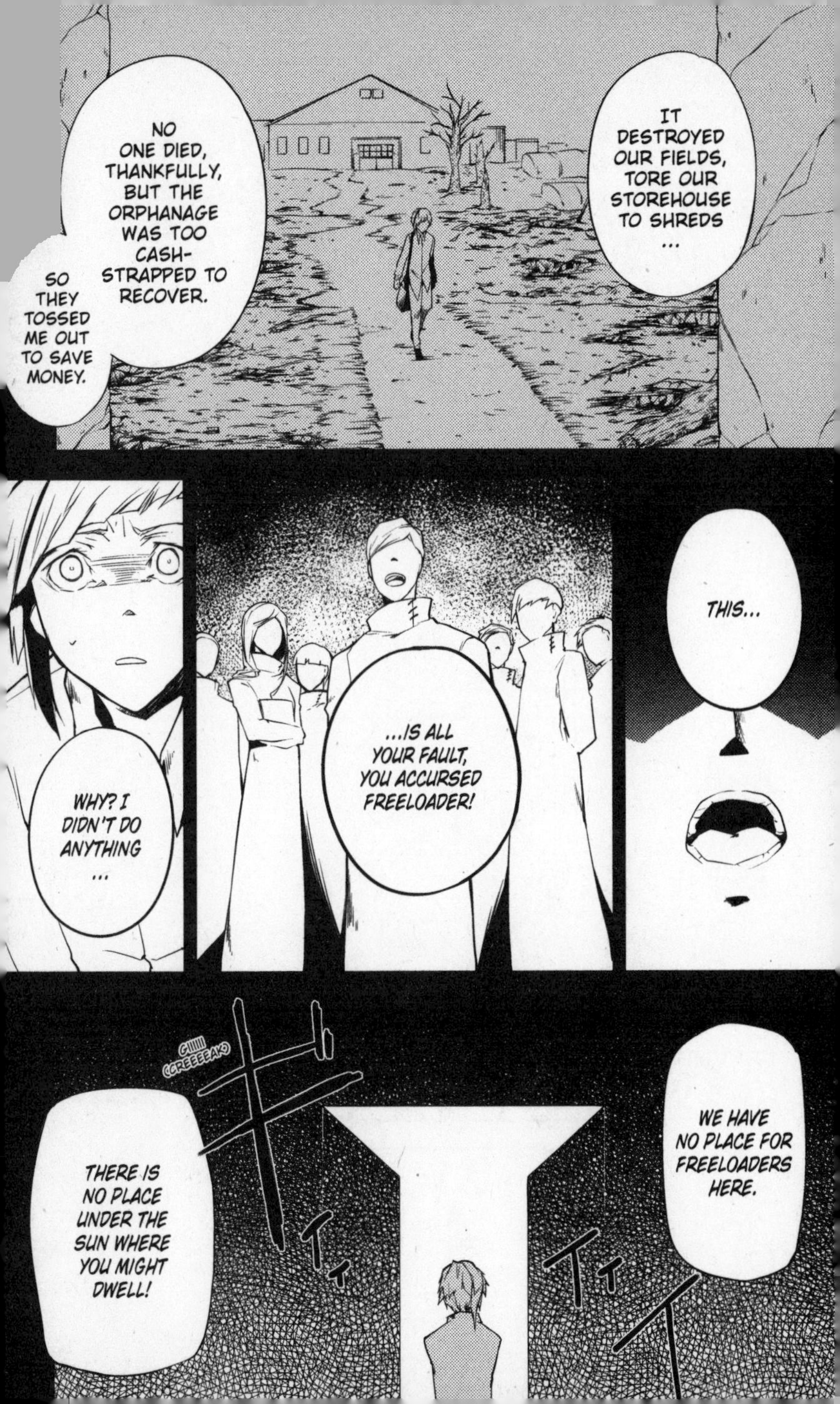
IT DESTROYED OUR FIELDS, TORE OUR STOREHOUSE TO SHREDS ...
NO ONE DIED, THANKFULLY, BUT THE ORPHANAGE WAS TOO CASH-STRAPPED TO RECOVER.
SO THEY TOSSED ME OUT TO SAVE MONEY.
THIS...
...IS ALL YOUR FAULT, YOU ACCURSED FREELOADER!
WHY? I DIDN'T DO ANYTHING ...
WE HAVE NO PLACE FOR FREELOADERS HERE.
(CREEEEAK)
THERE IS NO PLACE UNDER THE SUN WHERE YOU MIGHT DWELL!

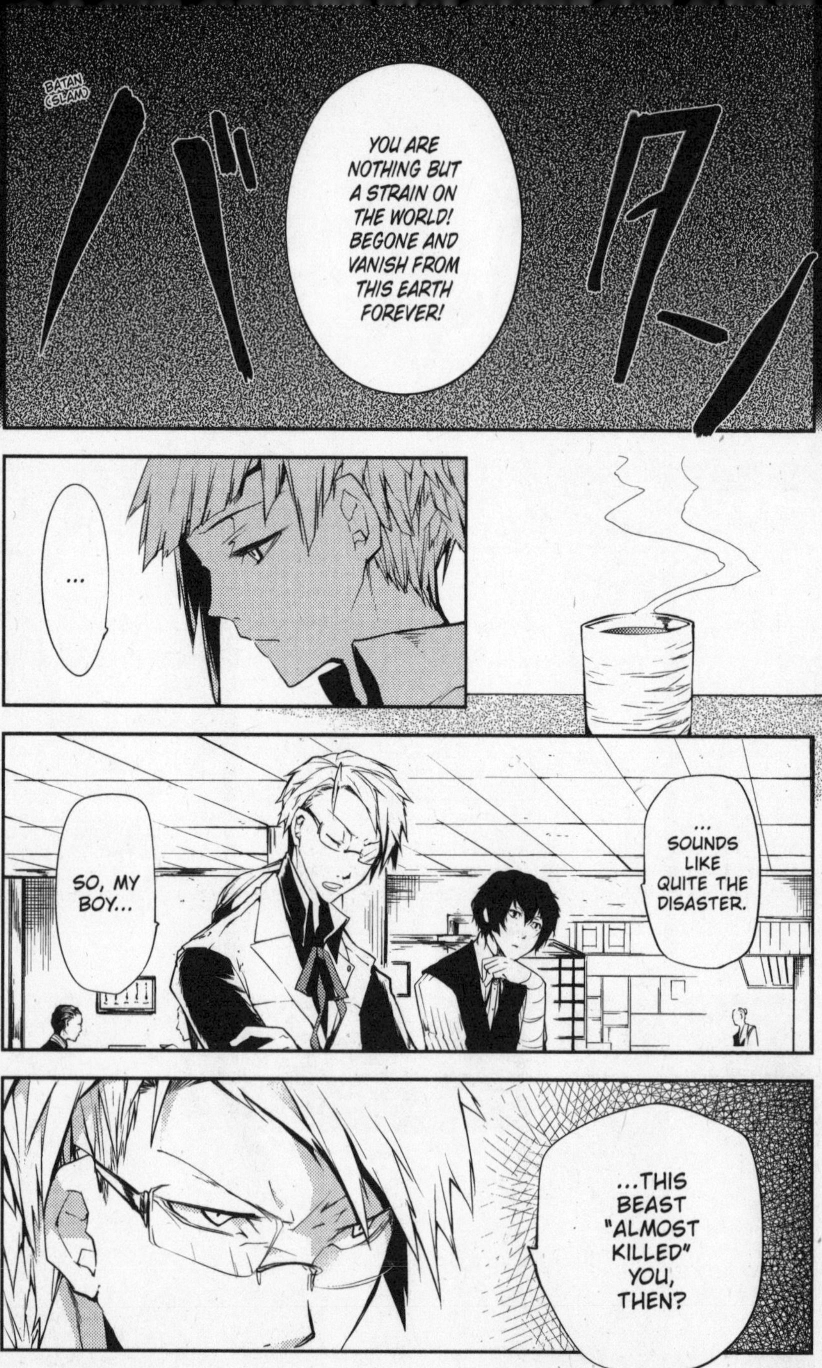
BATAN (SLAM)
YOU ARE NOTHING BUT A STRAIN ON THE WORLD! BEGONE AND VANISH FROM THIS EARTH FOREVER!
...
...SOUNDS LIKE QUITE THE DISASTER.
SO, MY BOY...
...THIS BEAST "ALMOST KILLED" YOU, THEN?

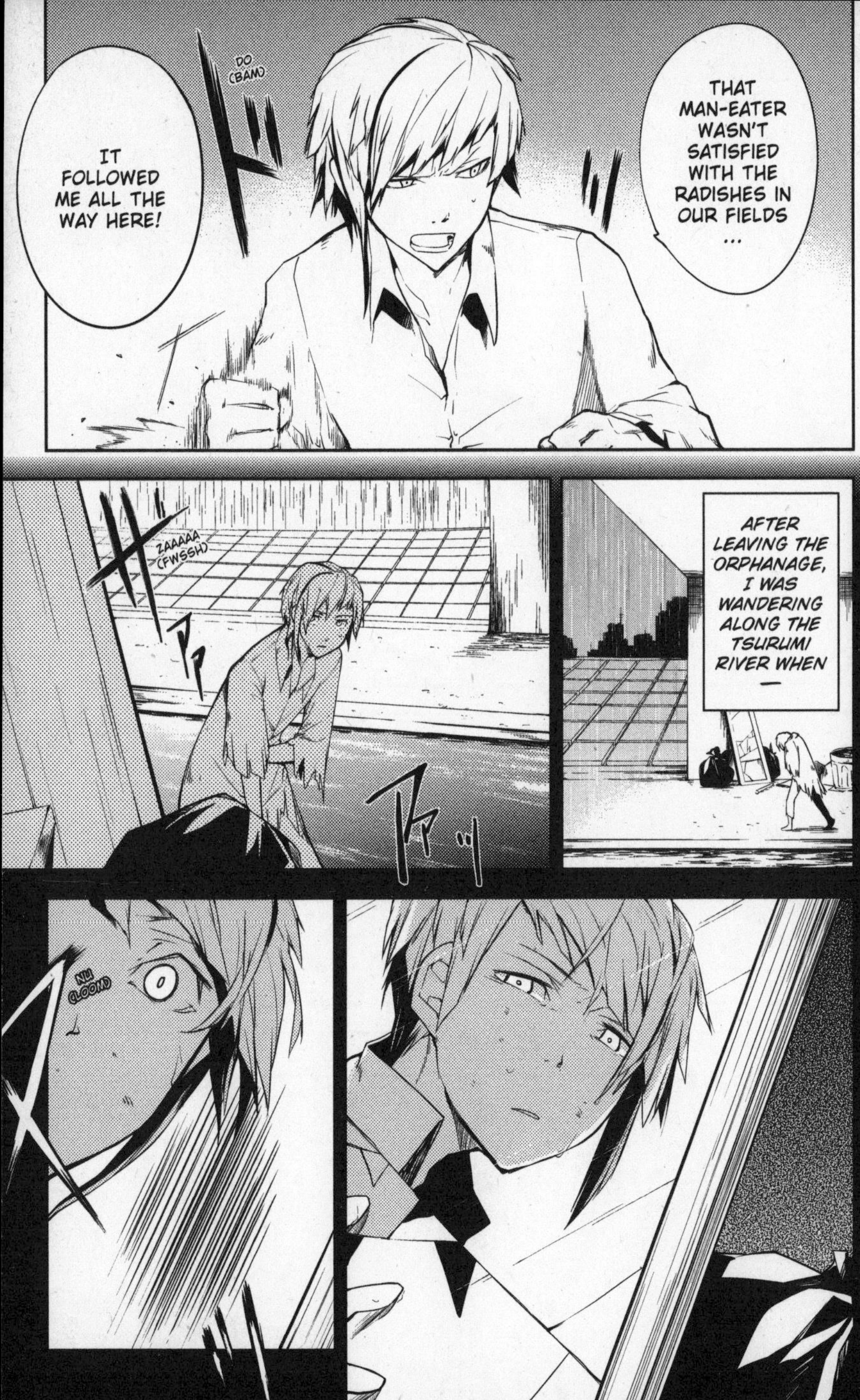
THAT MAN-EATER WASN'T SATISFIED WITH THE RADISHES IN OUR FIELDS ...
DO (BAM)
IT FOLLOWED ME ALL THE WAY HERE!
AFTER LEAVING THE ORPHANAGE, I WAS WANDERING ALONG THE TSURUMI RIVER WHEN —
ZAAAAA (FWSSH)
NU (LOOM)

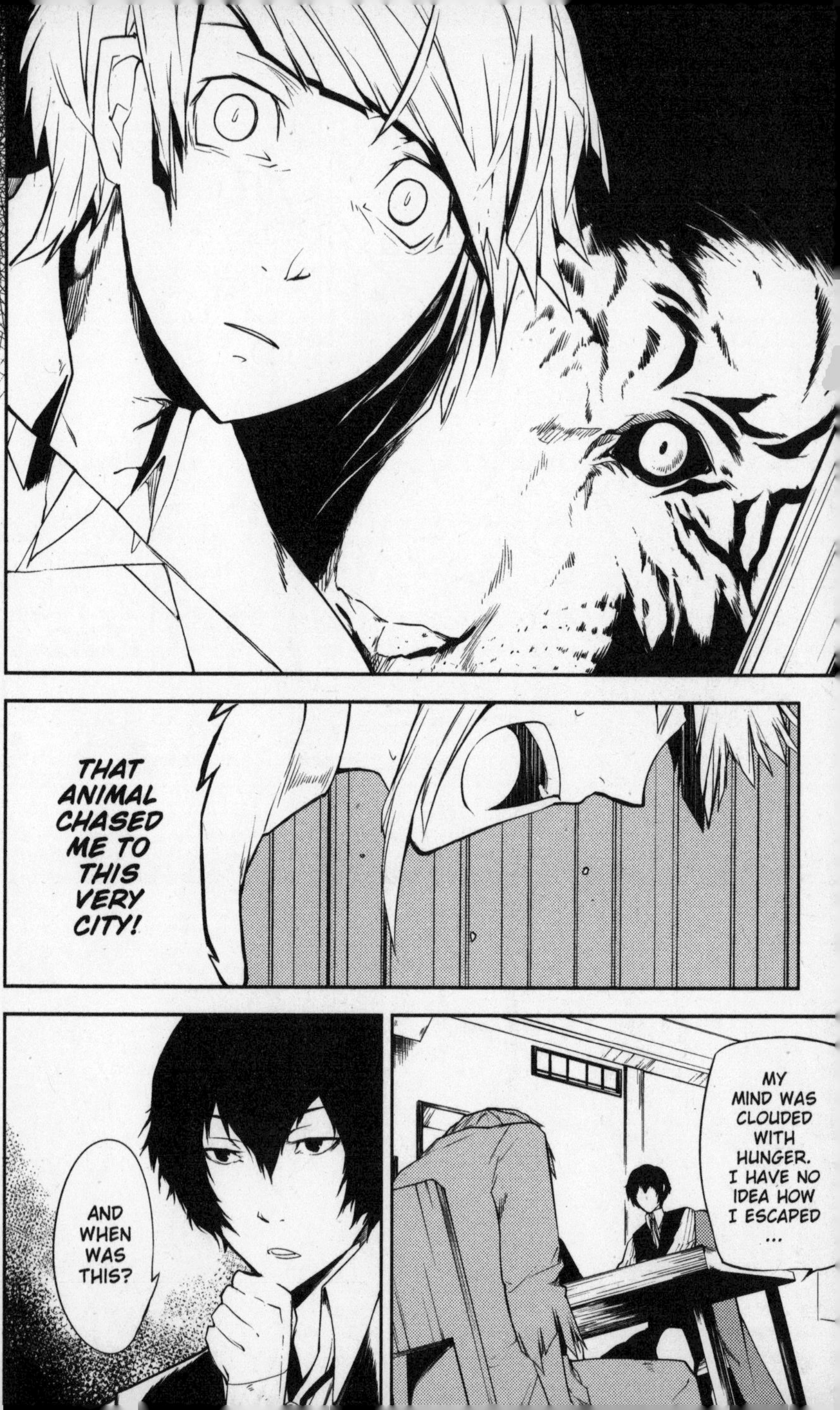
THAT ANIMAL CHASED ME TO THIS VERY CITY!
MY MIND WAS CLOUDED WITH HUNGER. I HAVE NO IDEA HOW I ESCAPED ...
AND WHEN WAS THIS?

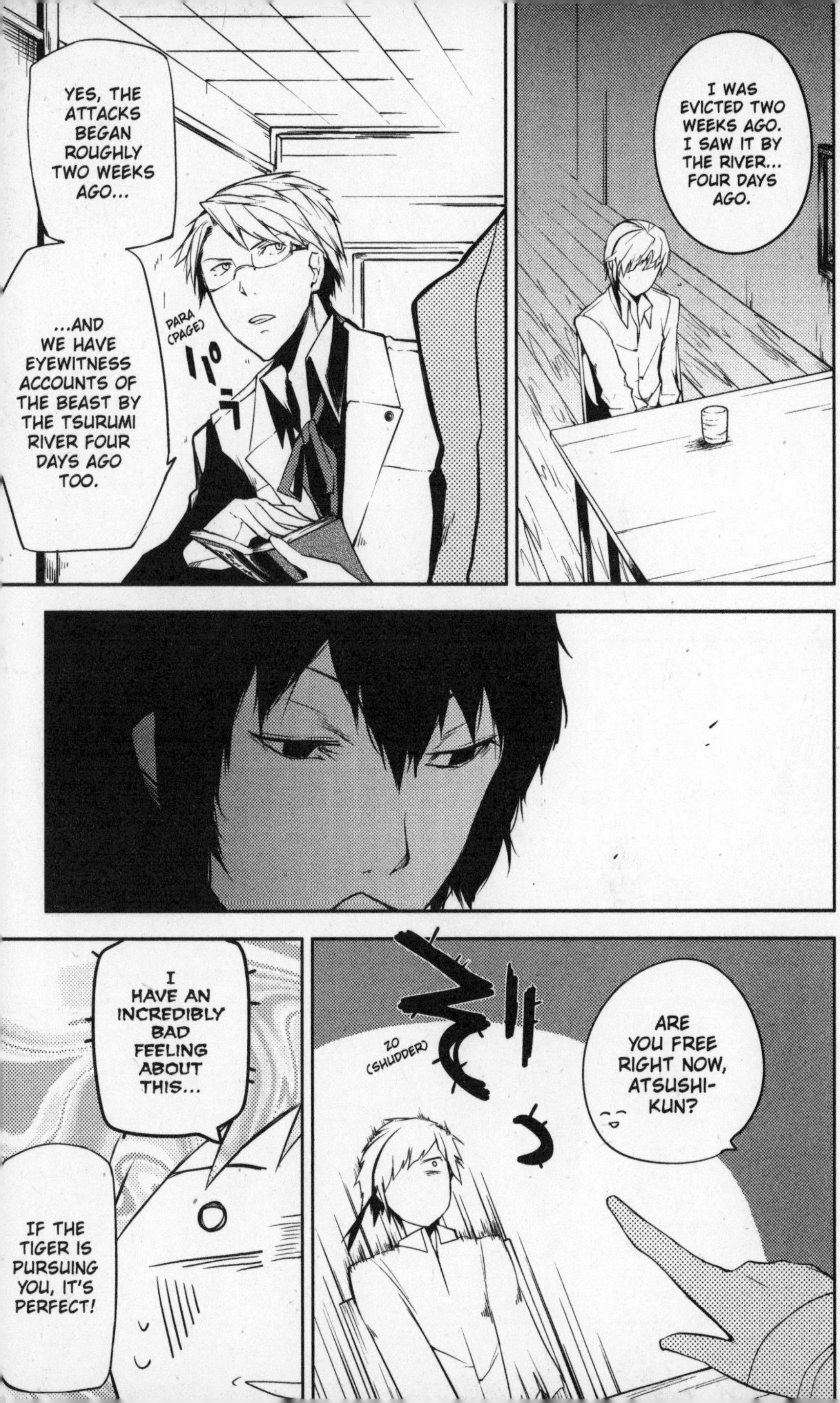
I WAS EVICTED TWO WEEKS AGO. I SAW IT BY THE RIVER... FOUR DAYS AGO.
YES, THE ATTACKS BEGAN ROUGHLY TWO WEEKS AGO...
PARA (PAGE)
...AND WE HAVE EYEWITNESS ACCOUNTS OF THE BEAST BY THE TSURUMI RIVER FOUR DAYS AGO TOO.
ARE YOU FREE RIGHT NOW, ATSUSHI-KUN?
ZO (SHUDDER)
I HAVE AN INCREDIBLY BAD FEELING ABOUT THIS...
IF THE TIGER IS PURSUING YOU, IT'S PERFECT!

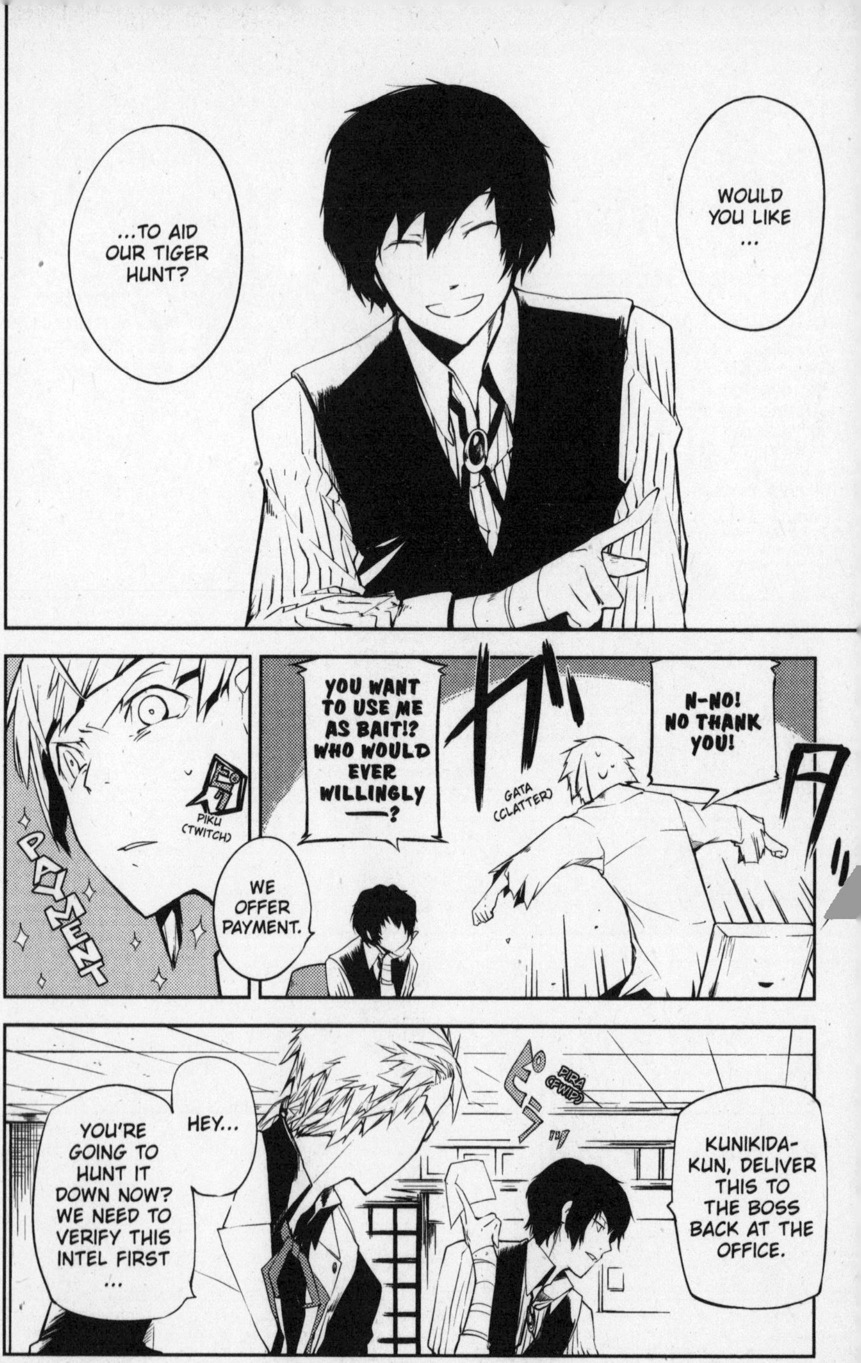
WOULD YOU LIKE ...
...TO AID OUR TIGER HUNT?
N-NO! NO THANK YOU!
GATA (CLATTER)
YOU WANT TO USE ME AS BAIT!? WHO WOULD EVER WILLINGLY —?
WE OFFER PAYMENT.
PIKU (TWITCH)
PAYMENT
KUNIKIDA-KUN, DELIVER THIS TO THE BOSS BACK AT THE OFFICE.
PIRA (PWIP)
HEY...
YOU'RE GOING TO HUNT IT DOWN NOW? WE NEED TO VERIFY THIS INTEL FIRST ...

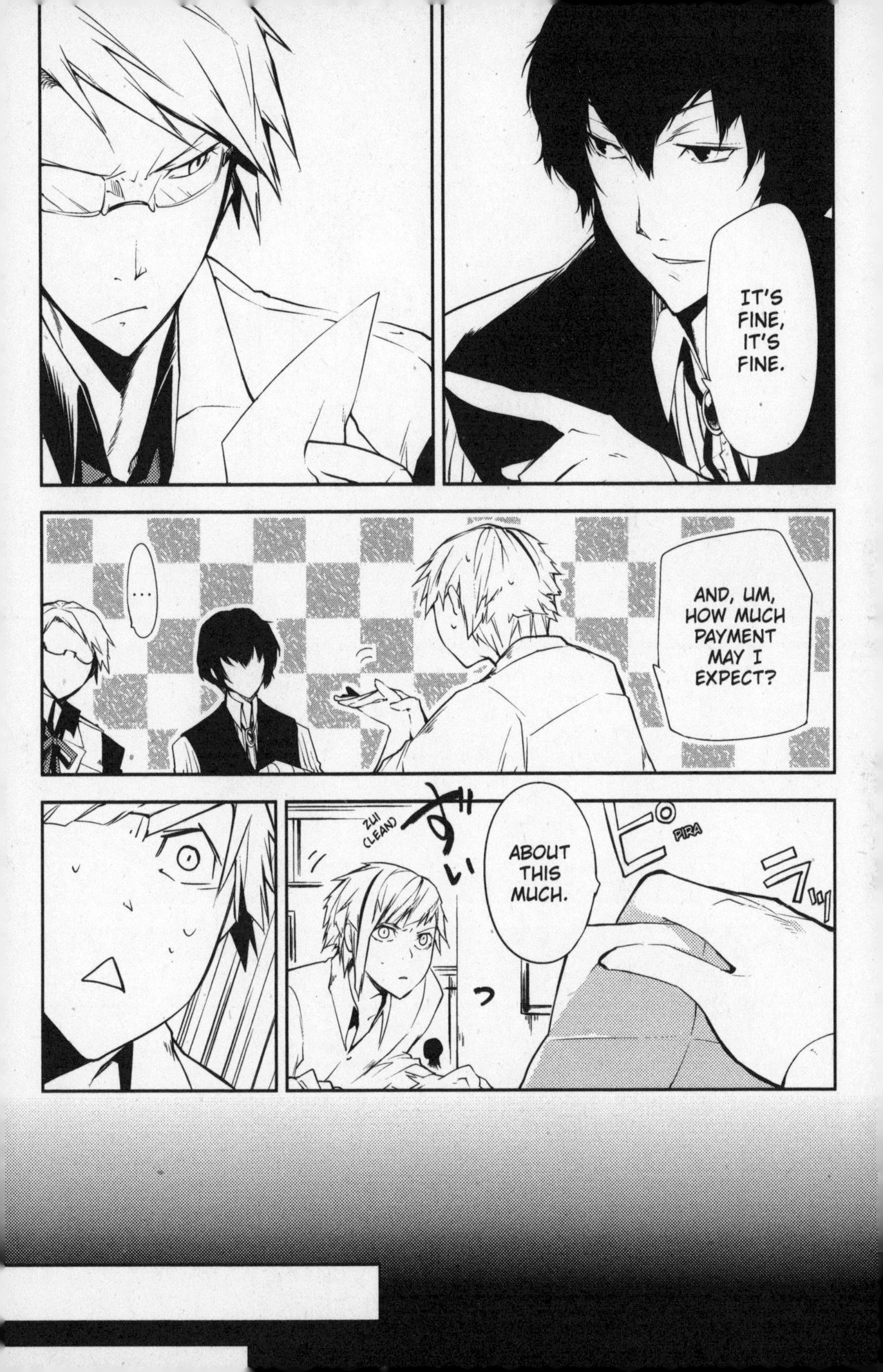
IT'S FINE, IT'S FINE.
AND, UM, HOW MUCH PAYMENT MAY I EXPECT?
...
PIRA
ABOUT THIS MUCH.
ZUI (CLEAN)

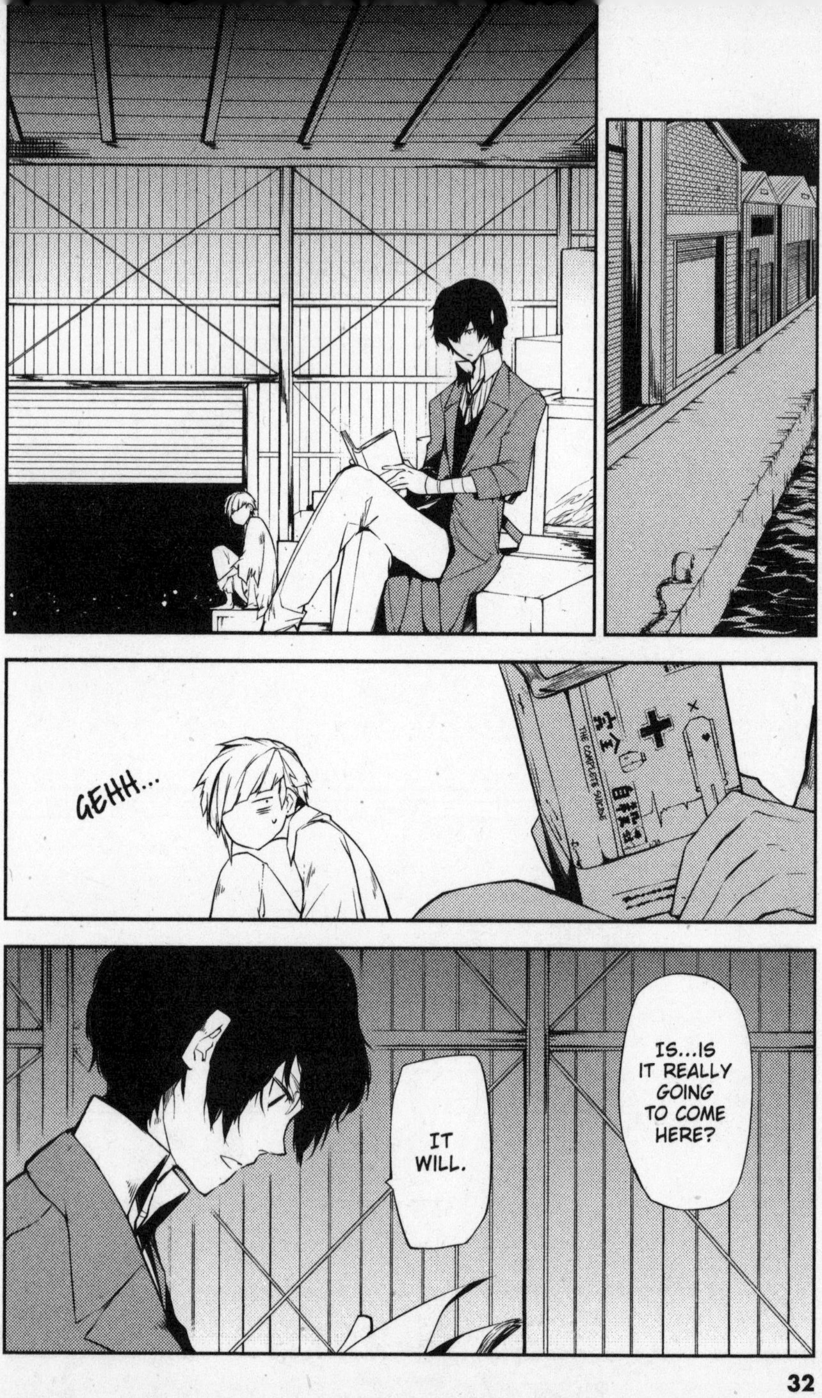
GEHH...
IS...IS IT REALLY GOING TO COME HERE?
IT WILL.

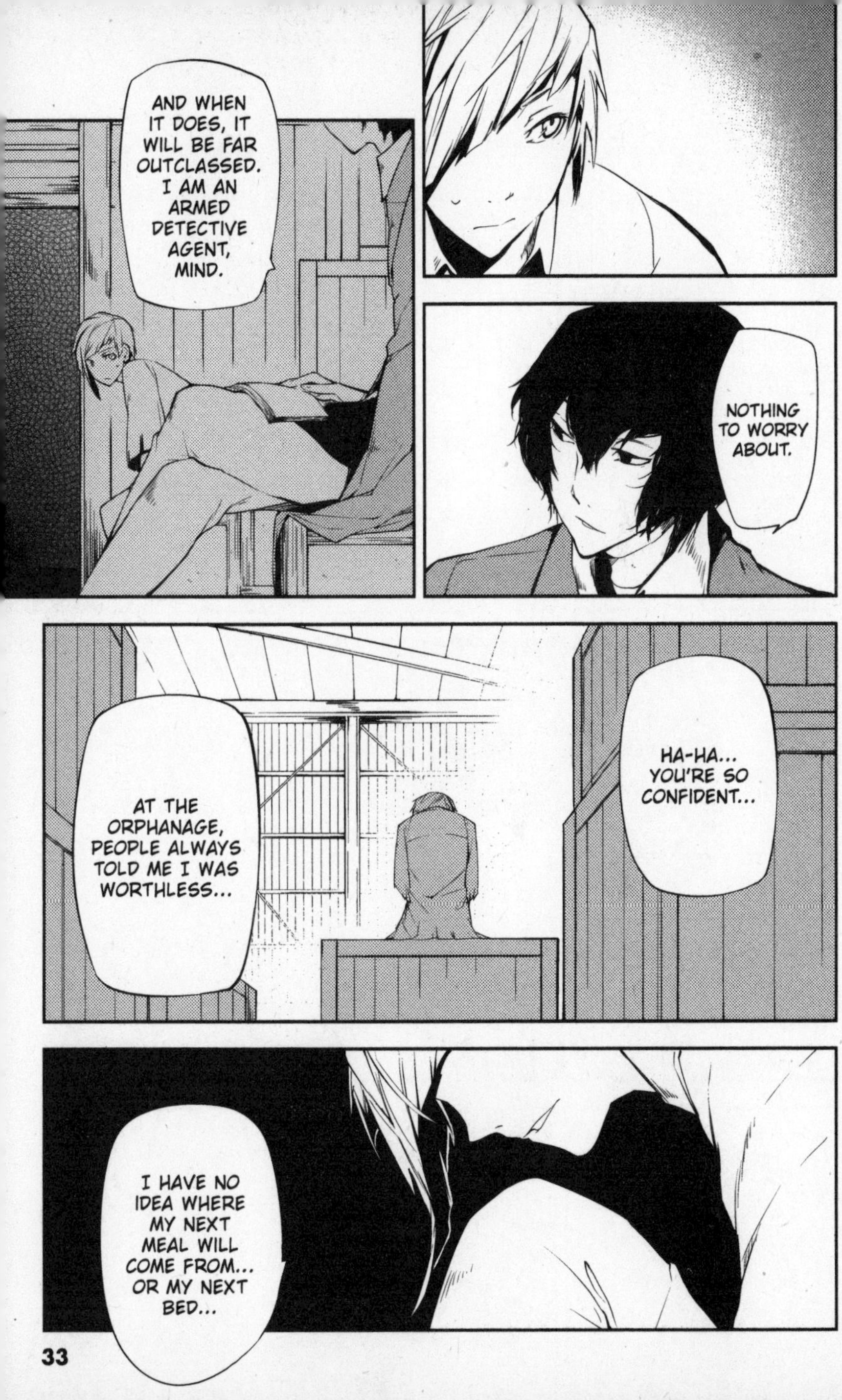

NOTHING TO WORRY ABOUT.
AND WHEN IT DOES, IT WILL BE FAR OUTCLASSED. I AM AN ARMED DETECTIVE AGENT, MIND.
HA-HA... YOU'RE SO CONFIDENT...
AT THE ORPHANAGE, PEOPLE ALWAYS TOLD ME I WAS WORTHLESS...
I HAVE NO IDEA WHERE MY NEXT MEAL WILL COME FROM... OR MY NEXT BED...

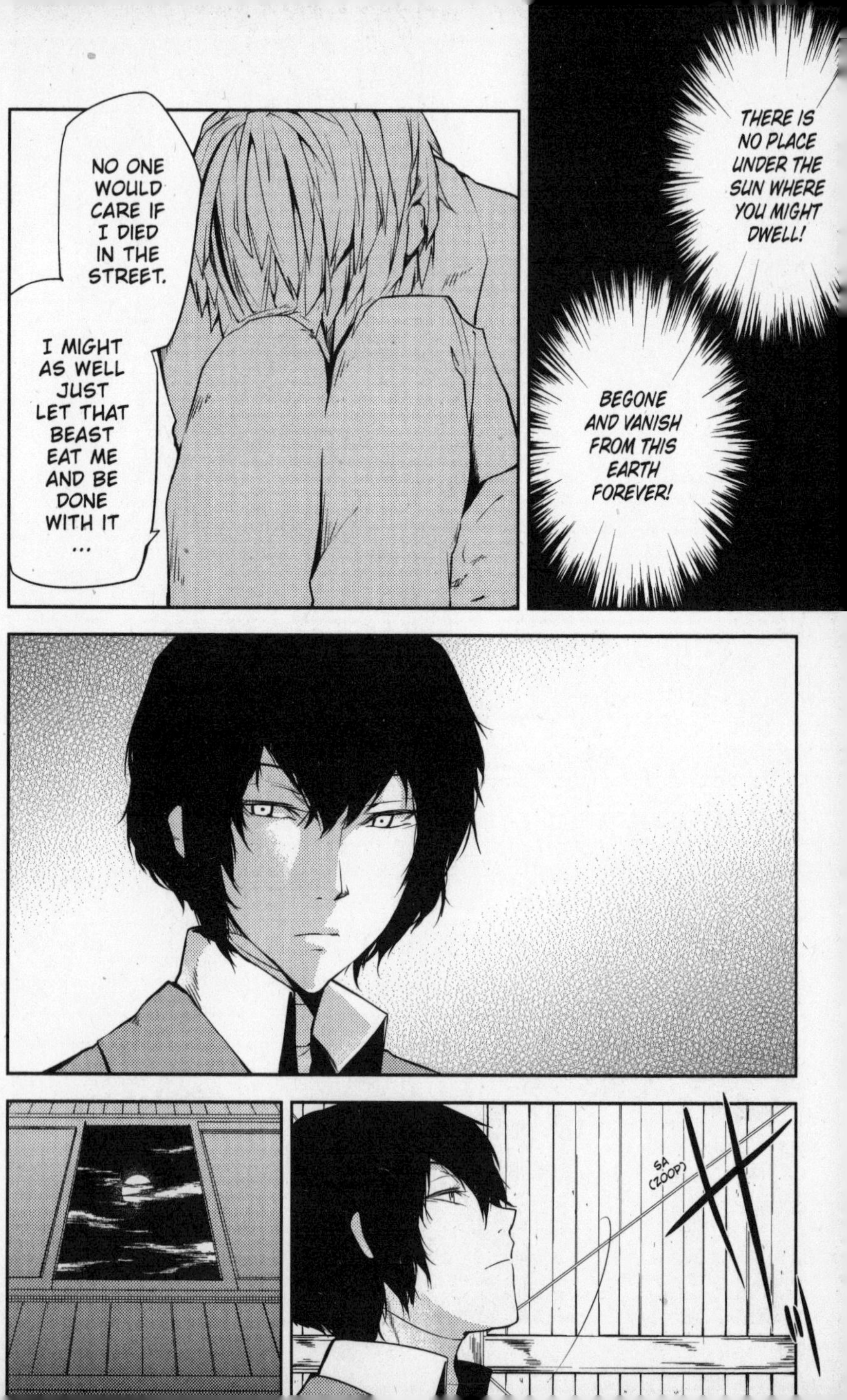
THERE IS NO PLACE UNDER THE SUN WHERE YOU MIGHT DWELL!
BEGONE AND VANISH FROM THIS EARTH FOREVER!
NO ONE WOULD CARE IF I DIED IN THE STREET.
I MIGHT AS WELL JUST LET THAT BEAST EAT ME AND BE DONE WITH IT ...
SA (ZOOP)

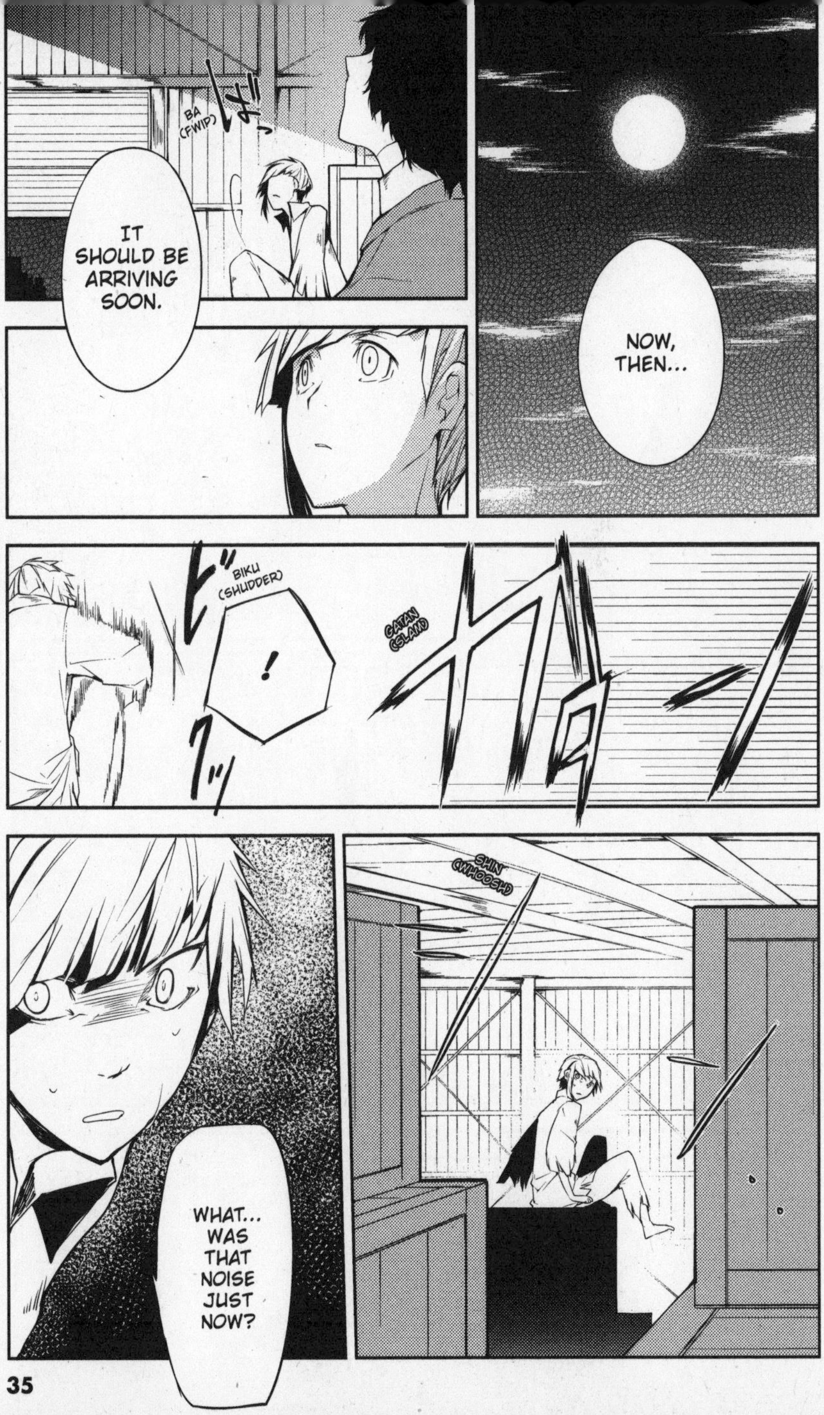
NOW, THEN...
BA (FWIP)
IT SHOULD BE ARRIVING SOON.
GATAN (SLAM)
BIKU (SHUDDER)
!
SHIN (WHOOSH)
WHAT... WAS THAT NOISE JUST NOW?

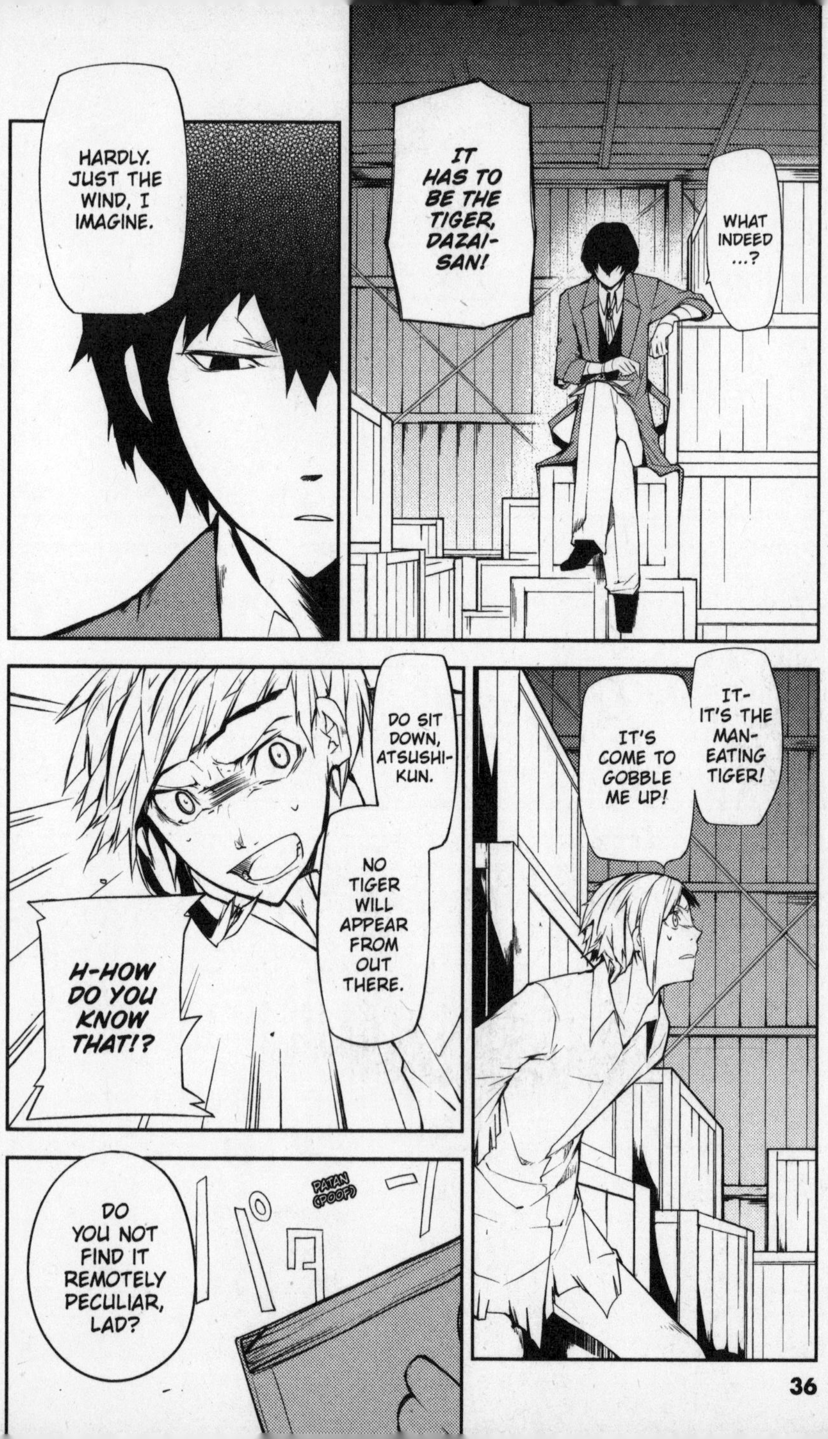
WHAT INDEED ...?
IT HAS TO BE THE TIGER, DAZAI-SAN!
HARDLY. JUST THE WIND, I IMAGINE.
IT- IT'S THE MAN-EATING TIGER!
IT'S COME TO GOBBLE ME UP!
DO SIT DOWN, ATSUSHI-KUN.
NO TIGER WILL APPEAR FROM OUT THERE.
H-HOW DO YOU KNOW THAT!?
PATAN (POOF)
DO YOU NOT FIND IT REMOTELY PECULIAR, LAD?

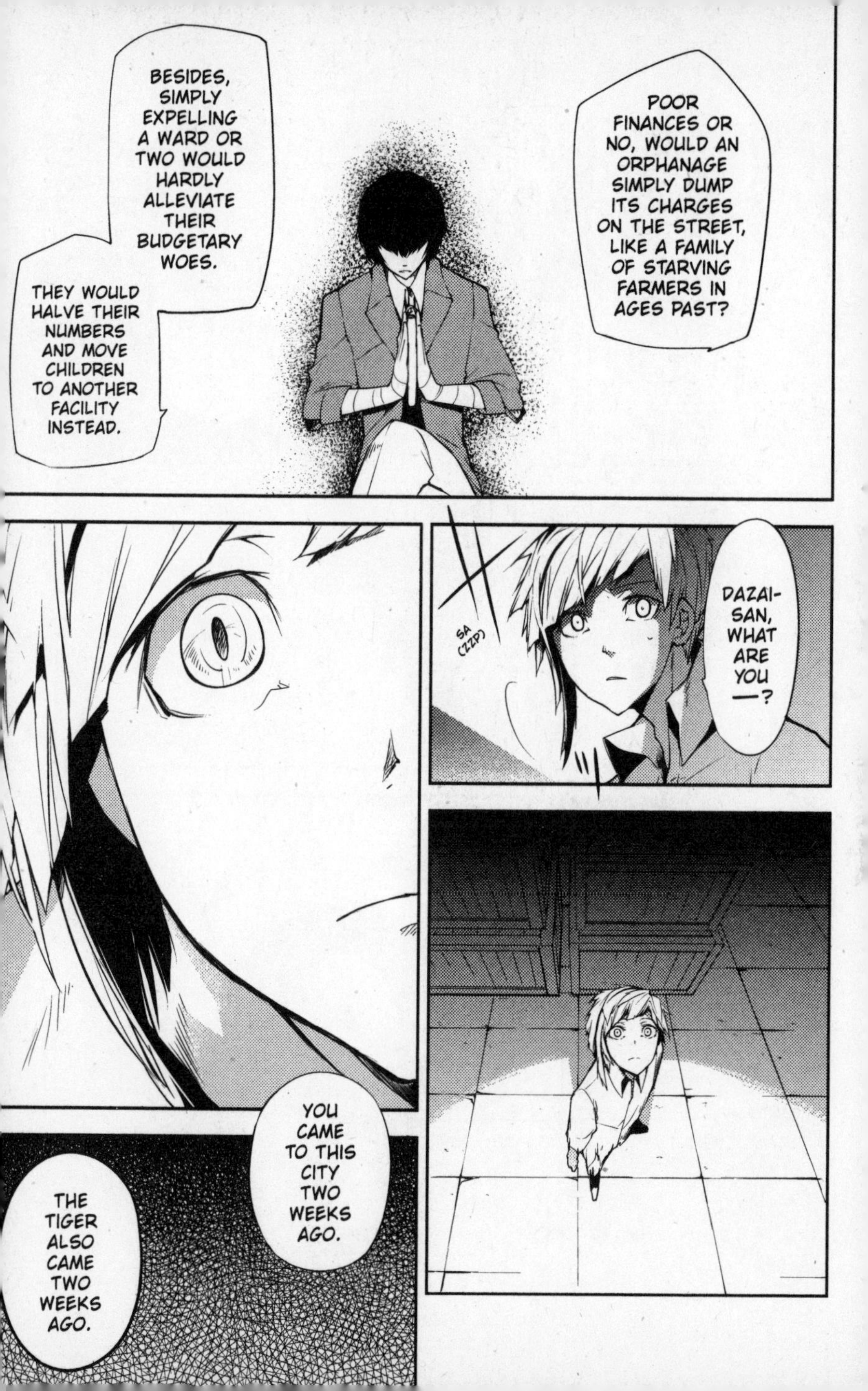
POOR FINANCES OR NO, WOULD AN ORPHANAGE SIMPLY DUMP ITS CHARGES ON THE STREET, LIKE A FAMILY OF STARVING FARMERS IN AGES PAST?
BESIDES, SIMPLY EXPELLING A WARD OR TWO WOULD HARDLY ALLEVIATE THEIR BUDGETARY WOES.
THEY WOULD HALVE THEIR NUMBERS AND MOVE CHILDREN TO ANOTHER FACILITY INSTEAD.
DAZAI-SAN, WHAT ARE YOU—?
SA (ZZP)
YOU CAME TO THIS CITY TWO WEEKS AGO.
THE TIGER ALSO CAME TWO WEEKS AGO.

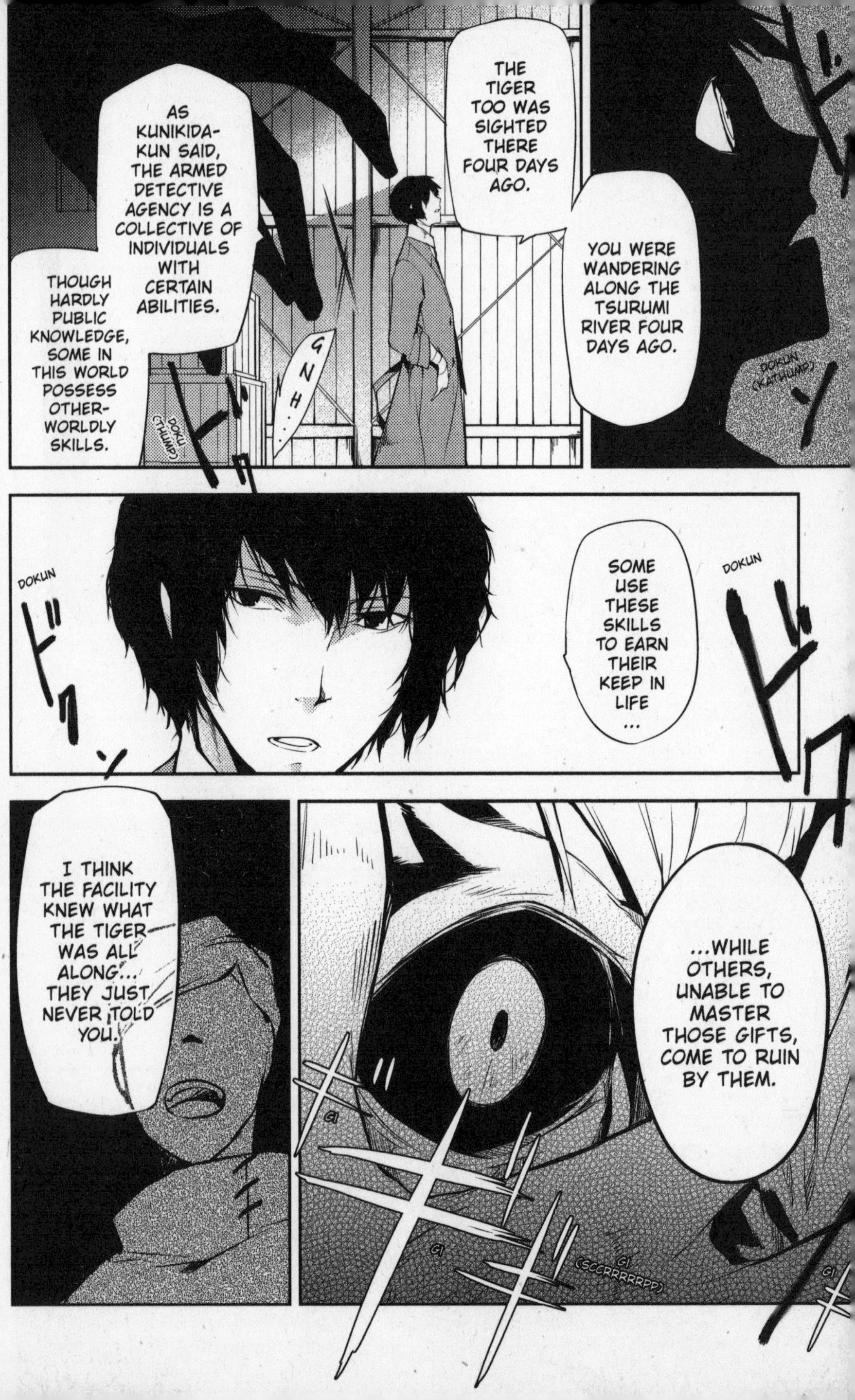
DOKUN (KATHUMP)
YOU WERE WANDERING ALONG THE TSURUMI RIVER FOUR DAYS AGO.
THE TIGER TOO WAS SIGHTED THERE FOUR DAYS AGO.
AS KUNIKIDA-KUN SAID, THE ARMED DETECTIVE AGENCY IS A COLLECTIVE OF INDIVIDUALS WITH CERTAIN ABILITIES.
GNH...
THOUGH HARDLY PUBLIC KNOWLEDGE, SOME IN THIS WORLD POSSESS OTHER-WORLDLY SKILLS.
DOKU (THUMP)
DOKUN
SOME USE THESE SKILLS TO EARN THEIR KEEP IN LIFE...
DOKUN
...WHILE OTHERS, UNABLE TO MASTER THOSE GIFTS, COME TO RUIN BY THEM.
GI
GI
GI (SCCRRRRRRPP)
GI
I THINK THE FACILITY KNEW WHAT THE TIGER WAS ALL ALONG... THEY JUST NEVER TOLD YOU.

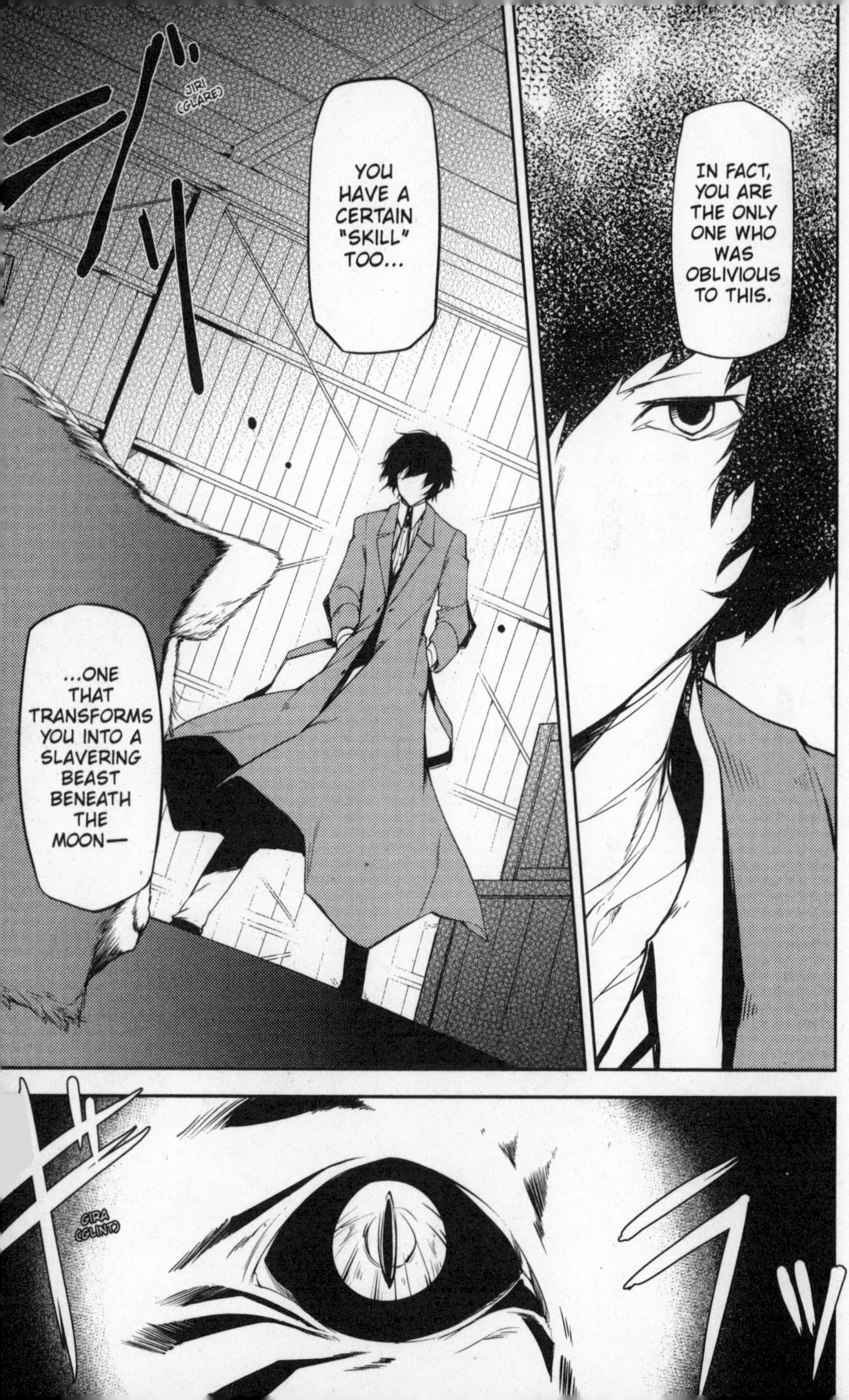
IN FACT, YOU ARE THE ONLY ONE WHO WAS OBLIVIOUS TO THIS.
YOU HAVE A CERTAIN "SKILL" TOO...
JIRI (GLARE)
...ONE THAT TRANSFORMS YOU INTO A SLAVERING BEAST BENEATH THE MOON—
GIRA (GLINT)

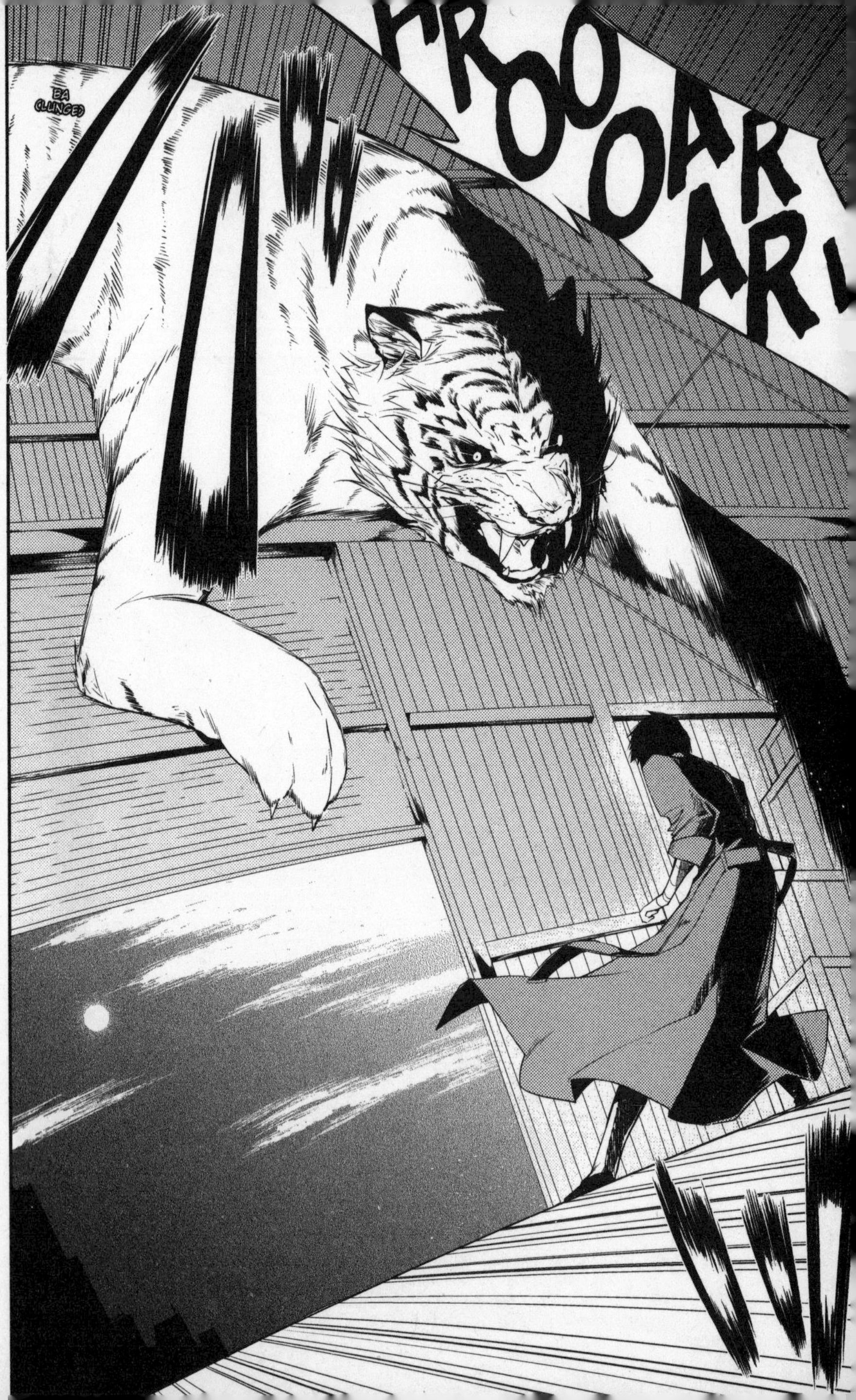
FROOOOARAR!
BA
(LUNGE)

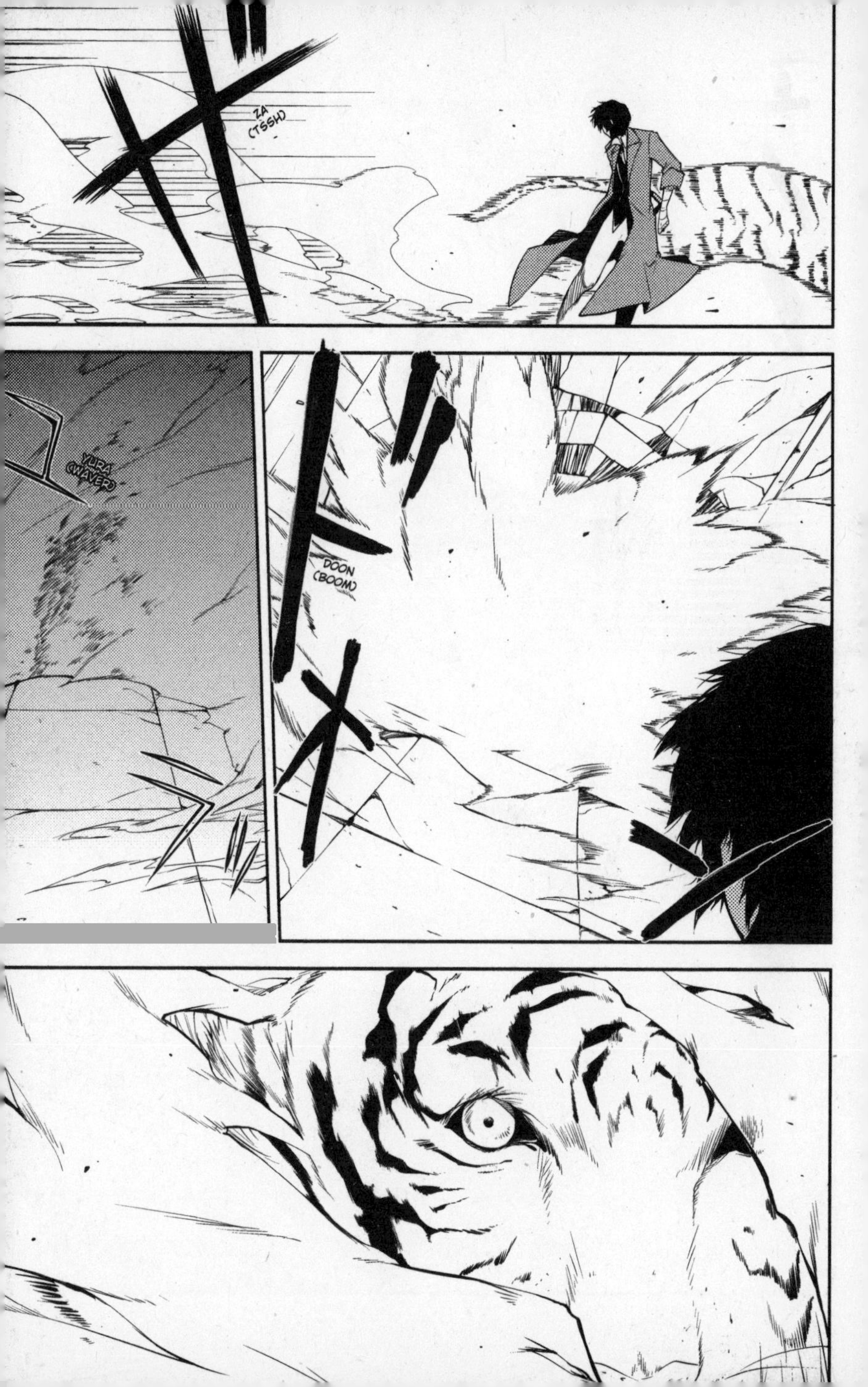
ZA
(TSSH)
DOON
(BOOM)
YURA
(WAVER)

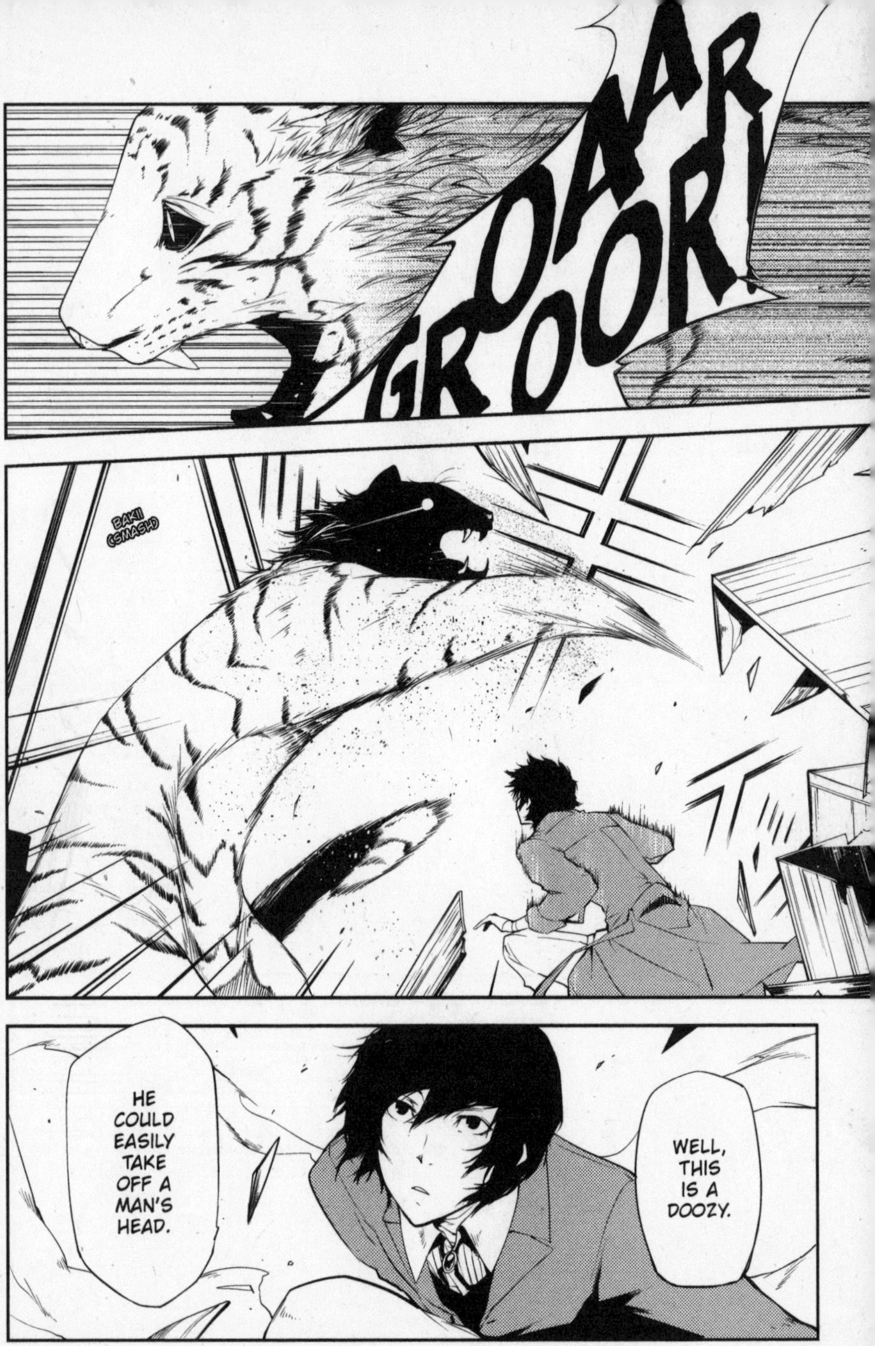
GROOOAAR!
BAKII (SMASH)
WELL, THIS IS A DOOZY.
HE COULD EASILY TAKE OFF A MAN'S HEAD.

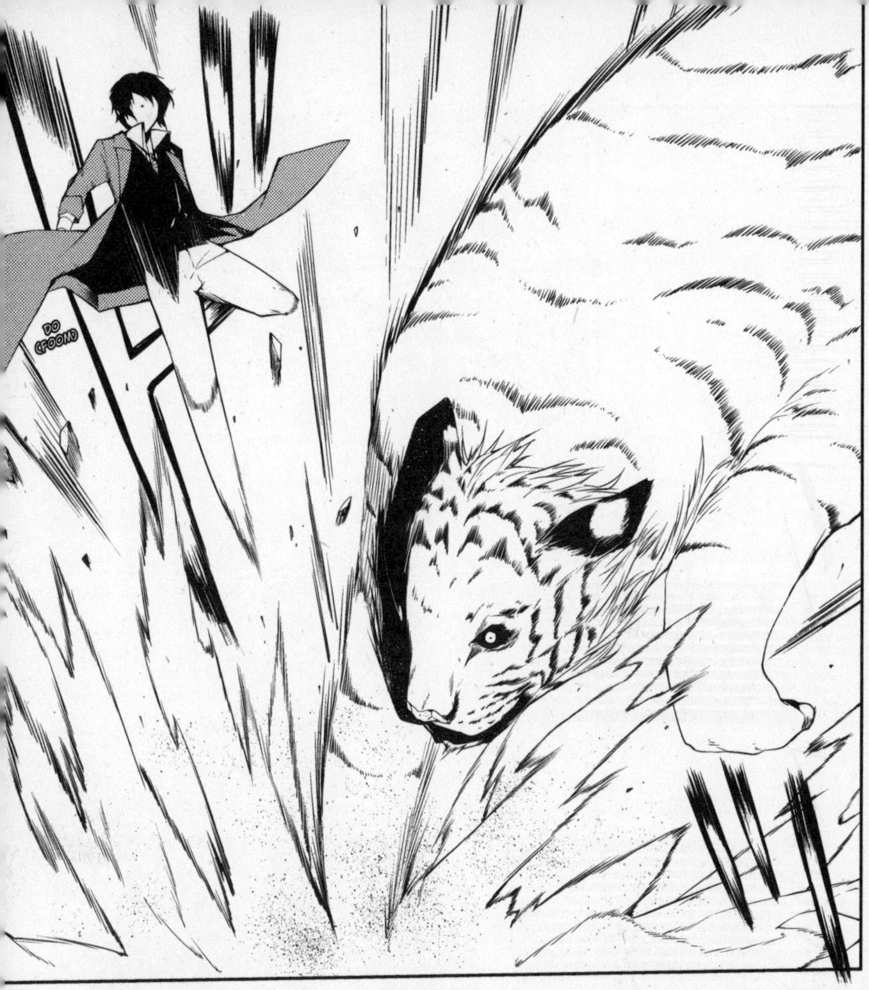
DO
(FOOM)
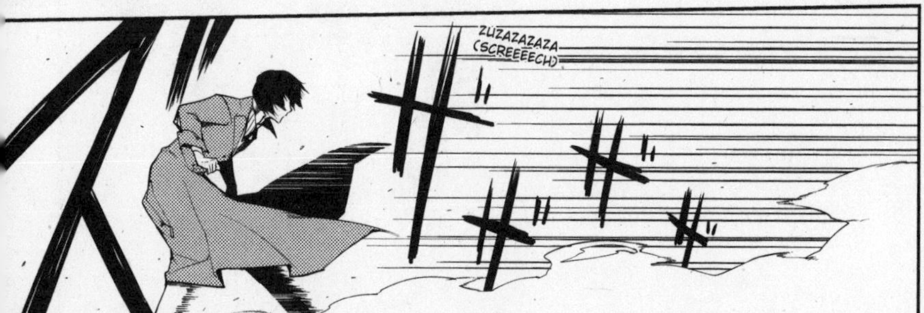
ZUZAZAZAZA
(SCREEEECH)

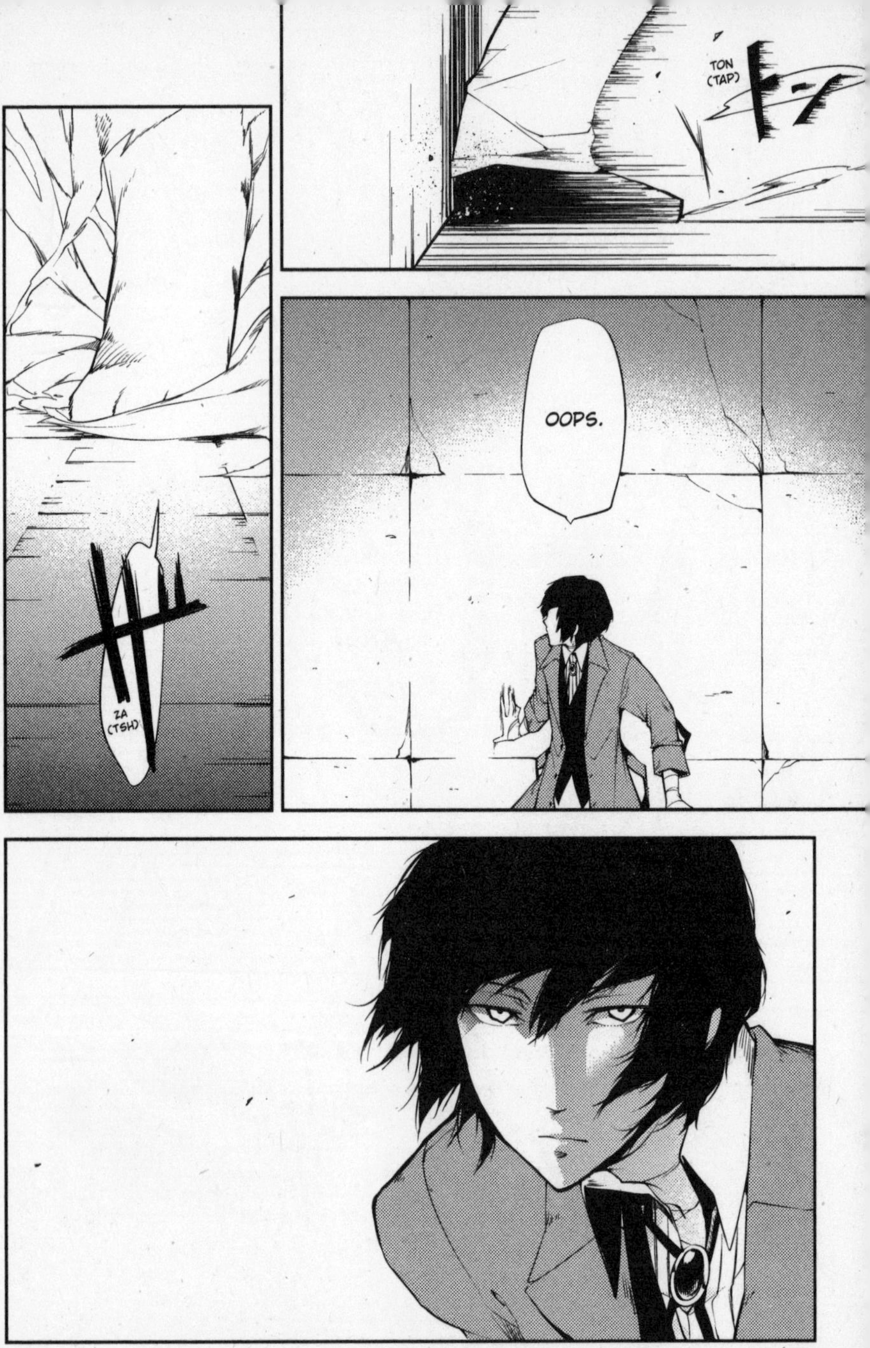
TON (TAP)
OOPS.
ZA (TSH)

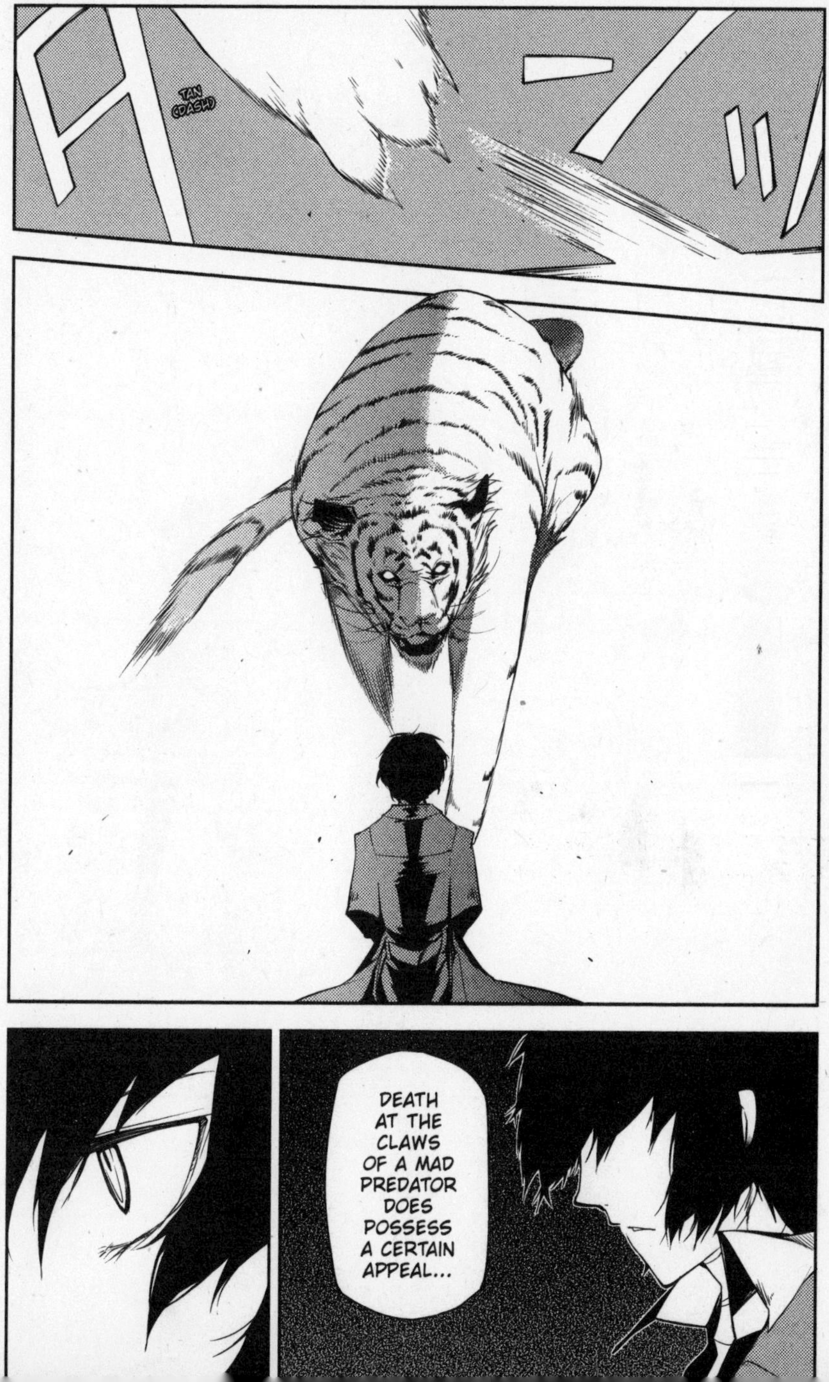
TAN (DASH)
DEATH AT THE CLAWS OF A MAD PREDATOR DOES POSSESS A CERTAIN APPEAL...

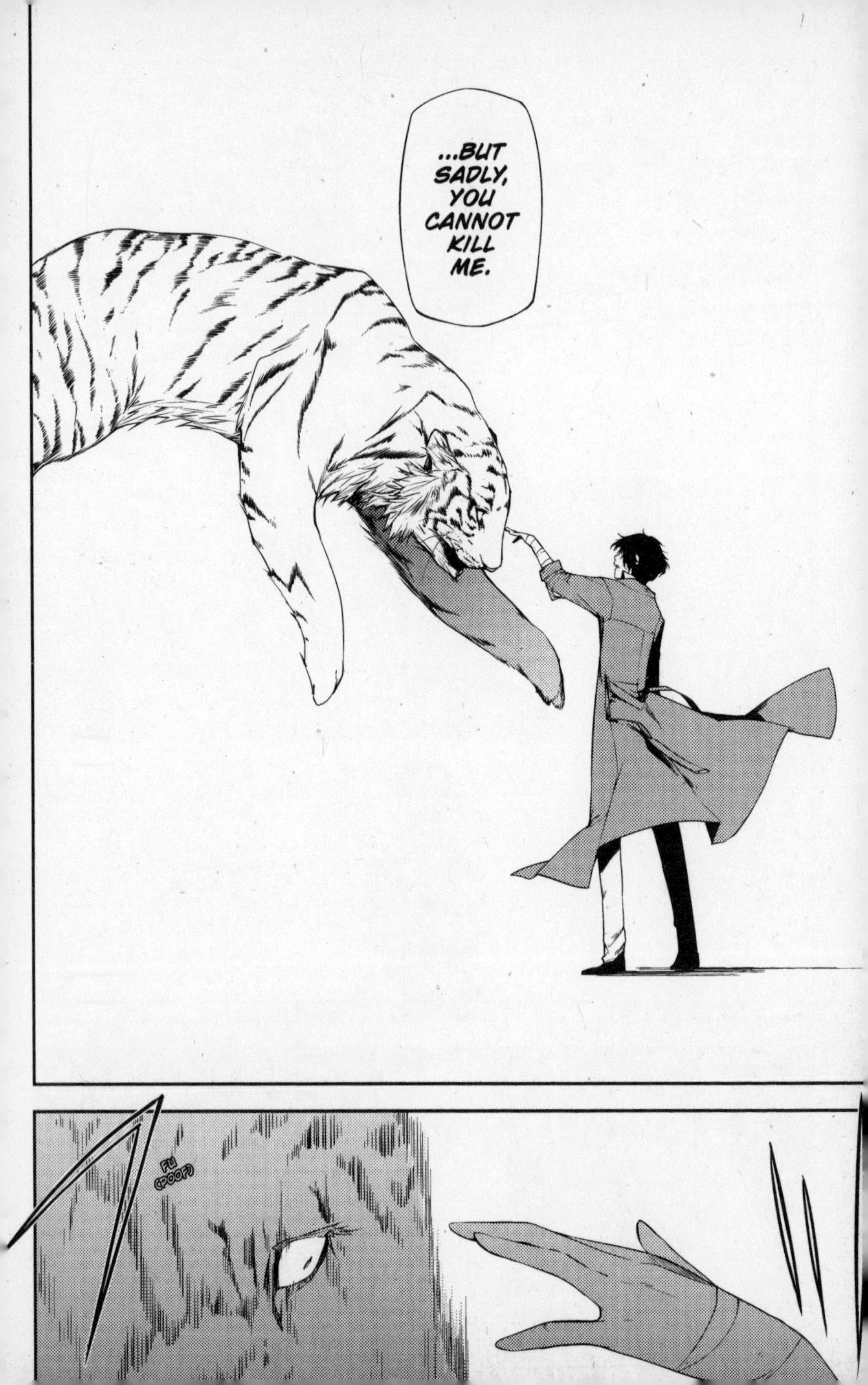
...BUT SADLY, YOU CANNOT KILL ME.
FU (POOF)

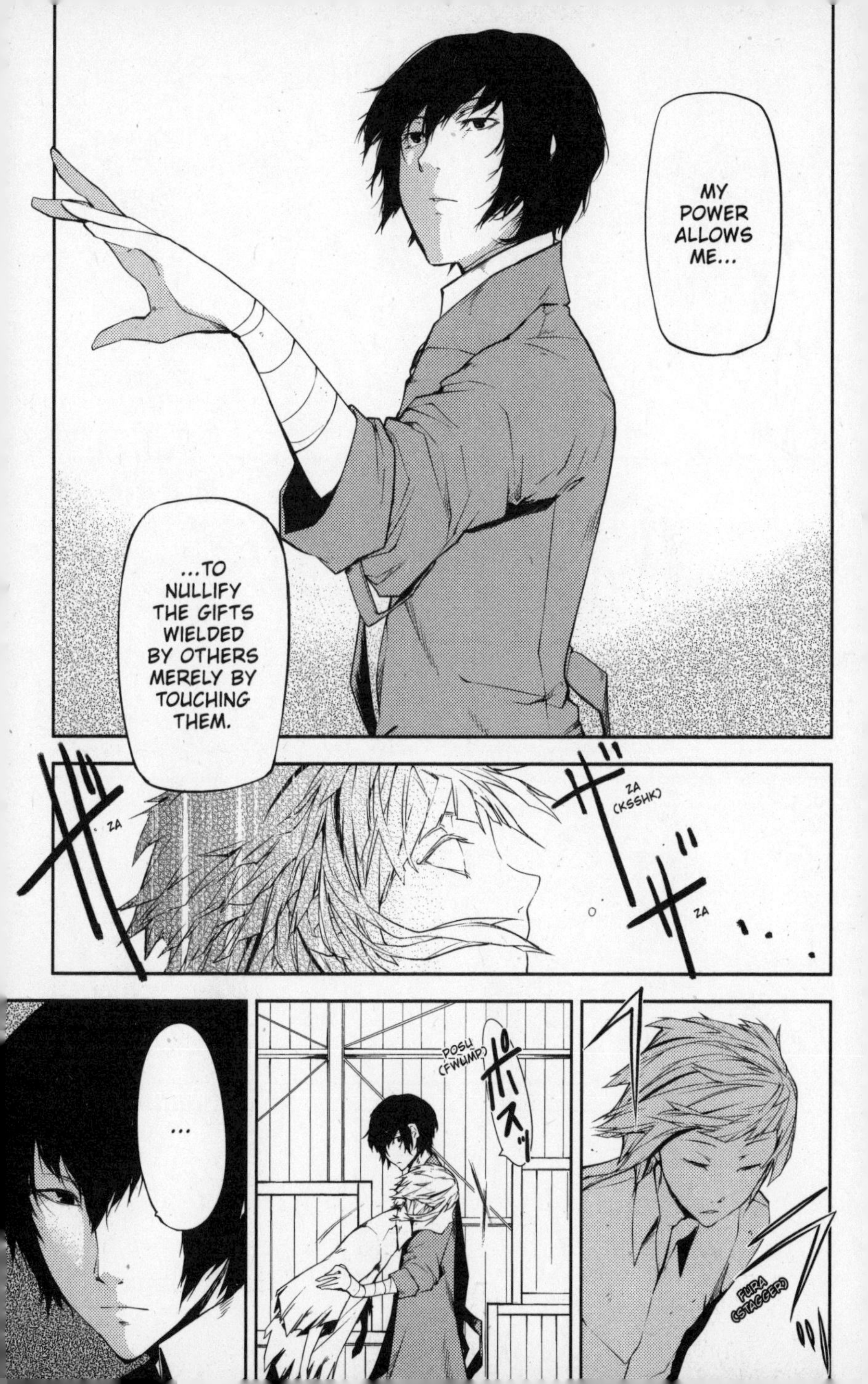
MY POWER ALLOWS ME...
...TO NULLIFY THE GIFTS WIELDED BY OTHERS MERELY BY TOUCHING THEM.
ZA (KSSHK)
ZA
ZA
FURA (STAGGER)
POSU (FWUMP)
...

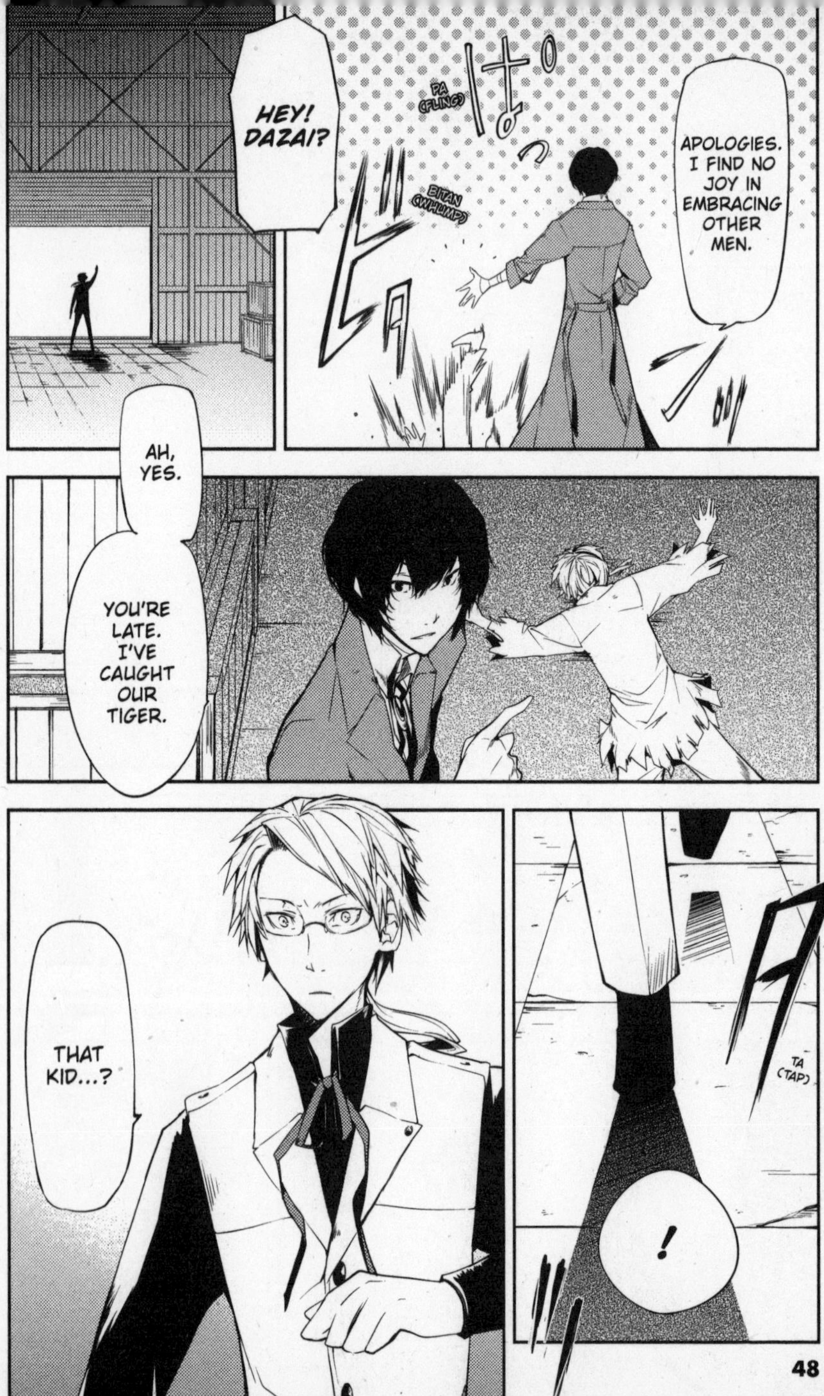
APOLOGIES. I FIND NO JOY IN EMBRACING OTHER MEN.
ぱっ
PA (FLING)
BITAN (WHUMP)
HEY! DAZAI?
AH, YES.
YOU'RE LATE. I'VE CAUGHT OUR TIGER.
TA (TAP)
!
THAT KID...?

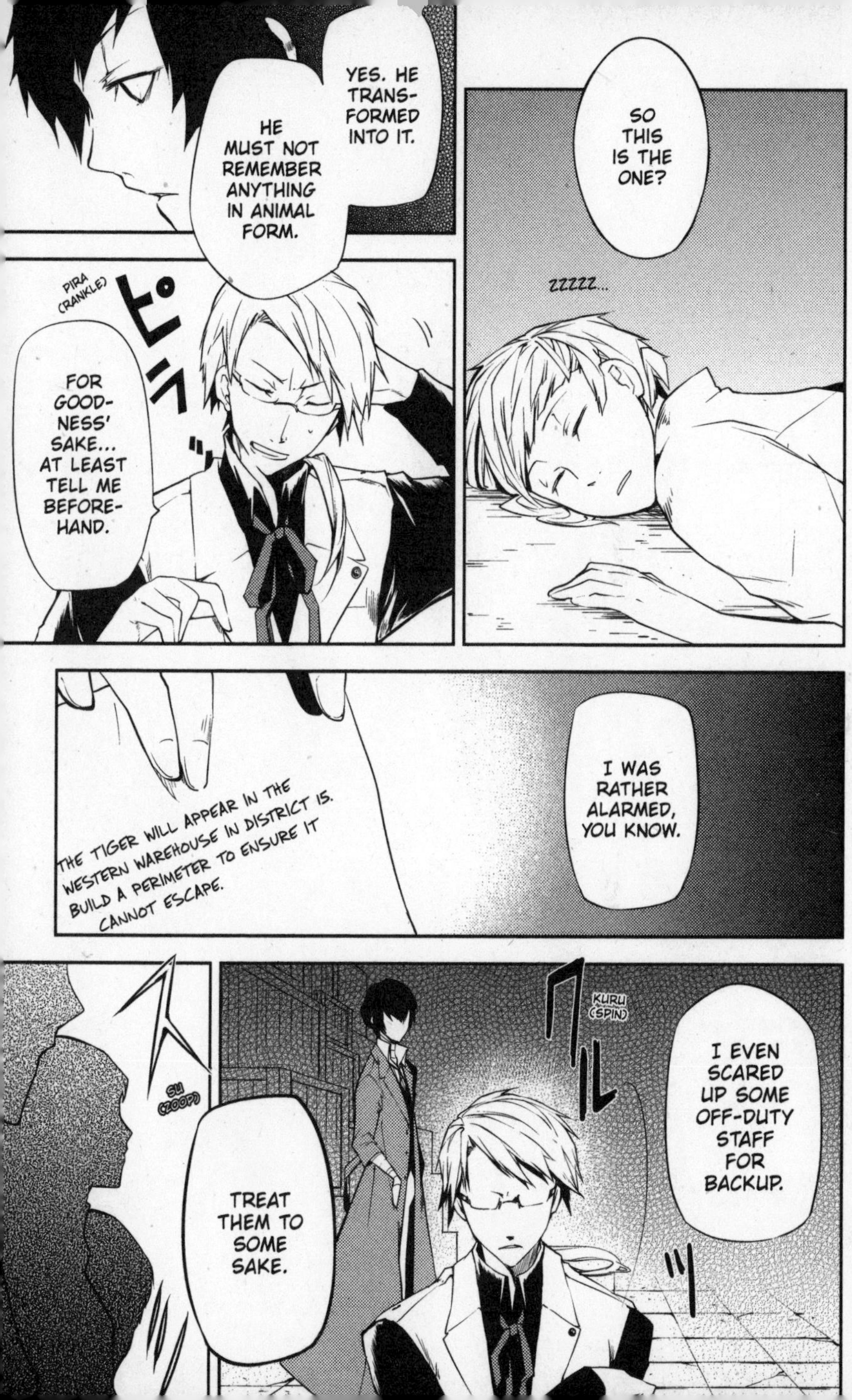
SO THIS IS THE ONE?
ZZZZZ...
YES. HE TRANS-FORMED INTO IT.
HE MUST NOT REMEMBER ANYTHING IN ANIMAL FORM.
PIRA (RANKLE)
FOR GOOD-NESS' SAKE... AT LEAST TELL ME BEFORE-HAND.
I WAS RATHER ALARMED, YOU KNOW.
THE TIGER WILL APPEAR IN THE WESTERN WAREHOUSE IN DISTRICT 15. BUILD A PERIMETER TO ENSURE IT CANNOT ESCAPE.
KURU (SPIN)
I EVEN SCARED UP SOME OFF-DUTY STAFF FOR BACKUP.
SU (ZOOP)
TREAT THEM TO SOME SAKE.

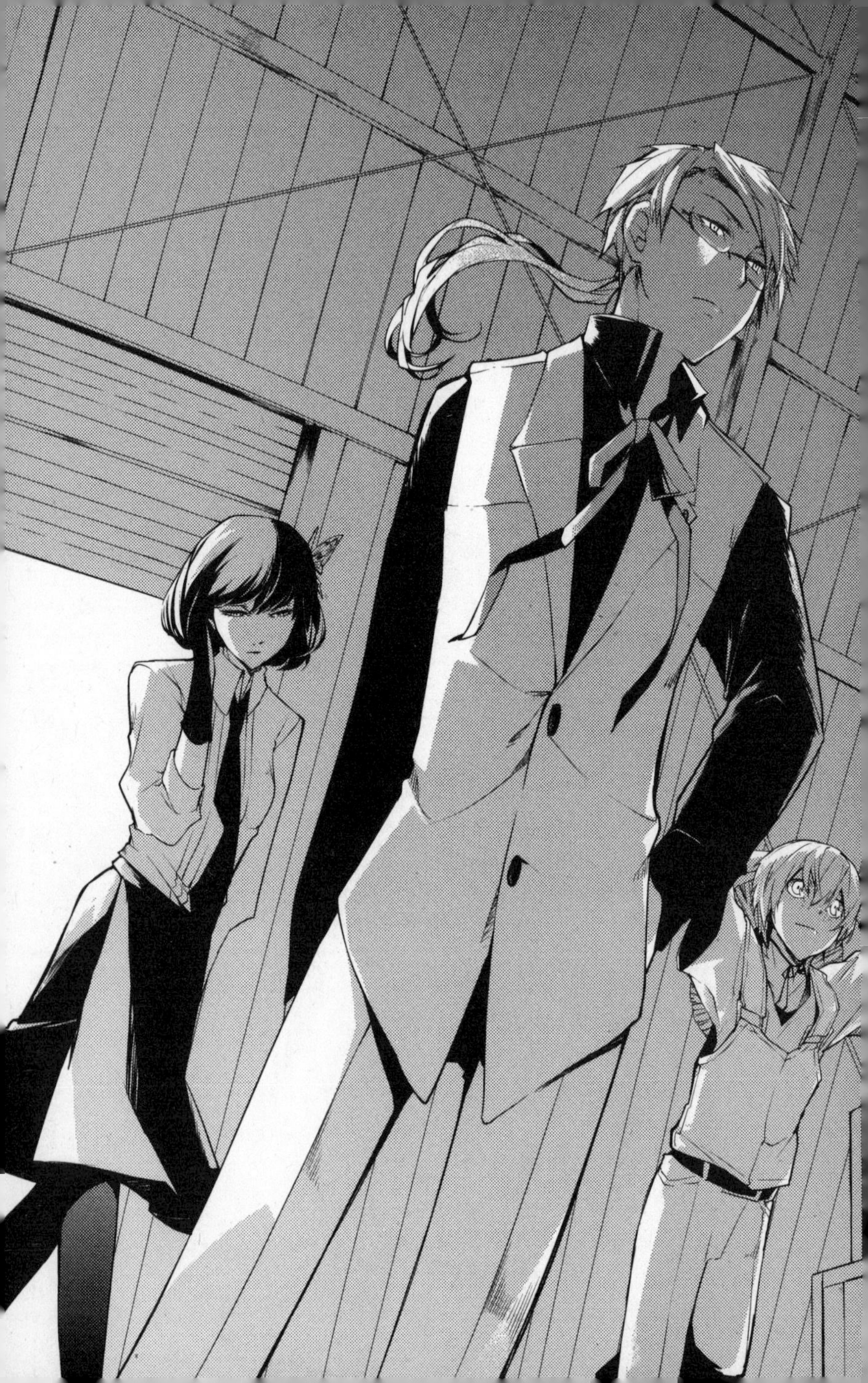

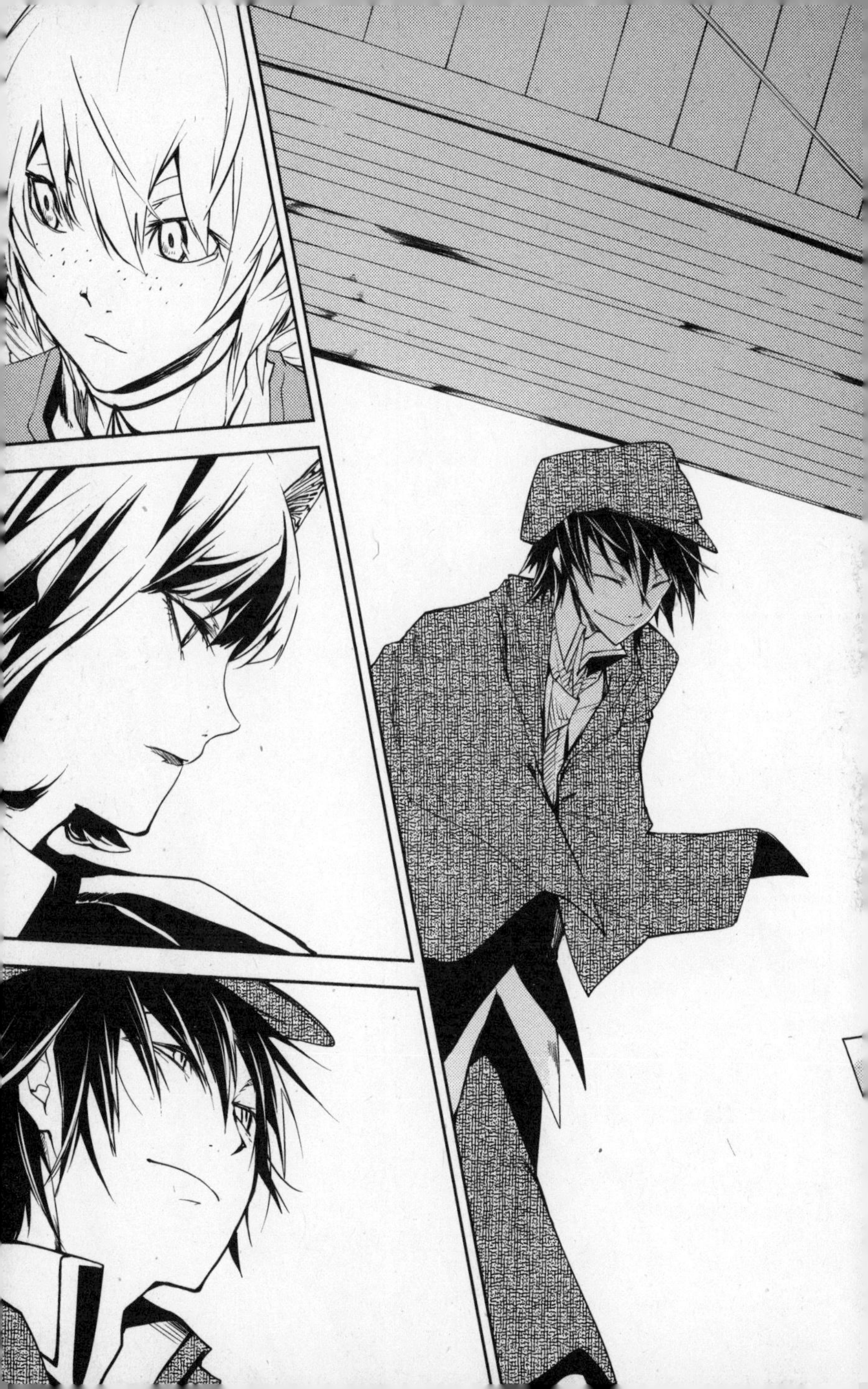

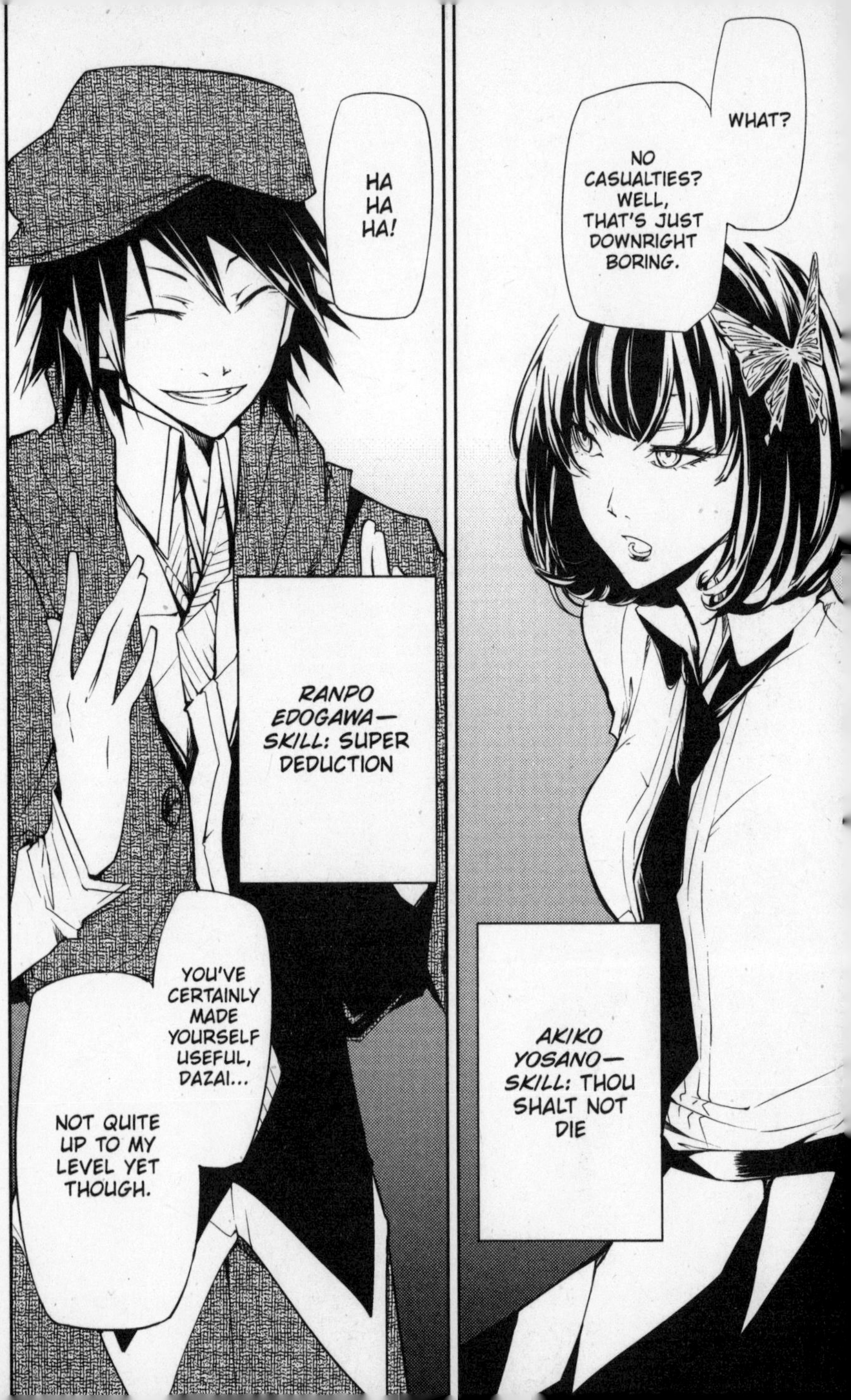
WHAT?
NO CASUALTIES? WELL, THAT'S JUST DOWNRIGHT BORING.
AKIKO YOSANO—SKILL: THOU SHALT NOT DIE
HA HA HA!
RANPO EDOGAWA—SKILL: SUPER DEDUCTION
YOU'VE CERTAINLY MADE YOURSELF USEFUL, DAZAI...
NOT QUITE UP TO MY LEVEL YET THOUGH.

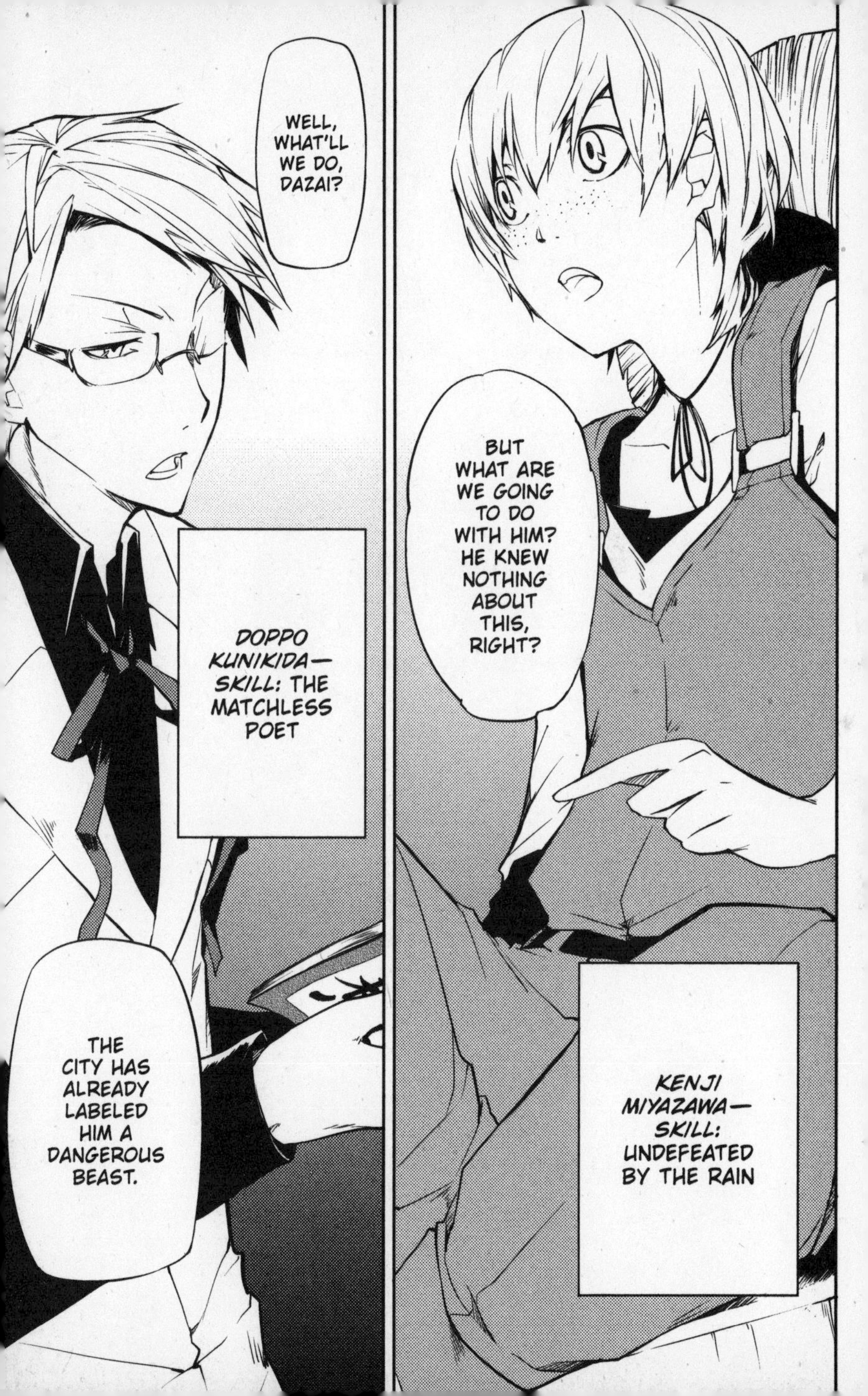
BUT WHAT ARE WE GOING TO DO WITH HIM? HE KNEW NOTHING ABOUT THIS, RIGHT?
KENJI MIYAZAWA—SKILL: UNDEFEATED BY THE RAIN
WELL, WHAT'LL WE DO, DAZAI?
DOPPO KUNIKIDA—SKILL: THE MATCHLESS POET
THE CITY HAS ALREADY LABELED HIM A DANGEROUS BEAST.

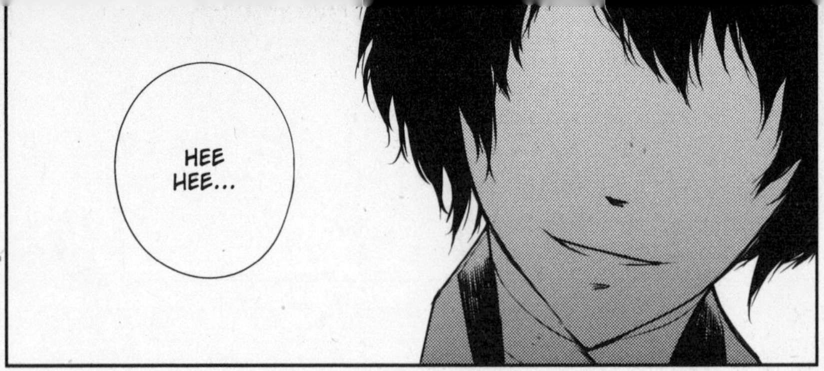
HEE HEE...

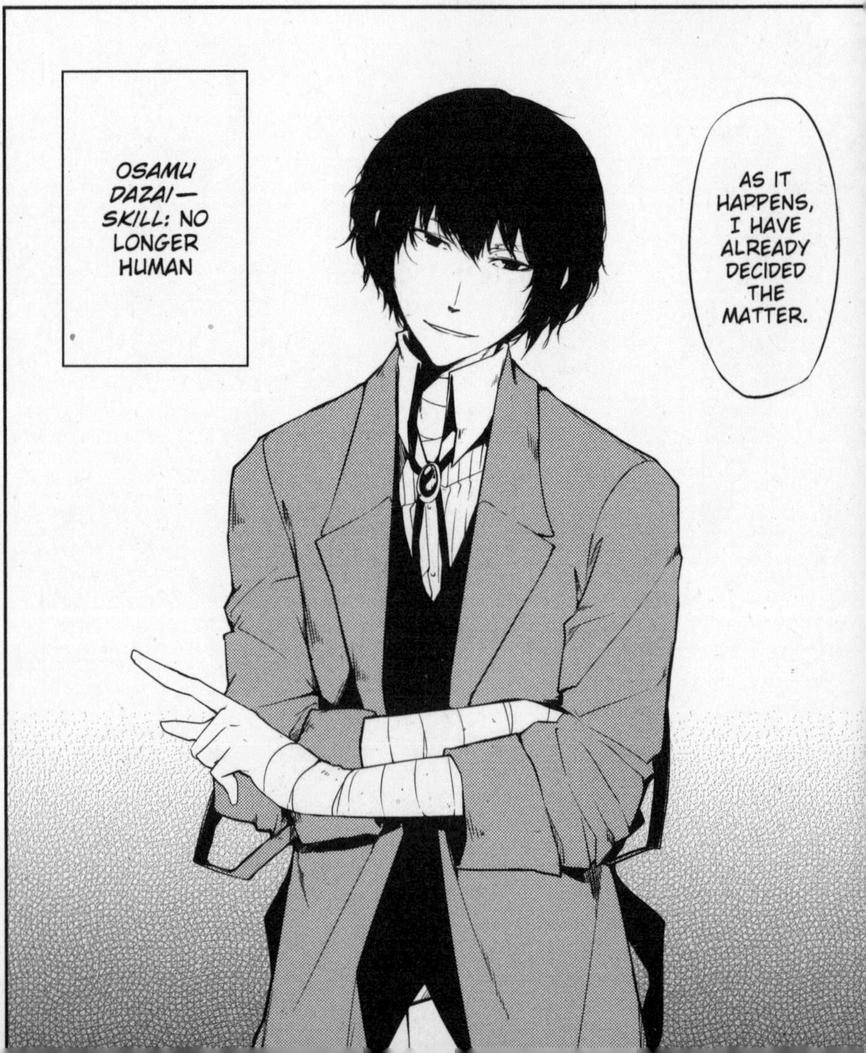
AS IT HAPPENS, I HAVE ALREADY DECIDED THE MATTER.
OSAMU DAZAI—
SKILL: NO LONGER HUMAN

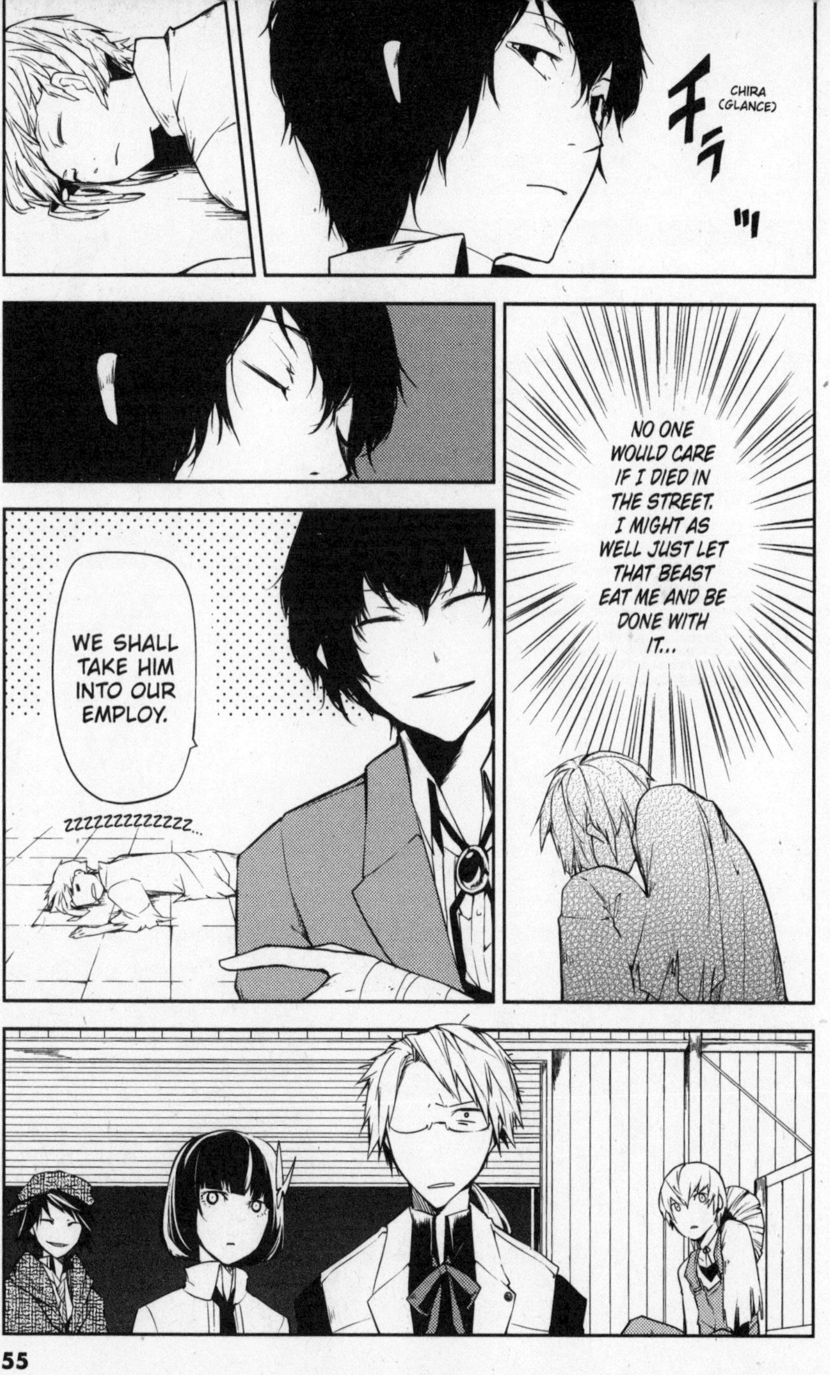
チラッ
CHIRA (GLANCE)
NO ONE WOULD CARE IF I DIED IN THE STREET. I MIGHT AS WELL JUST LET THAT BEAST EAT ME AND BE DONE WITH IT...
WE SHALL TAKE HIM INTO OUR EMPLOY.
ZZZZZZZZZZZZZ...

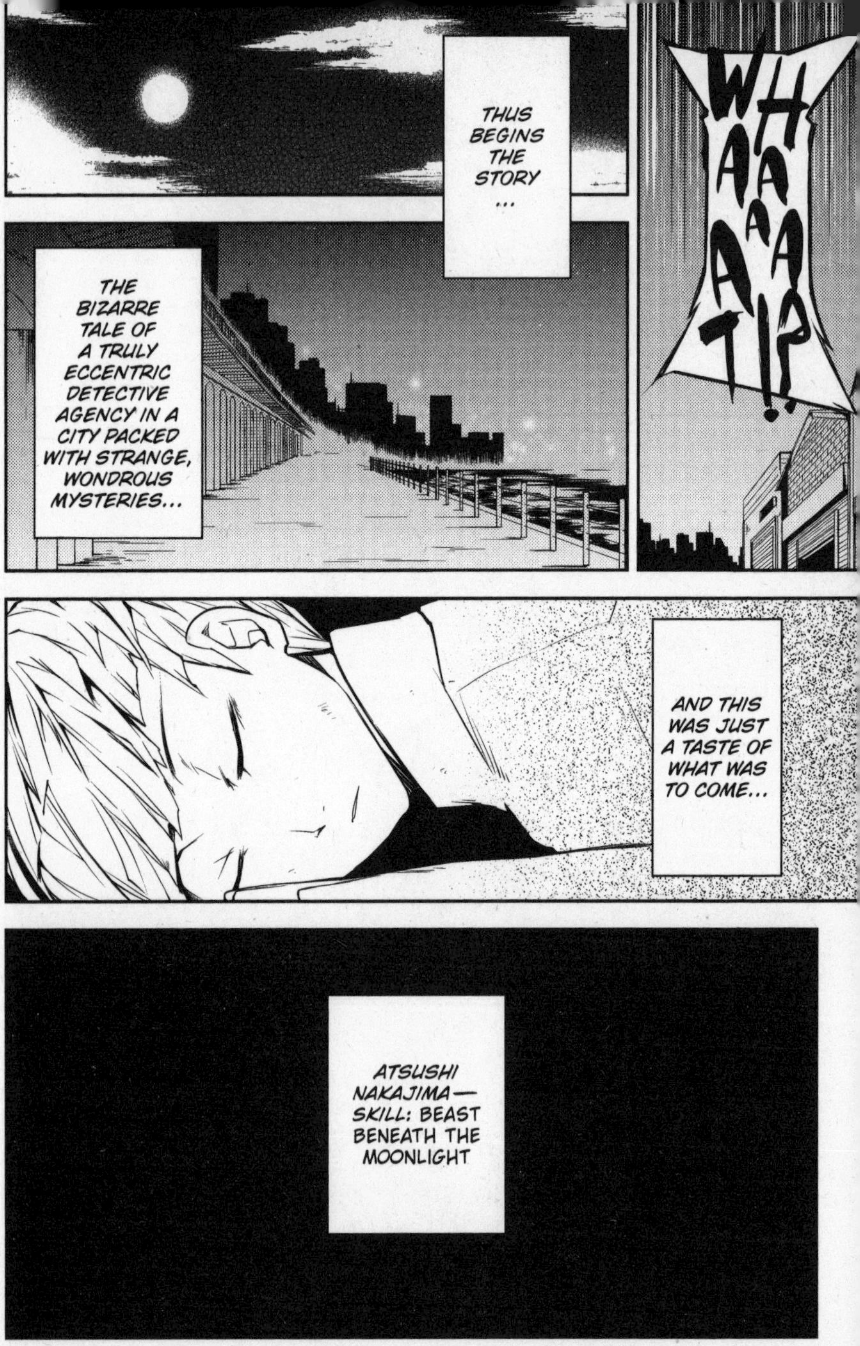
WHAAAAAAT!?
THUS BEGINS THE STORY...
THE BIZARRE TALE OF A TRULY ECCENTRIC DETECTIVE AGENCY IN A CITY PACKED WITH STRANGE, WONDROUS MYSTERIES...
AND THIS WAS JUST A TASTE OF WHAT WAS TO COME...
ATSUSHI NAKAJIMA—SKILL: BEAST BENEATH THE MOONLIGHT

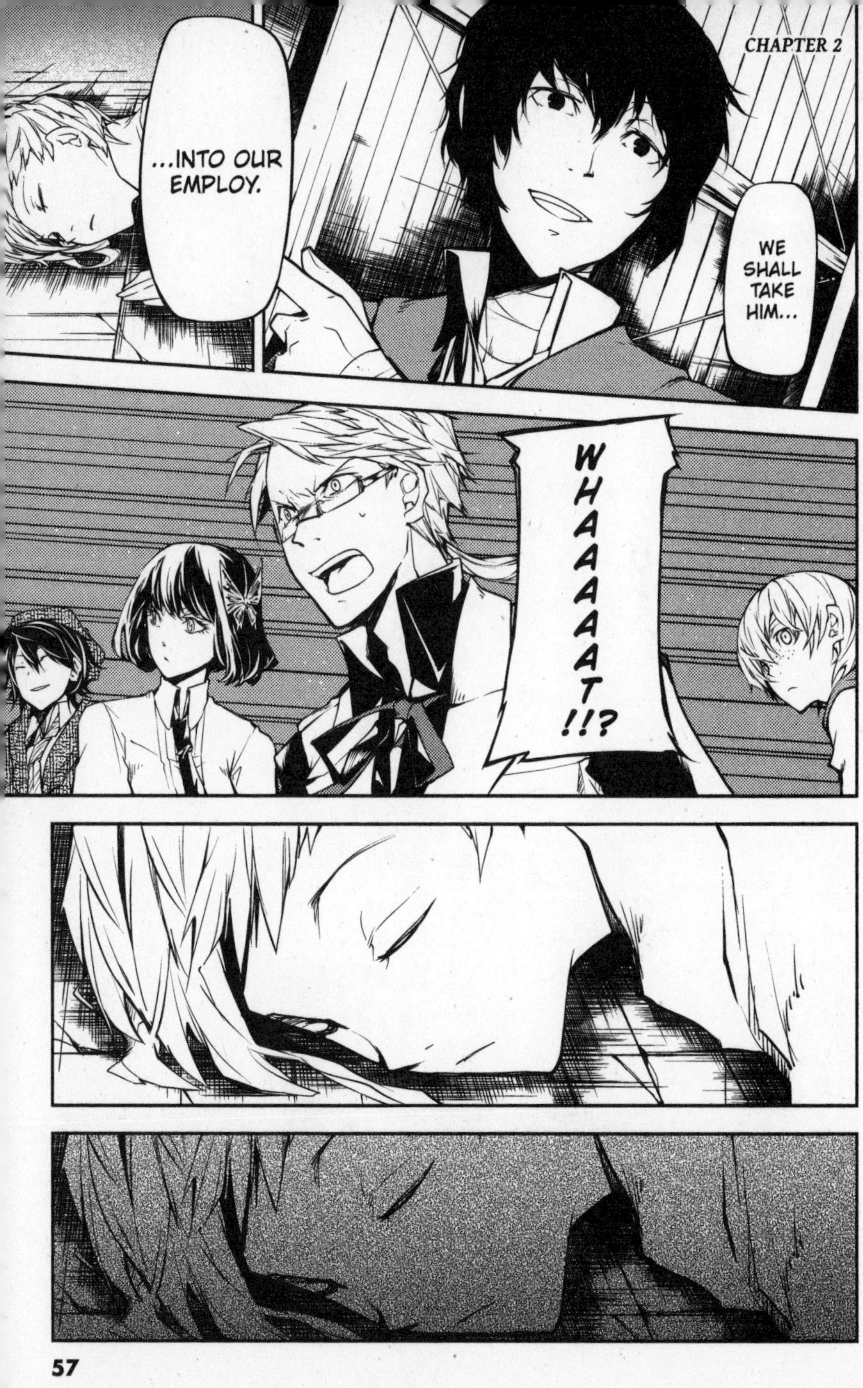
WE SHALL TAKE HIM...
...INTO OUR EMPLOY.
WHAAAAAAT!!?

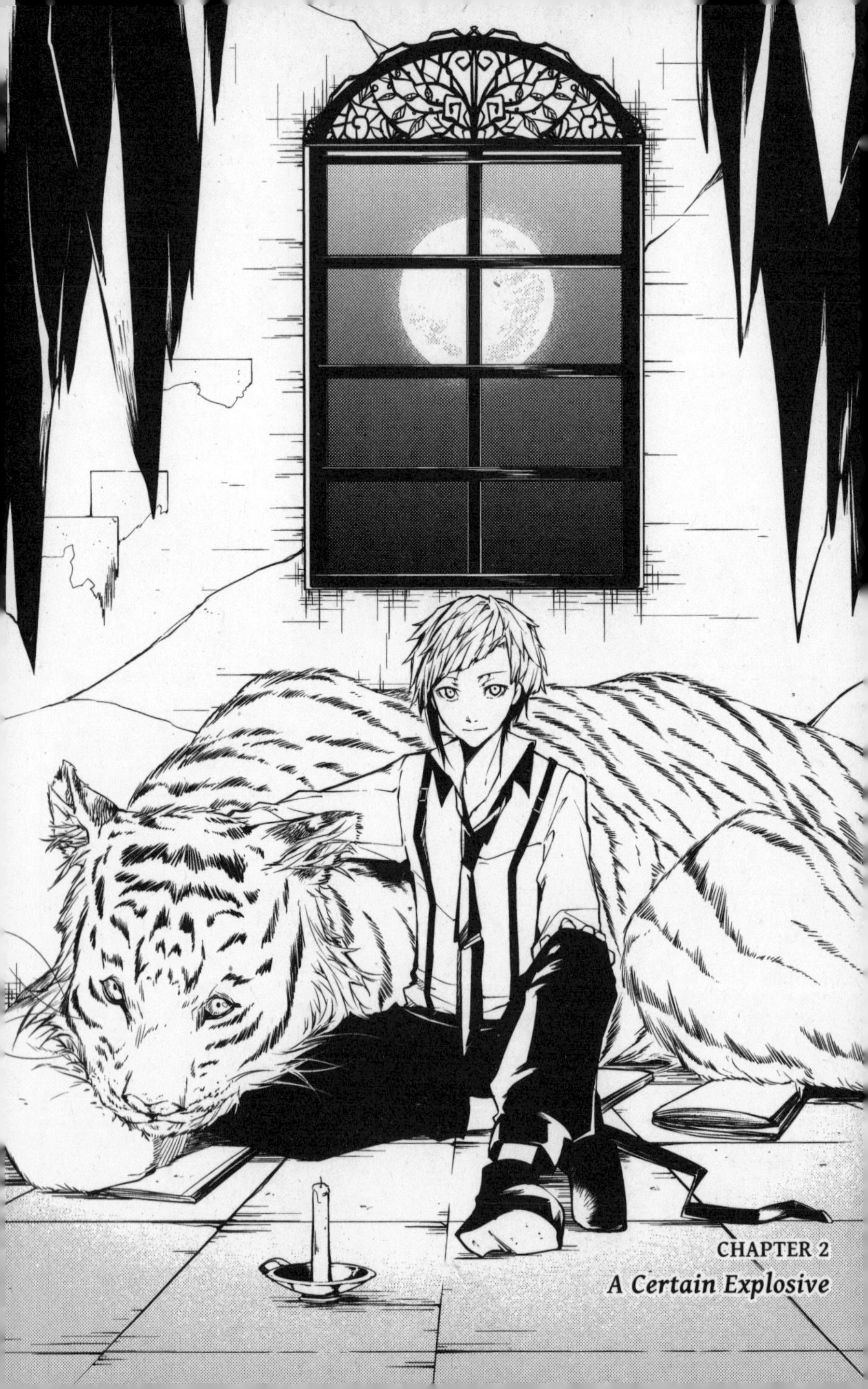

CHAPTER 2

A Certain Explosive

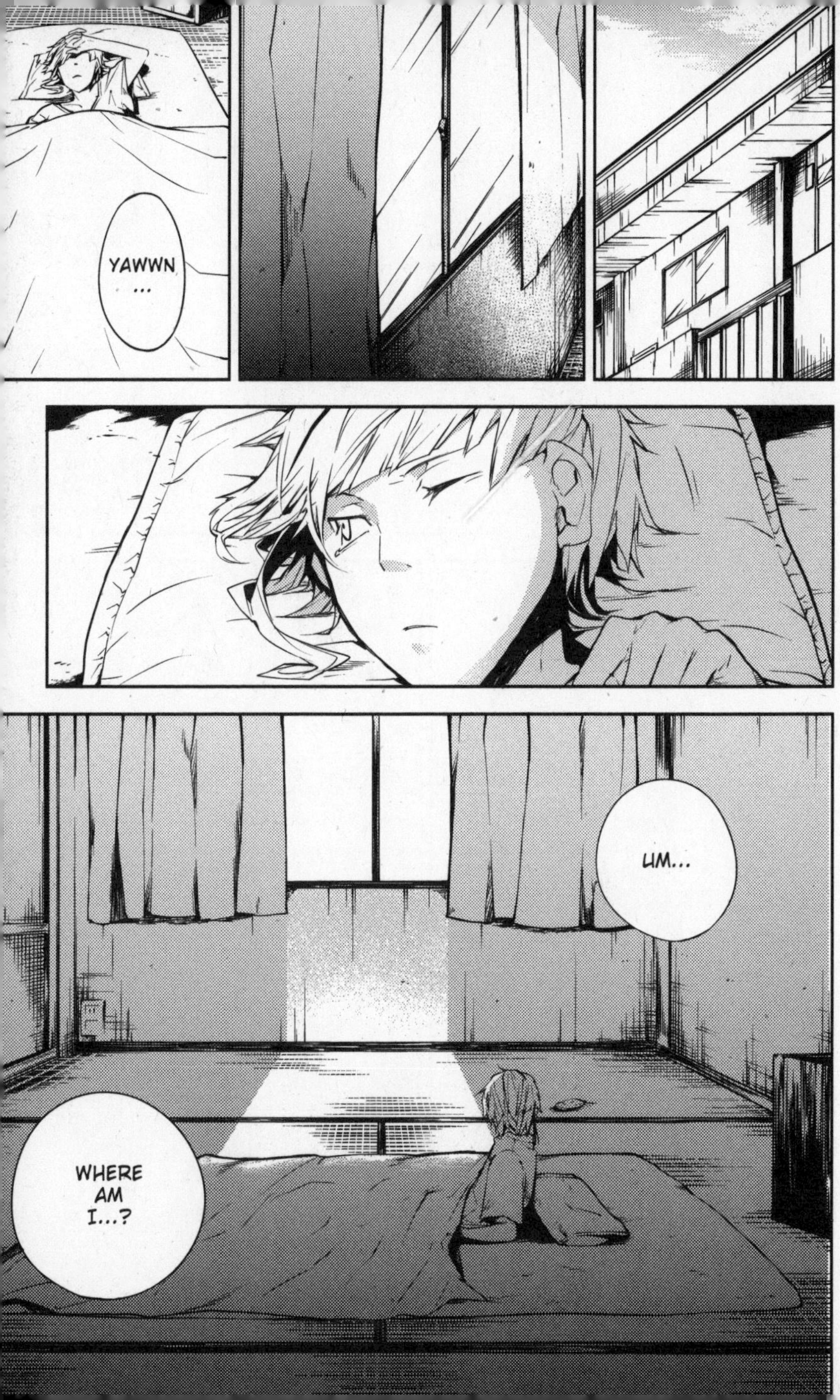
YAWWN
...
UM...
WHERE AM I...?

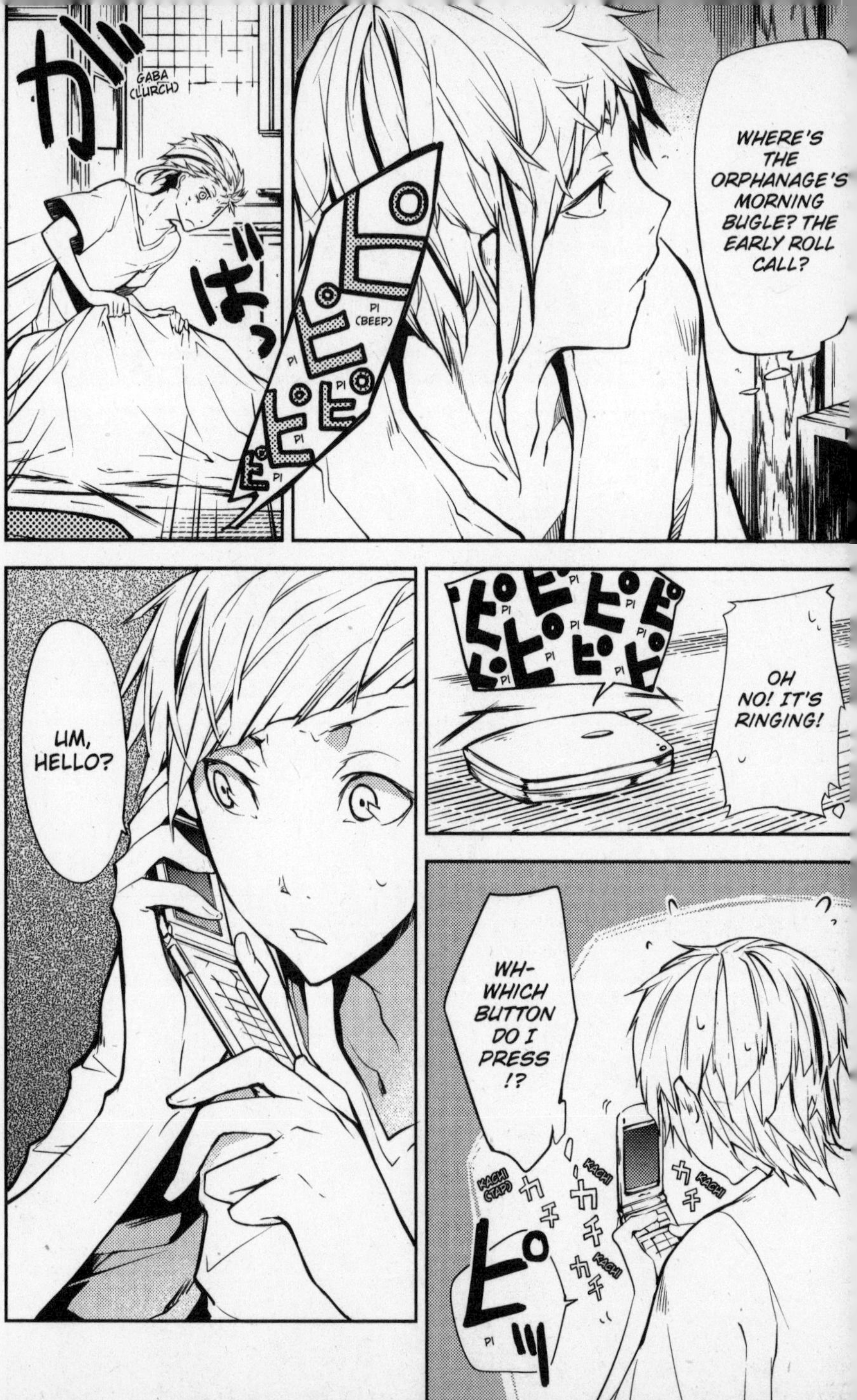
WHERE'S THE ORPHANAGE'S MORNING BUGLE? THE EARLY ROLL CALL?
PI (BEEP)
PI
PI
PI
PI
GABA (LURCH)
PI PI PI PI PI PI PI PI
OH NO! IT'S RINGING!
WH-WHICH BUTTON DO I PRESS!?
KACHI
KACHI
KACHI
KACHI (TAP)
PI
UM, HELLO?

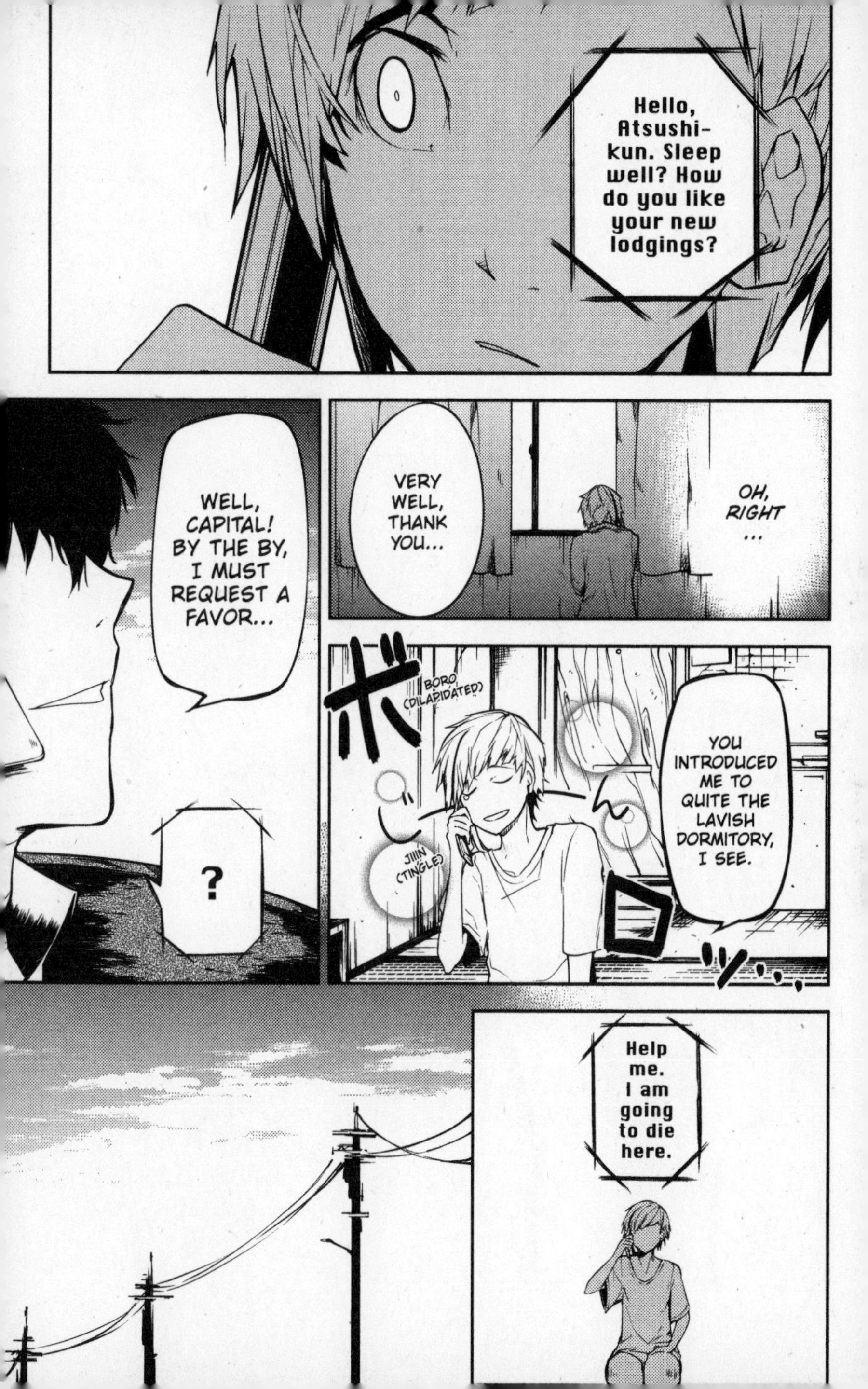
Hello, Atsushi-kun. Sleep well? How do you like your new lodgings?
OH, RIGHT...
VERY WELL, THANK YOU...
YOU INTRODUCED ME TO QUITE THE LAVISH DORMITORY, I SEE.
BORO (DILAPIDATED)
JIIIN (TINGLE)
WELL, CAPITAL! BY THE BY, I MUST REQUEST A FAVOR...
?
Help me. I am going to die here.

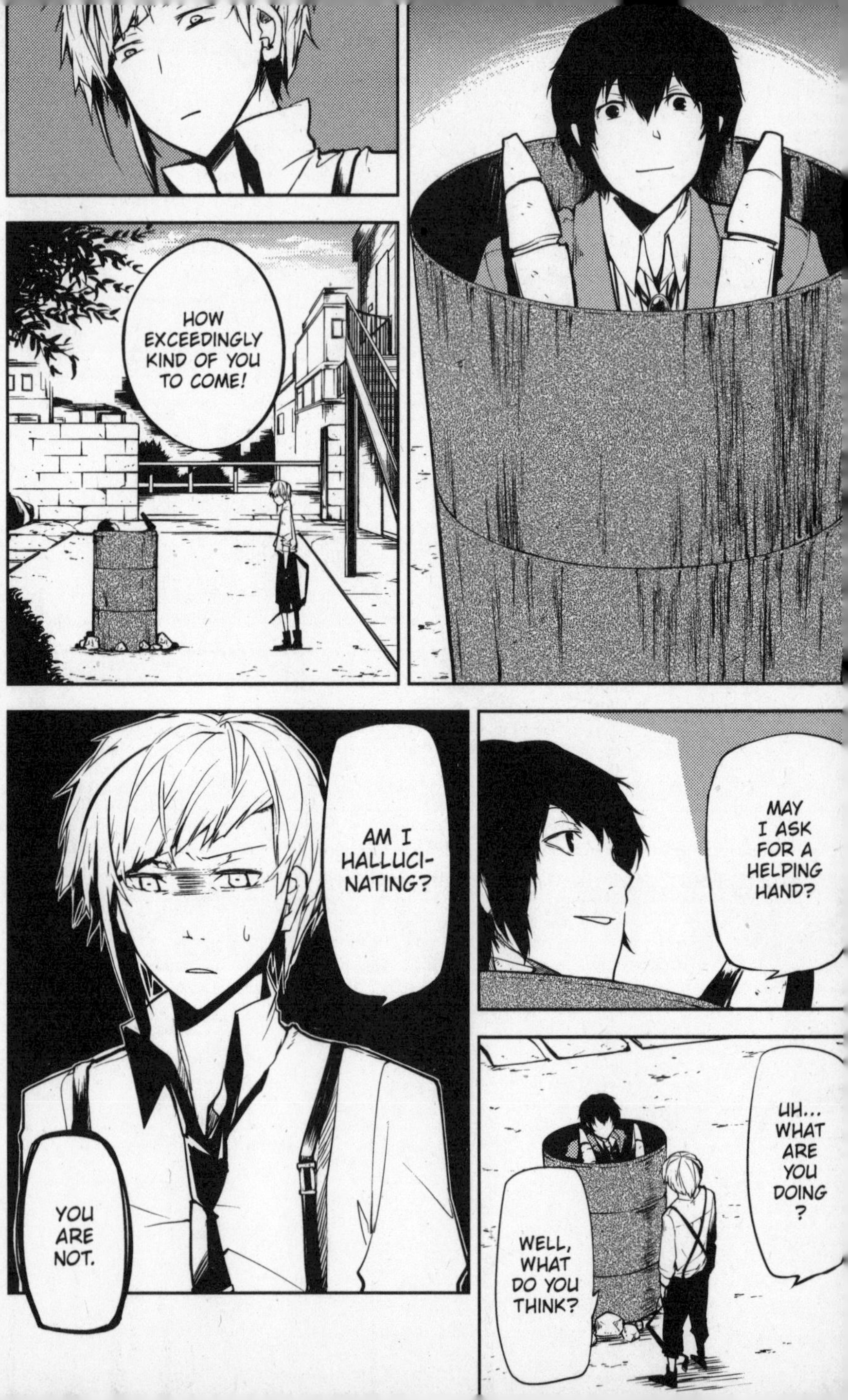
HOW EXCEEDINGLY KIND OF YOU TO COME!
MAY I ASK FOR A HELPING HAND?
UH... WHAT ARE YOU DOING?
WELL, WHAT DO YOU THINK?
AM I HALLUCI-NATING?
YOU ARE NOT.

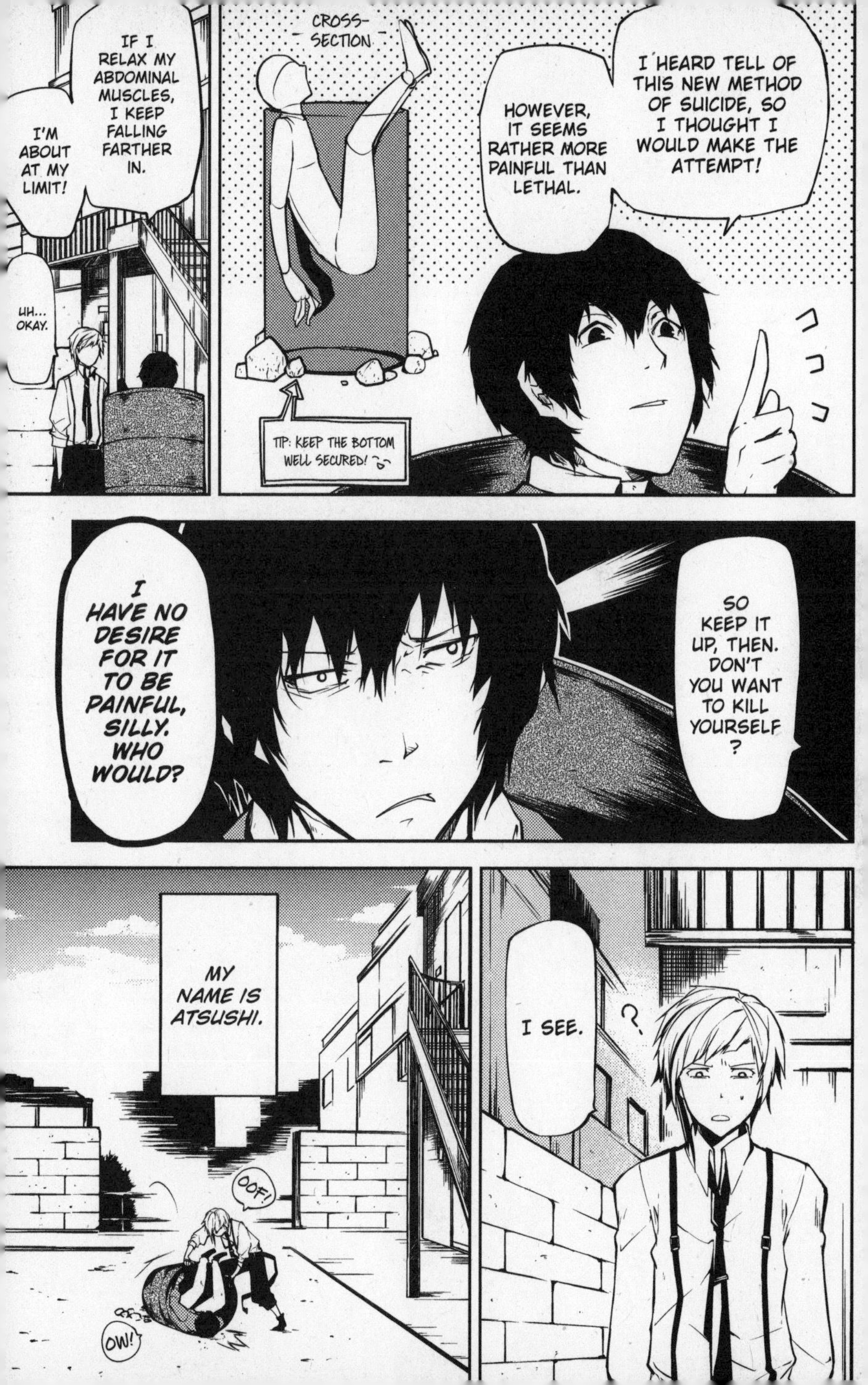
I HEARD TELL OF THIS NEW METHOD OF SUICIDE, SO I THOUGHT I WOULD MAKE THE ATTEMPT!
HOWEVER, IT SEEMS RATHER MORE PAINFUL THAN LETHAL.
CROSS-SECTION
TIP: KEEP THE BOTTOM WELL SECURED!
IF I RELAX MY ABDOMINAL MUSCLES, I KEEP FALLING FARTHER IN.
I'M ABOUT AT MY LIMIT!
UH... OKAY.
SO KEEP IT UP, THEN. DON'T YOU WANT TO KILL YOURSELF?
I HAVE NO DESIRE FOR IT TO BE PAINFUL, SILLY. WHO WOULD?
I SEE.
MY NAME IS ATSUSHI.
OOF!
OW!

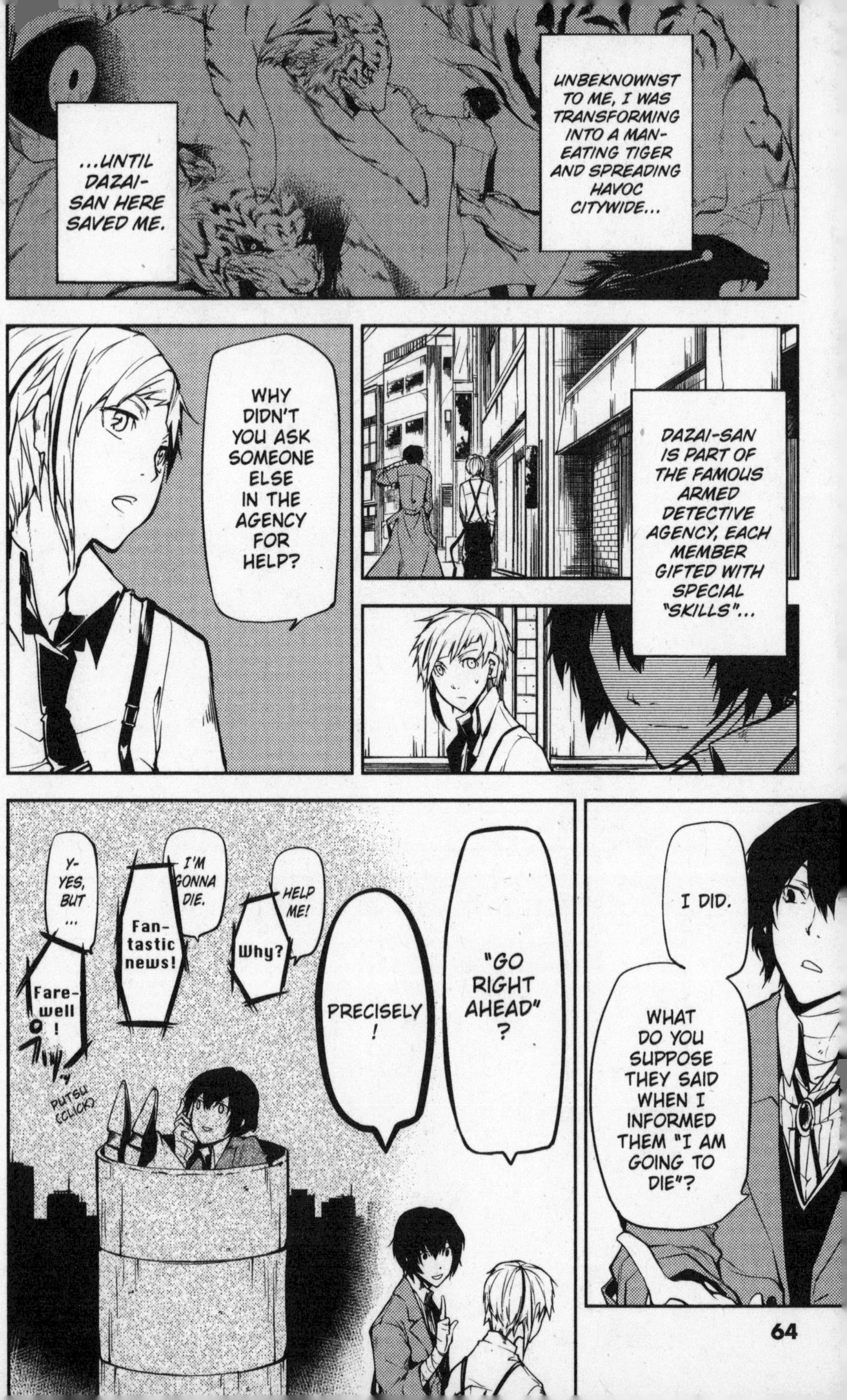
UNBEKNOWNST TO ME, I WAS TRANSFORMING INTO A MAN-EATING TIGER AND SPREADING HAVOC CITYWIDE...
...UNTIL DAZAI-SAN HERE SAVED ME.
DAZAI-SAN IS PART OF THE FAMOUS ARMED DETECTIVE AGENCY, EACH MEMBER GIFTED WITH SPECIAL "SKILLS"...
WHY DIDN'T YOU ASK SOMEONE ELSE IN THE AGENCY FOR HELP?
I DID.
WHAT DO YOU SUPPOSE THEY SAID WHEN I INFORMED THEM "I AM GOING TO DIE"?
"GO RIGHT AHEAD"?
PRECISELY!
HELP ME!
Why?
I'M GONNA DIE.
Fantastic news!
Y-YES, BUT...
Farewell!
PUTSU (CLICK)

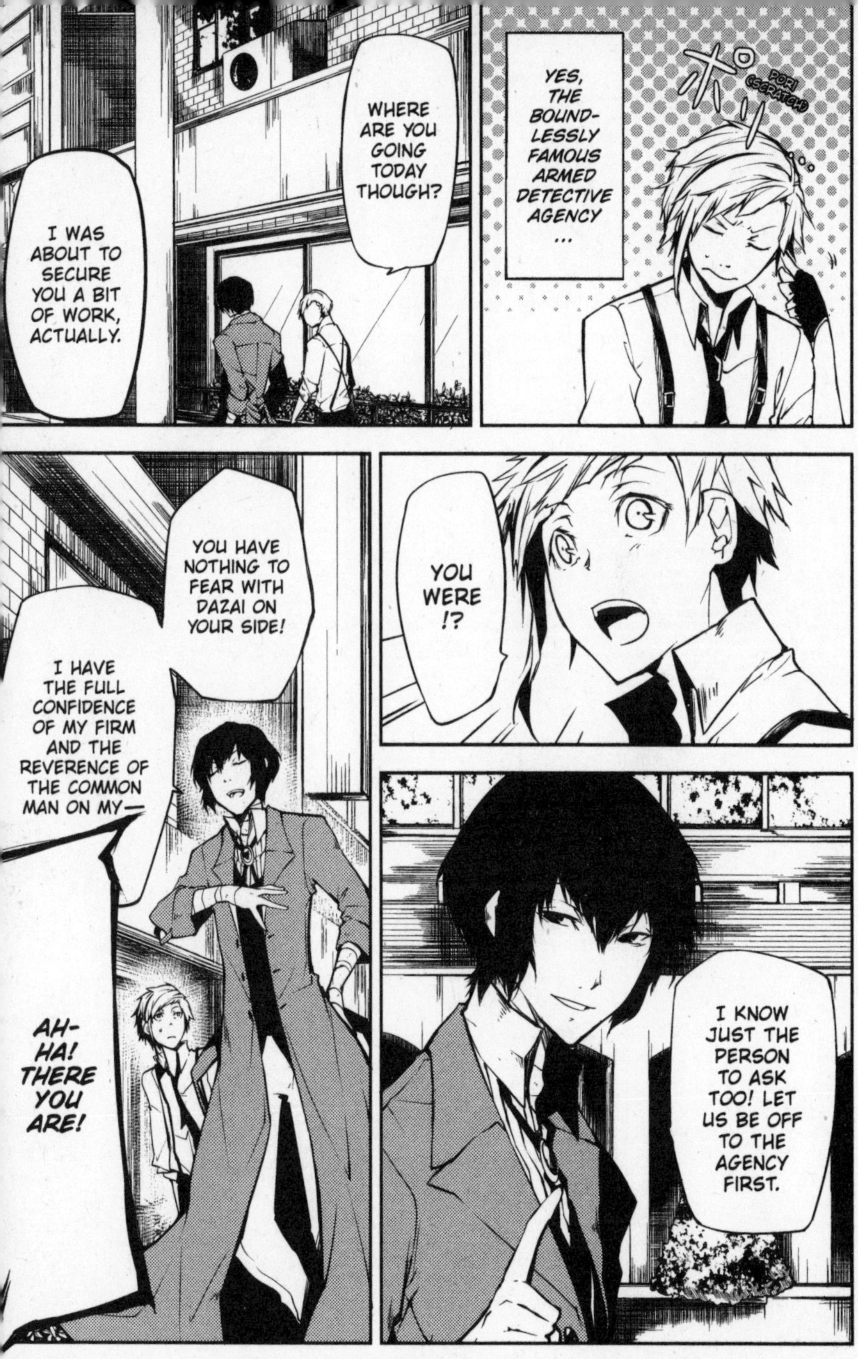
YES, THE BOUNDLESSLY FAMOUS ARMED DETECTIVE AGENCY ...
PORI (SCRATCH)
WHERE ARE YOU GOING TODAY THOUGH?
I WAS ABOUT TO SECURE YOU A BIT OF WORK, ACTUALLY.
YOU WERE !?
I KNOW JUST THE PERSON TO ASK TOO! LET US BE OFF TO THE AGENCY FIRST.
YOU HAVE NOTHING TO FEAR WITH DAZAI ON YOUR SIDE!
I HAVE THE FULL CONFIDENCE OF MY FIRM AND THE REVERENCE OF THE COMMON MAN ON MY—
AH-HA! THERE YOU ARE!

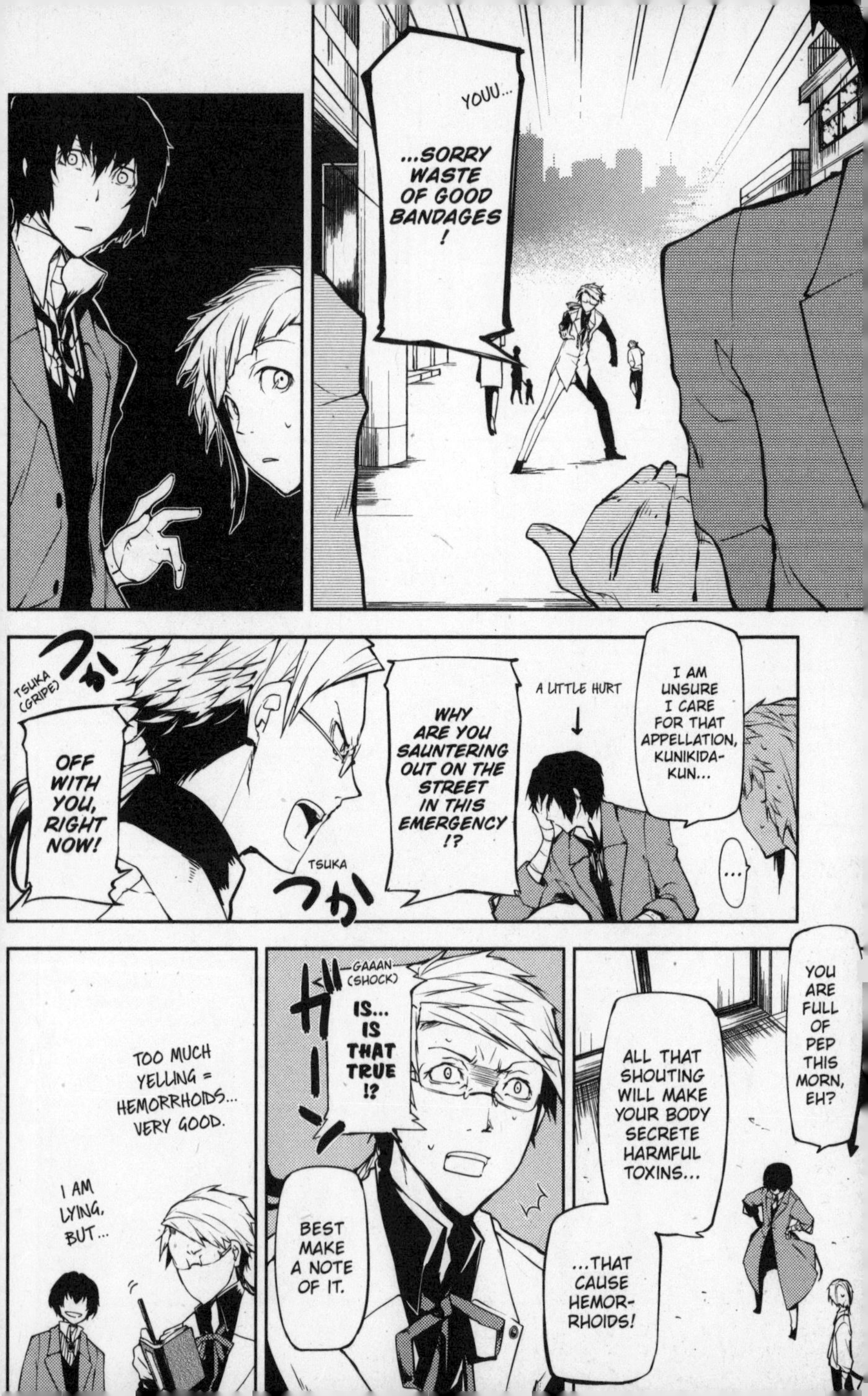
YOUU...
...SORRY WASTE OF GOOD BANDAGES!
I AM UNSURE I CARE FOR THAT APPELLATION, KUNIKIDA-KUN...
A LITTLE HURT
...
WHY ARE YOU SAUNTERING OUT ON THE STREET IN THIS EMERGENCY!?
つか
TSUKA
つか
TSUKA (GRIPE)
OFF WITH YOU, RIGHT NOW!
YOU ARE FULL OF PEP THIS MORN, EH?
ALL THAT SHOUTING WILL MAKE YOUR BODY SECRETE HARMFUL TOXINS...
...THAT CAUSE HEMORRHOIDS!
GAAAN (SHOCK)
IS... IS THAT TRUE!?
BEST MAKE A NOTE OF IT.
TOO MUCH YELLING = HEMORRHOIDS... VERY GOOD.
I AM LYING, BUT...

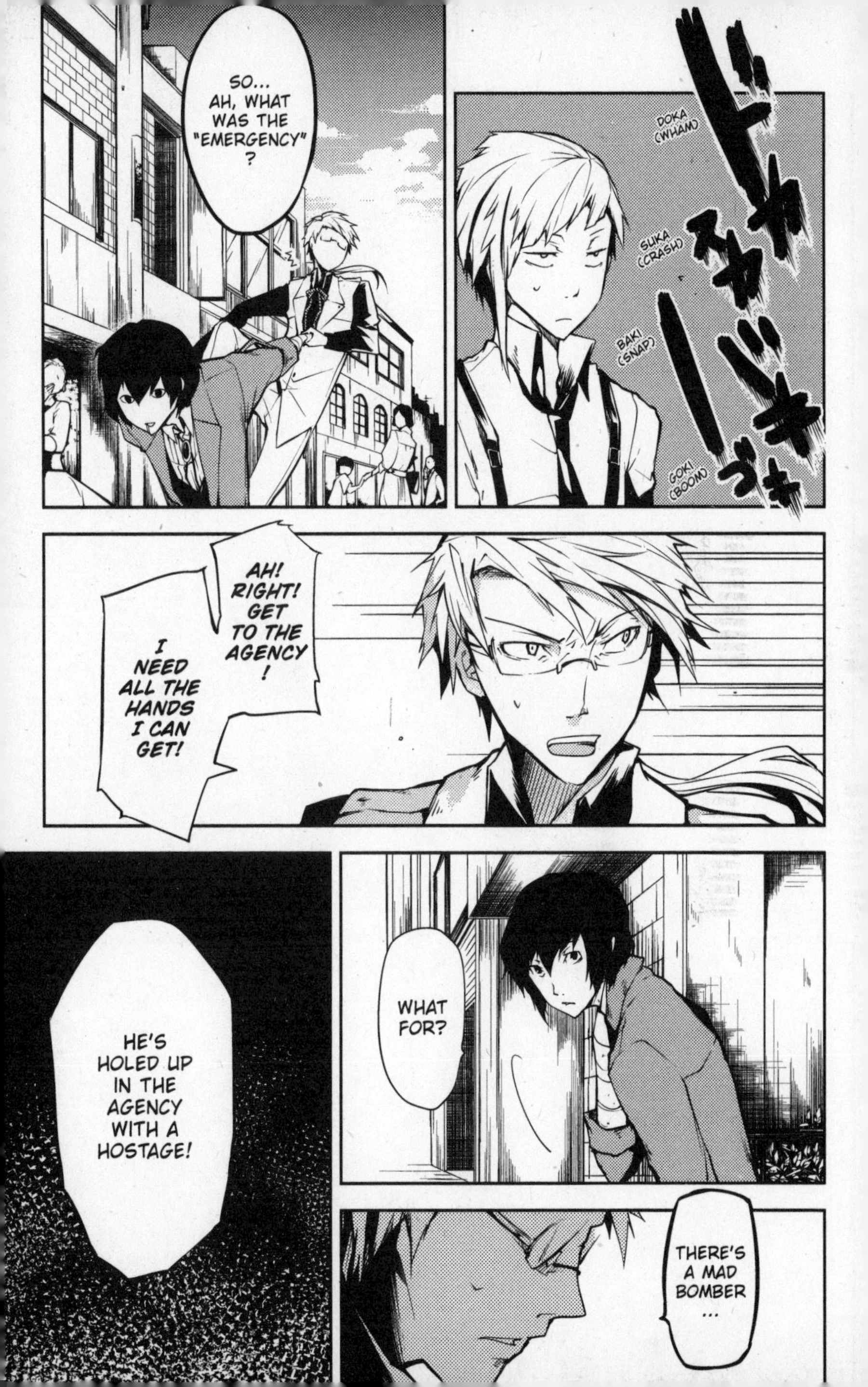
DOKA (WHAM)
SUKA (CRASH)
BAKI (SNAP)
GOKI (BOOM)
SO... AH, WHAT WAS THE "EMERGENCY"?
AH! RIGHT! GET TO THE AGENCY!
I NEED ALL THE HANDS I CAN GET!
WHAT FOR?
THERE'S A MAD BOMBER...
HE'S HOLED UP IN THE AGENCY WITH A HOSTAGE!

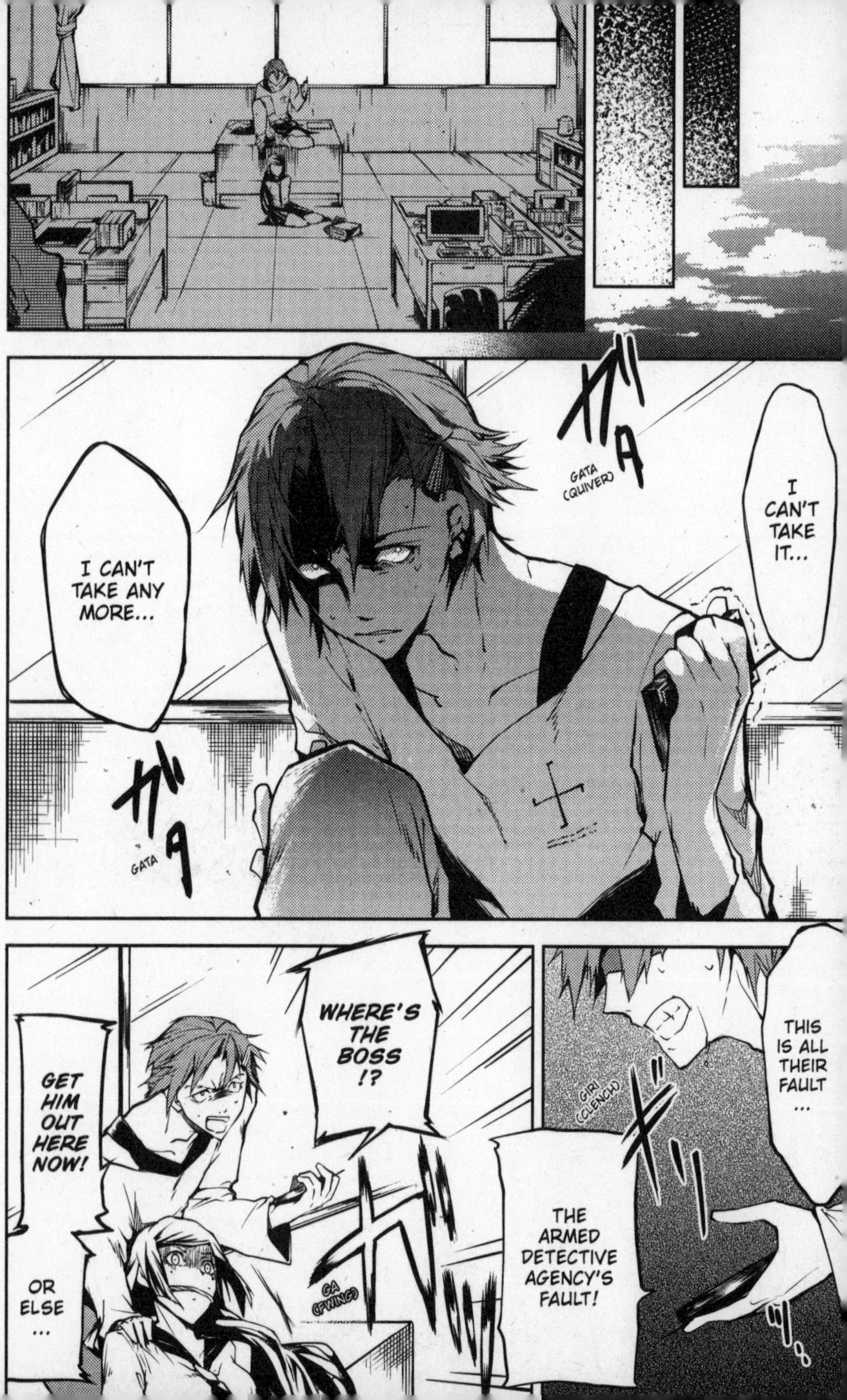

I CAN'T TAKE IT...
GATA (QUIVER)
I CAN'T TAKE ANY MORE...
GATA
THIS IS ALL THEIR FAULT...
GIRI (CLENCH)
THE ARMED DETECTIVE AGENCY'S FAULT!
WHERE'S THE BOSS!?
GET HIM OUT HERE NOW!
GA (FWING)
OR ELSE...

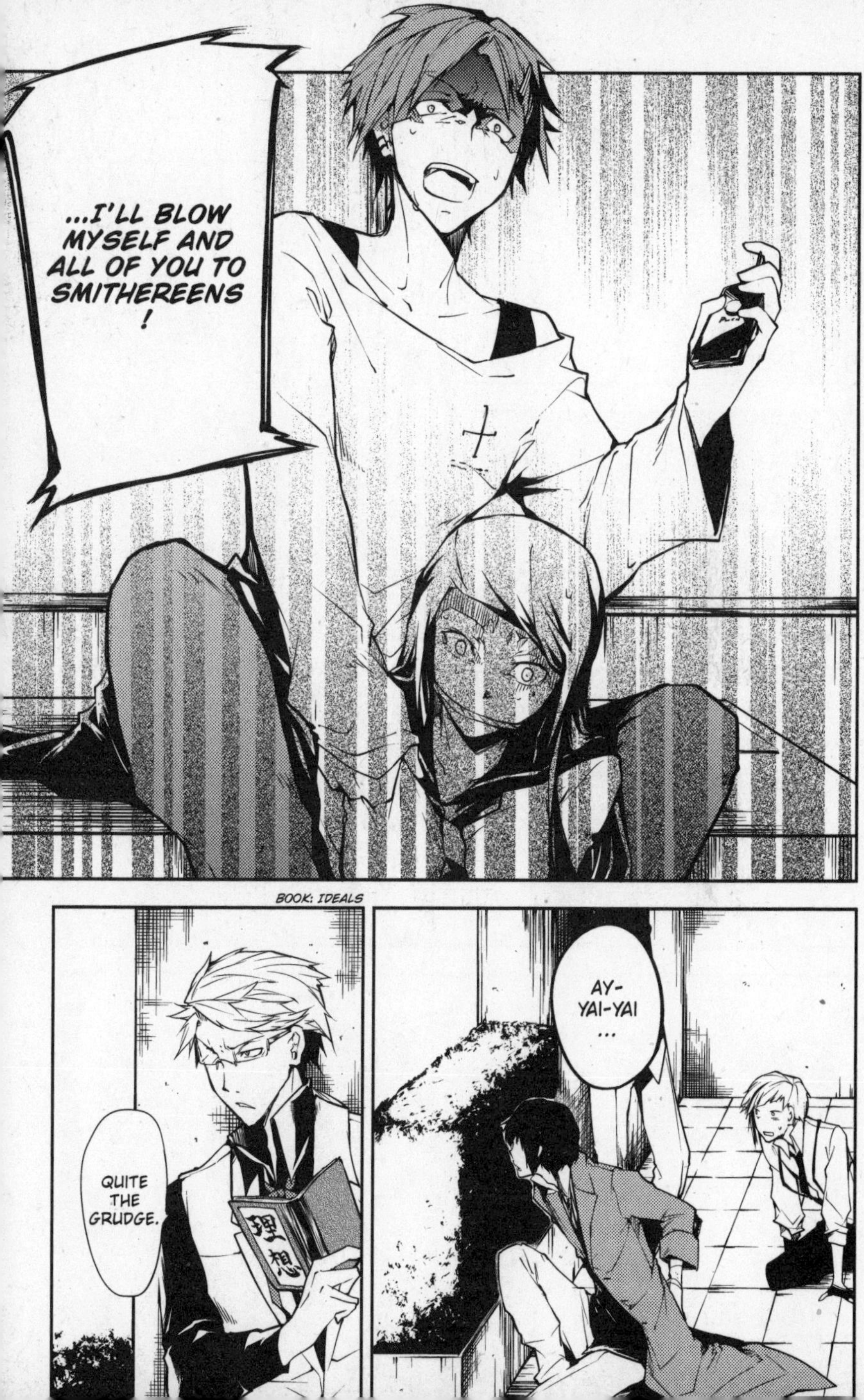
...I'LL BLOW MYSELF AND ALL OF YOU TO SMITHEREENS!
BOOK: IDEALS
AY-YAI-YAI...
QUITE THE GRUDGE.
理想

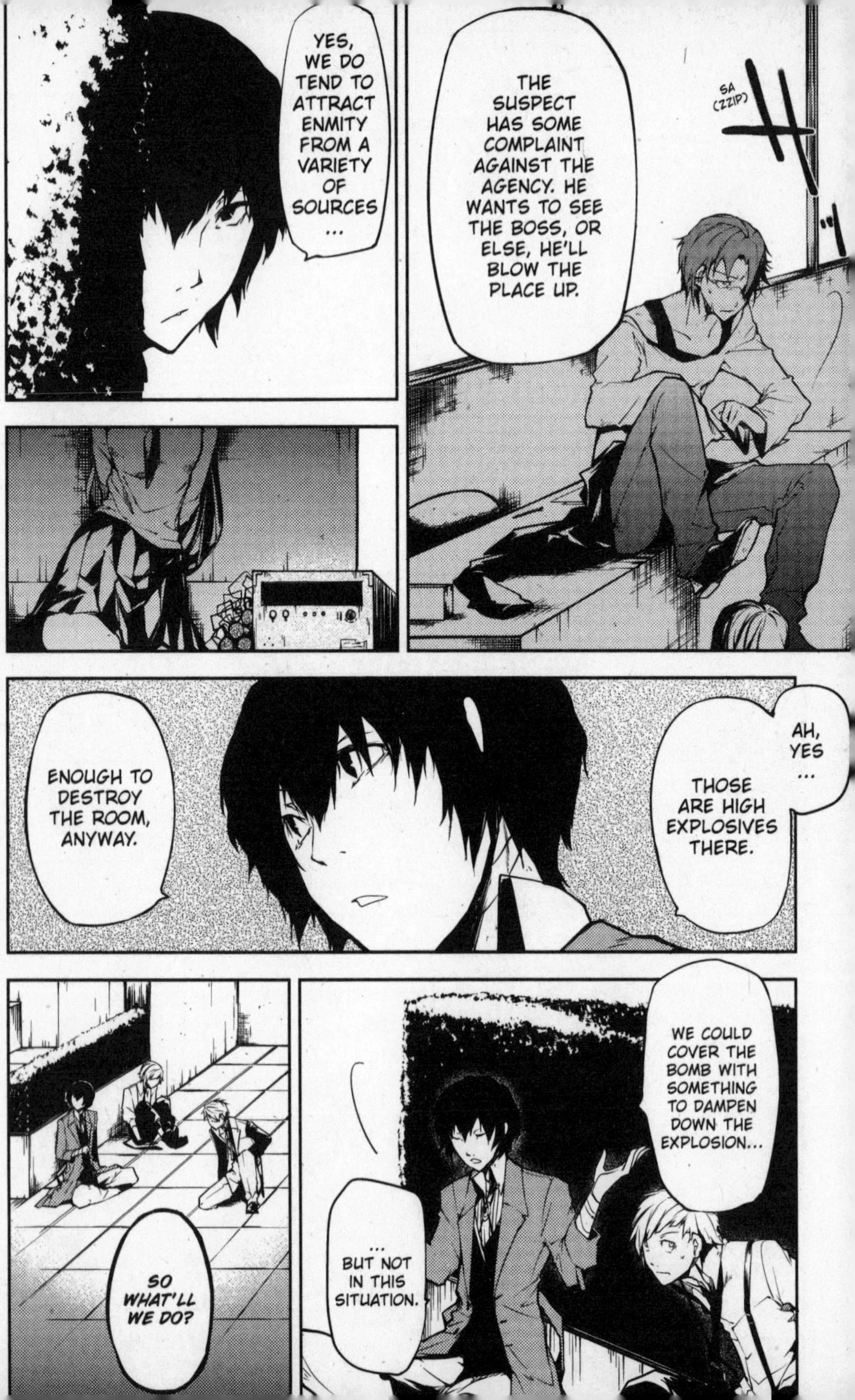
SA (ZZIP)
THE SUSPECT HAS SOME COMPLAINT AGAINST THE AGENCY. HE WANTS TO SEE THE BOSS, OR ELSE, HE'LL BLOW THE PLACE UP.
YES, WE DO TEND TO ATTRACT ENMITY FROM A VARIETY OF SOURCES ...
AH, YES ...
THOSE ARE HIGH EXPLOSIVES THERE.
ENOUGH TO DESTROY THE ROOM, ANYWAY.
WE COULD COVER THE BOMB WITH SOMETHING TO DAMPEN DOWN THE EXPLOSION...
... BUT NOT IN THIS SITUATION.
SO WHAT'LL WE DO?

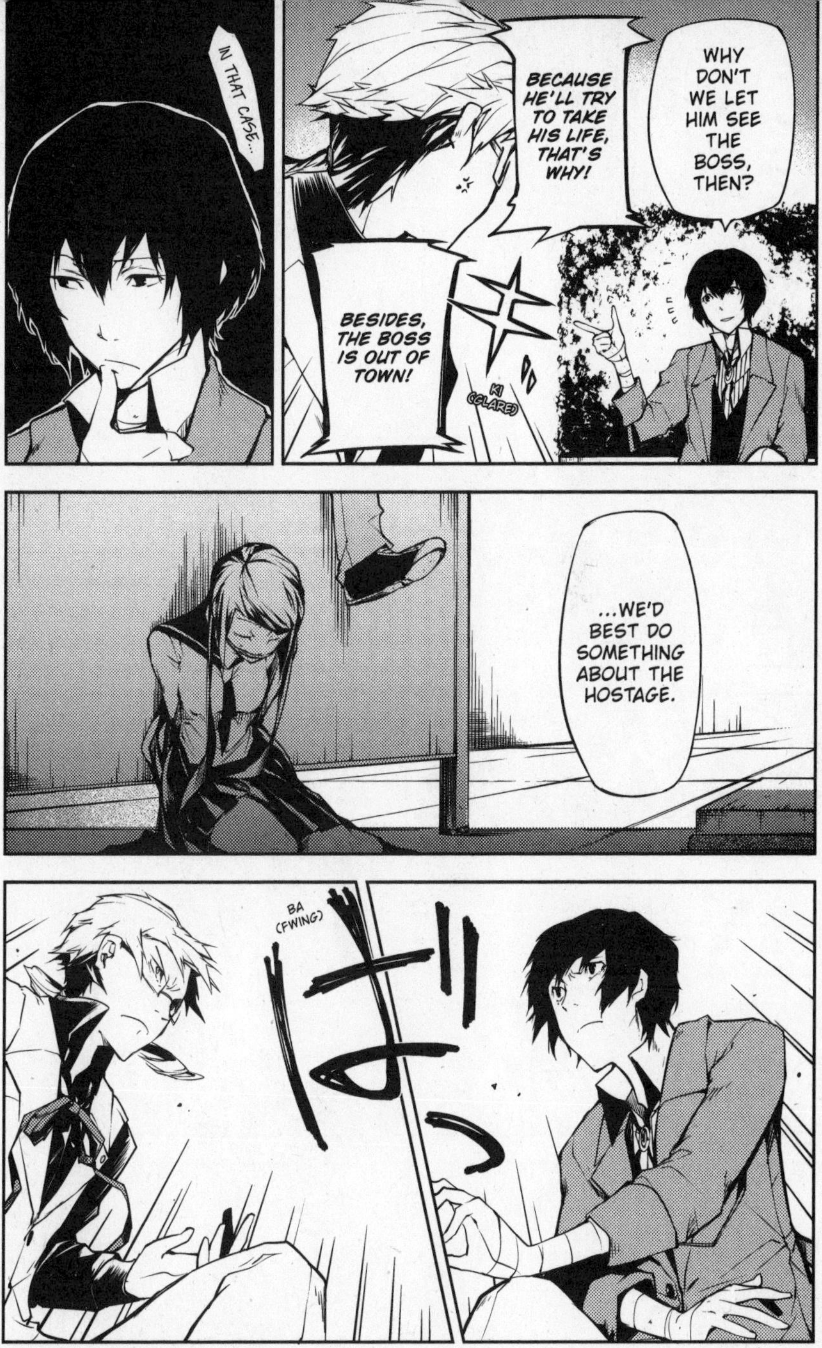
WHY DON'T WE LET HIM SEE THE BOSS, THEN?
BECAUSE HE'LL TRY TO TAKE HIS LIFE, THAT'S WHY!
BESIDES, THE BOSS IS OUT OF TOWN!
KI (GLARE)
IN THAT CASE...
...WE'D BEST DO SOMETHING ABOUT THE HOSTAGE.
BA (FWING)

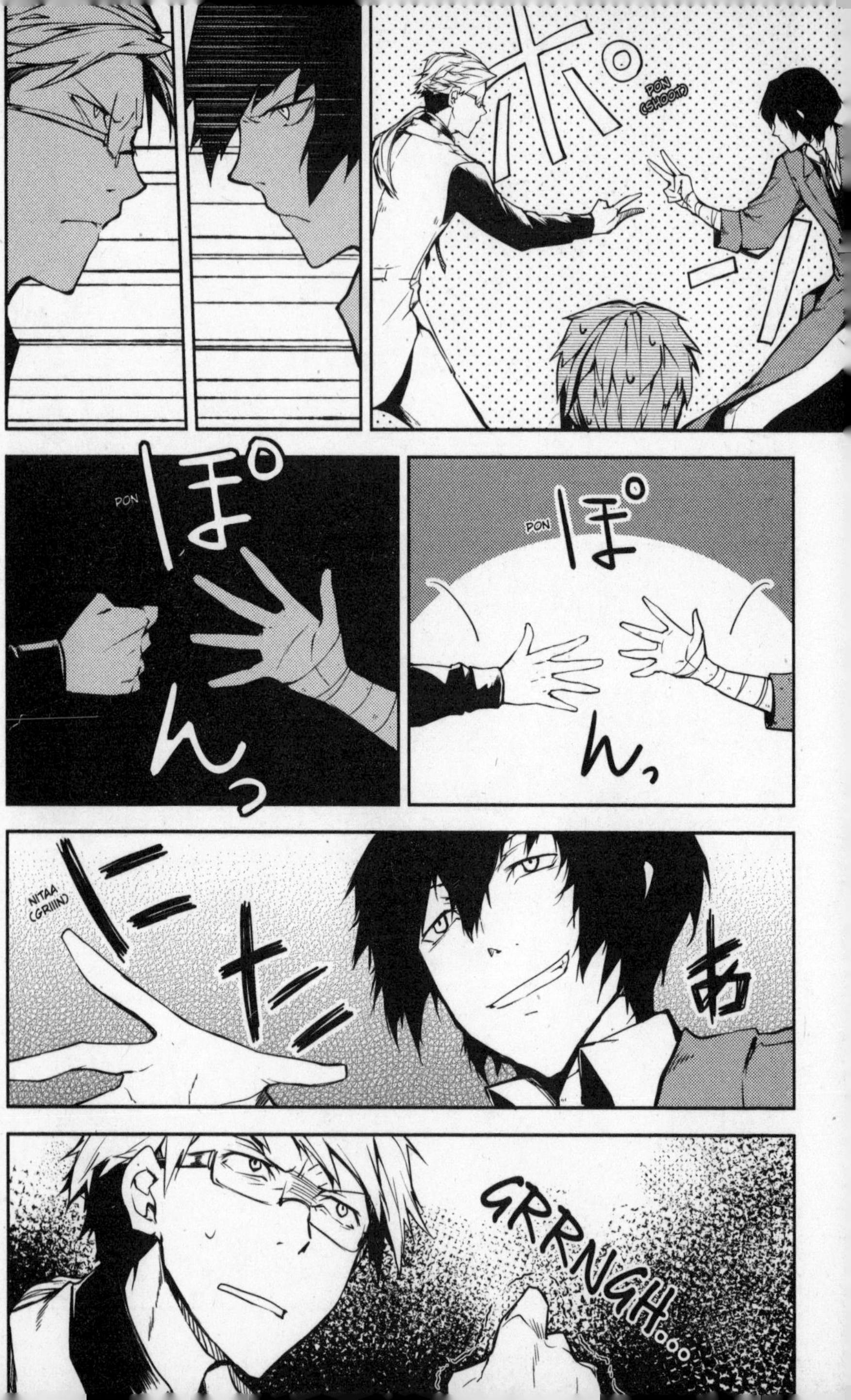
PON (SHOOT!)
ぽんっ
PON
ぽんっ
PON
NITAA (GRIIIN)
GRRNGH...

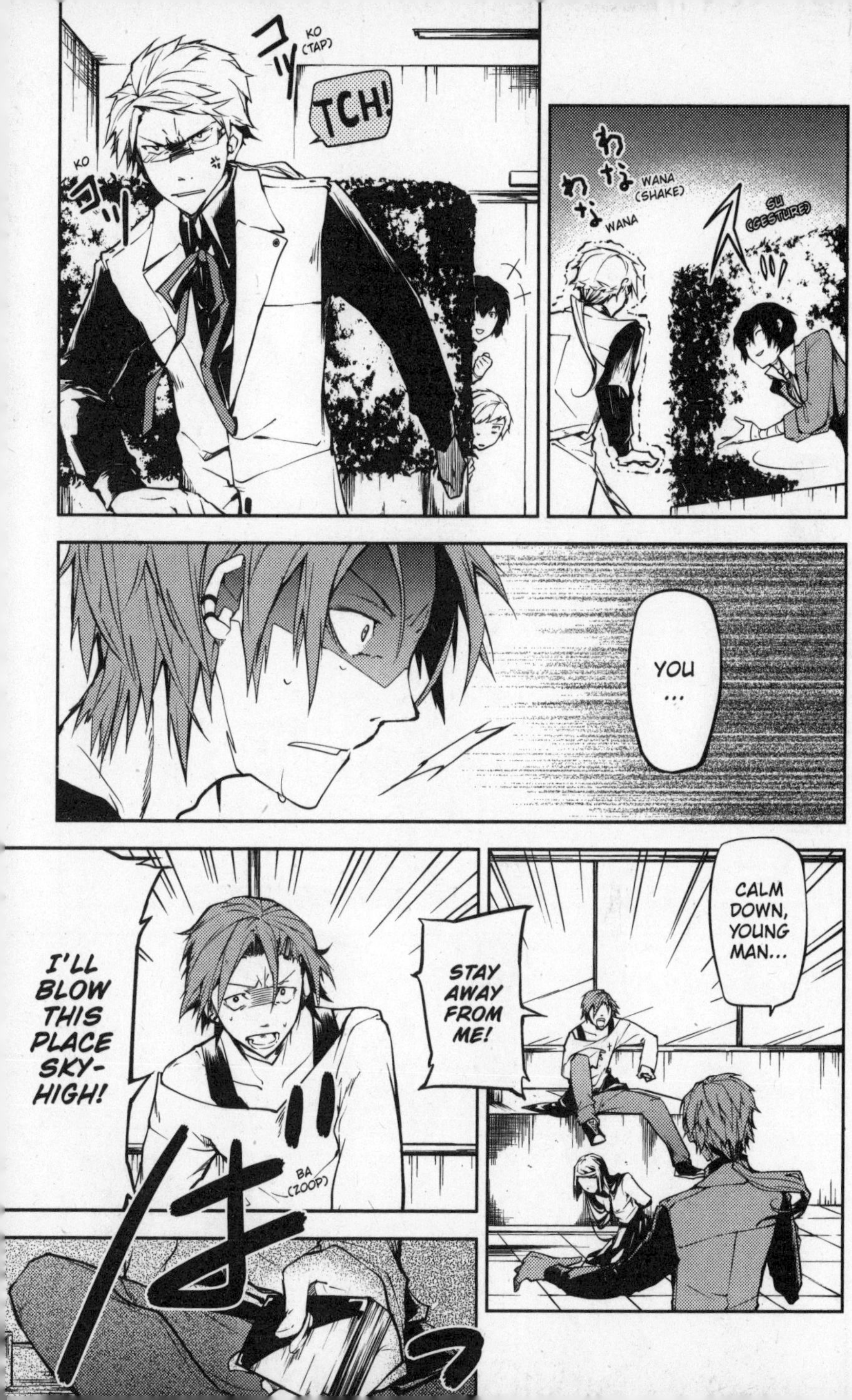
わな
わな
WANA (SHAKE)
WANA
SU (GESTURE)
KO (TAP)
TCH!
KO
YOU ...
CALM DOWN, YOUNG MAN...
STAY AWAY FROM ME!
I'LL BLOW THIS PLACE SKY-HIGH!
BA (ZOOP)

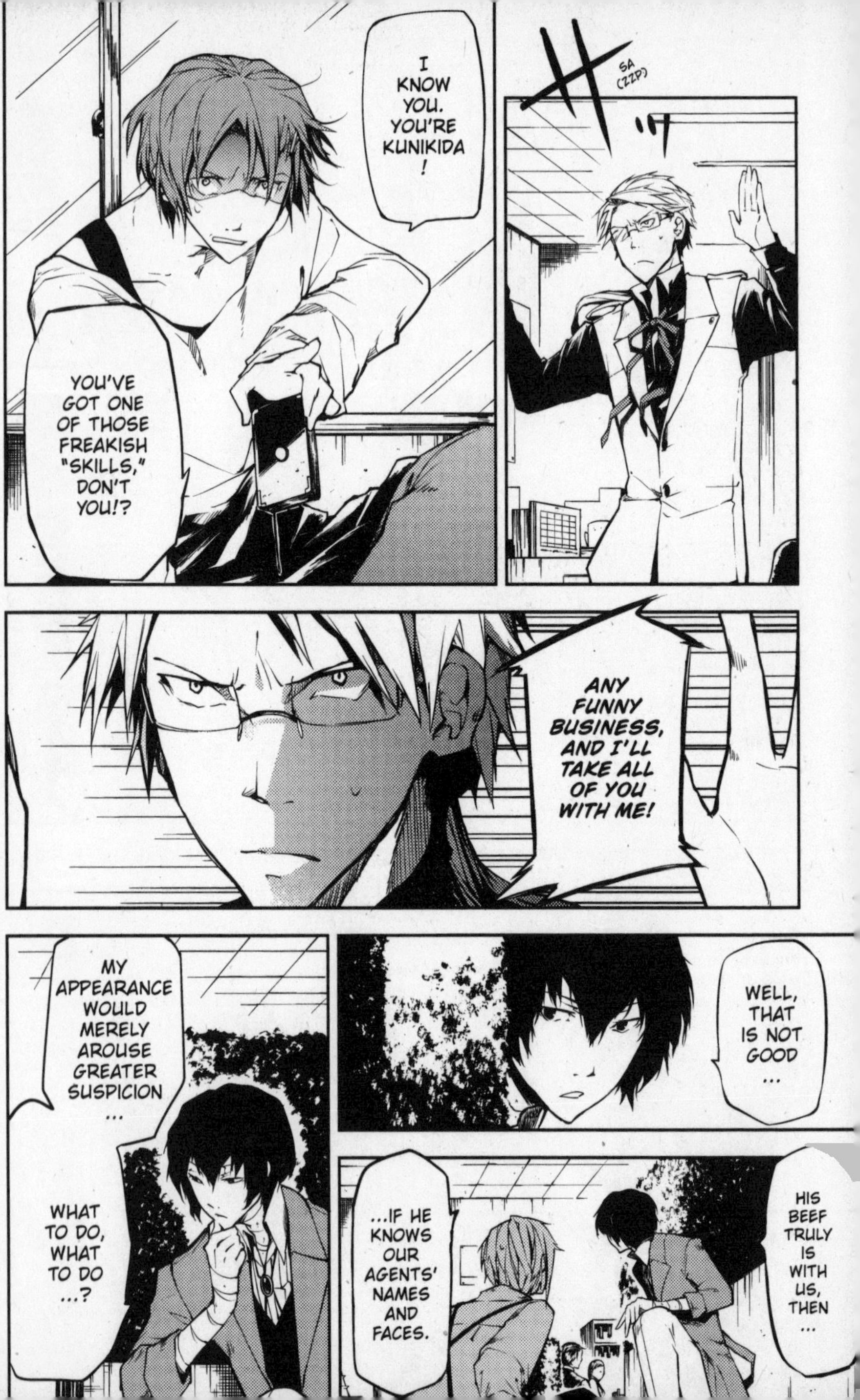

SA (ZZP)
I KNOW YOU. YOU'RE KUNIKIDA!
YOU'VE GOT ONE OF THOSE FREAKISH "SKILLS," DON'T YOU!?
ANY FUNNY BUSINESS, AND I'LL TAKE ALL OF YOU WITH ME!
WELL, THAT IS NOT GOOD...
HIS BEEF TRULY IS WITH US, THEN...
...IF HE KNOWS OUR AGENTS' NAMES AND FACES.
MY APPEARANCE WOULD MERELY AROUSE GREATER SUSPICION...
WHAT TO DO, WHAT TO DO...?

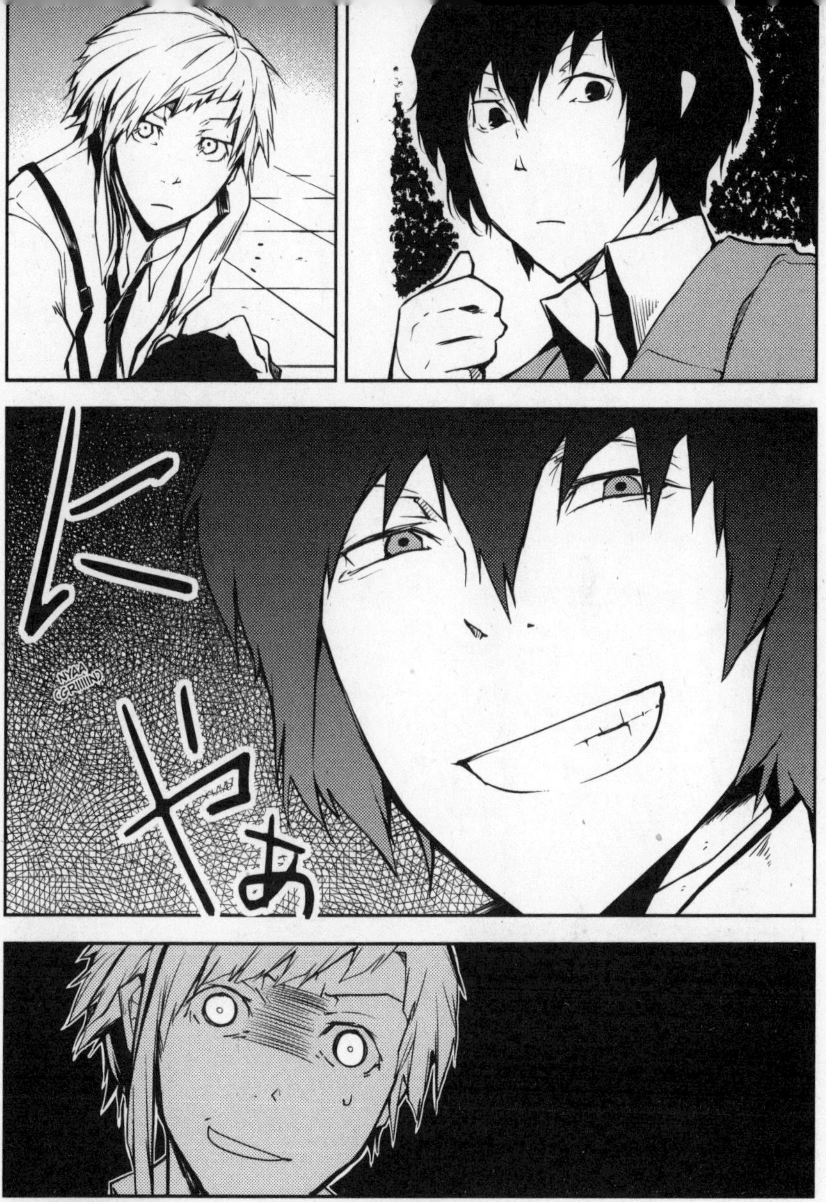
にーやあ
NYAA (GRIIIIN)

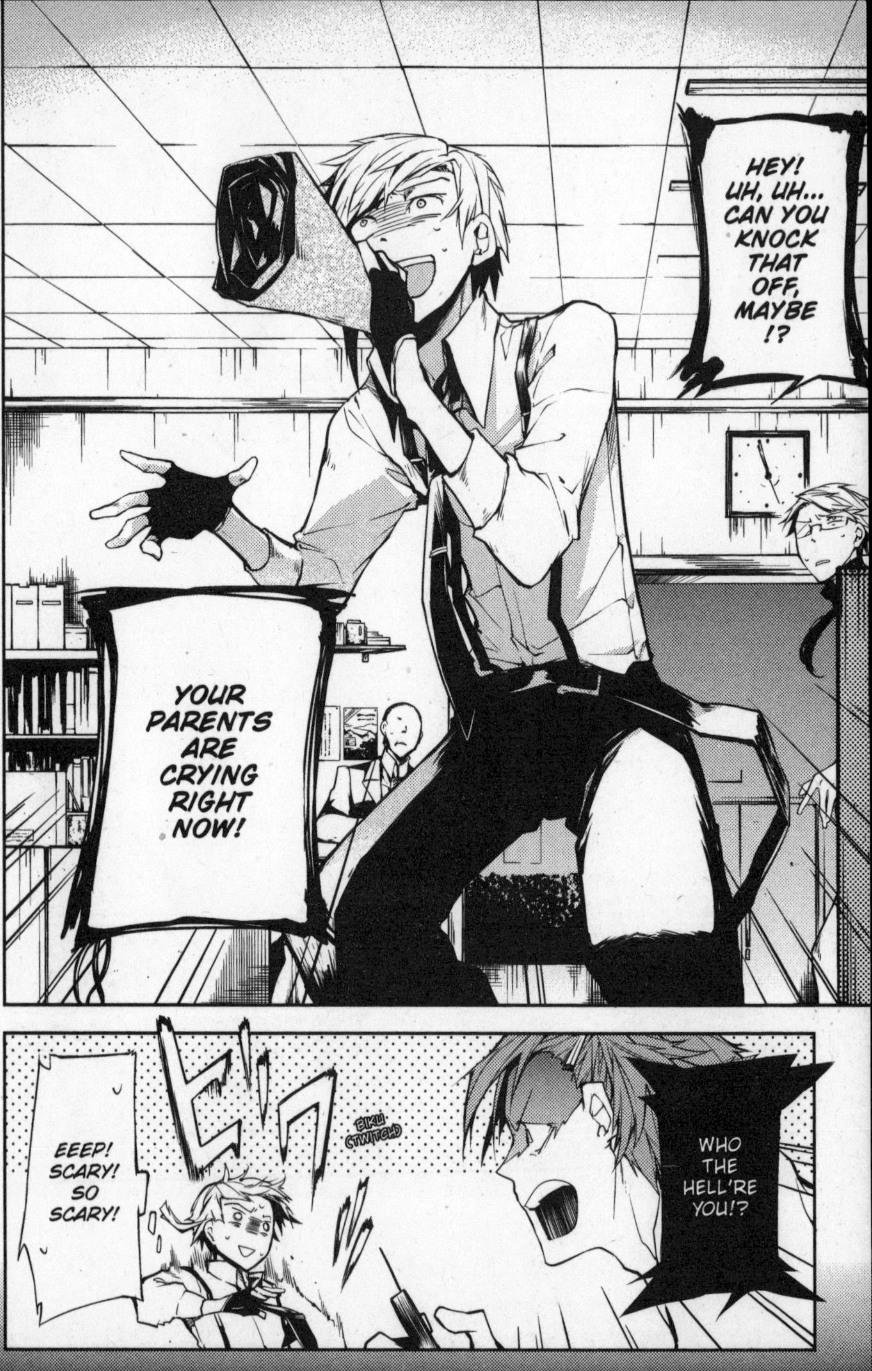

HEY! UH, UH... CAN YOU KNOCK THAT OFF, MAYBE!?
YOUR PARENTS ARE CRYING RIGHT NOW!
WHO THE HELL'RE YOU!?
EIKU (TWITCH)
EEEP! SCARY! SO SCARY!

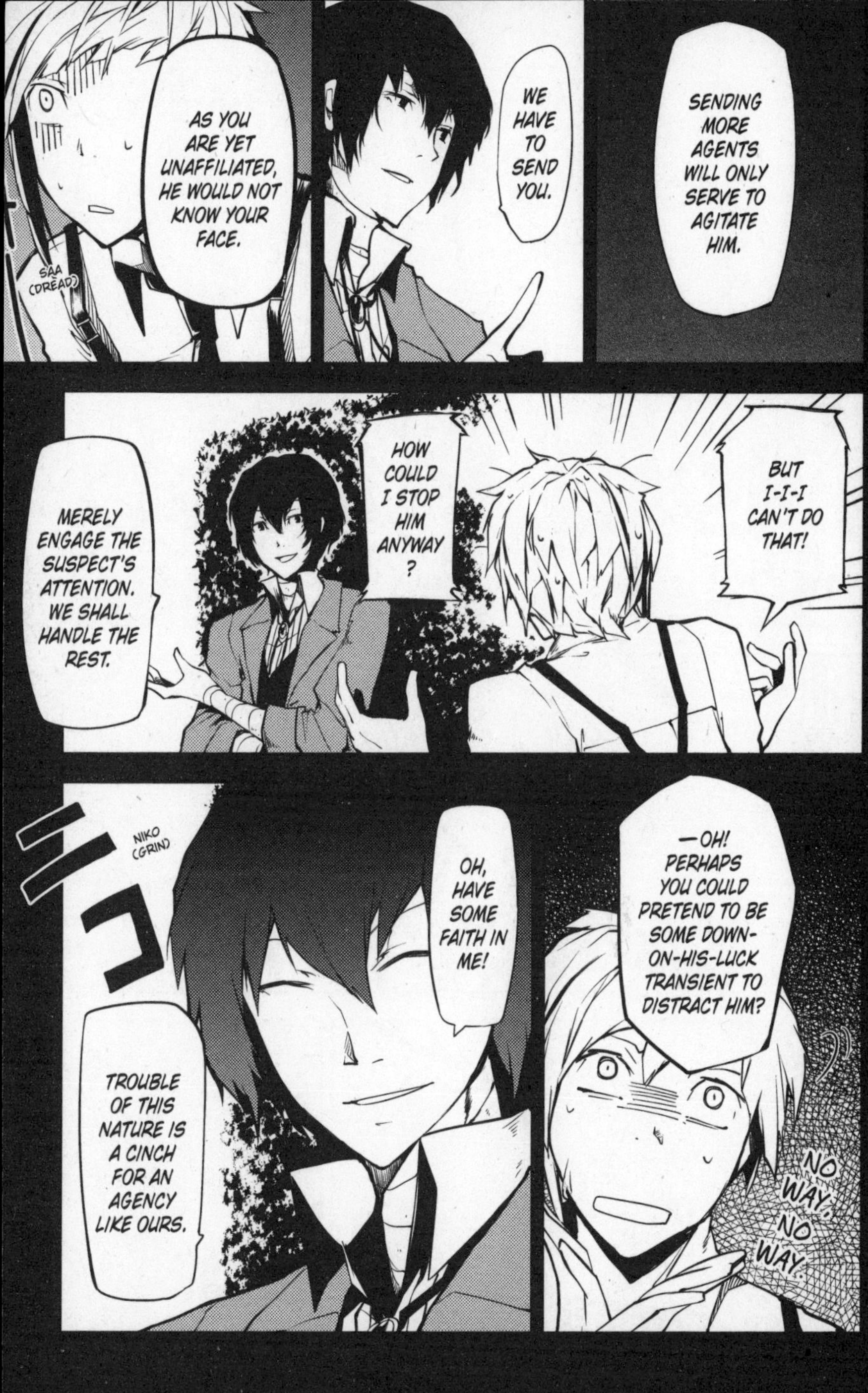
SENDING MORE AGENTS WILL ONLY SERVE TO AGITATE HIM.
WE HAVE TO SEND YOU.
AS YOU ARE YET UNAFFILIATED, HE WOULD NOT KNOW YOUR FACE.
SAA (DREAD)
BUT I-I-I CAN'T DO THAT!
HOW COULD I STOP HIM ANYWAY?
MERELY ENGAGE THE SUSPECT'S ATTENTION. WE SHALL HANDLE THE REST.
—OH! PERHAPS YOU COULD PRETEND TO BE SOME DOWN-ON-HIS-LUCK TRANSIENT TO DISTRACT HIM?
NO WAY, NO WAY.
OH, HAVE SOME FAITH IN ME!
NIKO (GRIN)
TROUBLE OF THIS NATURE IS A CINCH FOR AN AGENCY LIKE OURS.

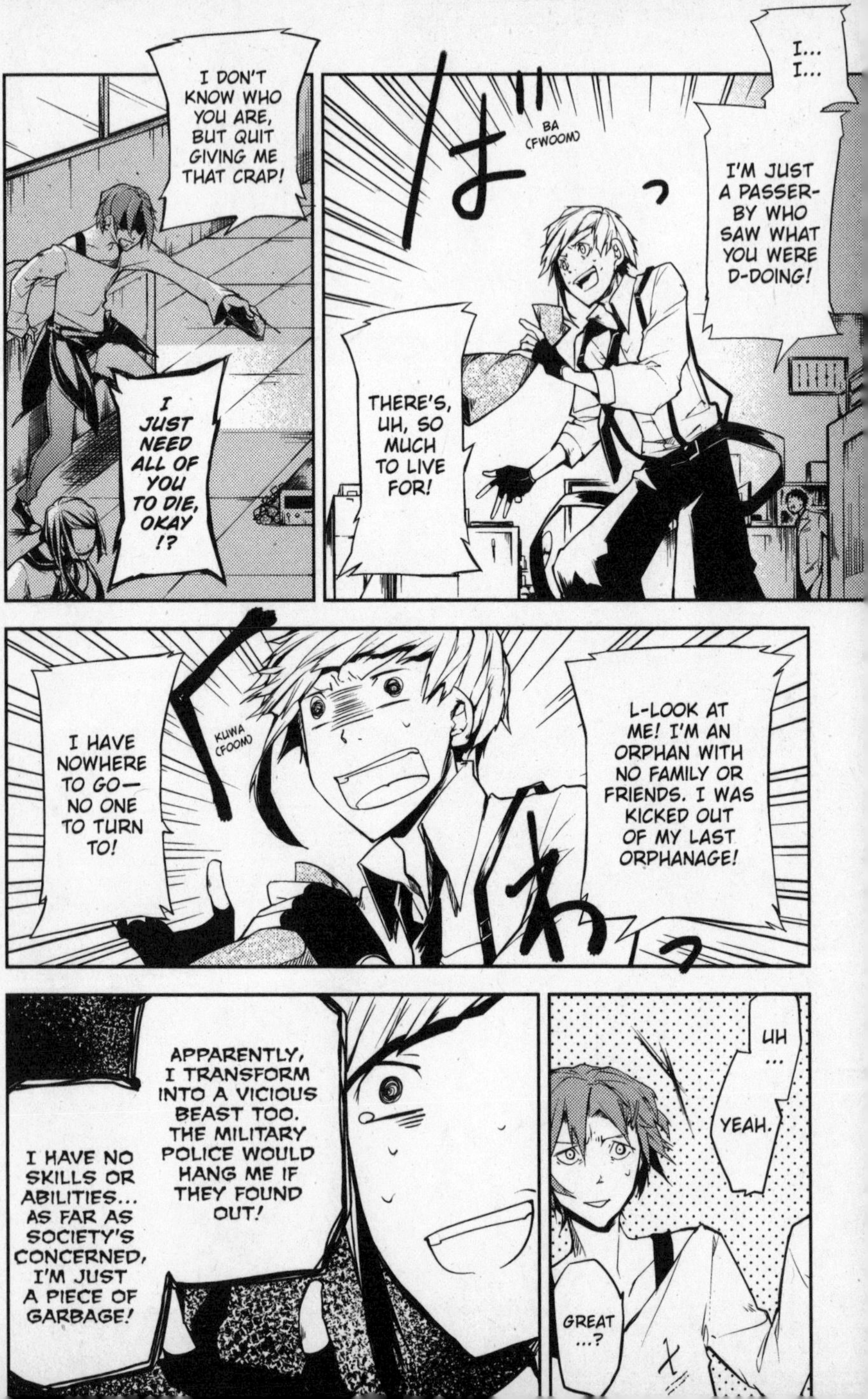
I... I...
I'M JUST A PASSER-BY WHO SAW WHAT YOU WERE D-DOING!
BA (FWOOM)
THERE'S, UH, SO MUCH TO LIVE FOR!
I DON'T KNOW WHO YOU ARE, BUT QUIT GIVING ME THAT CRAP!
I JUST NEED ALL OF YOU TO DIE, OKAY!?
L-LOOK AT ME! I'M AN ORPHAN WITH NO FAMILY OR FRIENDS. I WAS KICKED OUT OF MY LAST ORPHANAGE!
KUWA (FOOM)
I HAVE NOWHERE TO GO— NO ONE TO TURN TO!
UH ...
YEAH.
GREAT ...?
APPARENTLY, I TRANSFORM INTO A VICIOUS BEAST TOO. THE MILITARY POLICE WOULD HANG ME IF THEY FOUND OUT!
I HAVE NO SKILLS OR ABILITIES... AS FAR AS SOCIETY'S CONCERNED, I'M JUST A PIECE OF GARBAGE!

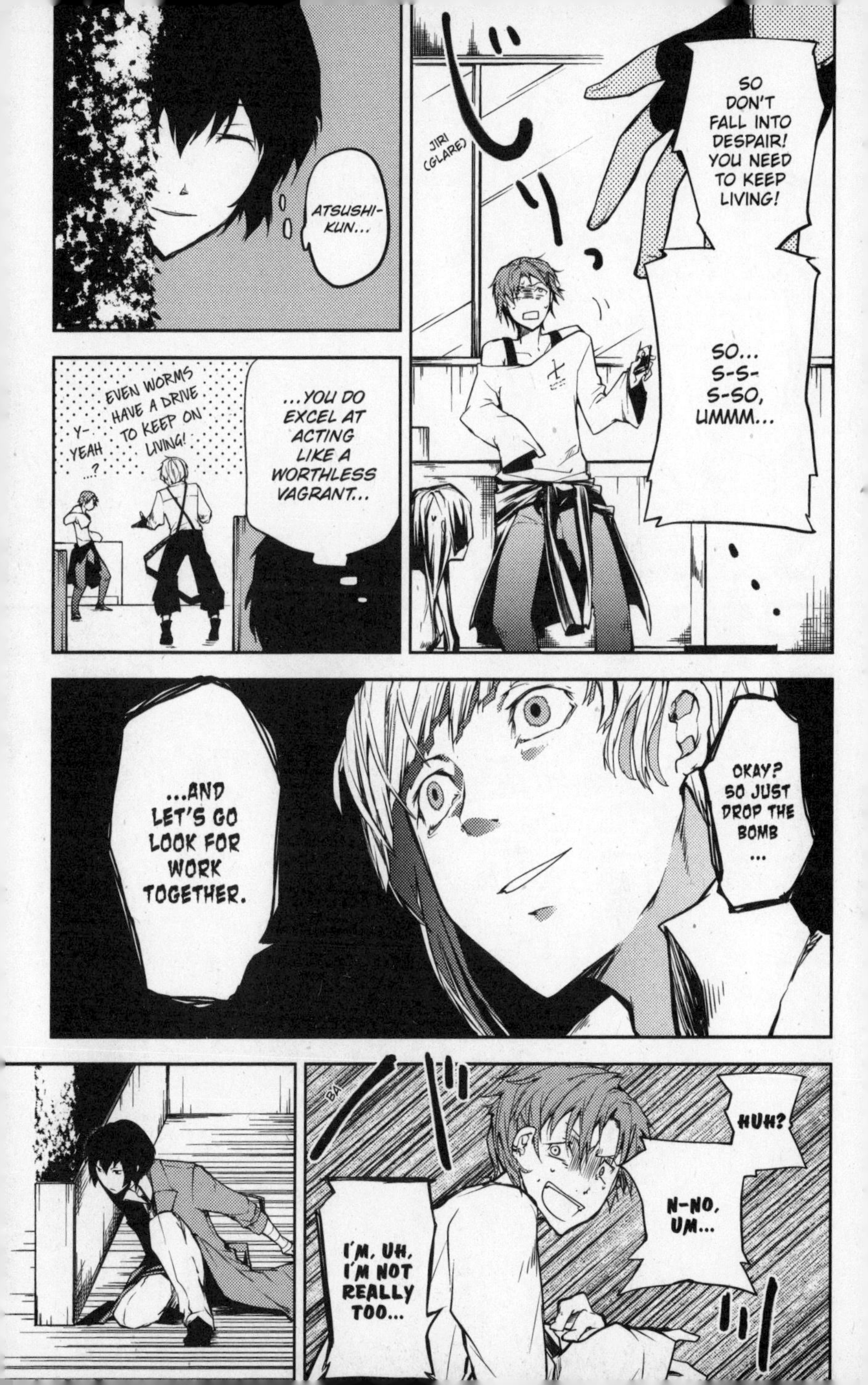

JIRI (GLARE)
SO DON'T FALL INTO DESPAIR! YOU NEED TO KEEP LIVING!
SO... S-S-S-SO, UMMM...
ATSUSHI-KUN...
...YOU DO EXCEL AT ACTING LIKE A WORTHLESS VAGRANT...
EVEN WORMS HAVE A DRIVE TO KEEP ON LIVING!
Y-YEAH ...?
OKAY? SO JUST DROP THE BOMB ...
...AND LET'S GO LOOK FOR WORK TOGETHER.
BA
HUH?
N-NO, UM...
I'M, UH, I'M NOT REALLY TOO...

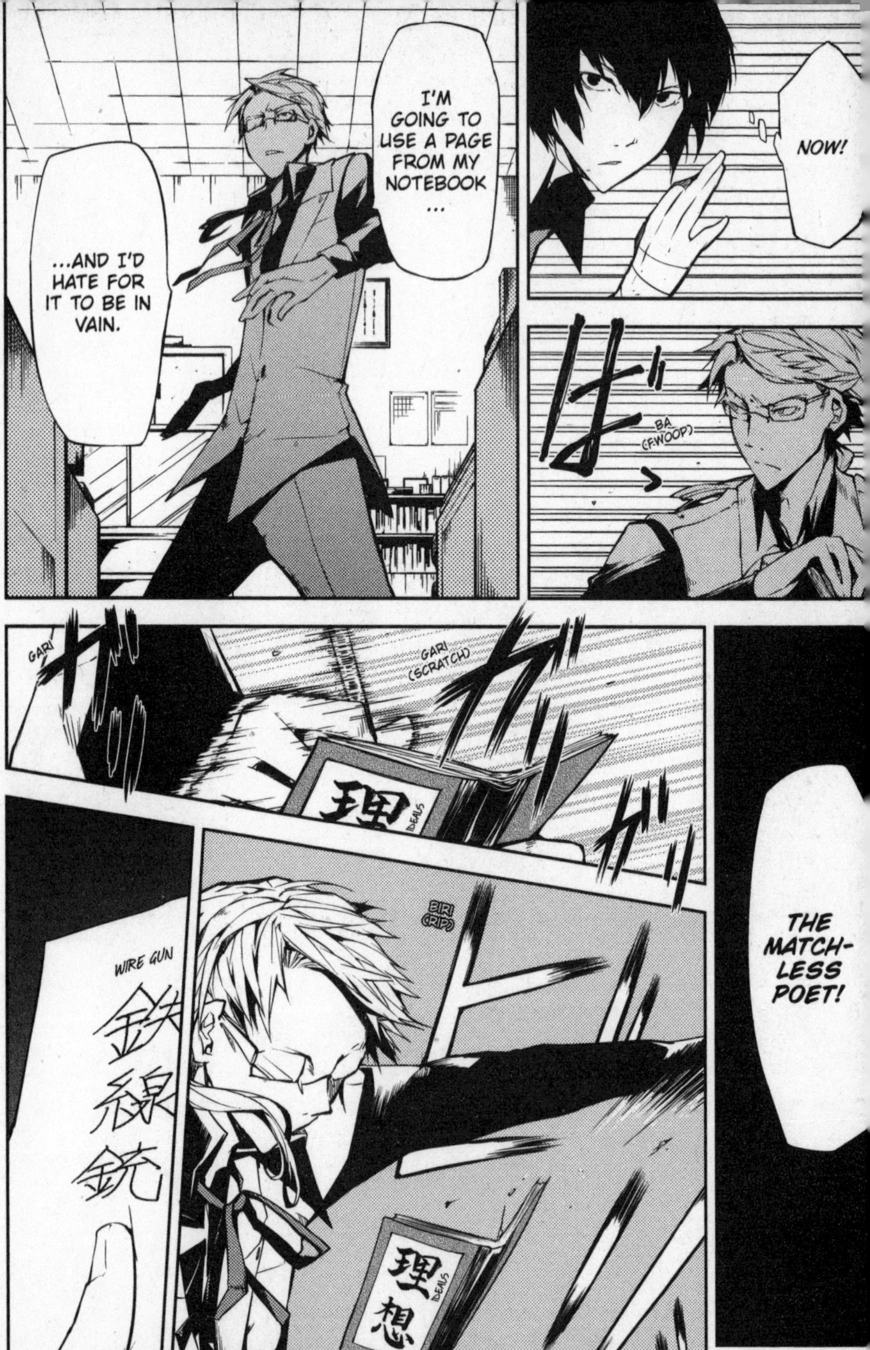
NOW!
BA (F-WOOP)
I'M GOING TO USE A PAGE FROM MY NOTEBOOK ...
...AND I'D HATE FOR IT TO BE IN VAIN.
THE MATCH-LESS POET!
GARI (SCRATCH)
GARI
理
IDEALS
BIRI (RIP)
WIRE GUN
鉄線銃
理想
IDEALS

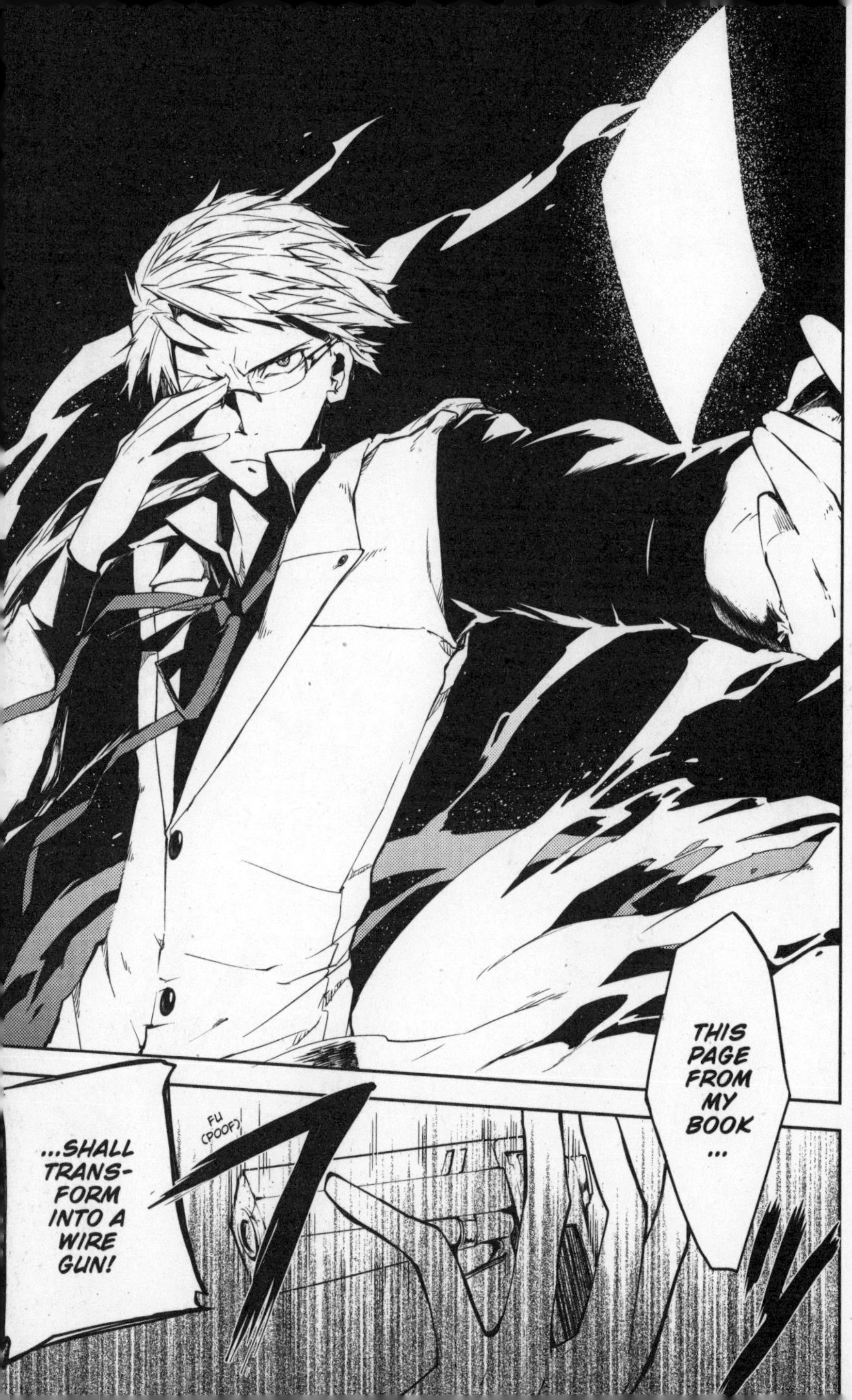
THIS PAGE FROM MY BOOK ...
FU (POOF)
...SHALL TRANS-FORM INTO A WIRE GUN!

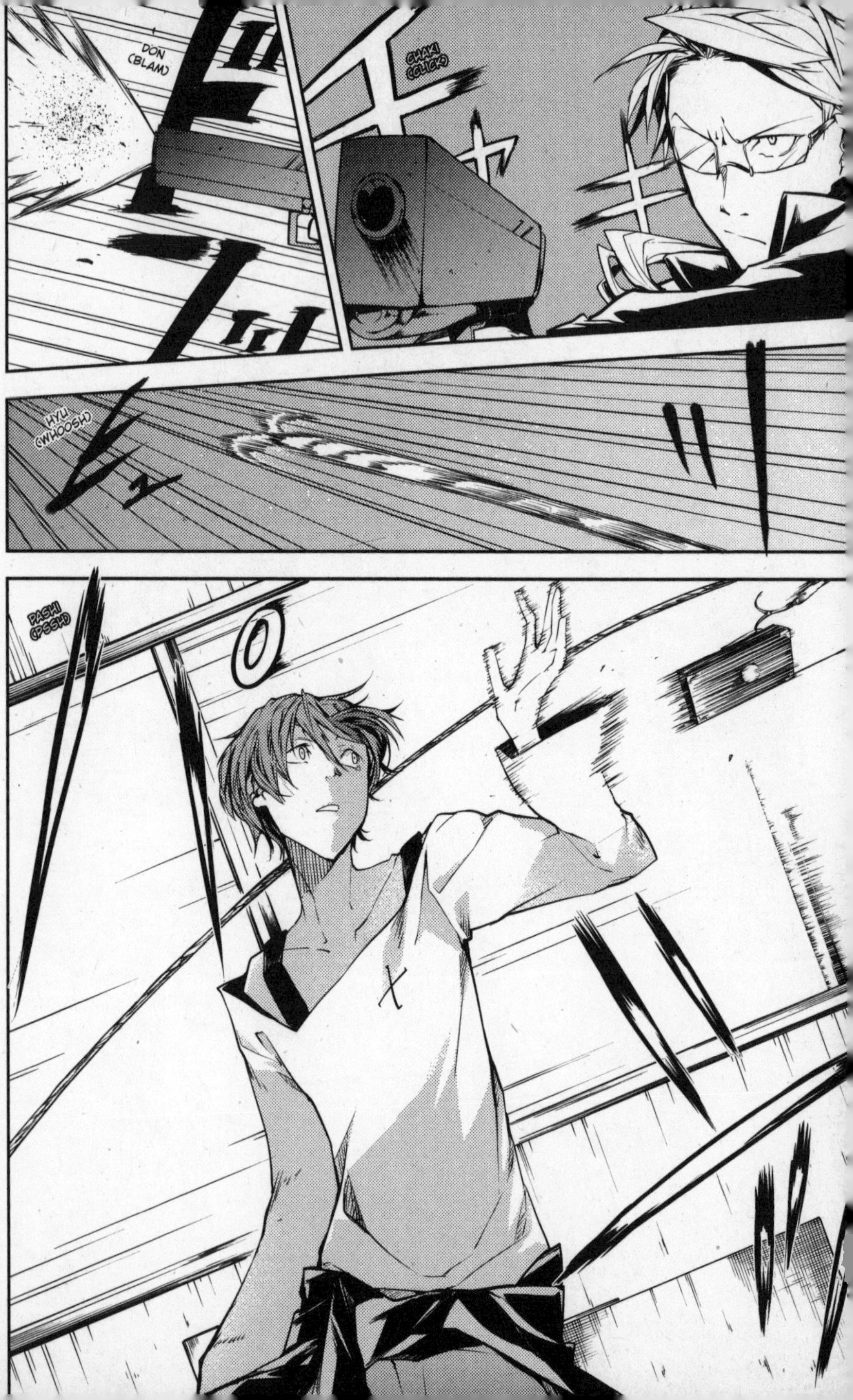
CHAKI (CLICK)
DON (BLAM)
HYU (WHOOSH)
PASHI (PSSH)

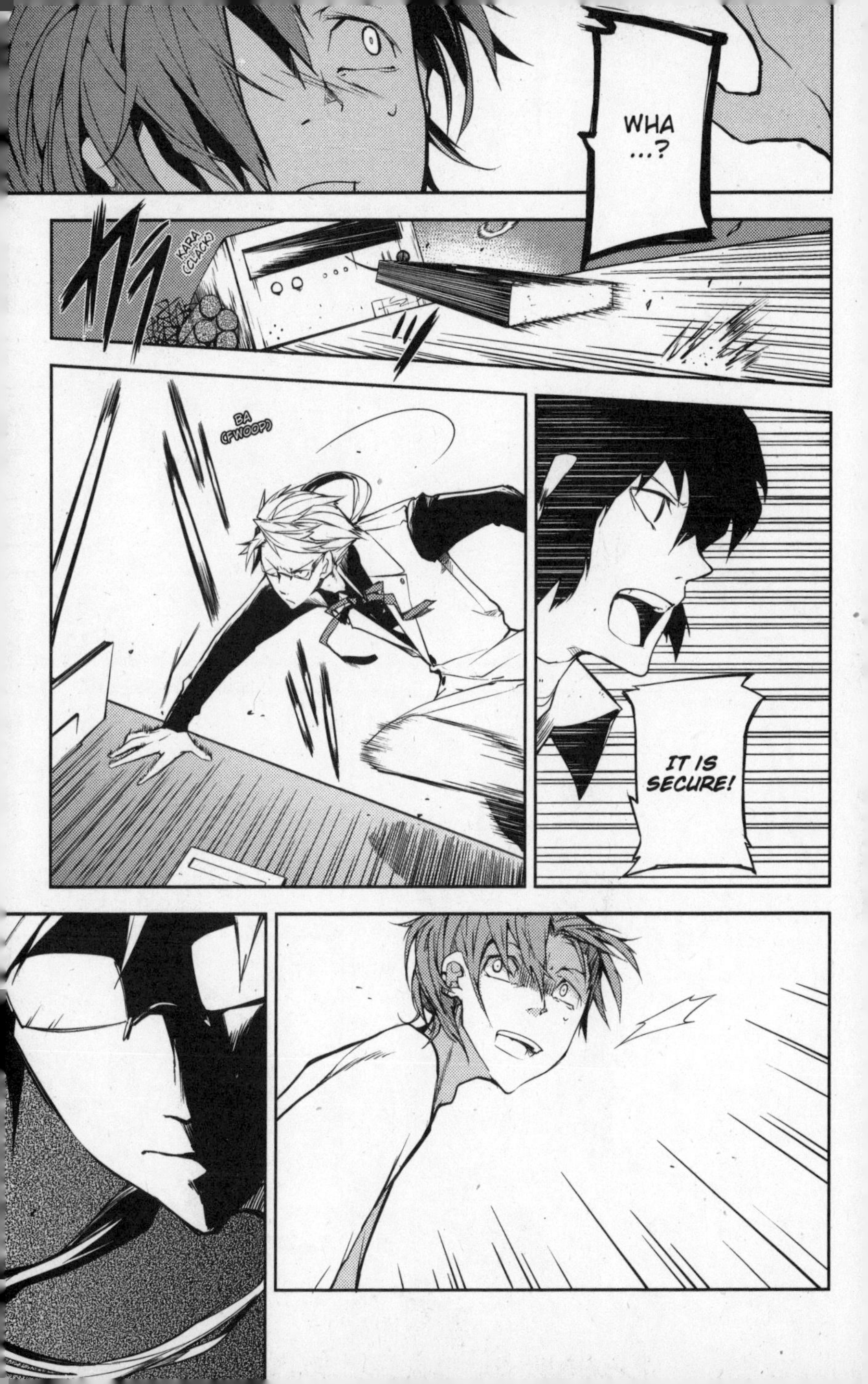
WHA ...?
KARA (CLACK)
IT IS SECURE!
BA (FWOOP)

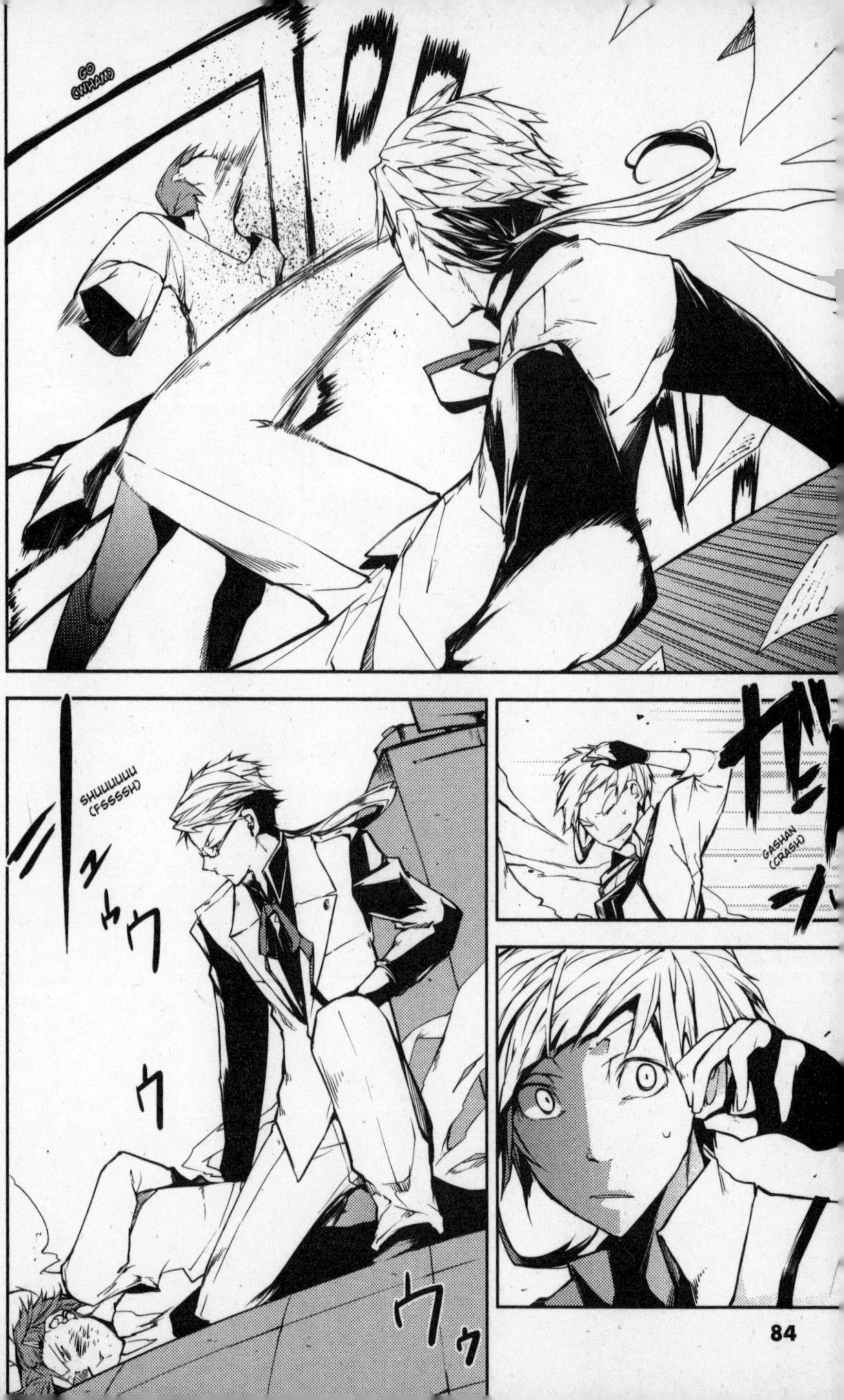
GO
(WHAM)
GASHAN
(CRASH)
SHUUUUUU
(FSSSSH)

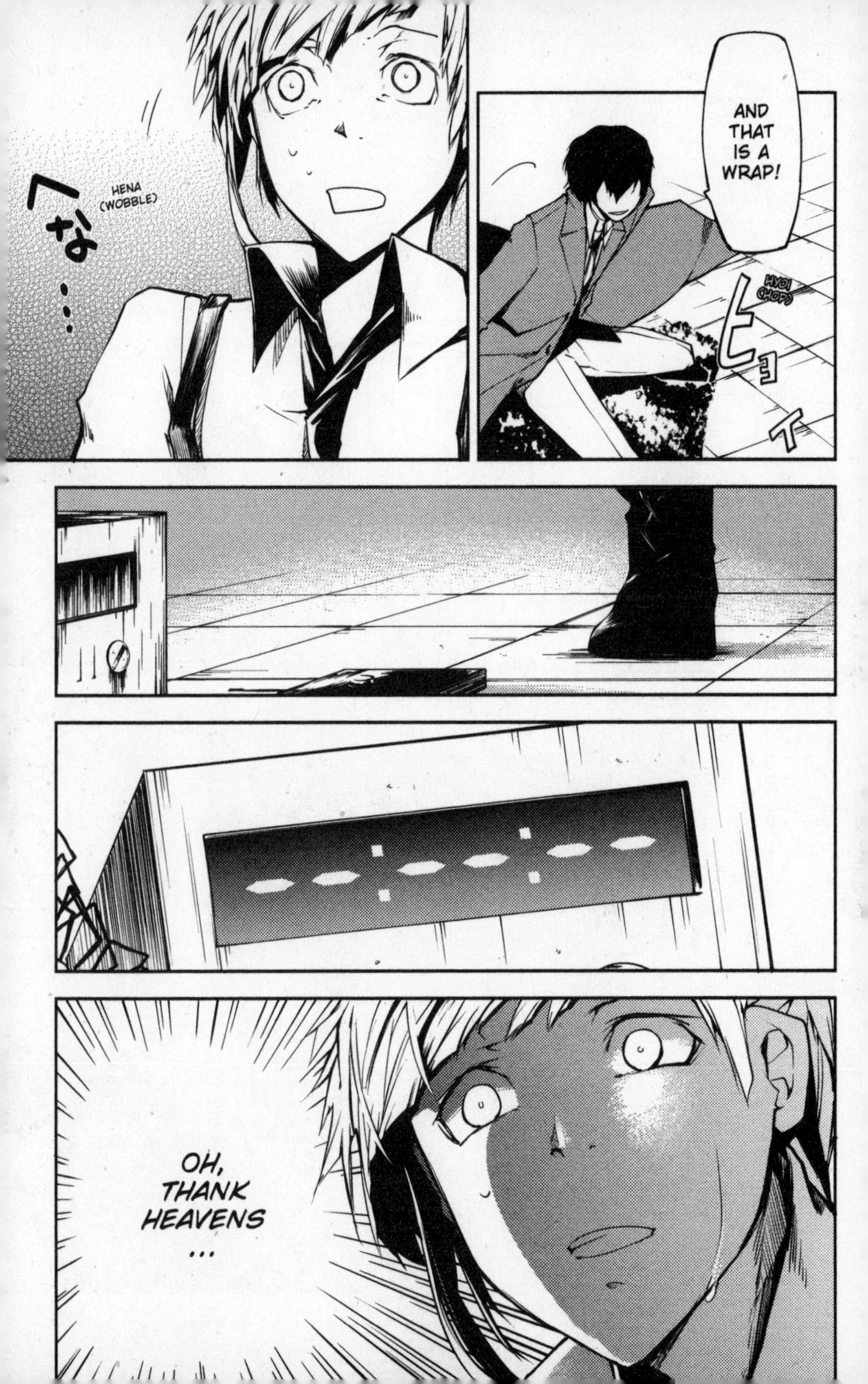
AND THAT IS A WRAP!
HYOI (HOP)
ヒョイ
HENA (WOBBLE)
へな…
OH, THANK HEAVENS...

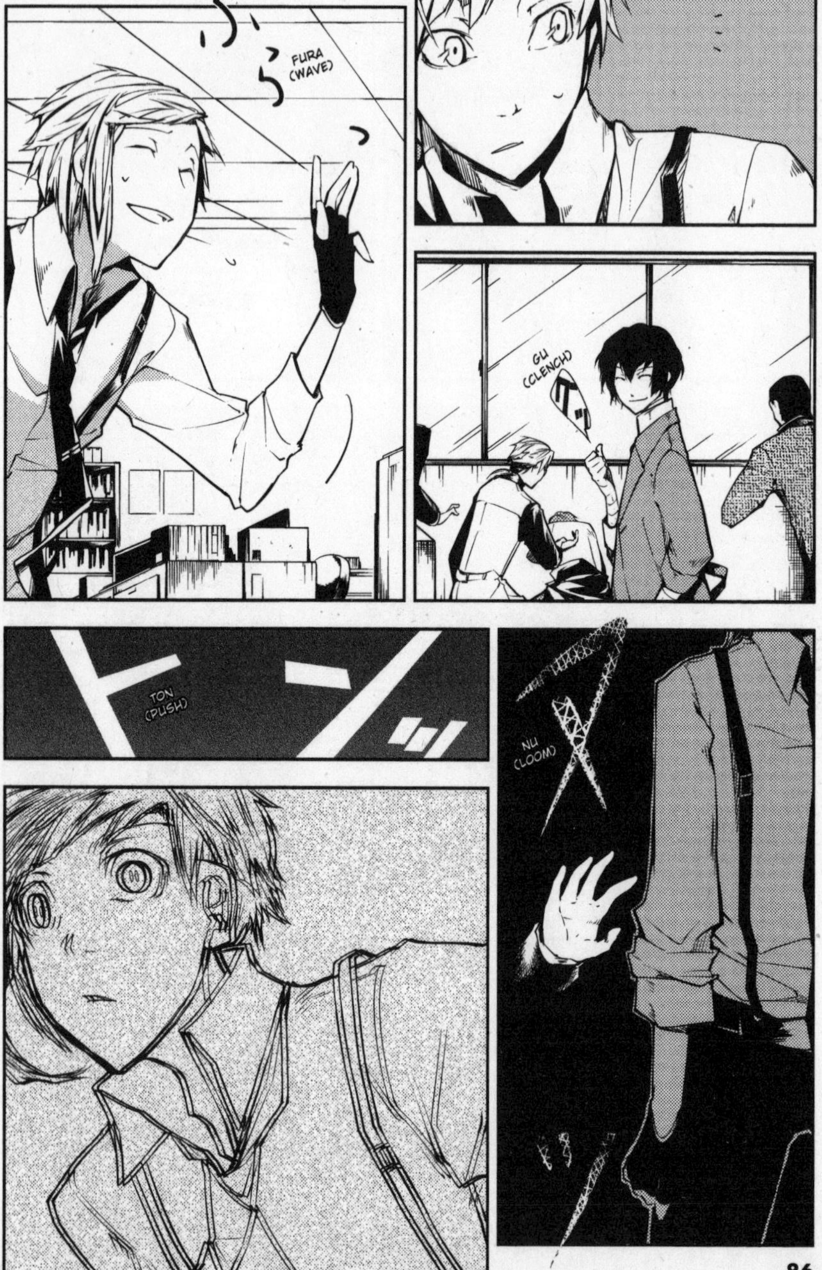
GU (CLENCH)
FURA (WAVE)
NU (LOOM)
TON (PUSH)

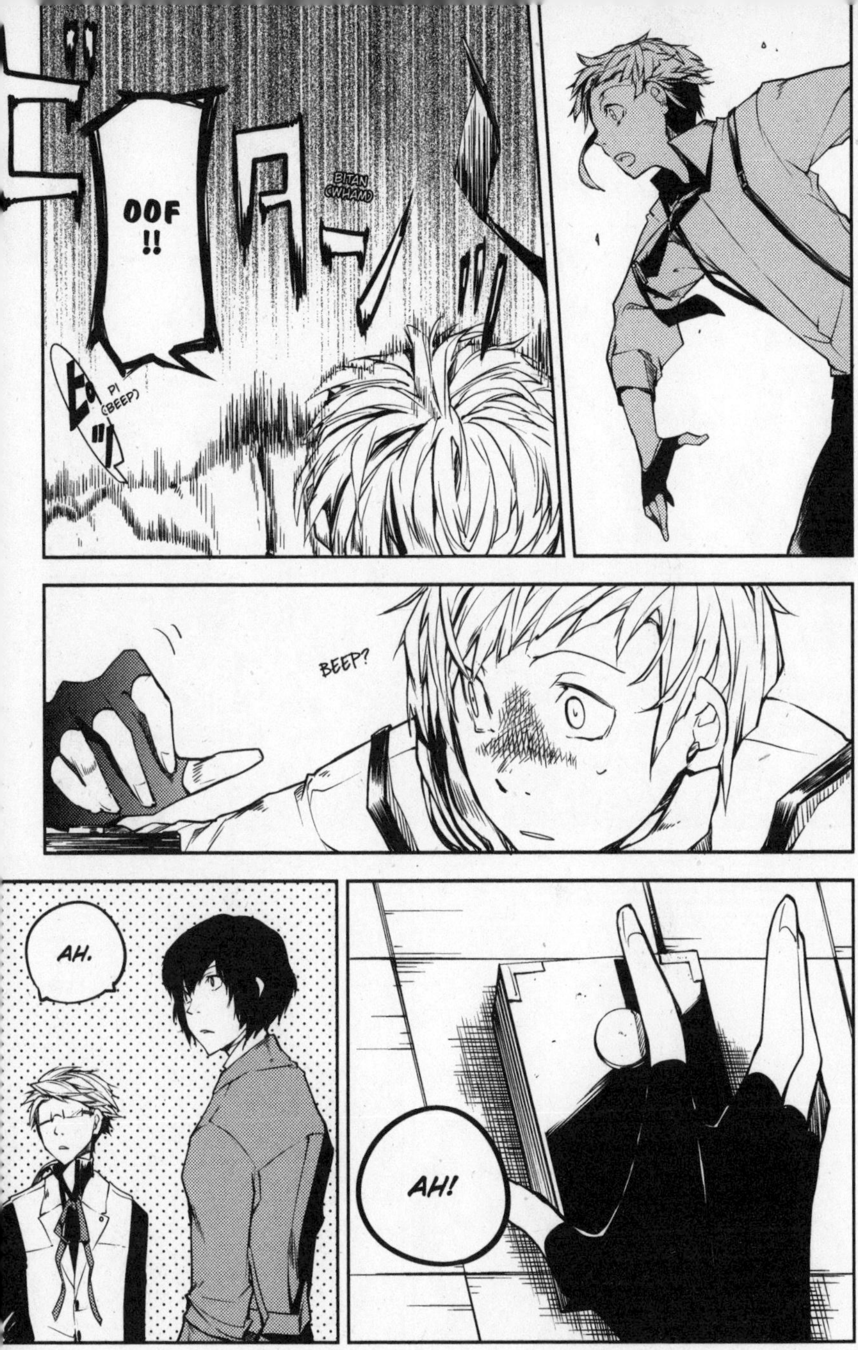
BITAN (WHAM)
OOF!!
PI (BEEP)
BEEP?
AH!
AH.

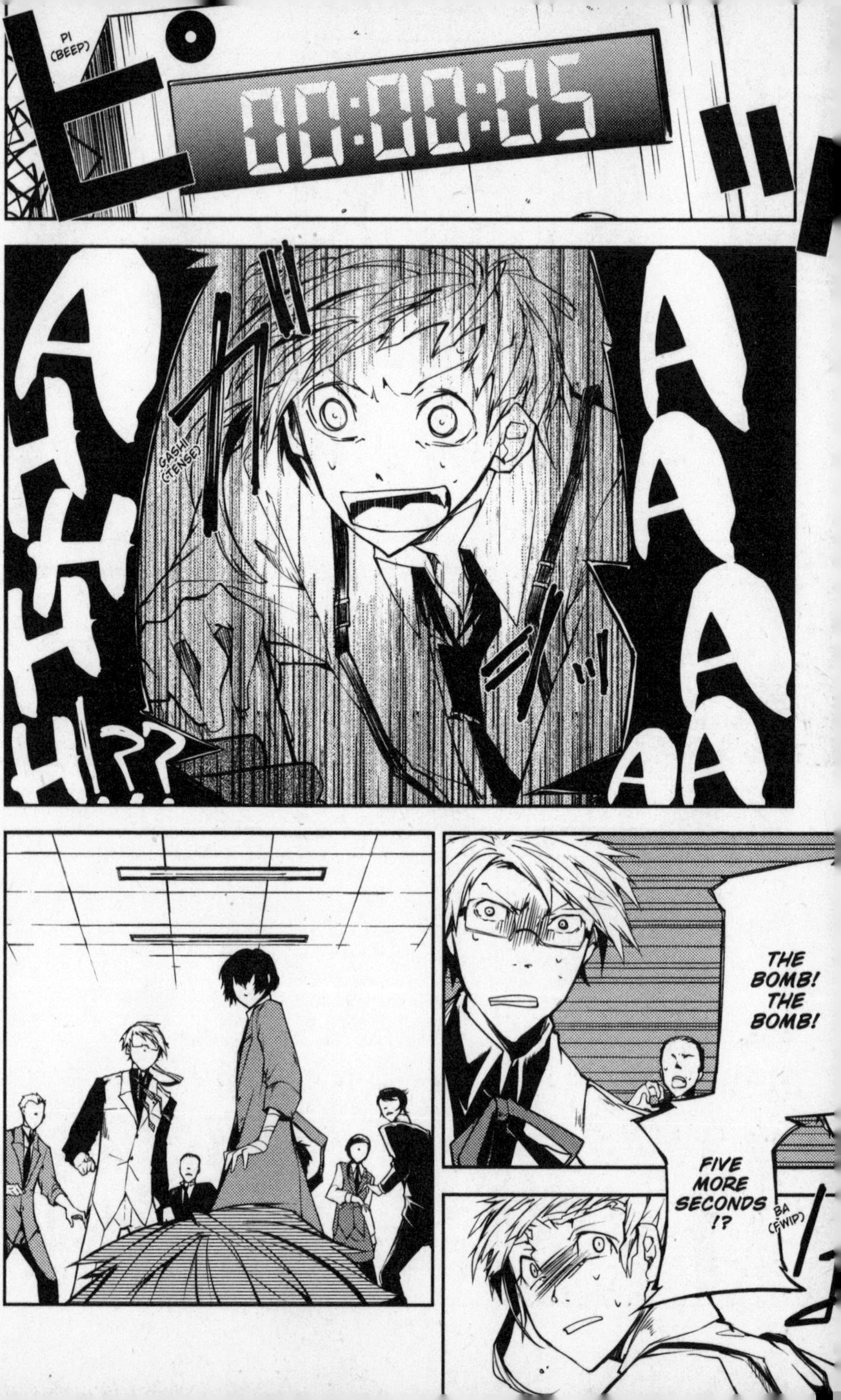
PI (BEEP)
00:00:05
GASHI (TENSE)
AAAAAA
AHHHH!??
THE BOMB! THE BOMB!
FIVE MORE SECONDS !?
BA (FWIP)

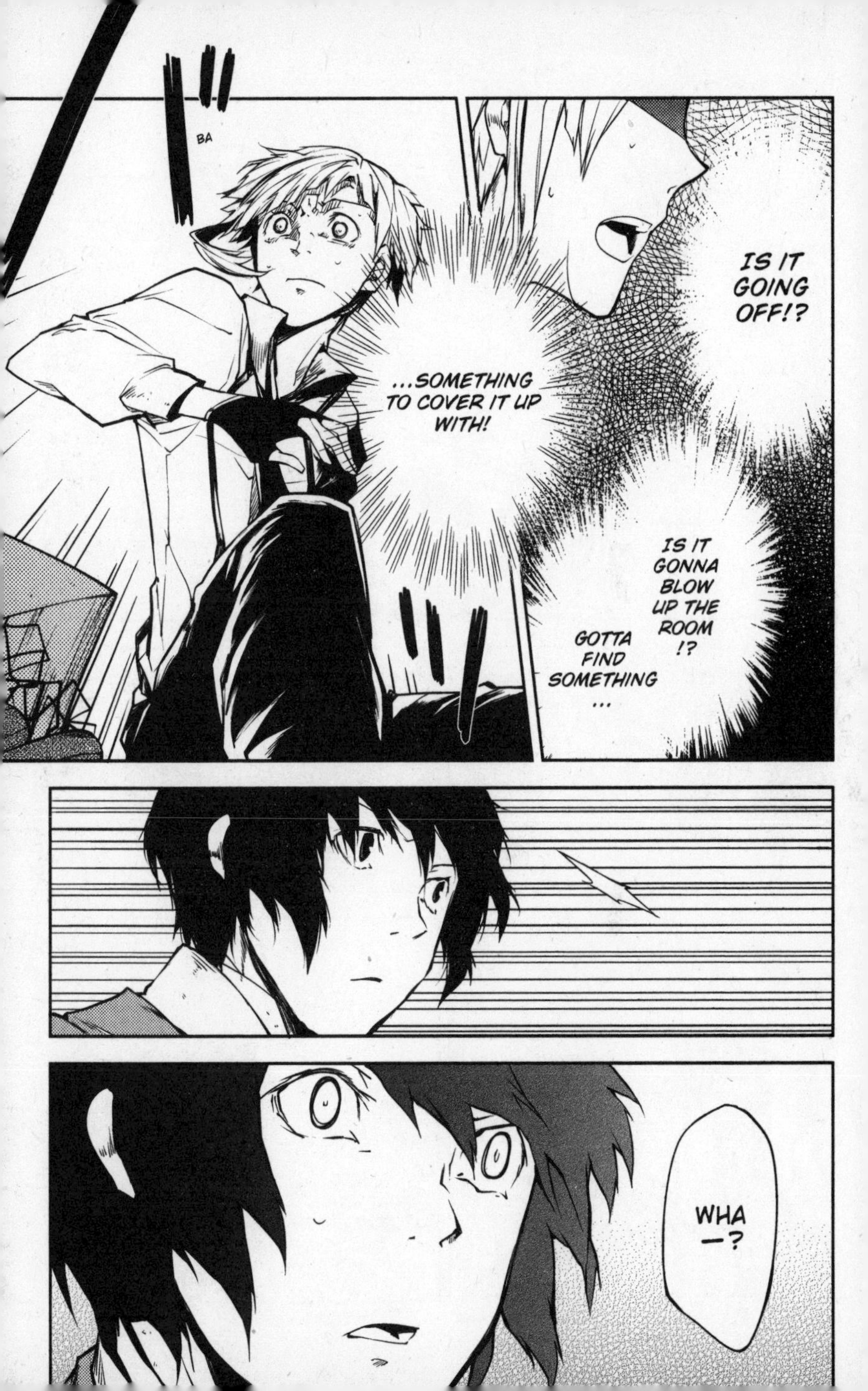

IS IT GOING OFF!?
BA
...SOMETHING TO COVER IT UP WITH!
IS IT GONNA BLOW UP THE ROOM!?
GOTTA FIND SOMETHING...
WHA—?

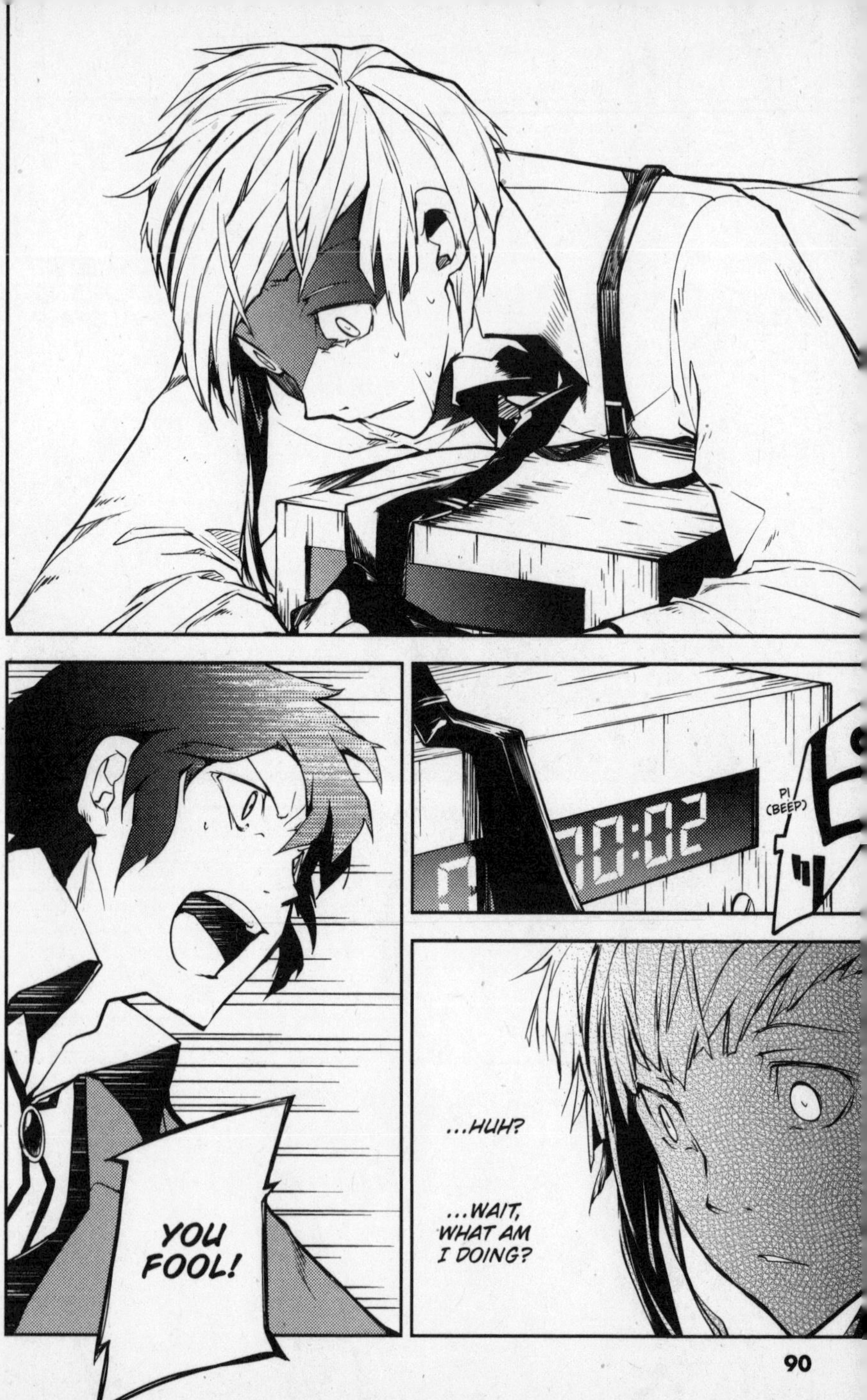

PI (BEEP)
...HUH?
...WAIT, WHAT AM I DOING?
YOU FOOL!

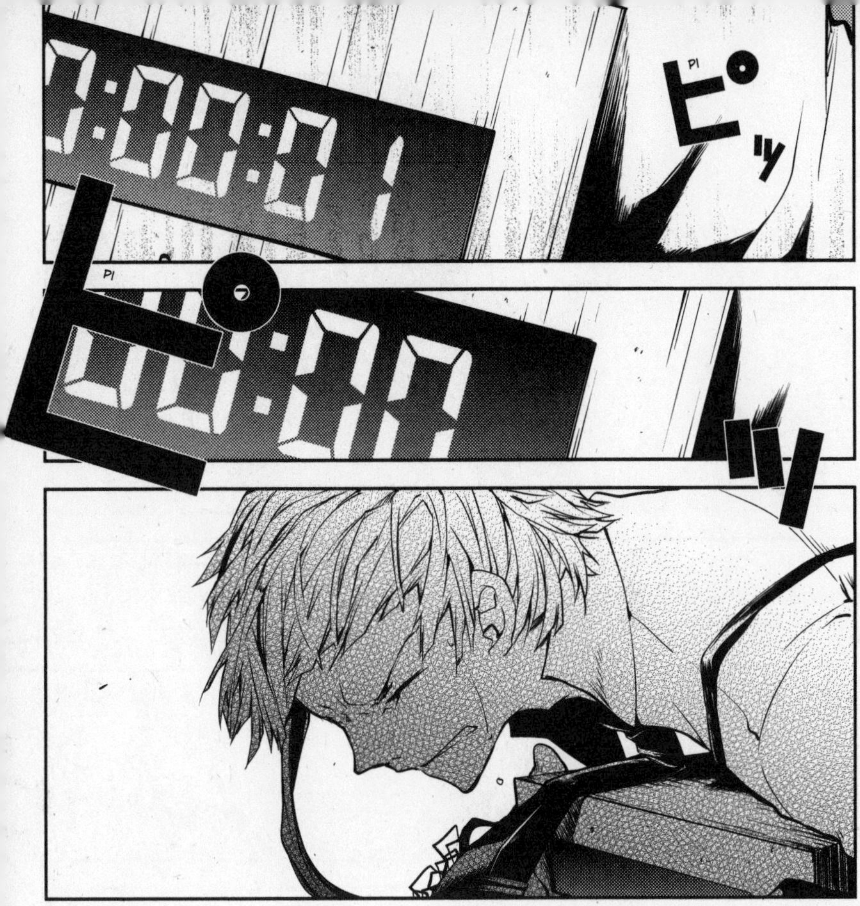
ピッ
PI
ピッ
PI

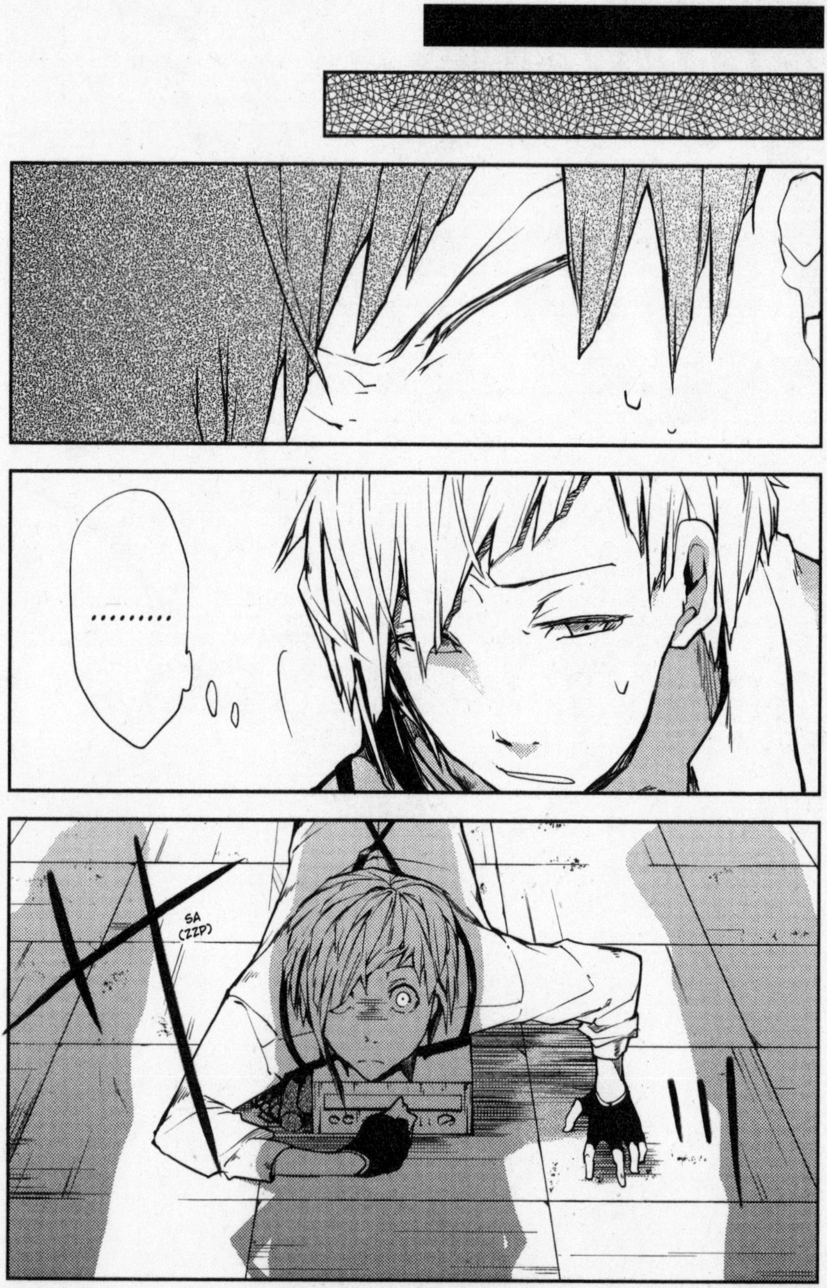
....
SA
(ZZP)

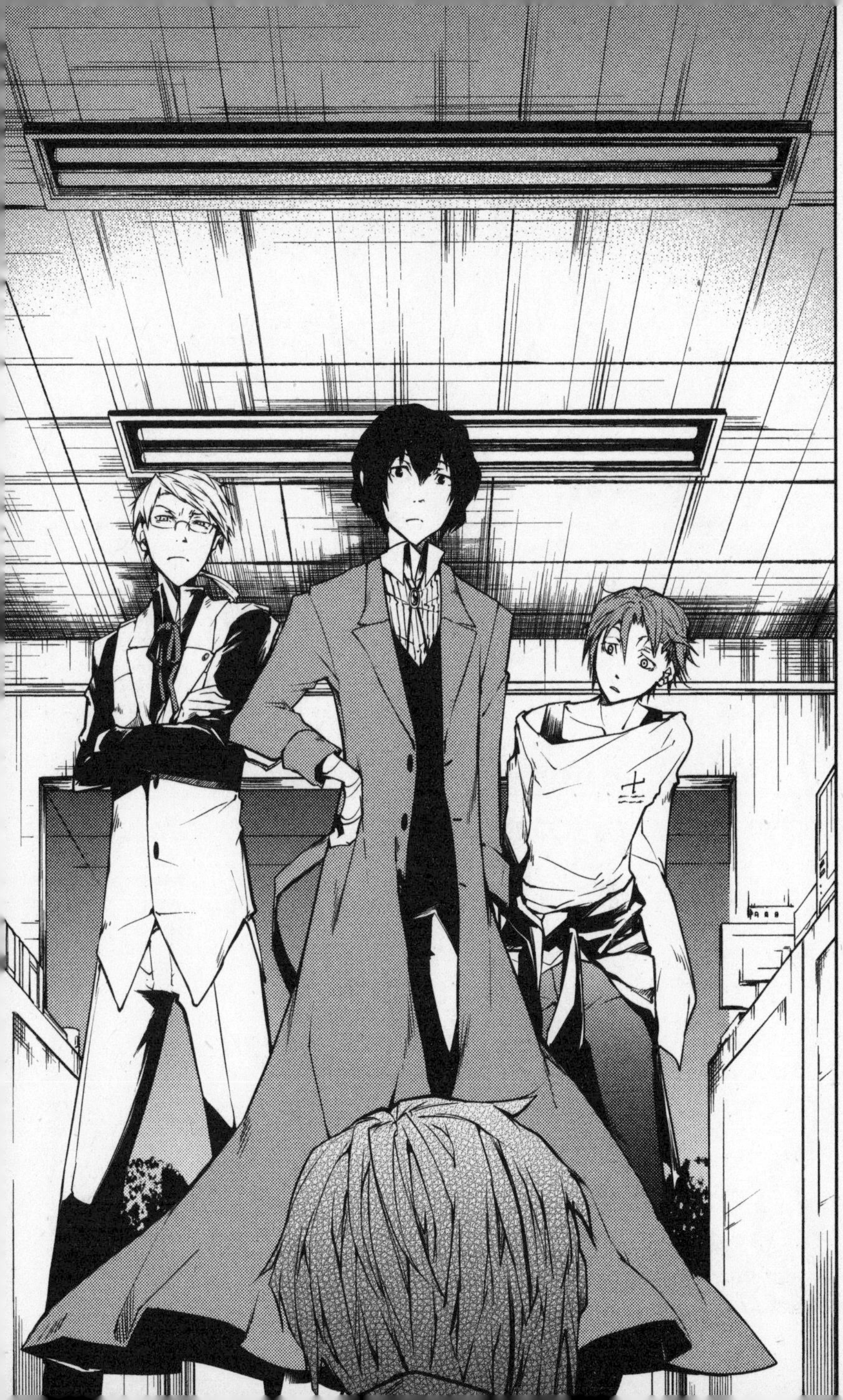

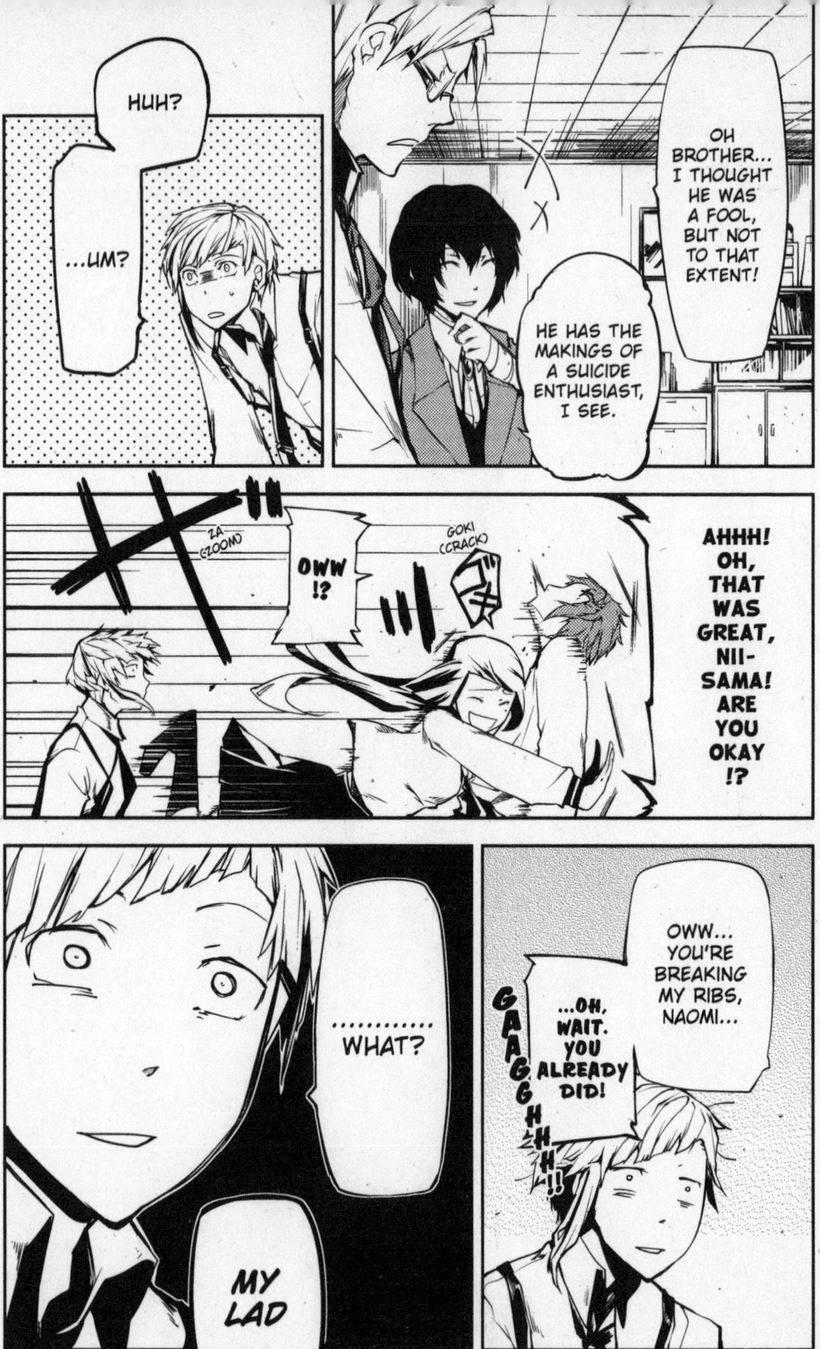
OH BROTHER... I THOUGHT HE WAS A FOOL, BUT NOT TO THAT EXTENT!
HE HAS THE MAKINGS OF A SUICIDE ENTHUSIAST, I SEE.
HUH?
...UM?
AHHH! OH, THAT WAS GREAT, NII-SAMA! ARE YOU OKAY !?
GOKI (CRACK)
OWW !?
ZA (ZOOM)
OWW... YOU'RE BREAKING MY RIBS, NAOMI...
...OH, WAIT. YOU ALREADY DID!
GAAGGHHH!!
.... WHAT?
MY LAD ...

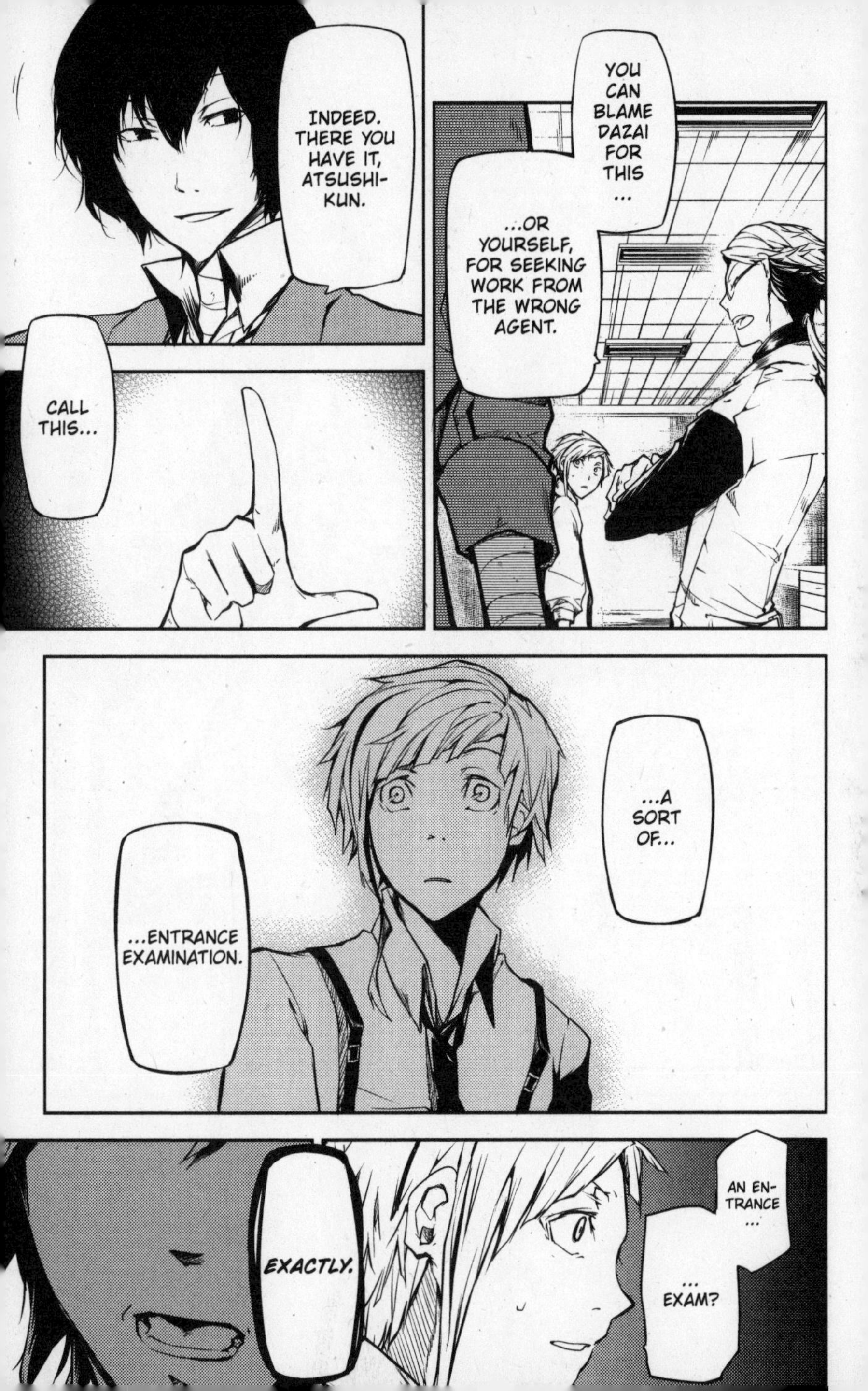
YOU CAN BLAME DAZAI FOR THIS...
...OR YOURSELF, FOR SEEKING WORK FROM THE WRONG AGENT.
INDEED. THERE YOU HAVE IT, ATSUSHI-KUN.
CALL THIS...
...A SORT OF...
...ENTRANCE EXAMINATION.
AN EN-TRANCE...
...EXAM?
EXACTLY.

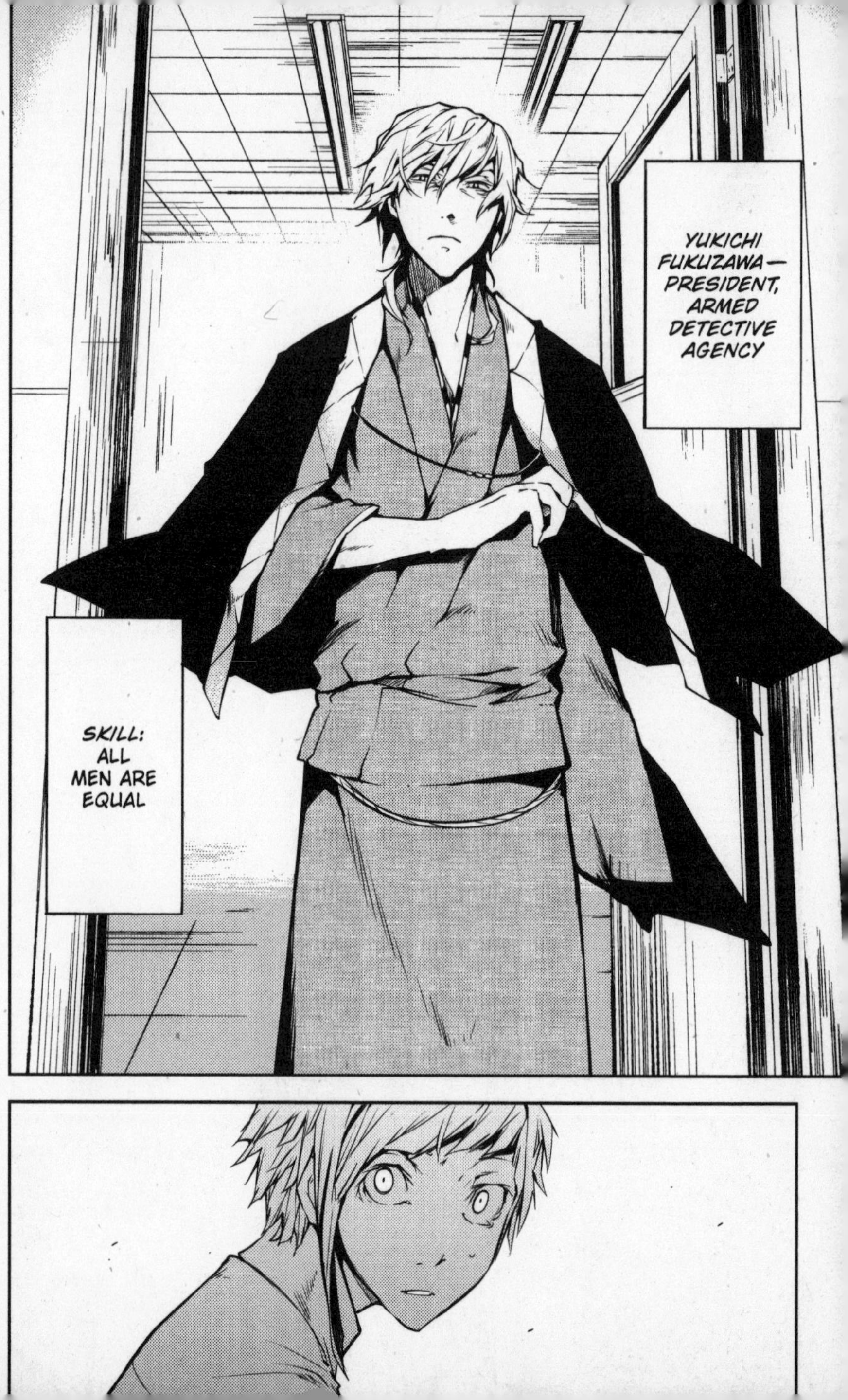
YUKICHI FUKUZAWA—PRESIDENT, ARMED DETECTIVE AGENCY
SKILL: ALL MEN ARE EQUAL

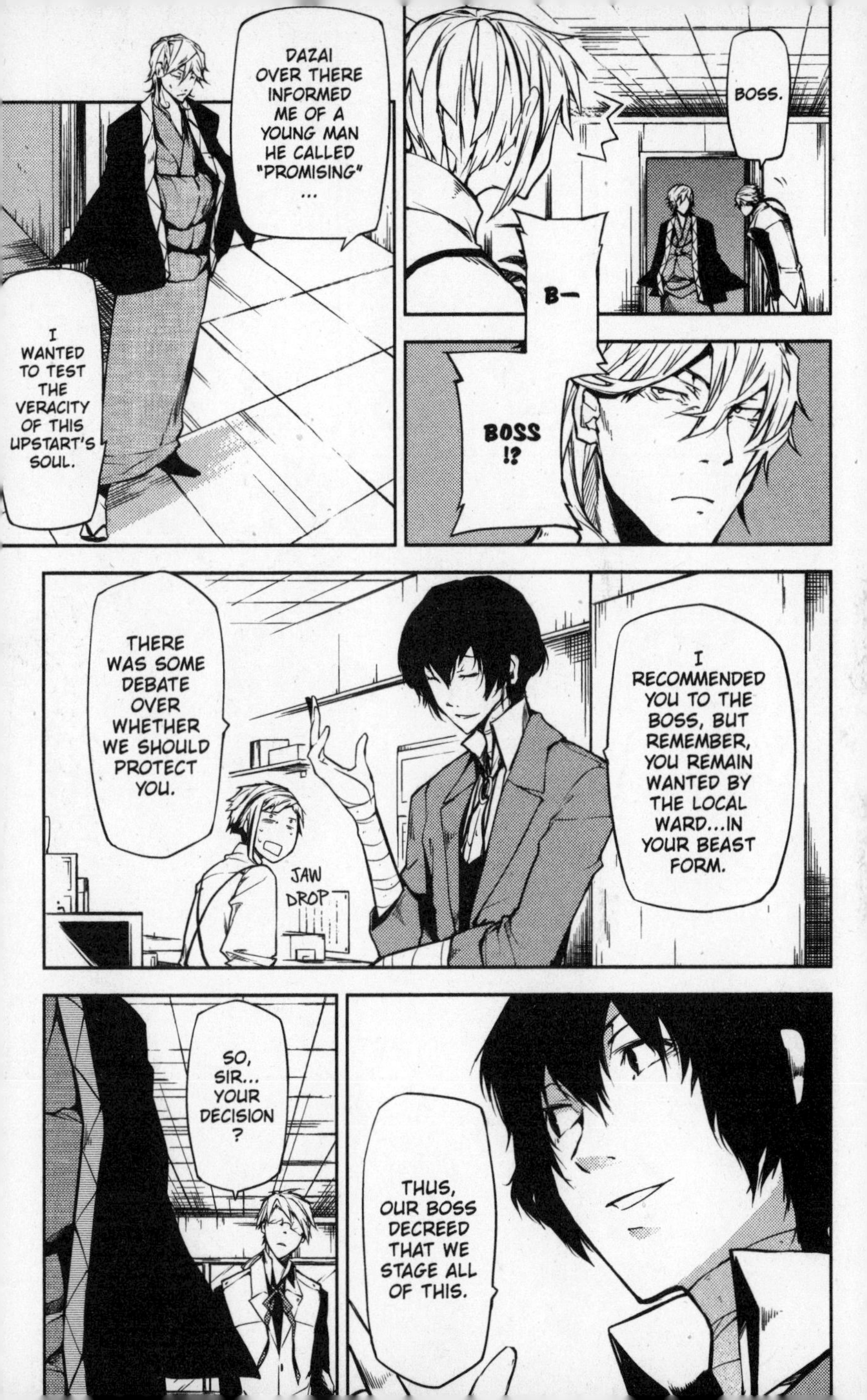
BOSS.
B—
BOSS !?
DAZAI OVER THERE INFORMED ME OF A YOUNG MAN HE CALLED "PROMISING" ...
I WANTED TO TEST THE VERACITY OF THIS UPSTART'S SOUL.
I RECOMMENDED YOU TO THE BOSS, BUT REMEMBER, YOU REMAIN WANTED BY THE LOCAL WARD...IN YOUR BEAST FORM.
THERE WAS SOME DEBATE OVER WHETHER WE SHOULD PROTECT YOU.
JAW DROP
THUS, OUR BOSS DECREED THAT WE STAGE ALL OF THIS.
SO, SIR... YOUR DECISION ?

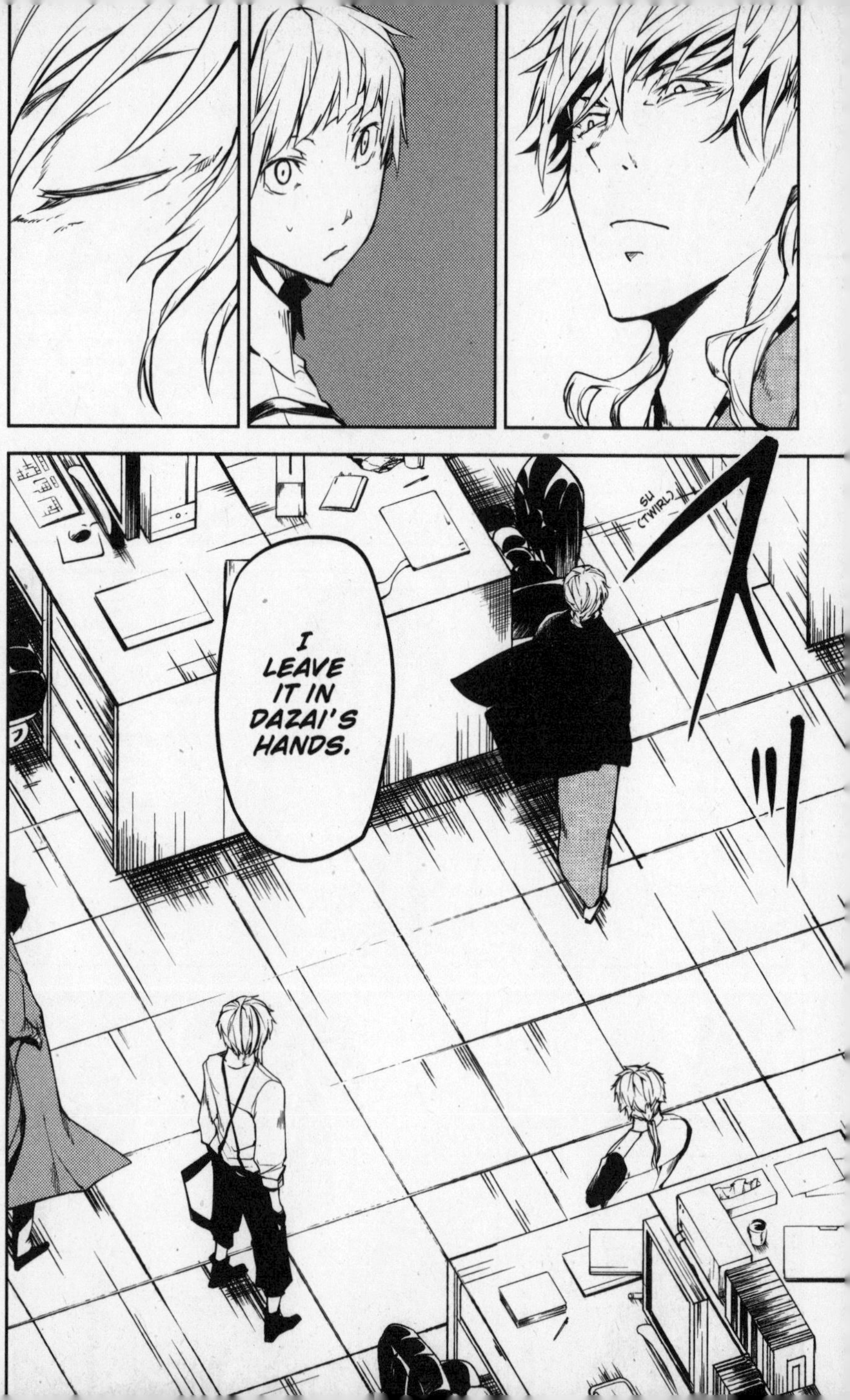
SU (TWIRL)
I LEAVE IT IN DAZAI'S HANDS.

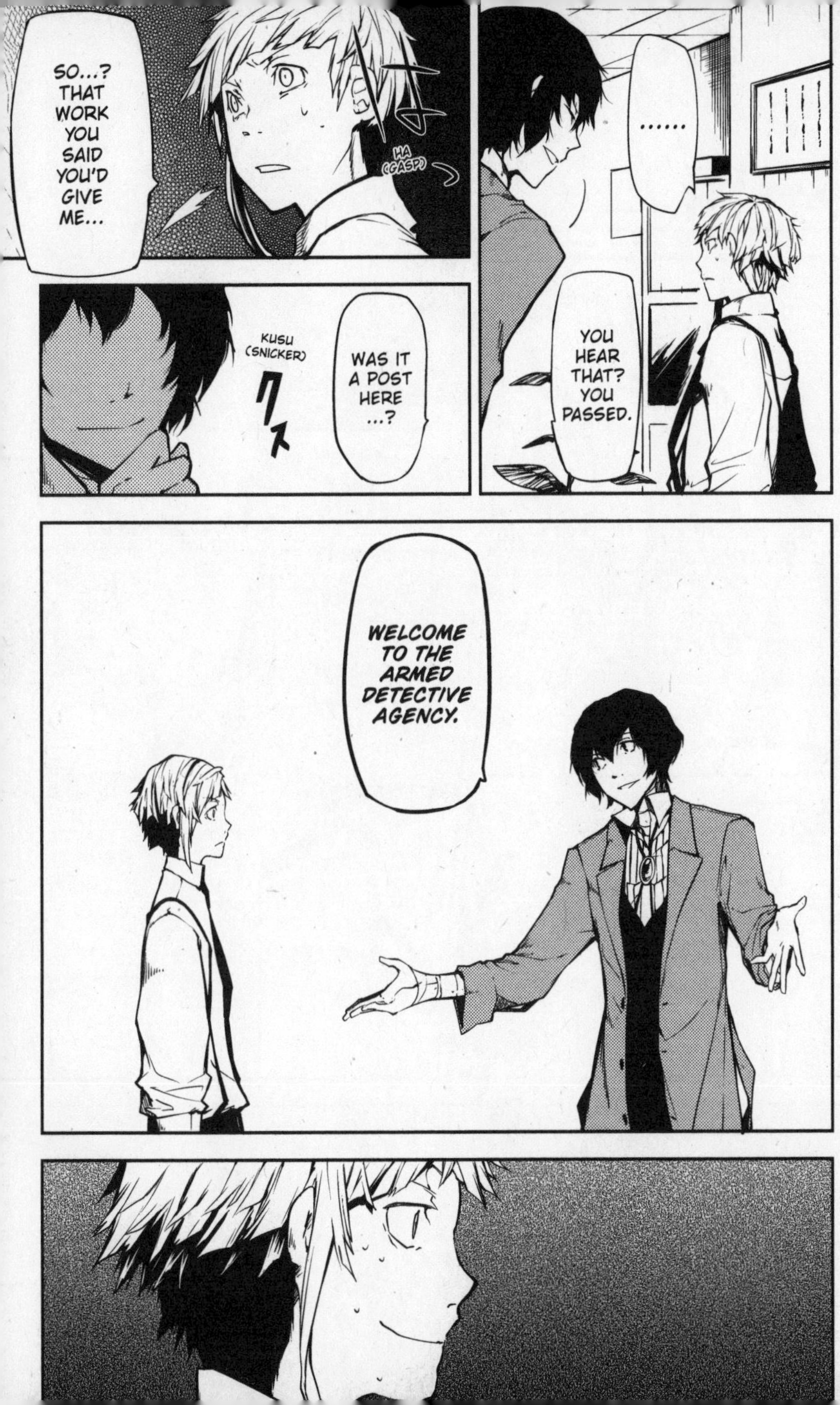
......
YOU HEAR THAT? YOU PASSED.
HA (GASP)
SO...? THAT WORK YOU SAID YOU'D GIVE ME...
WAS IT A POST HERE ...?
KUSU (SNICKER)
クス
WELCOME TO THE ARMED DETECTIVE AGENCY.

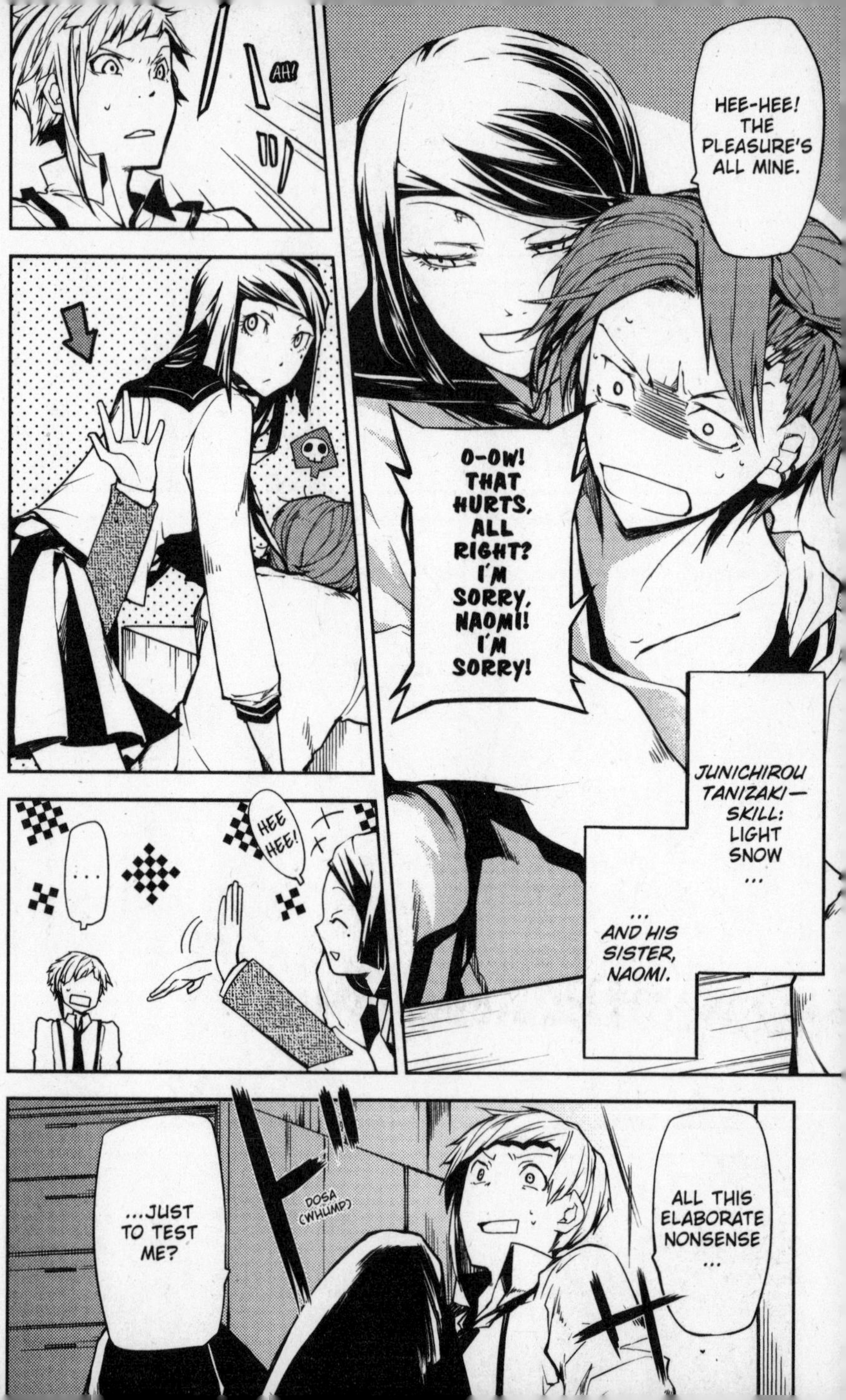
HEE-HEE! THE PLEASURE'S ALL MINE.
O-OW! THAT HURTS, ALL RIGHT? I'M SORRY, NAOMI! I'M SORRY!
JUNICHIROU TANIZAKI—SKILL: LIGHT SNOW ...
... AND HIS SISTER, NAOMI.
AH!
HEE HEE!
...
ALL THIS ELABORATE NONSENSE ...
DOSA (WHUMP)
...JUST TO TEST ME?

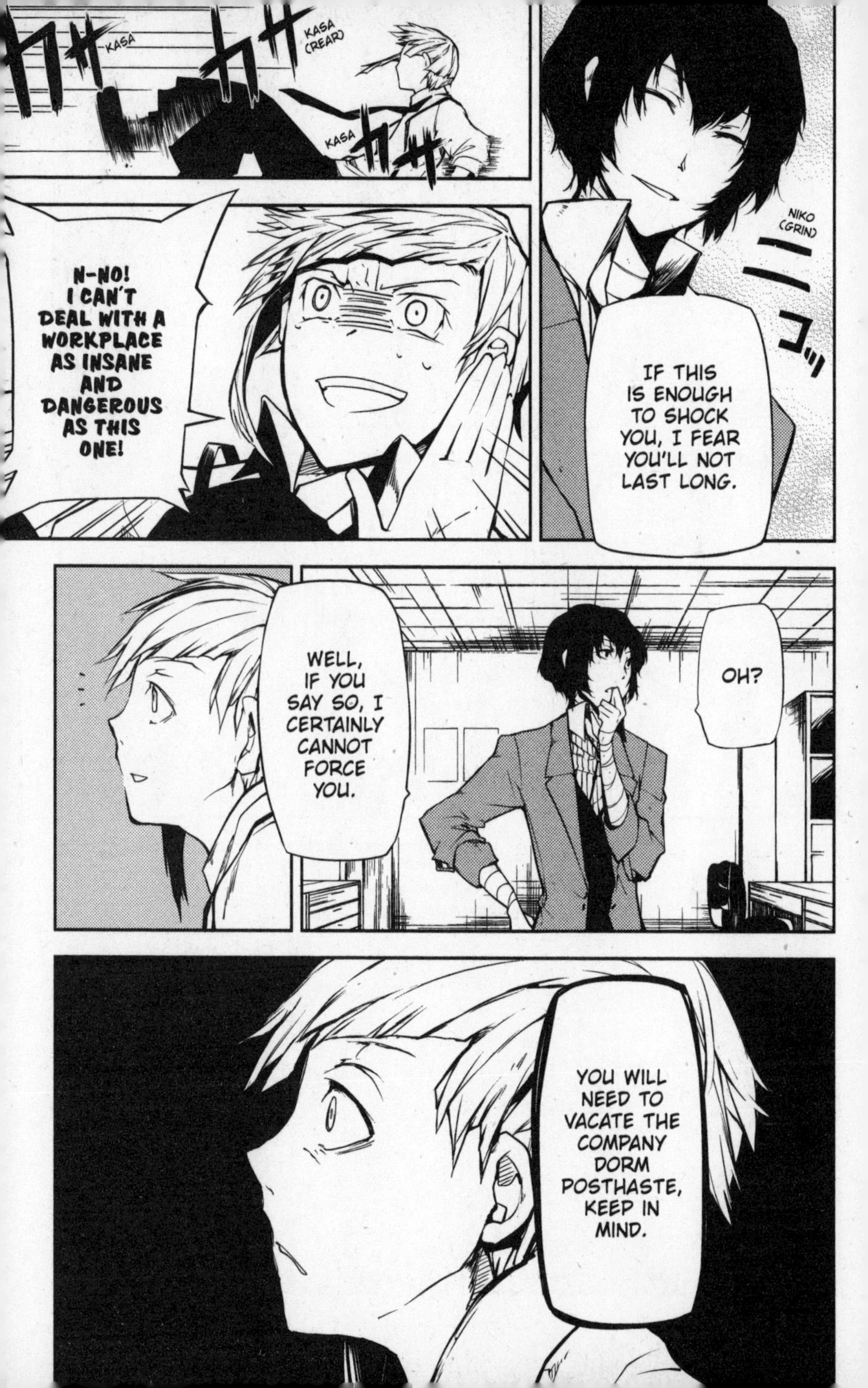
NIKO (GRIN)
IF THIS IS ENOUGH TO SHOCK YOU, I FEAR YOU'LL NOT LAST LONG.
KASA (REAR)
KASA
KASA
N-NO! I CAN'T DEAL WITH A WORKPLACE AS INSANE AND DANGEROUS AS THIS ONE!
OH?
WELL, IF YOU SAY SO, I CERTAINLY CANNOT FORCE YOU.
YOU WILL NEED TO VACATE THE COMPANY DORM POSTHASTE, KEEP IN MIND.

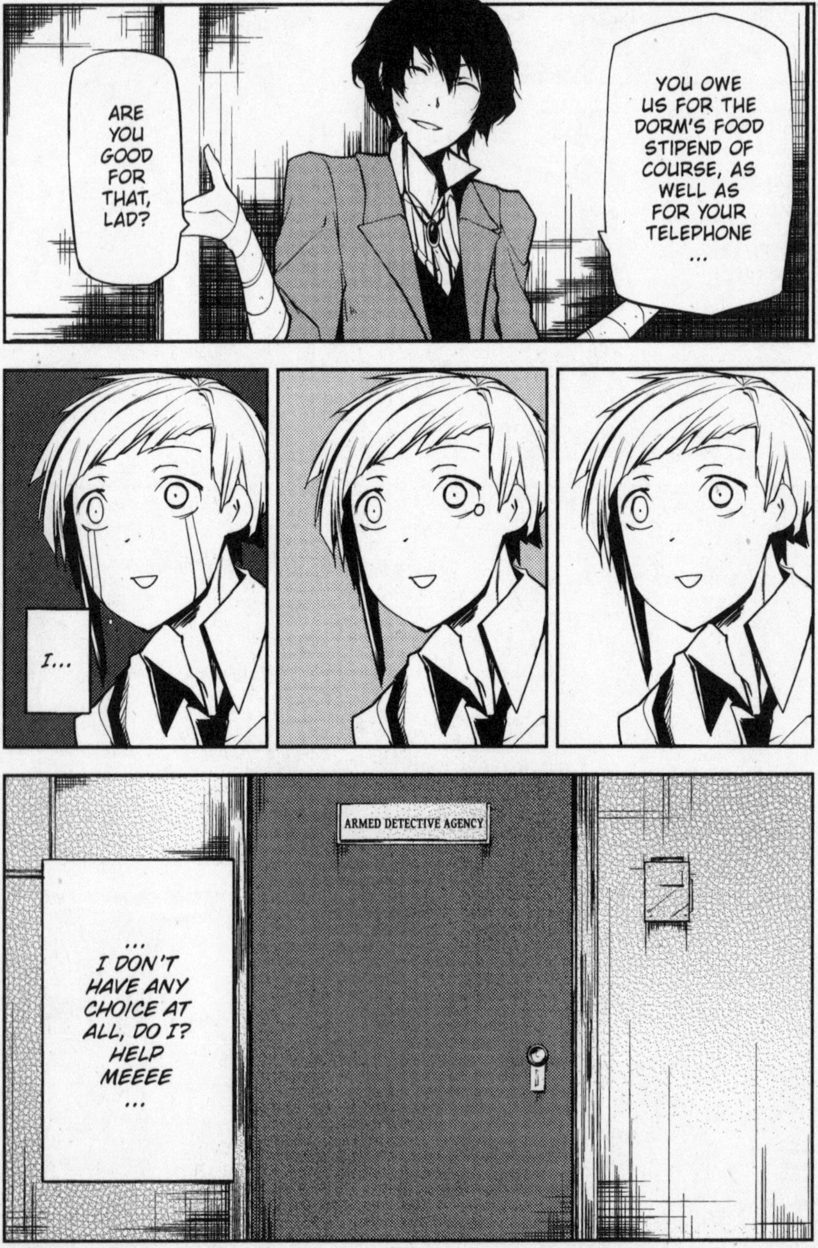
YOU OWE US FOR THE DORM'S FOOD STIPEND OF COURSE, AS WELL AS FOR YOUR TELEPHONE ...
ARE YOU GOOD FOR THAT, LAD?
I...
ARMED DETECTIVE AGENCY
... I DON'T HAVE ANY CHOICE AT ALL, DO I? HELP MEEEE ...

CHAPTER 3

Yokohama Gangster Paradise, Part 1

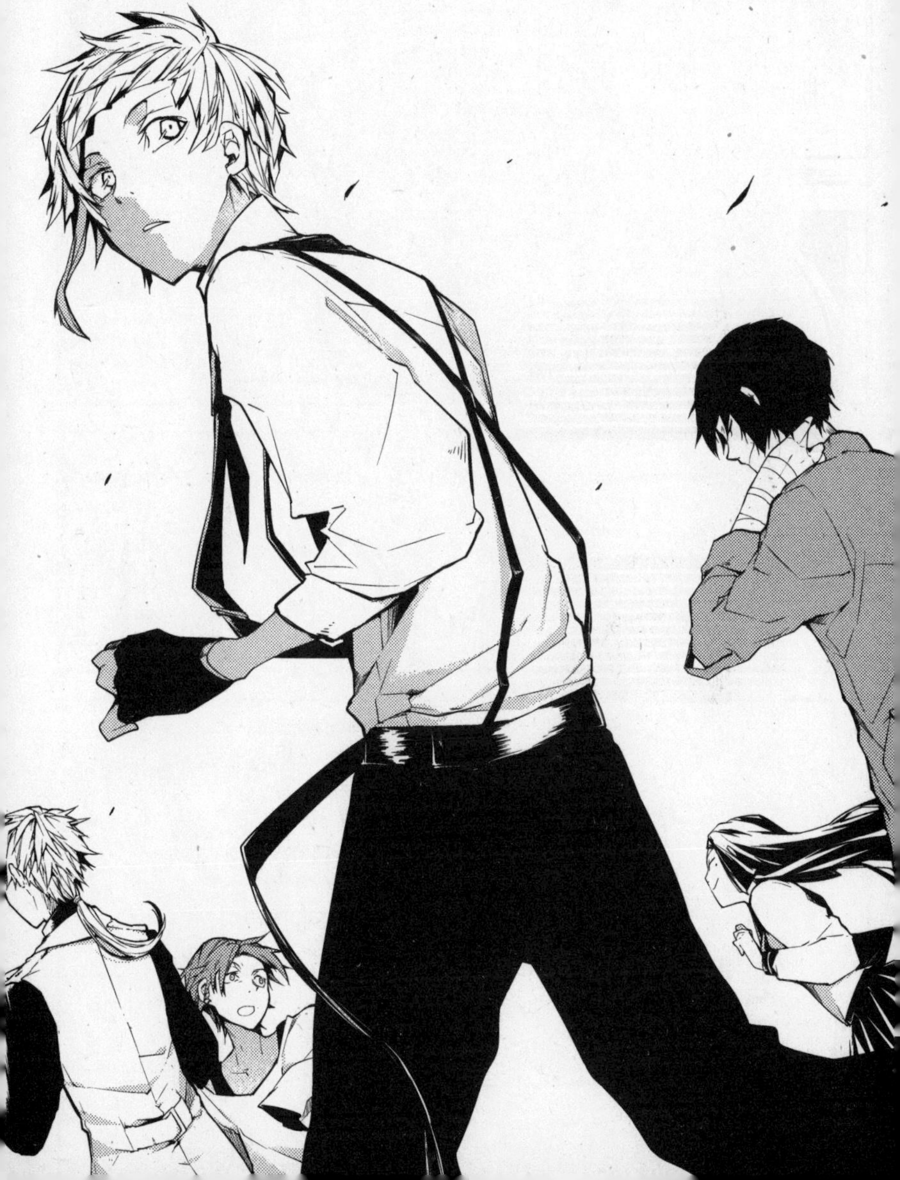

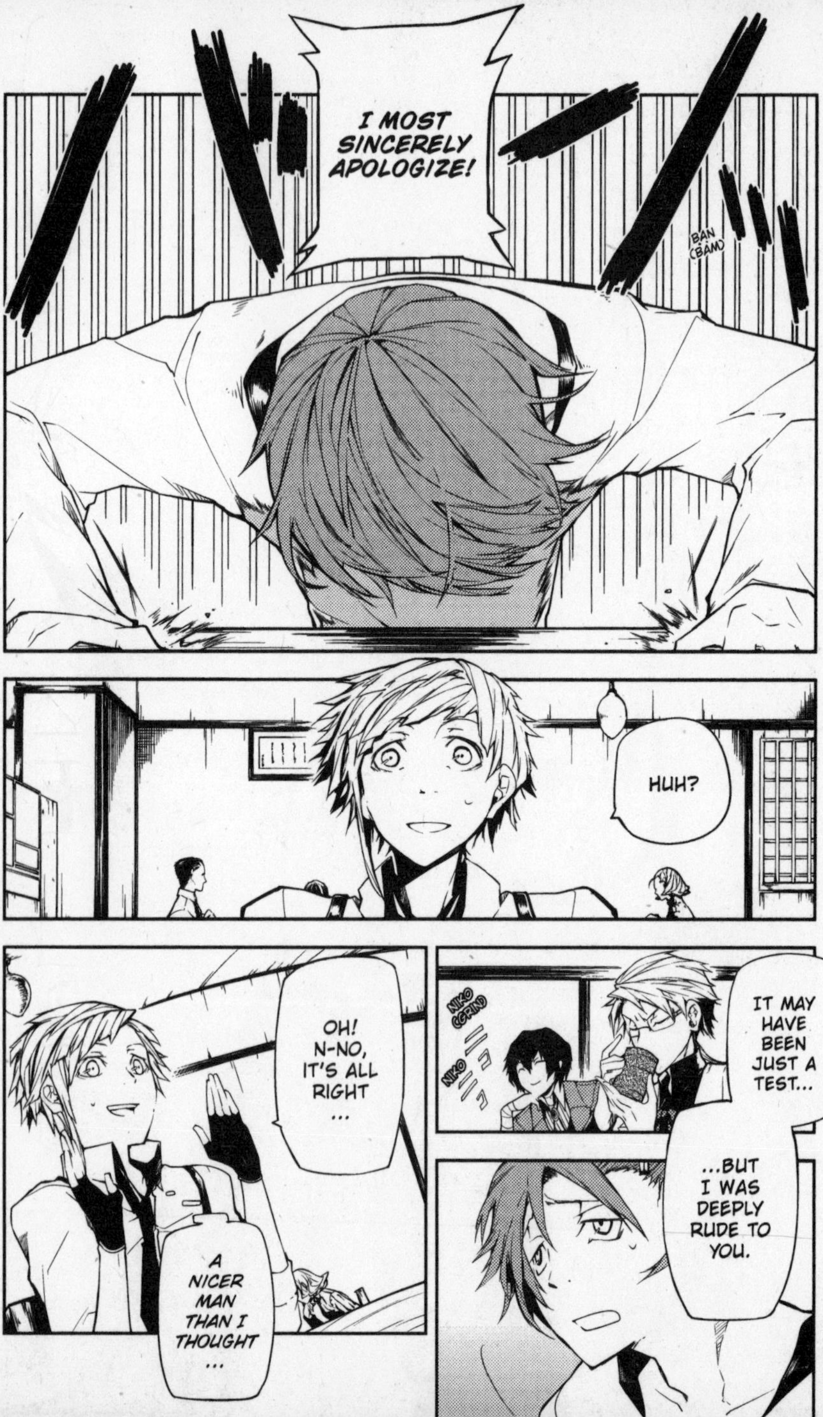
I MOST SINCERELY APOLOGIZE!
BAN (BAM)
HUH?
IT MAY HAVE BEEN JUST A TEST...
NIKO (GRIN)
NIKO
...BUT I WAS DEEPLY RUDE TO YOU.
OH! N-NO, IT'S ALL RIGHT ...
A NICER MAN THAN I THOUGHT ...

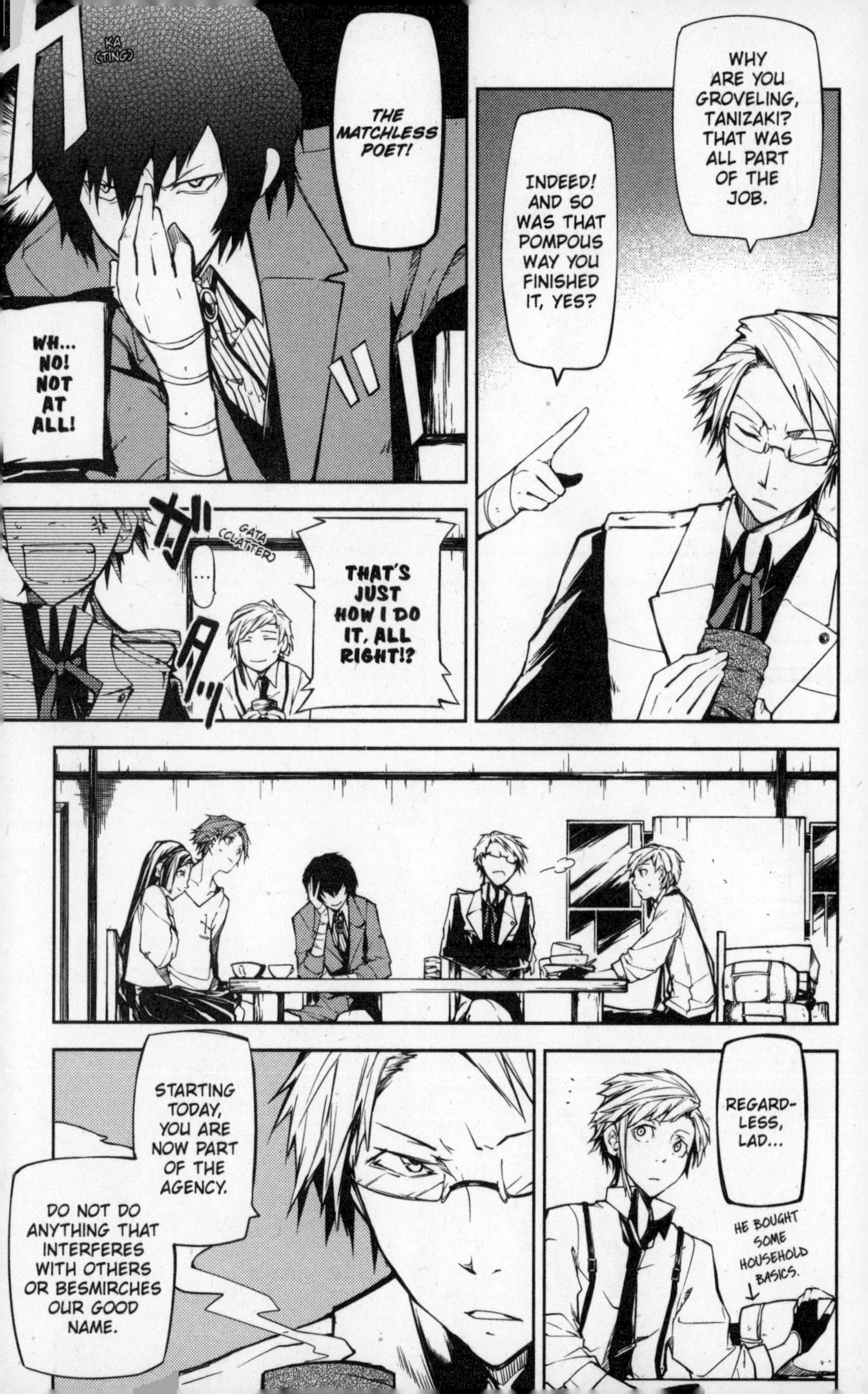
WHY ARE YOU GROVELING, TANIZAKI? THAT WAS ALL PART OF THE JOB.
INDEED! AND SO WAS THAT POMPOUS WAY YOU FINISHED IT, YES?
THE MATCHLESS POET!
KA (TING)
WH... NO! NOT AT ALL!
GATA (CLATTER)
THAT'S JUST HOW I DO IT, ALL RIGHT!?
...
REGARDLESS, LAD...
HE BOUGHT SOME HOUSEHOLD BASICS.
STARTING TODAY, YOU ARE NOW PART OF THE AGENCY.
DO NOT DO ANYTHING THAT INTERFERES WITH OTHERS OR BESMIRCHES OUR GOOD NAME.

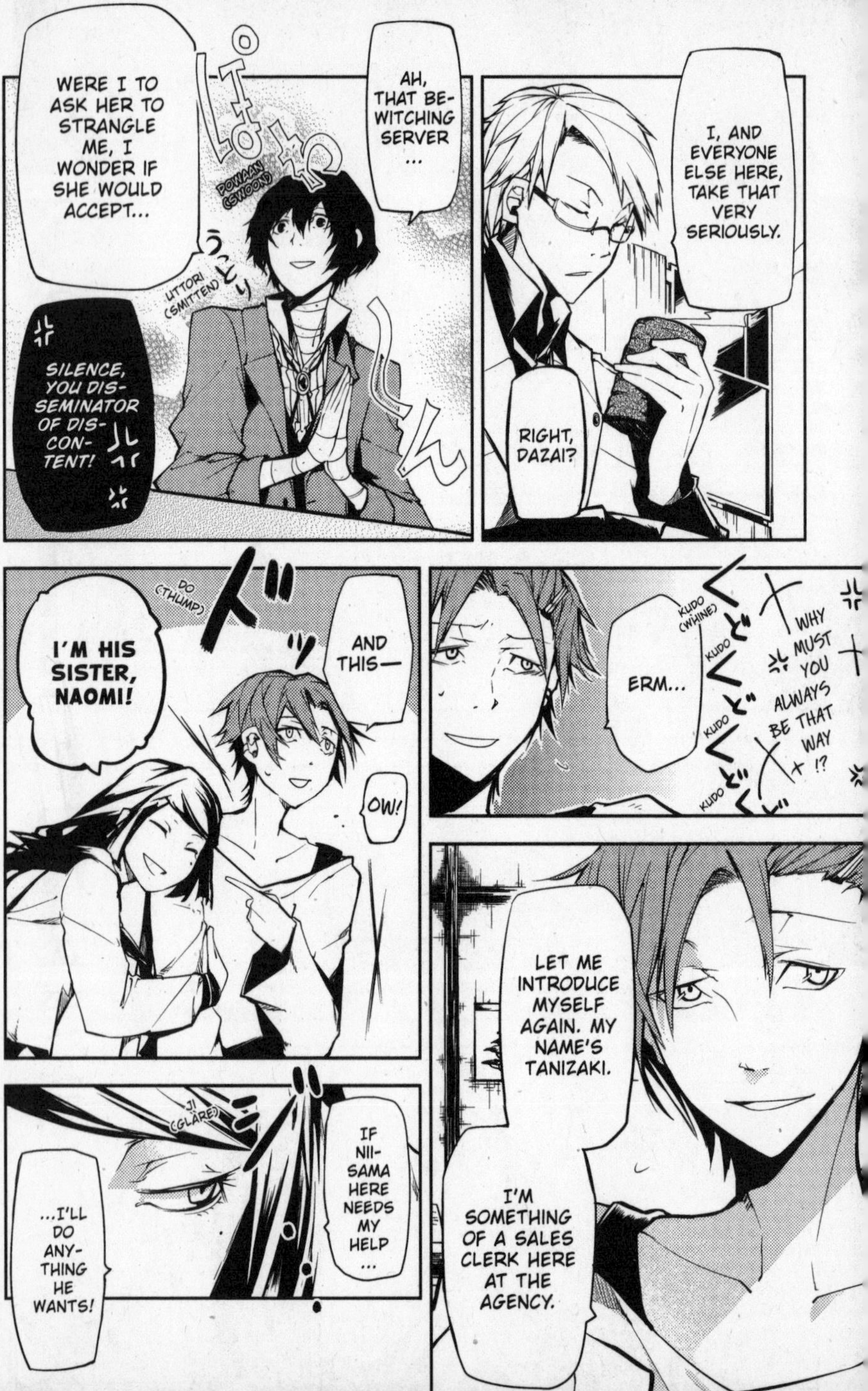
I, AND EVERYONE ELSE HERE, TAKE THAT VERY SERIOUSLY.
RIGHT, DAZAI?
AH, THAT BEWITCHING SERVER...
POWAAN (SWOON)
WERE I TO ASK HER TO STRANGLE ME, I WONDER IF SHE WOULD ACCEPT...
UTTORI (SMITTEN)
SILENCE, YOU DISSEMINATOR OF DISCONTENT!
KUDO (WHINE)
KUDO
KUDO
KUDO
WHY MUST YOU ALWAYS BE THAT WAY!?
ERM...
AND THIS—
DO (THUMP)
I'M HIS SISTER, NAOMI!
OW!
LET ME INTRODUCE MYSELF AGAIN. MY NAME'S TANIZAKI.
I'M SOMETHING OF A SALES CLERK HERE AT THE AGENCY.
JI (GLARE)
IF NII-SAMA HERE NEEDS MY HELP...
...I'LL DO ANYTHING HE WANTS!

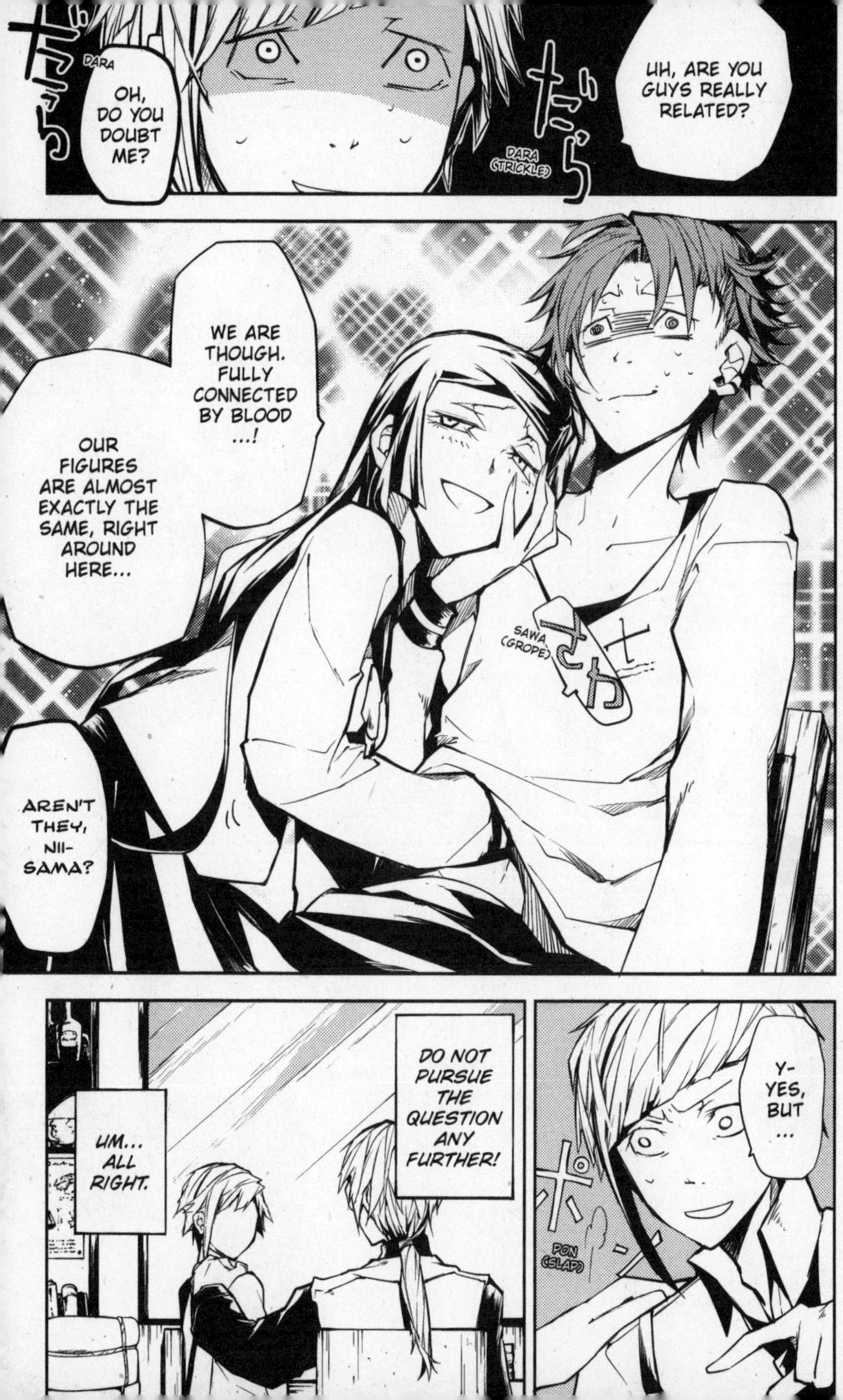
UH, ARE YOU GUYS REALLY RELATED?
DARA (TRICKLE)
DARA
OH, DO YOU DOUBT ME?
WE ARE THOUGH. FULLY CONNECTED BY BLOOD ...!
OUR FIGURES ARE ALMOST EXACTLY THE SAME, RIGHT AROUND HERE...
SAWA (GROPE)
AREN'T THEY, NII-SAMA?
Y-YES, BUT ...
PON (SLAP)
DO NOT PURSUE THE QUESTION ANY FURTHER!
UM... ALL RIGHT.

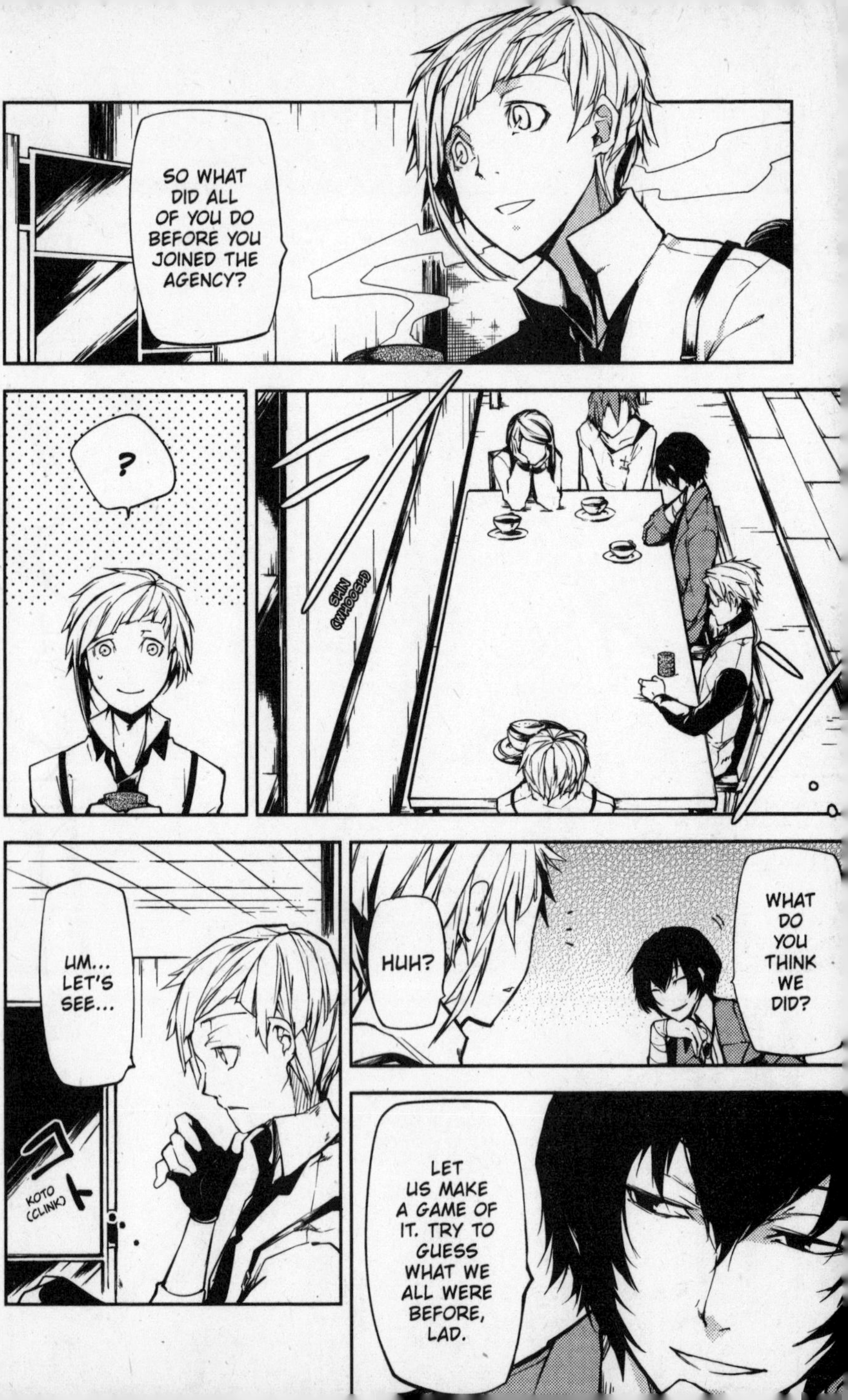
SO WHAT DID ALL OF YOU DO BEFORE YOU JOINED THE AGENCY?
SHIN (WHOOSH)
?
WHAT DO YOU THINK WE DID?
HUH?
LET US MAKE A GAME OF IT. TRY TO GUESS WHAT WE ALL WERE BEFORE, LAD.
UM... LET'S SEE...
KOTO (CLINK)

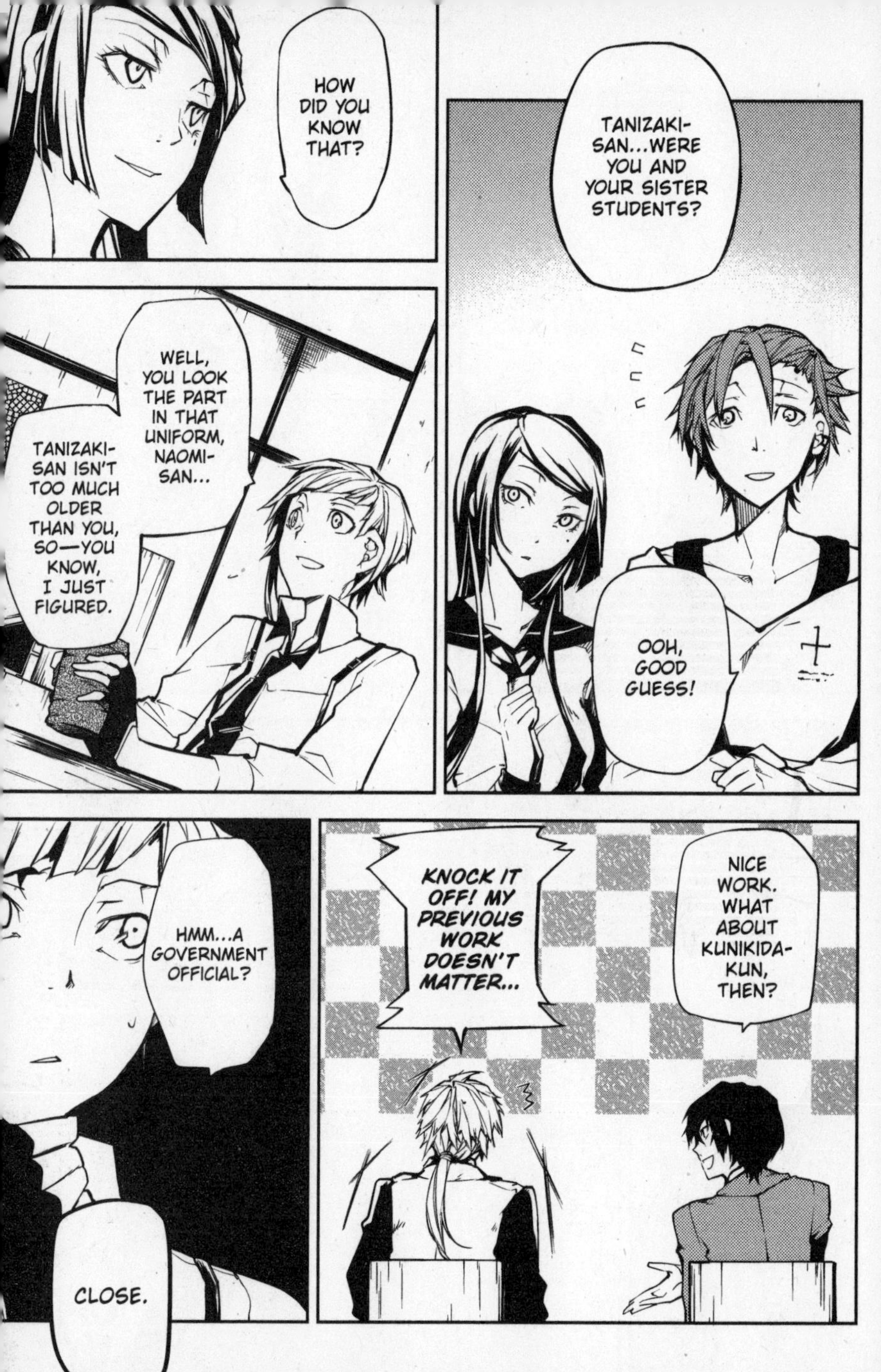
TANIZAKI-SAN...WERE YOU AND YOUR SISTER STUDENTS?
OOH, GOOD GUESS!
HOW DID YOU KNOW THAT?
WELL, YOU LOOK THE PART IN THAT UNIFORM, NAOMI-SAN...
TANIZAKI-SAN ISN'T TOO MUCH OLDER THAN YOU, SO—YOU KNOW, I JUST FIGURED.
NICE WORK. WHAT ABOUT KUNIKIDA-KUN, THEN?
KNOCK IT OFF! MY PREVIOUS WORK DOESN'T MATTER...
HMM...A GOVERNMENT OFFICIAL?
CLOSE.

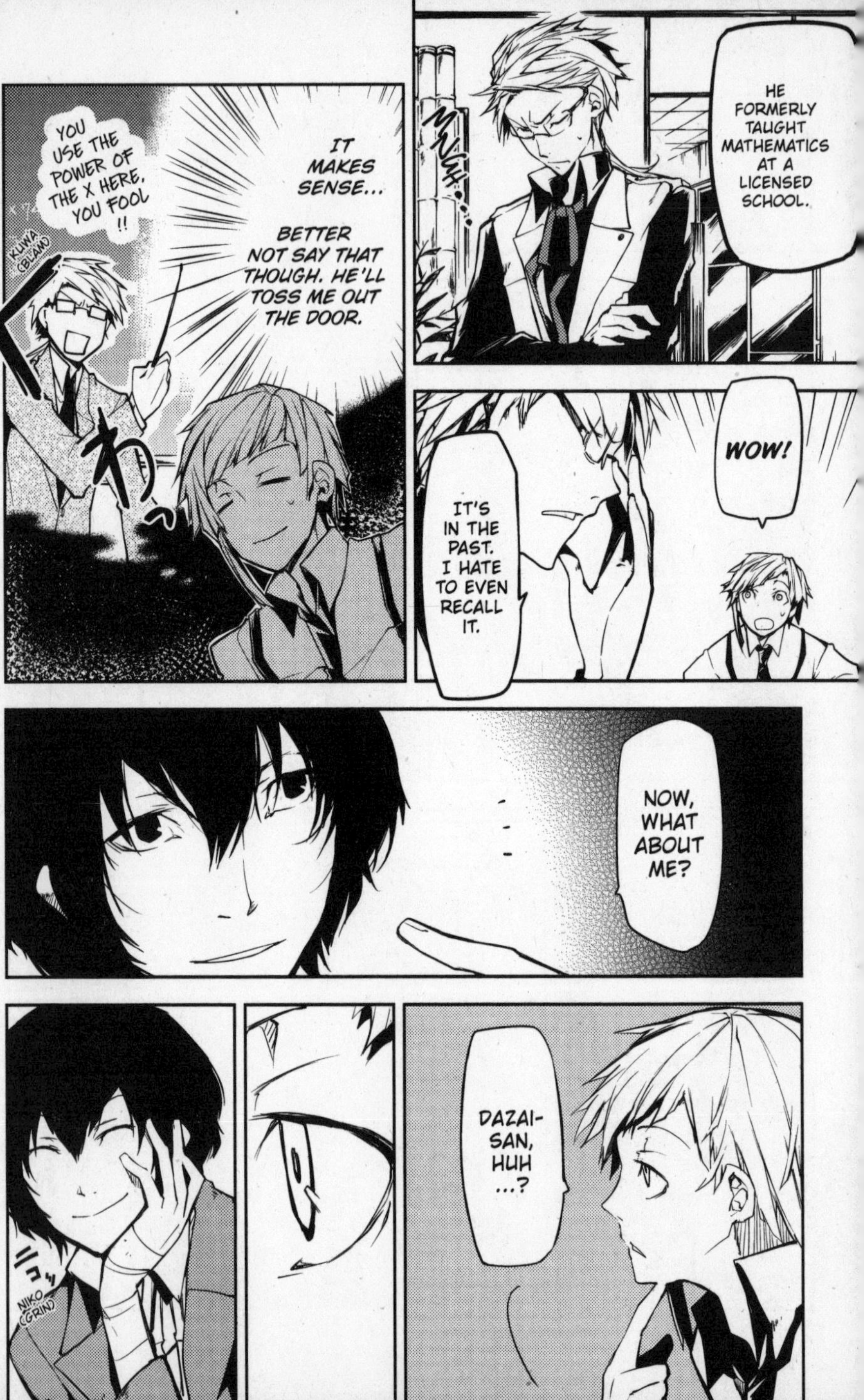
HE FORMERLY TAUGHT MATHEMATICS AT A LICENSED SCHOOL.
MUGH...
WOW!
IT'S IN THE PAST. I HATE TO EVEN RECALL IT.
IT MAKES SENSE...
BETTER NOT SAY THAT THOUGH. HE'LL TOSS ME OUT THE DOOR.
YOU USE THE POWER OF THE X HERE, YOU FOOL!!
KUWA (BLAM)
NOW, WHAT ABOUT ME?
DAZAI-SAN, HUH...?
NIKO (GRIN)

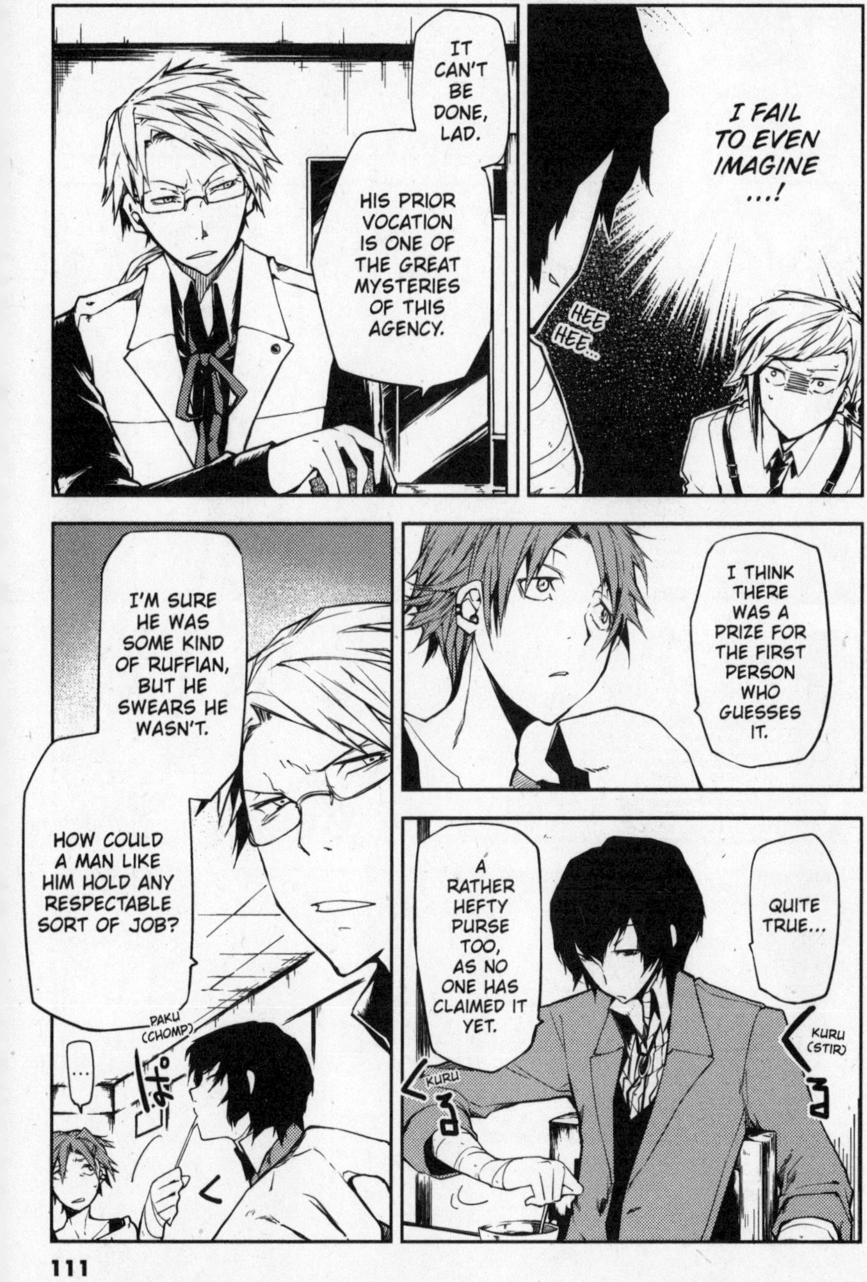
I FAIL TO EVEN IMAGINE ...!
HEE HEE...
IT CAN'T BE DONE, LAD.
HIS PRIOR VOCATION IS ONE OF THE GREAT MYSTERIES OF THIS AGENCY.
I THINK THERE WAS A PRIZE FOR THE FIRST PERSON WHO GUESSES IT.
QUITE TRUE...
A RATHER HEFTY PURSE TOO, AS NO ONE HAS CLAIMED IT YET.
KURU (STIR)
KURU
I'M SURE HE WAS SOME KIND OF RUFFIAN, BUT HE SWEARS HE WASN'T.
HOW COULD A MAN LIKE HIM HOLD ANY RESPECTABLE SORT OF JOB?
PAKU (CHOMP)
...

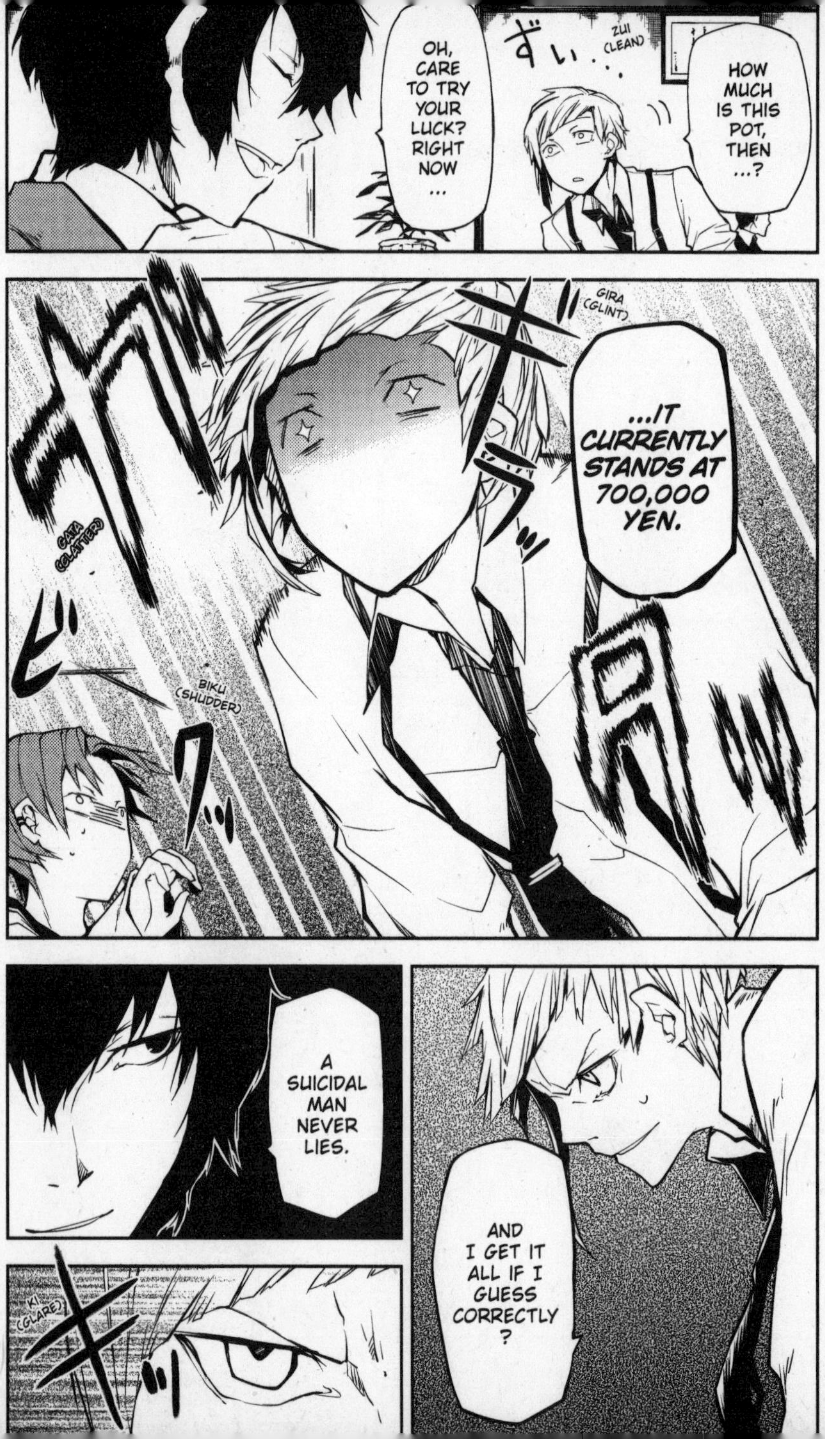
ZUI (LEAN)
HOW MUCH IS THIS POT, THEN ...?
OH, CARE TO TRY YOUR LUCK? RIGHT NOW ...
GIRA (GLINT)
...IT CURRENTLY STANDS AT 700,000 YEN.
GATA (CLATTER)
BIKU (SHUDDER)
AND I GET IT ALL IF I GUESS CORRECTLY ?
A SUICIDAL MAN NEVER LIES.
KI (GLARE)

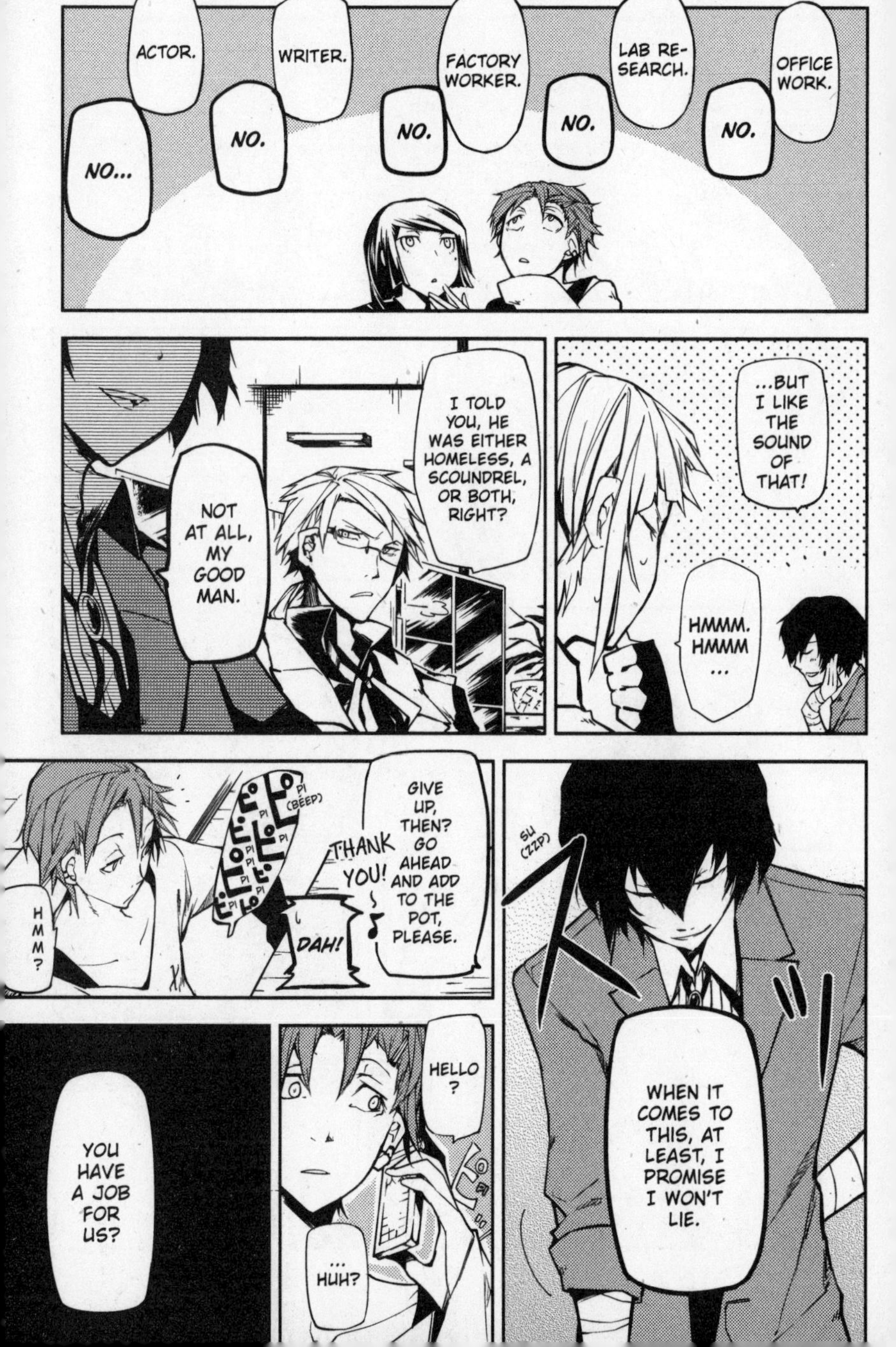
OFFICE WORK.
NO.
LAB RE-SEARCH.
NO.
FACTORY WORKER.
NO.
WRITER.
NO.
ACTOR.
NO...
...BUT I LIKE THE SOUND OF THAT!
HMMM. HMMM...
I TOLD YOU, HE WAS EITHER HOMELESS, A SCOUNDREL, OR BOTH, RIGHT?
NOT AT ALL, MY GOOD MAN.
SU (ZZZ)
WHEN IT COMES TO THIS, AT LEAST, I PROMISE I WON'T LIE.
GIVE UP, THEN? GO AHEAD AND ADD TO THE POT, PLEASE.
THANK YOU!
DAH!
PI (BEEP)
HMM?
HELLO?
...HUH?
YOU HAVE A JOB FOR US?

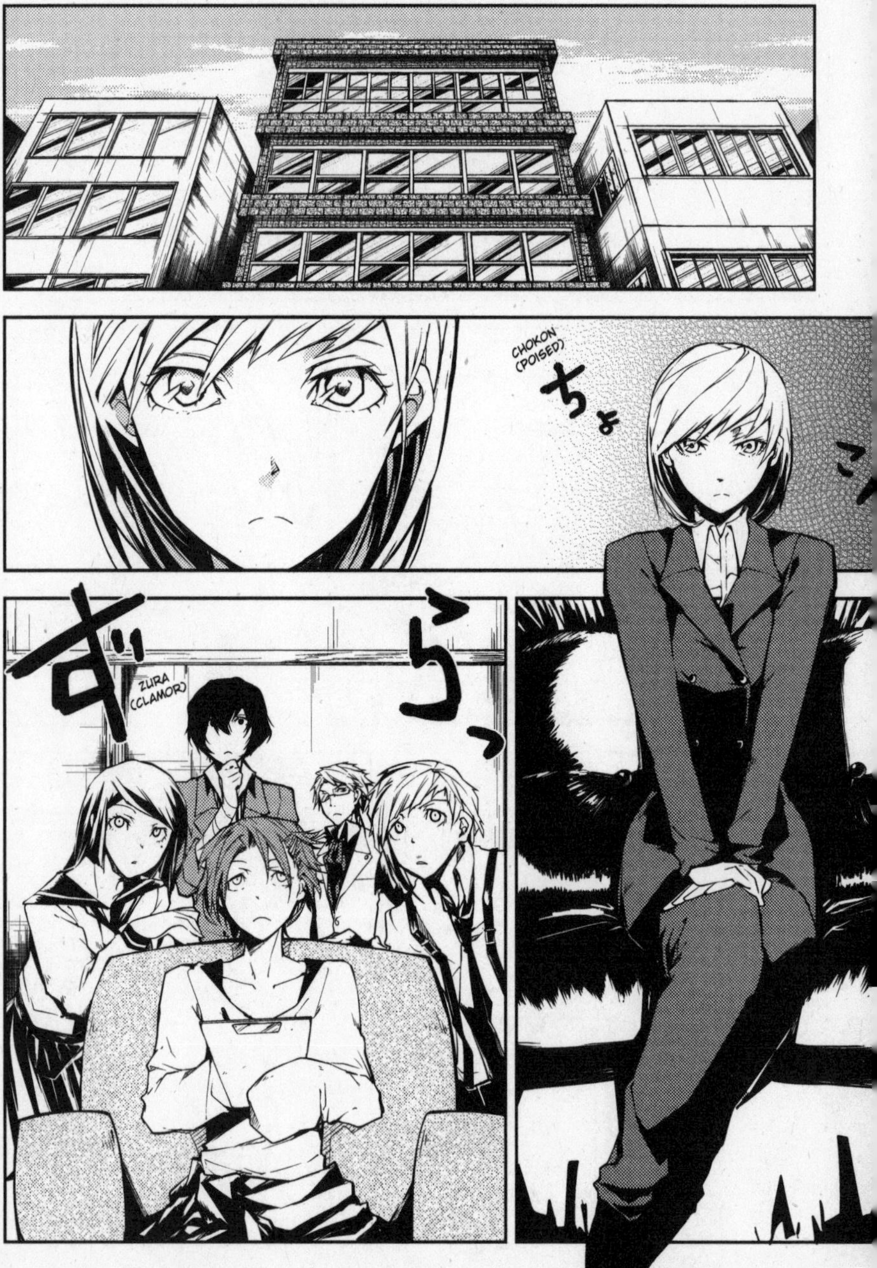
CHOKON (POISED)
ZURA (CLAMOR)

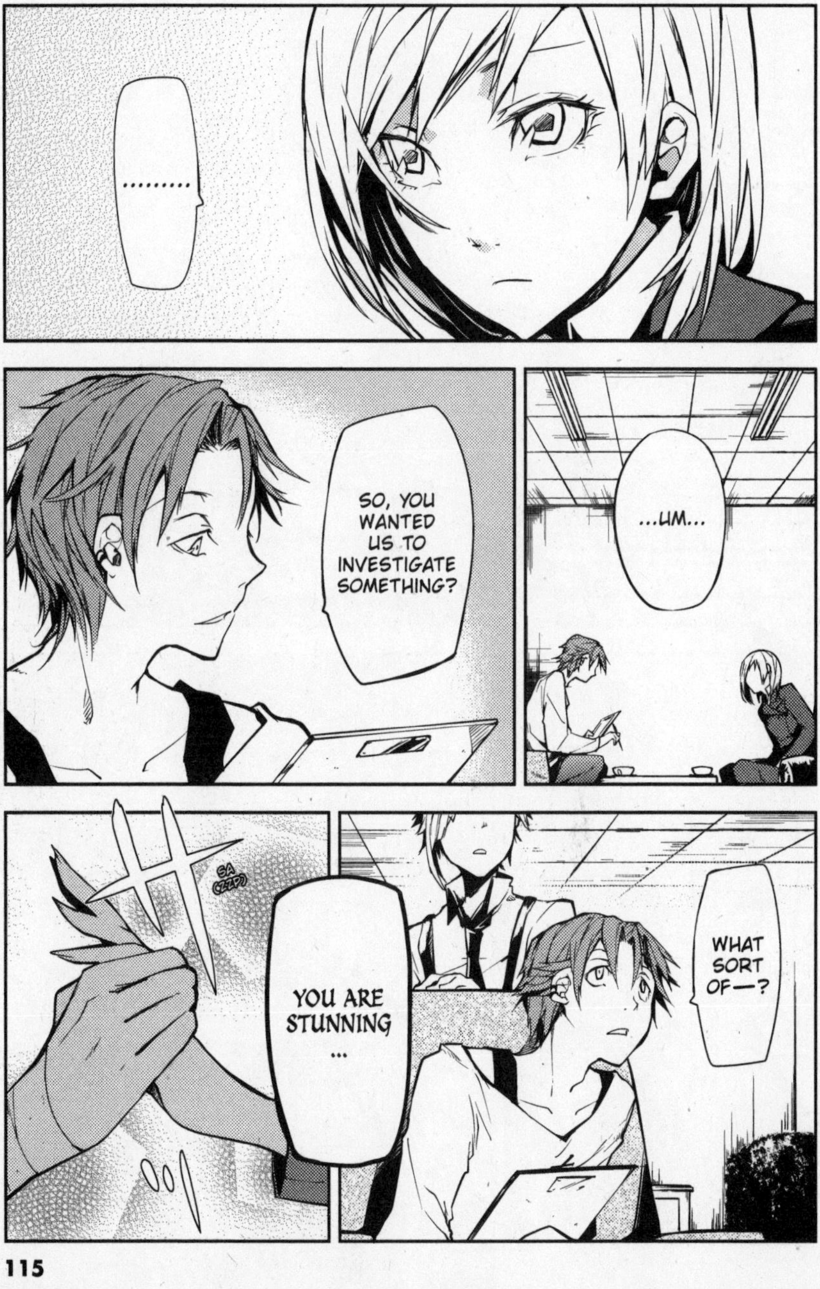
....
...UM...
SO, YOU WANTED US TO INVESTIGATE SOMETHING?
WHAT SORT OF—?
YOU ARE STUNNING ...
SA (ZZP)

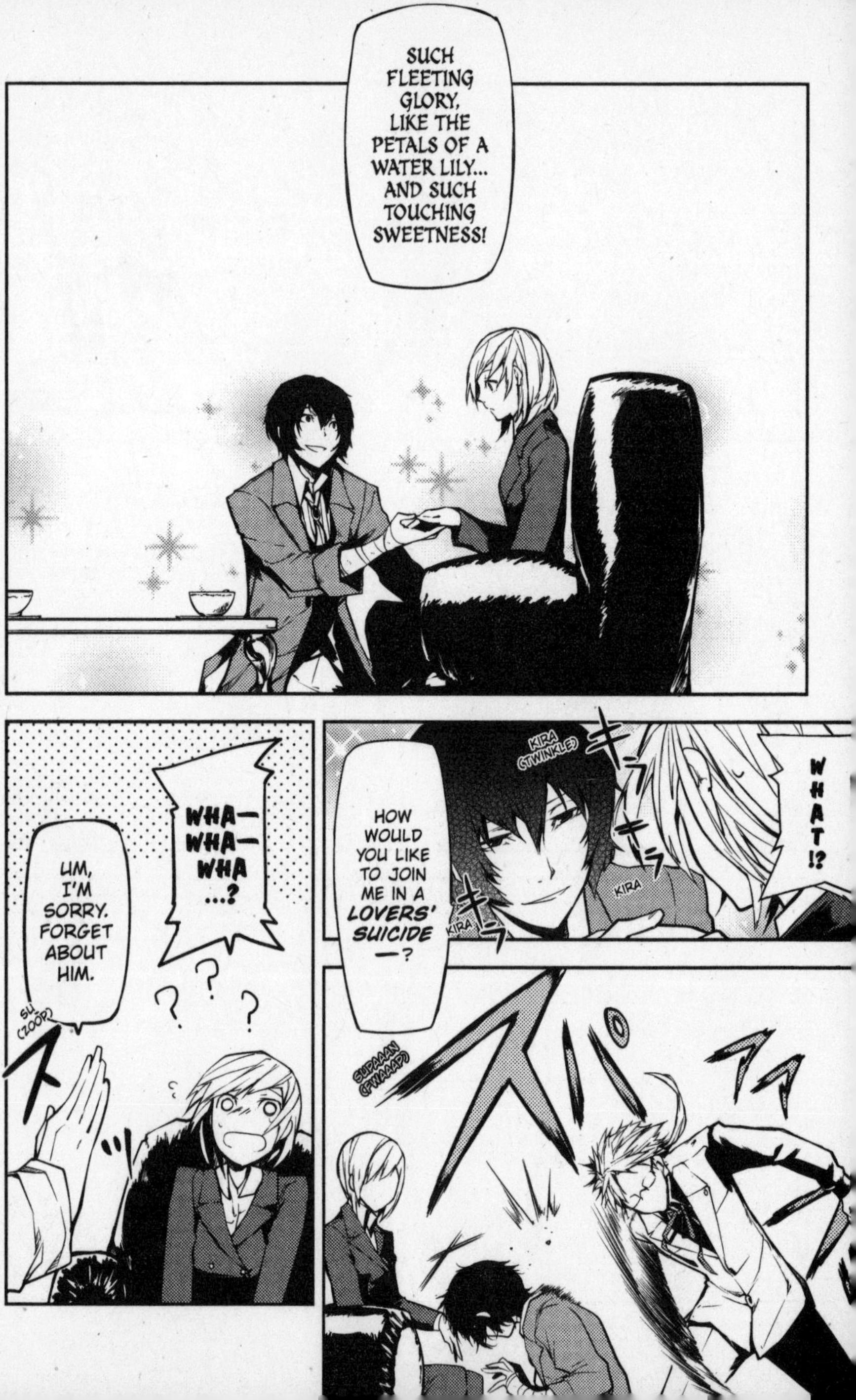
SUCH FLEETING GLORY, LIKE THE PETALS OF A WATER LILY... AND SUCH TOUCHING SWEETNESS!
WHAT!?
KIRA (TWINKLE)
KIRA
KIRA
HOW WOULD YOU LIKE TO JOIN ME IN A *LOVERS' SUICIDE*—?
SUPAAAN (FWAAAP)
WHA—WHA—WHA...?
UM, I'M SORRY. FORGET ABOUT HIM.
SU (ZOOP)

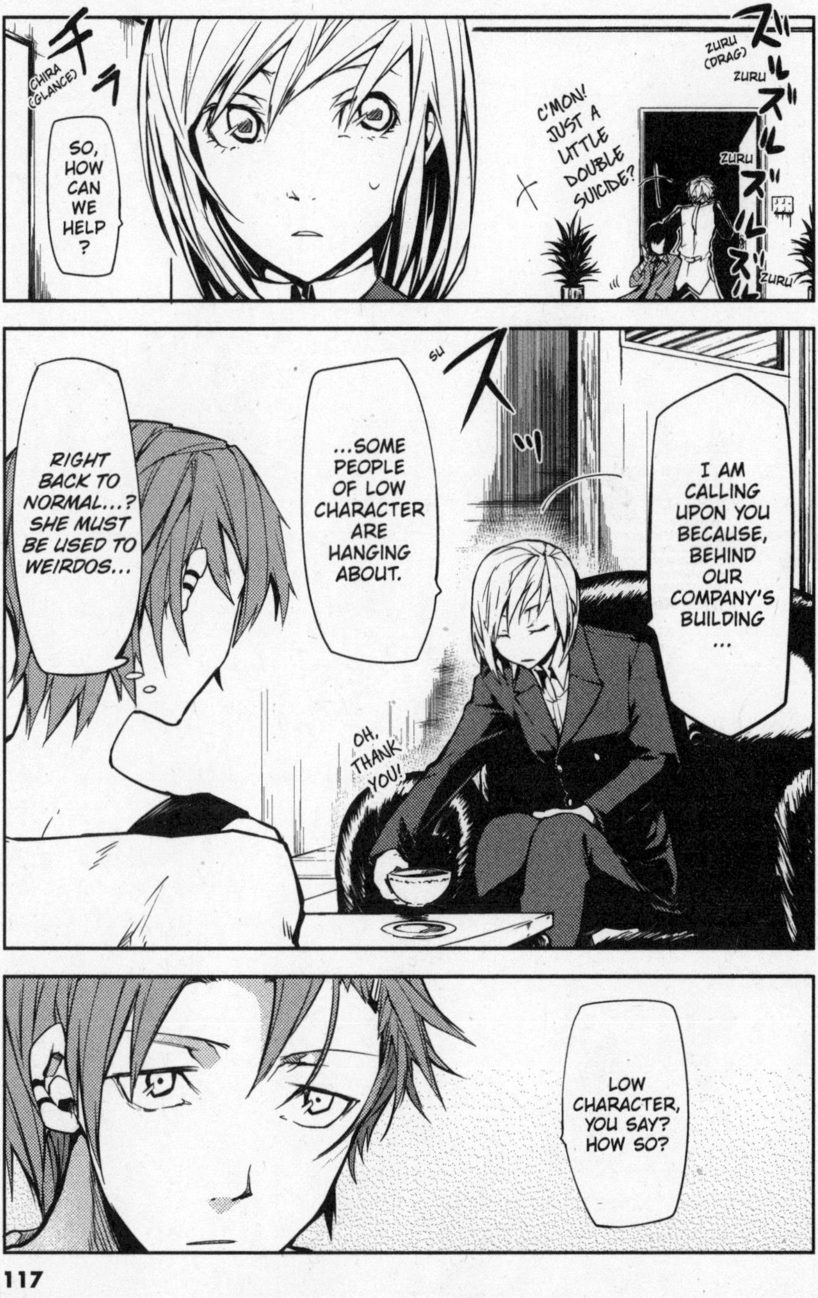
ZURU (DRAG)
ZURU
ZURU
ZURU
C'MON! JUST A LITTLE DOUBLE SUICIDE?
CHIRA (GLANCE)
SO, HOW CAN WE HELP?
SU
I AM CALLING UPON YOU BECAUSE, BEHIND OUR COMPANY'S BUILDING ...
...SOME PEOPLE OF LOW CHARACTER ARE HANGING ABOUT.
OH, THANK YOU!
RIGHT BACK TO NORMAL...? SHE MUST BE USED TO WEIRDOS...
LOW CHARACTER, YOU SAY? HOW SO?

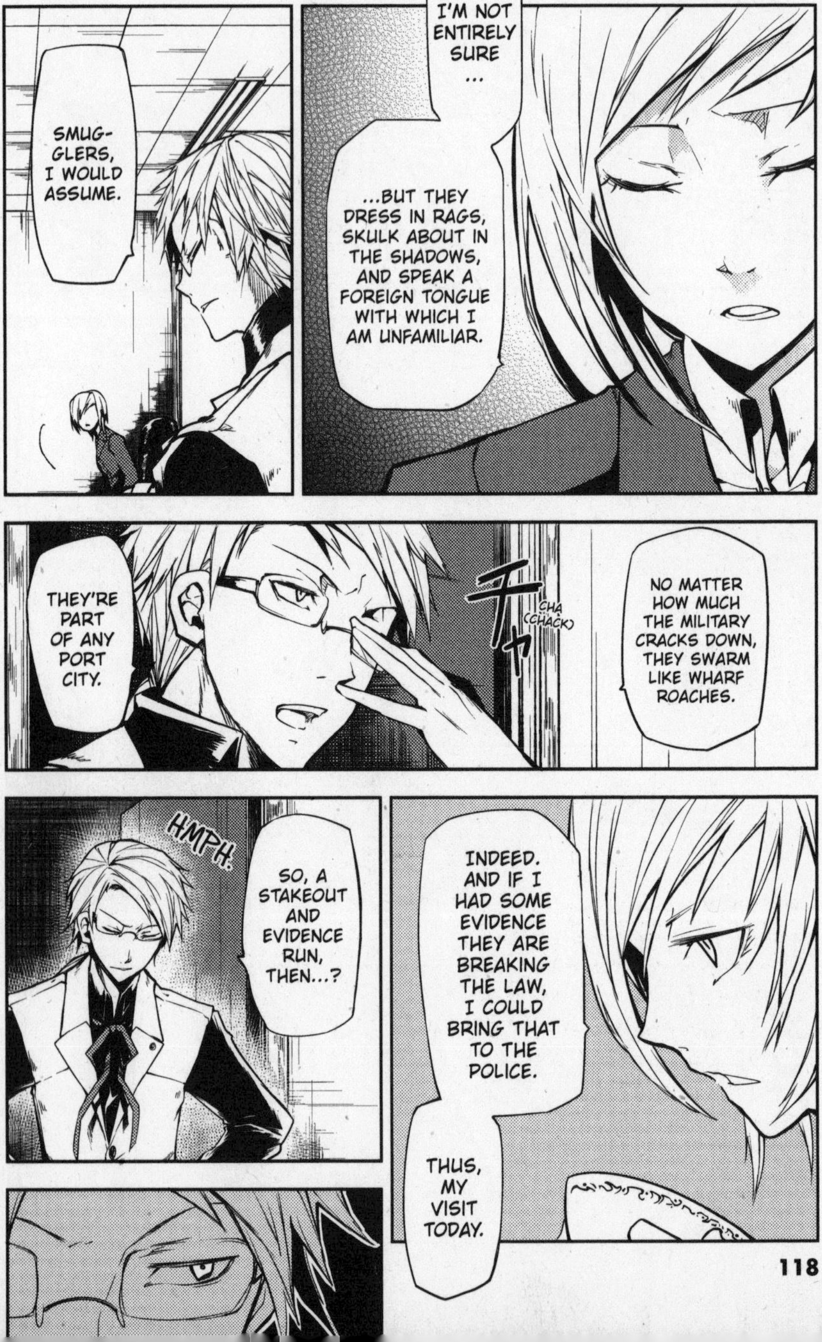
I'M NOT ENTIRELY SURE ...
...BUT THEY DRESS IN RAGS, SKULK ABOUT IN THE SHADOWS, AND SPEAK A FOREIGN TONGUE WITH WHICH I AM UNFAMILIAR.
SMUG-GLERS, I WOULD ASSUME.
NO MATTER HOW MUCH THE MILITARY CRACKS DOWN, THEY SWARM LIKE WHARF ROACHES.
チャ
CHA (CHACK)
THEY'RE PART OF ANY PORT CITY.
INDEED. AND IF I HAD SOME EVIDENCE THEY ARE BREAKING THE LAW, I COULD BRING THAT TO THE POLICE.
THUS, MY VISIT TODAY.
HMPH.
SO, A STAKEOUT AND EVIDENCE RUN, THEN...?

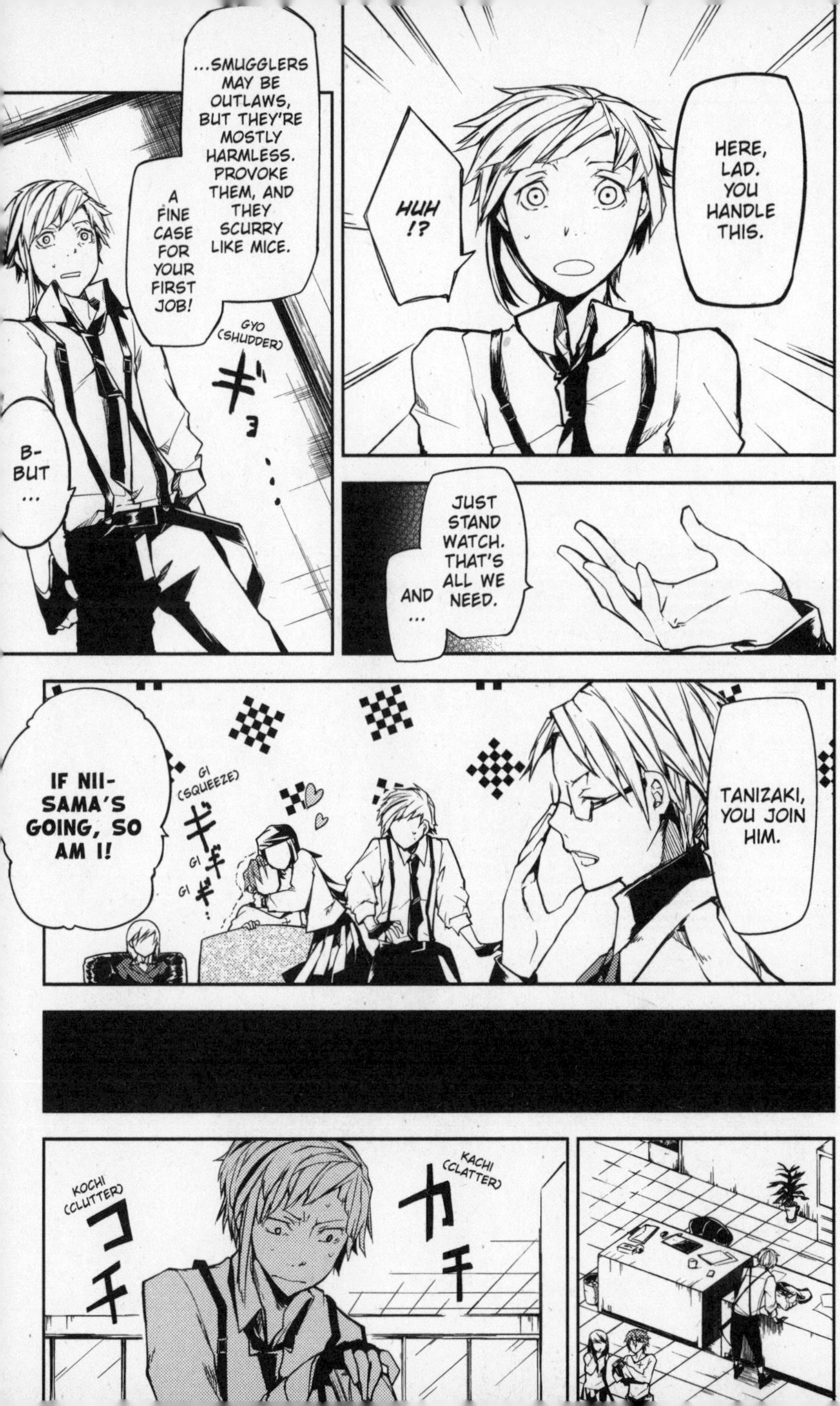
HERE, LAD. YOU HANDLE THIS.
HUH!?
JUST STAND WATCH. THAT'S ALL WE NEED.
AND ...
...SMUGGLERS MAY BE OUTLAWS, BUT THEY'RE MOSTLY HARMLESS. PROVOKE THEM, AND THEY SCURRY LIKE MICE.
A FINE CASE FOR YOUR FIRST JOB!
GYO (SHUDDER)
ギョ
B-BUT ...
TANIZAKI, YOU JOIN HIM.
GI (SQUEEZE)
ギ
GI
ギ
GI
ギ
IF NII-SAMA'S GOING, SO AM I!
KACHI (CLATTER)
カチ
KOCHI (CLUTTER)
コチ

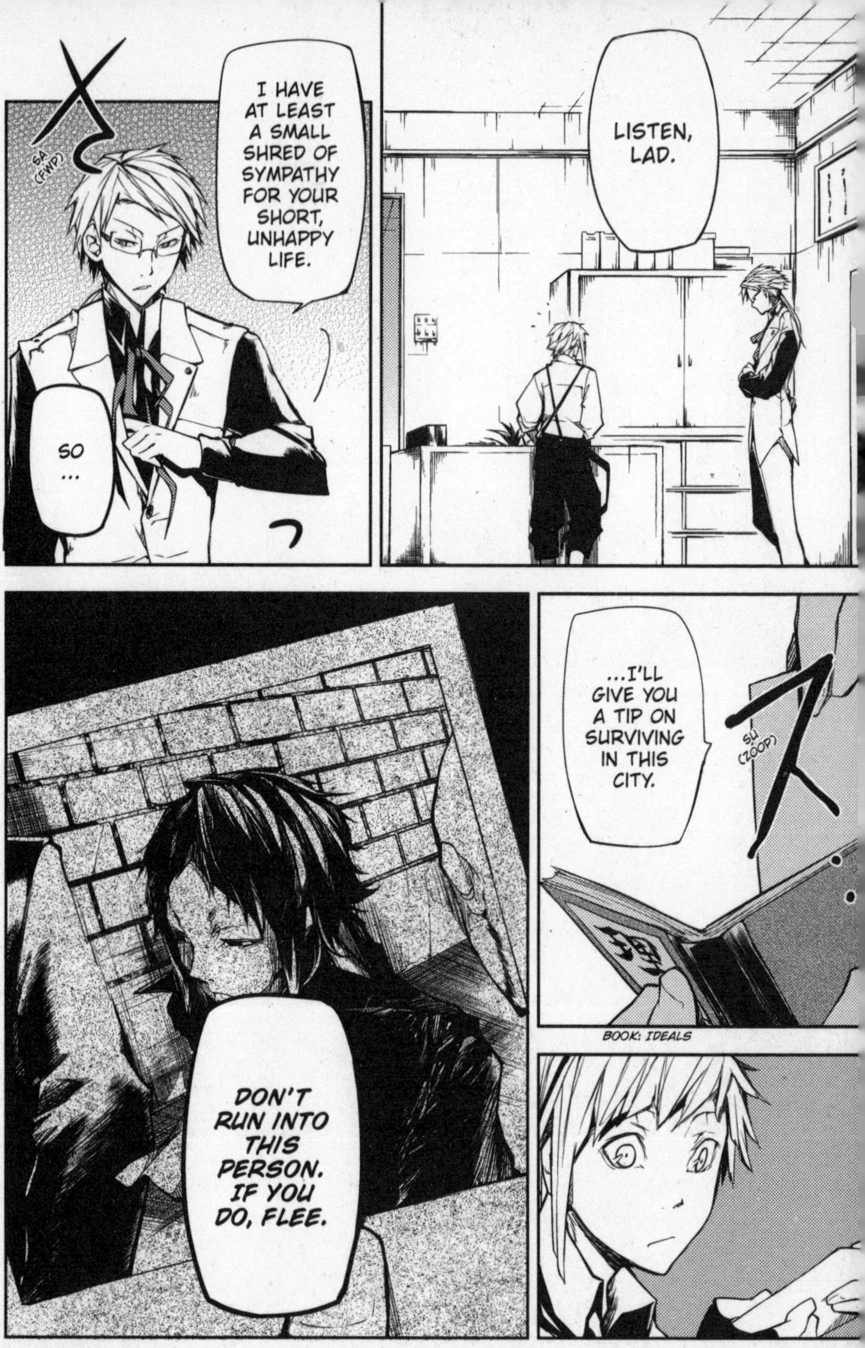
LISTEN, LAD.
I HAVE AT LEAST A SMALL SHRED OF SYMPATHY FOR YOUR SHORT, UNHAPPY LIFE.
SA (FWP)
SO ...
...I'LL GIVE YOU A TIP ON SURVIVING IN THIS CITY.
SU (ZOOP)
BOOK: IDEALS
DON'T RUN INTO THIS PERSON. IF YOU DO, FLEE.

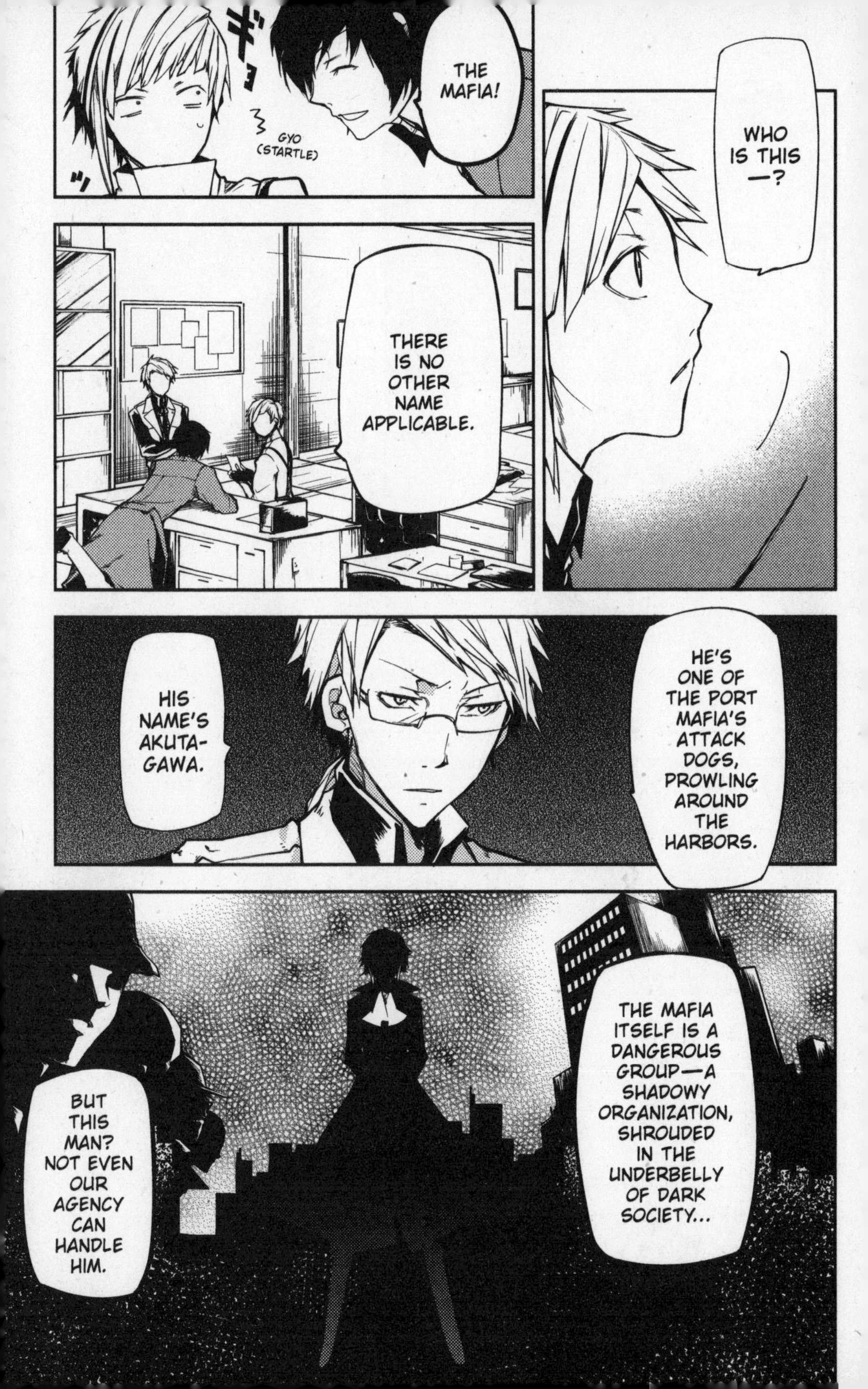

WHO IS THIS—?
THE MAFIA!
ギョッ
GYO (STARTLE)
THERE IS NO OTHER NAME APPLICABLE.
HE'S ONE OF THE PORT MAFIA'S ATTACK DOGS, PROWLING AROUND THE HARBORS.
HIS NAME'S AKUTA-GAWA.
THE MAFIA ITSELF IS A DANGEROUS GROUP—A SHADOWY ORGANIZATION, SHROUDED IN THE UNDERBELLY OF DARK SOCIETY...
BUT THIS MAN? NOT EVEN OUR AGENCY CAN HANDLE HIM.

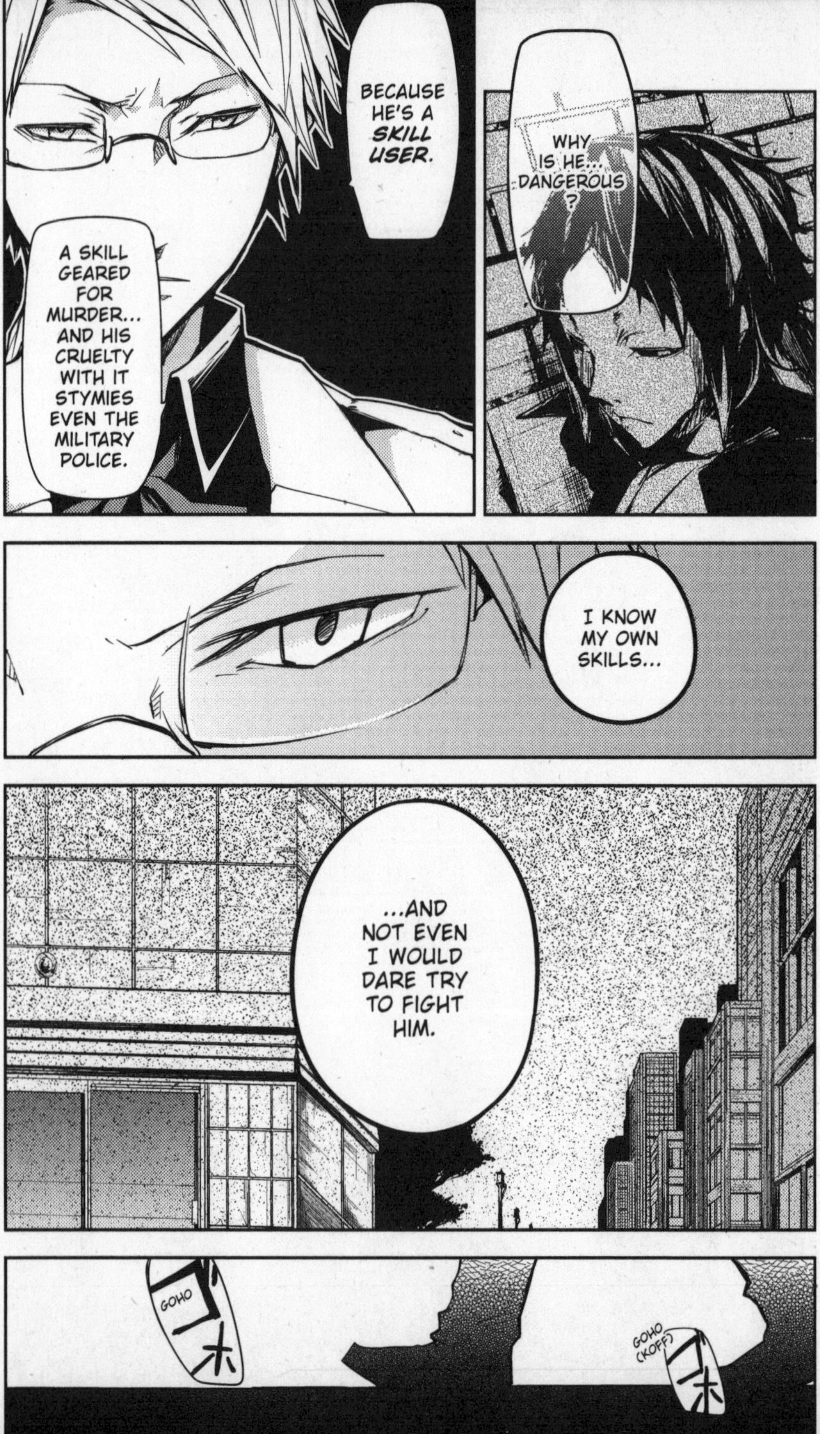

WHY IS HE... DANGEROUS?
BECAUSE HE'S A *SKILL USER*.
A SKILL GEARED FOR MURDER... AND HIS CRUELTY WITH IT STYMIES EVEN THE MILITARY POLICE.
I KNOW MY OWN SKILLS...
...AND NOT EVEN I WOULD DARE TRY TO FIGHT HIM.
GOHO (KOFF)
ゴホ
GOHO
ゴホ

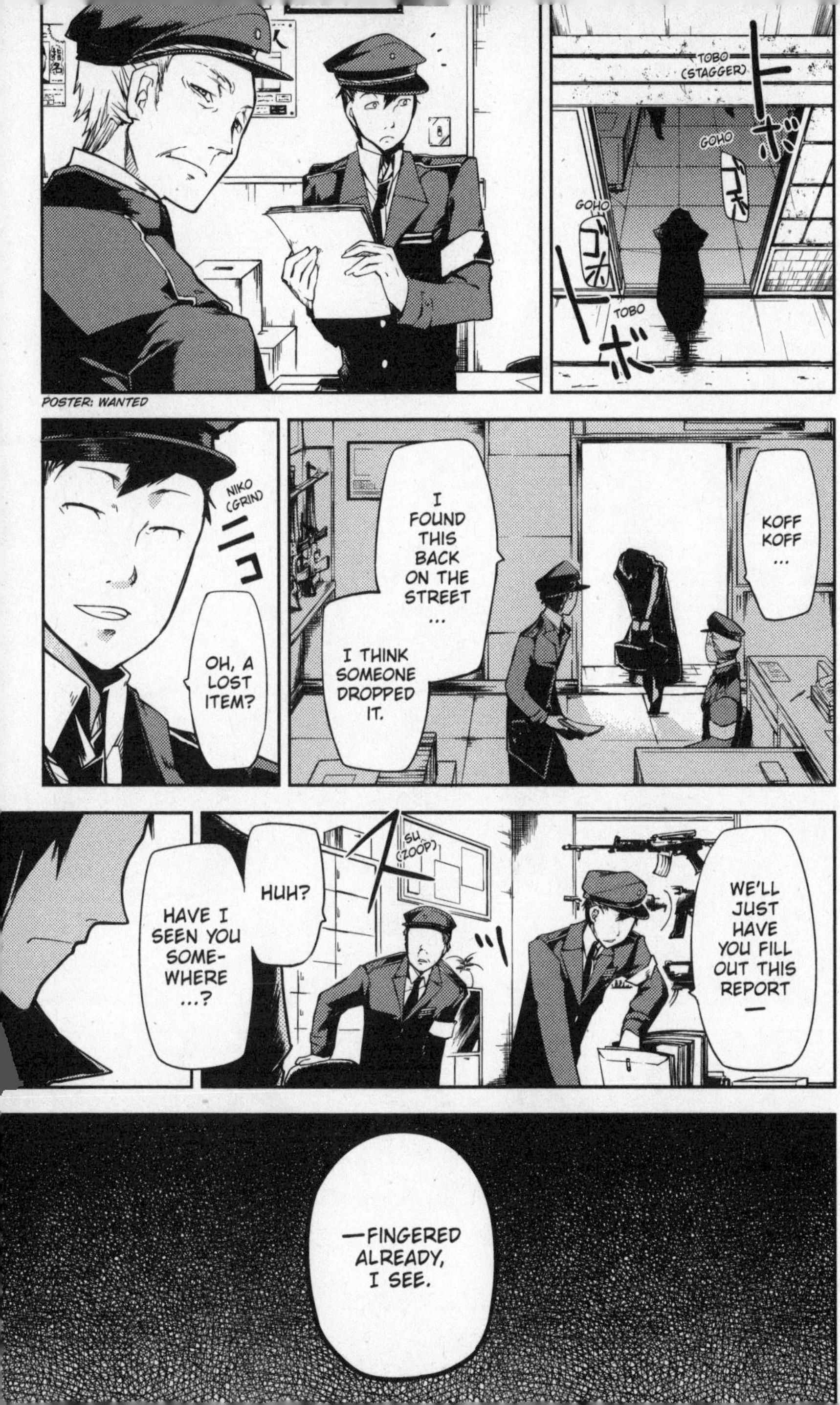
TOBO (STAGGER)
GOHO
GOHO
TOBO
POSTER: WANTED
KOFF KOFF ...
I FOUND THIS BACK ON THE STREET ...
I THINK SOMEONE DROPPED IT.
NIKO (GRIN)
OH, A LOST ITEM?
WE'LL JUST HAVE YOU FILL OUT THIS REPORT —
SU (ZOOP)
HUH?
HAVE I SEEN YOU SOME-WHERE ...?
—FINGERED ALREADY, I SEE.

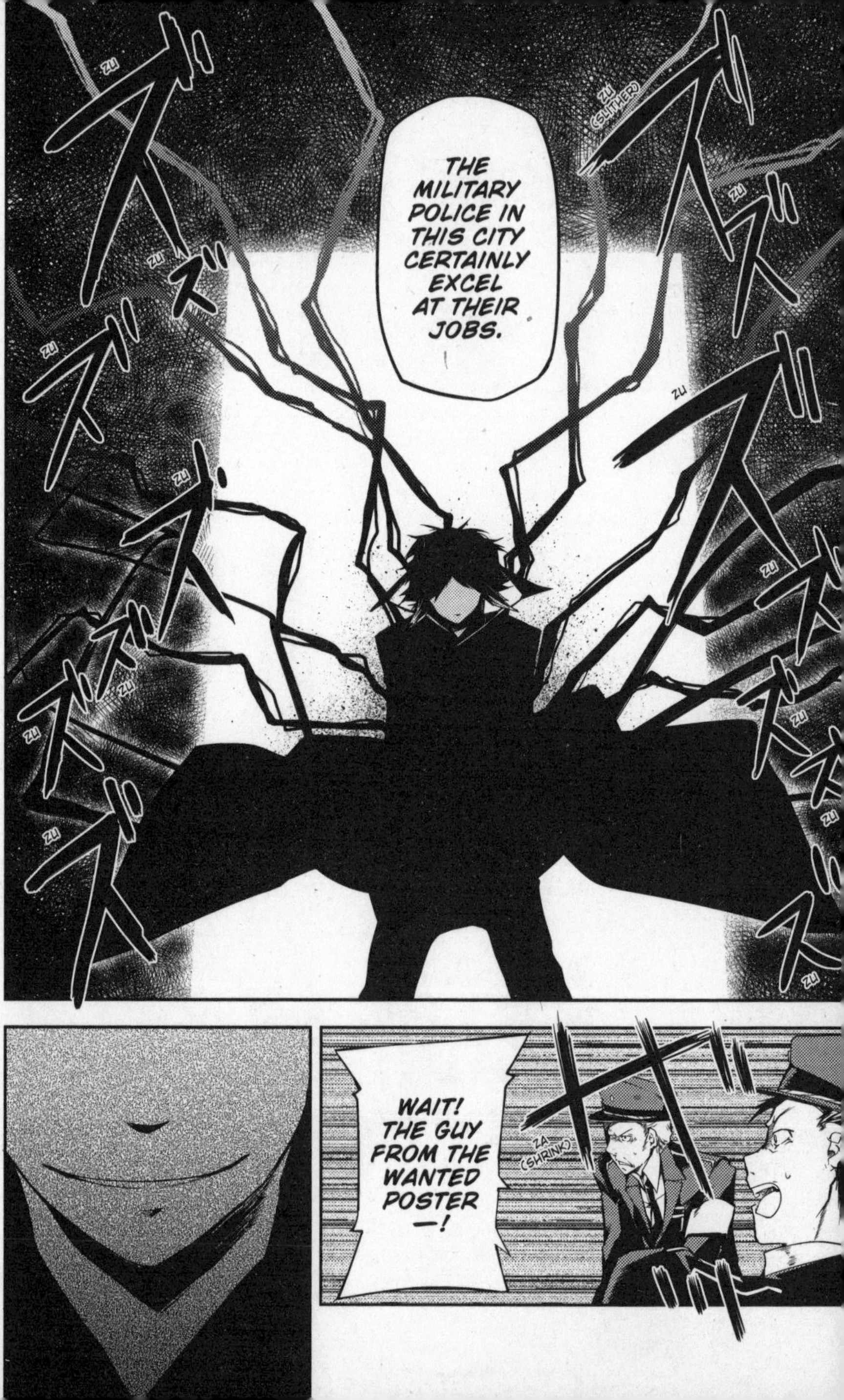
ZU (SLITHER)
ZU
ZU
ZU
THE MILITARY POLICE IN THIS CITY CERTAINLY EXCEL AT THEIR JOBS.
ZU
ZU
ZU
ZU
ZU
ZU
ZU
ZU
ZU
ZU
ZA (SHRINK)
WAIT! THE GUY FROM THE WANTED POSTER—!

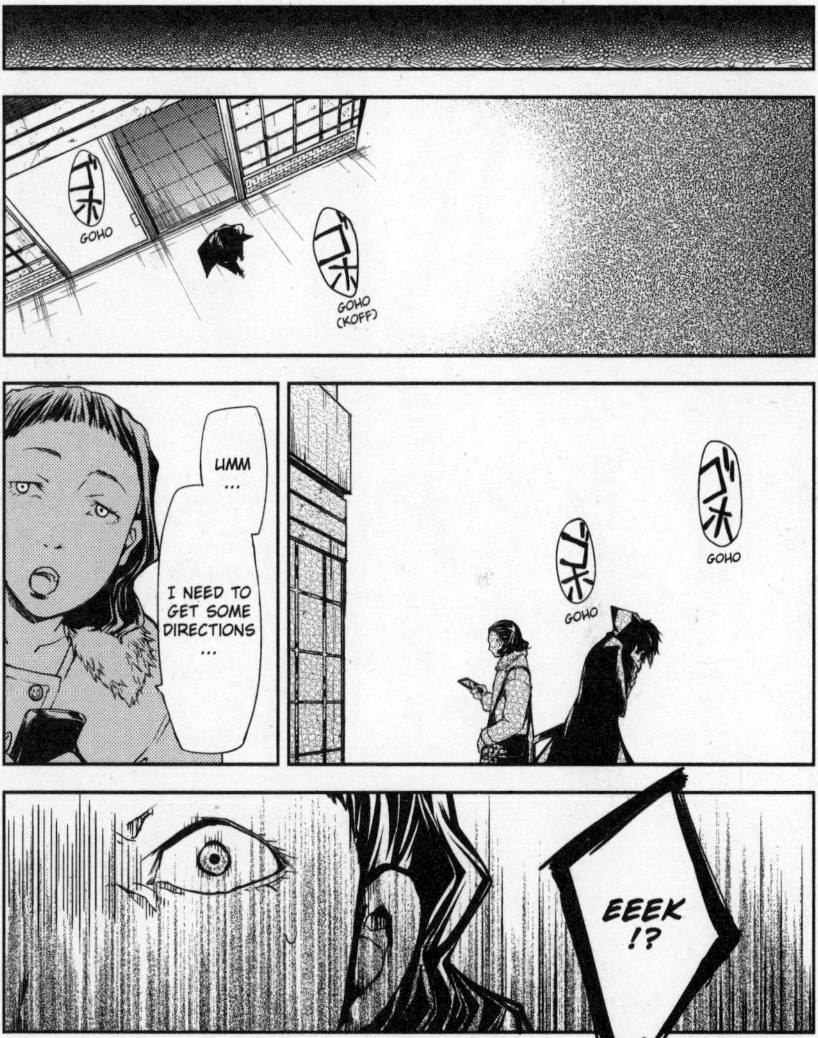
GOHO (KOFF)
GOHO
GOHO
GOHO
UMM ...
I NEED TO GET SOME DIRECTIONS ...
EEEK !?

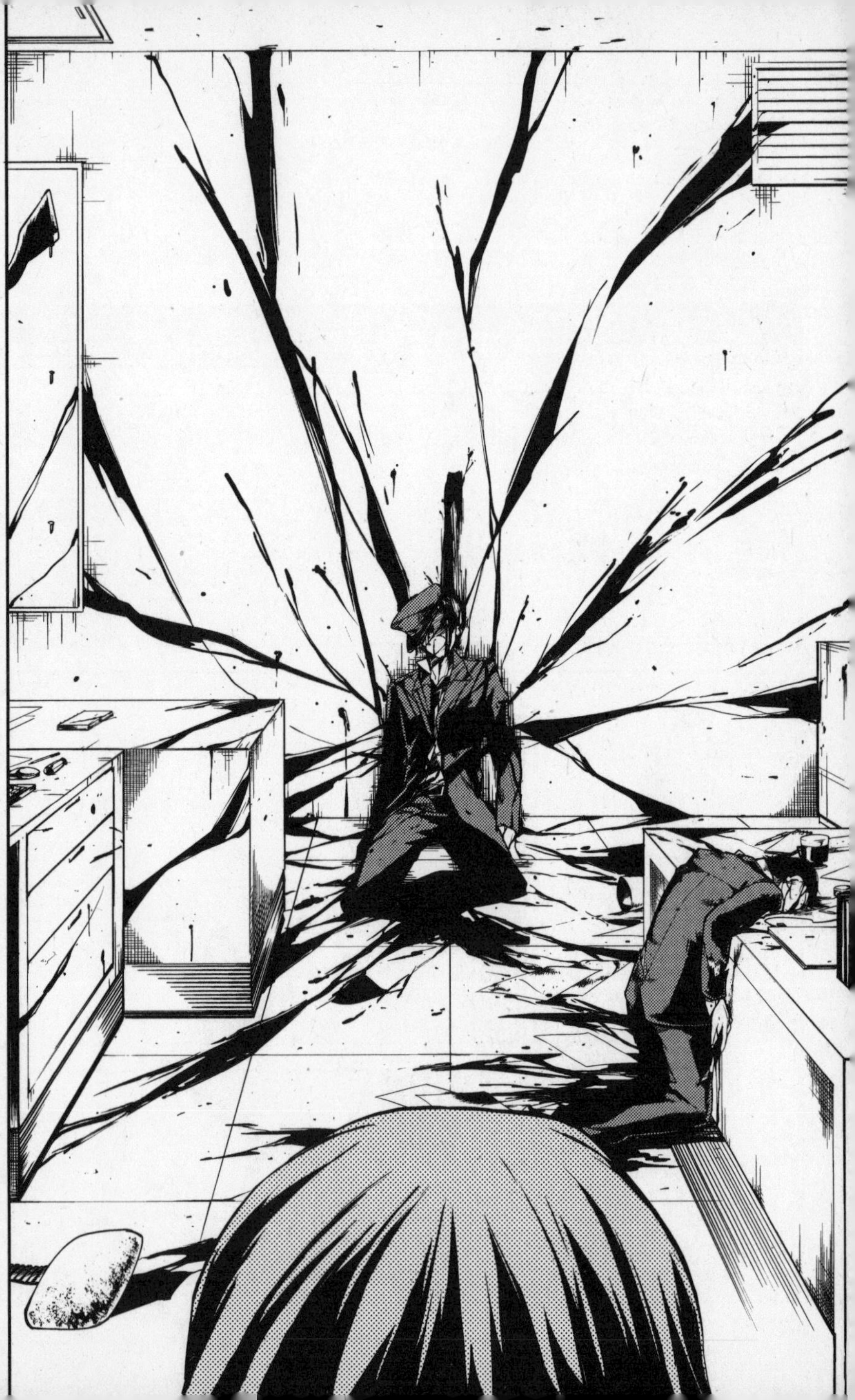

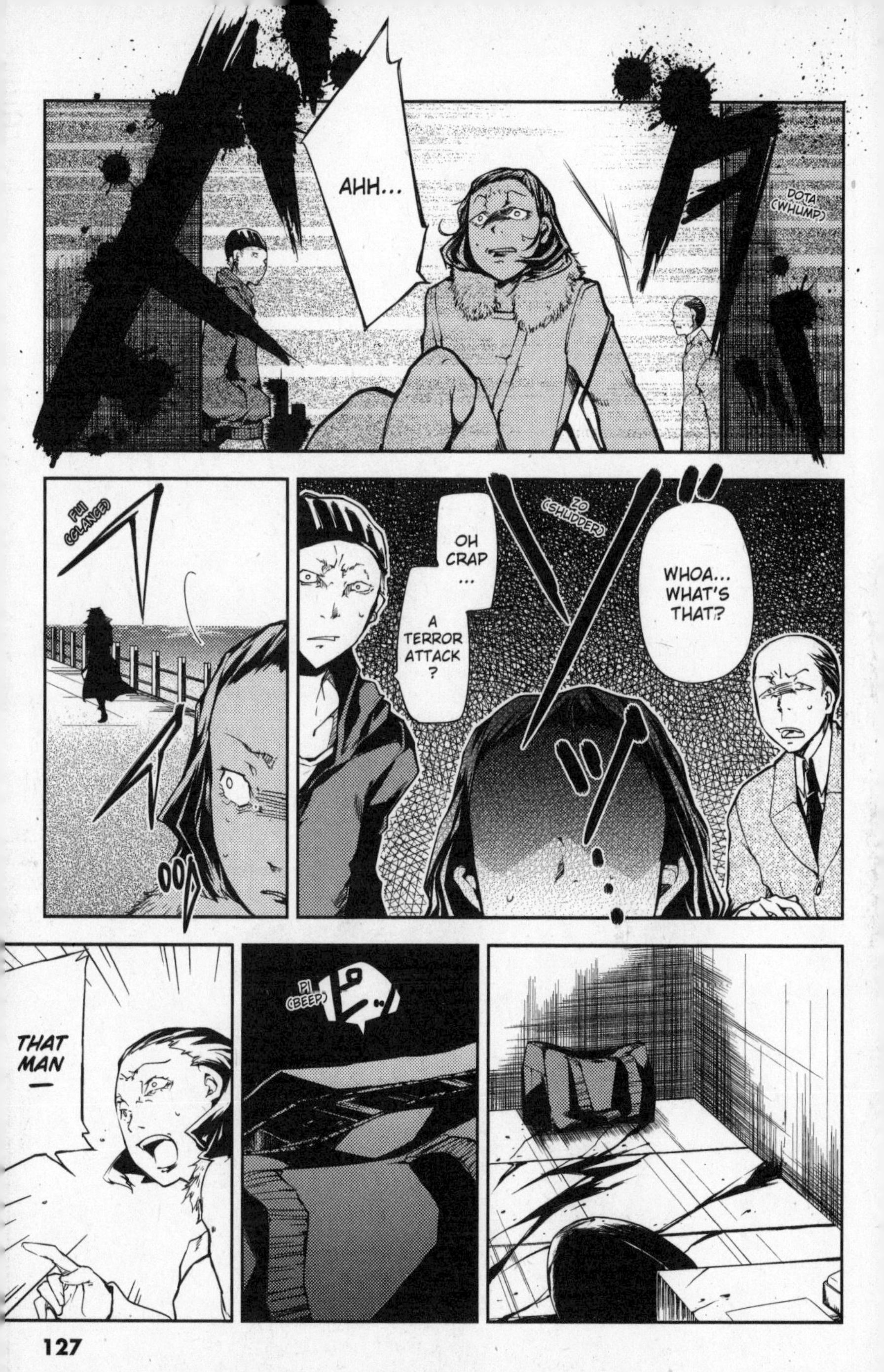
DOTA (WHUMP)
AHH...
WHOA... WHAT'S THAT?
ZO (SHUDDER)
OH CRAP ...
A TERROR ATTACK ?
FUI (GLANCE)
PI (BEEP)
THAT MAN —

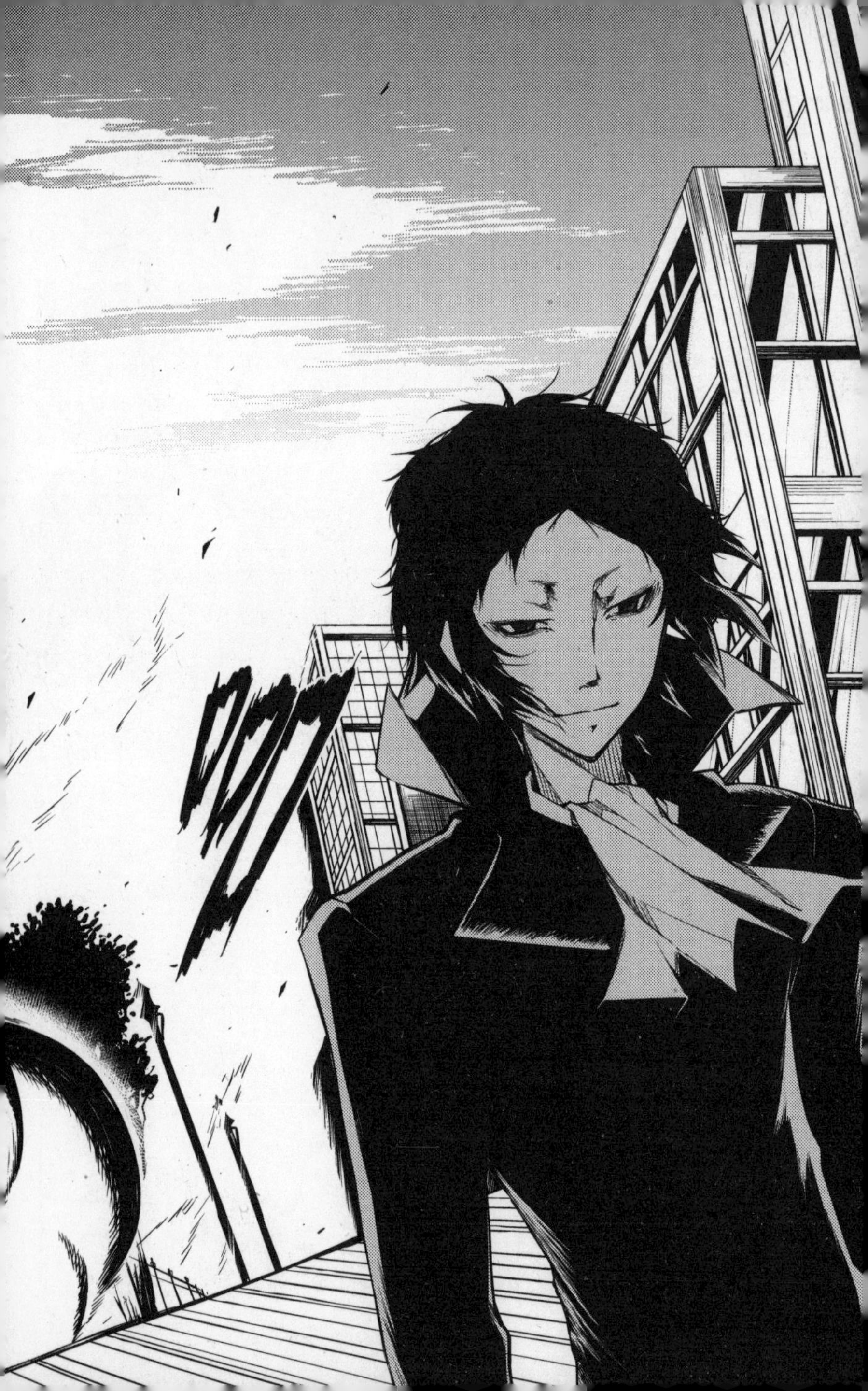

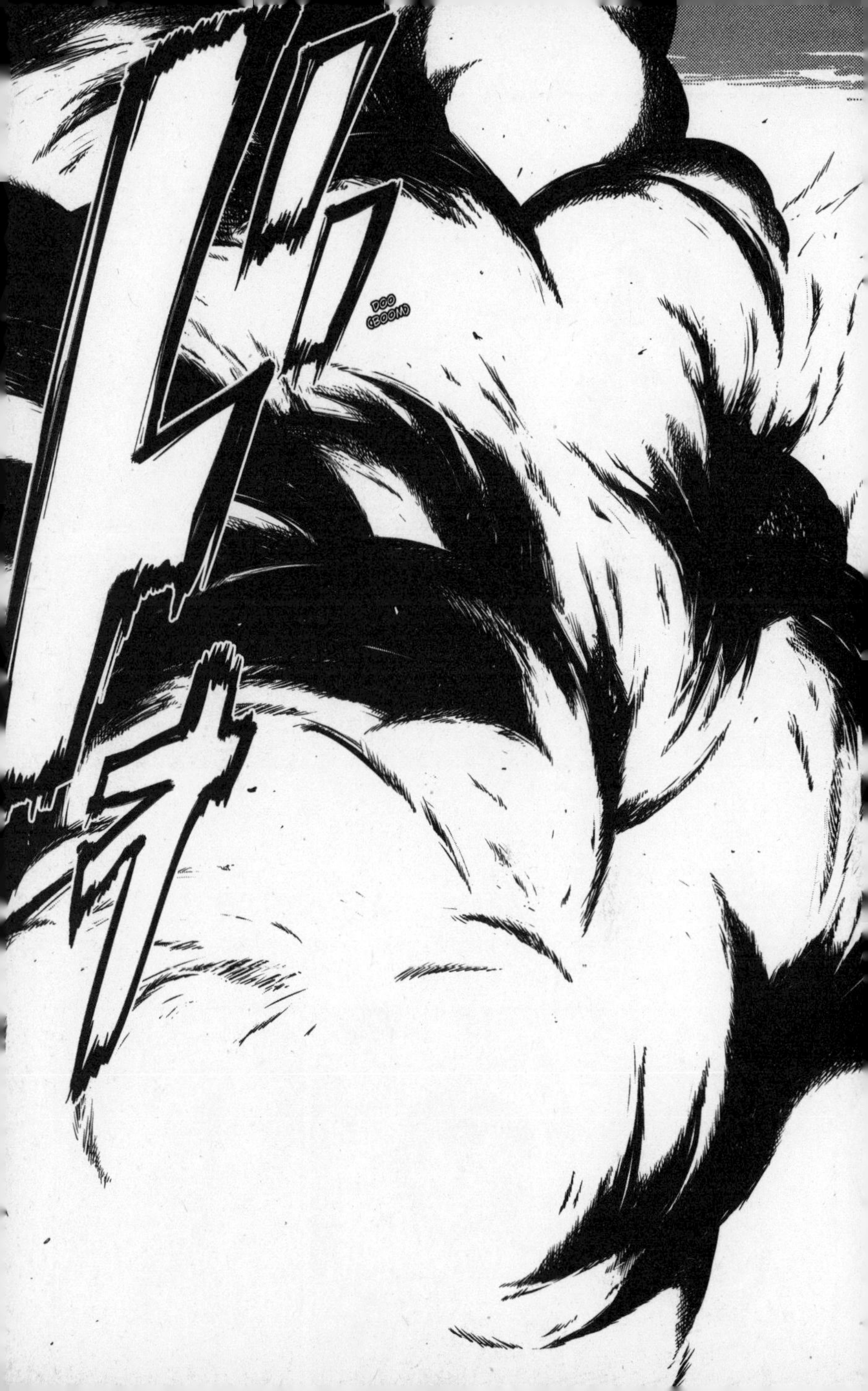
DOO
(BOOM)

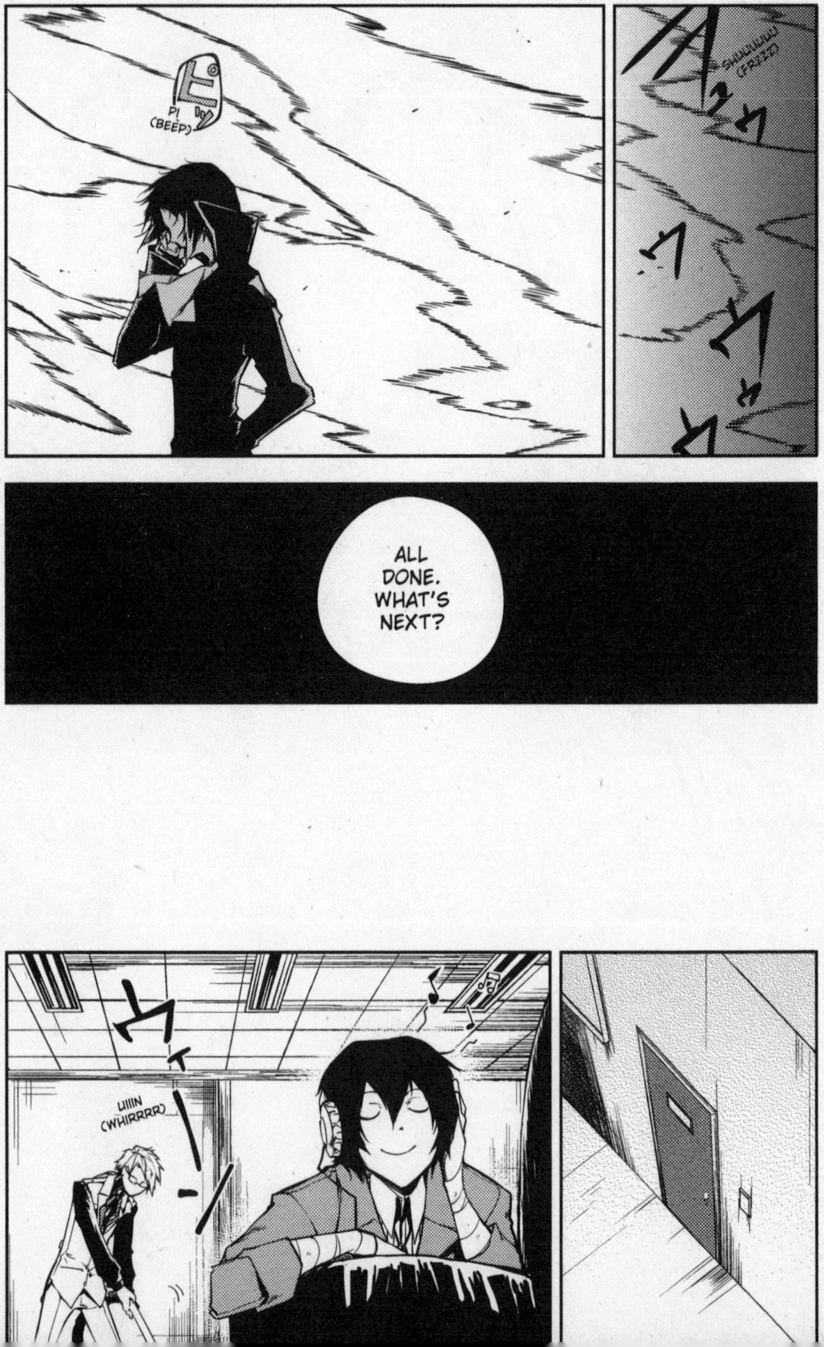
SHUUUUU (FRIZZ)
PI (BEEP)
ALL DONE. WHAT'S NEXT?
UIIIN (WHIRRRR)

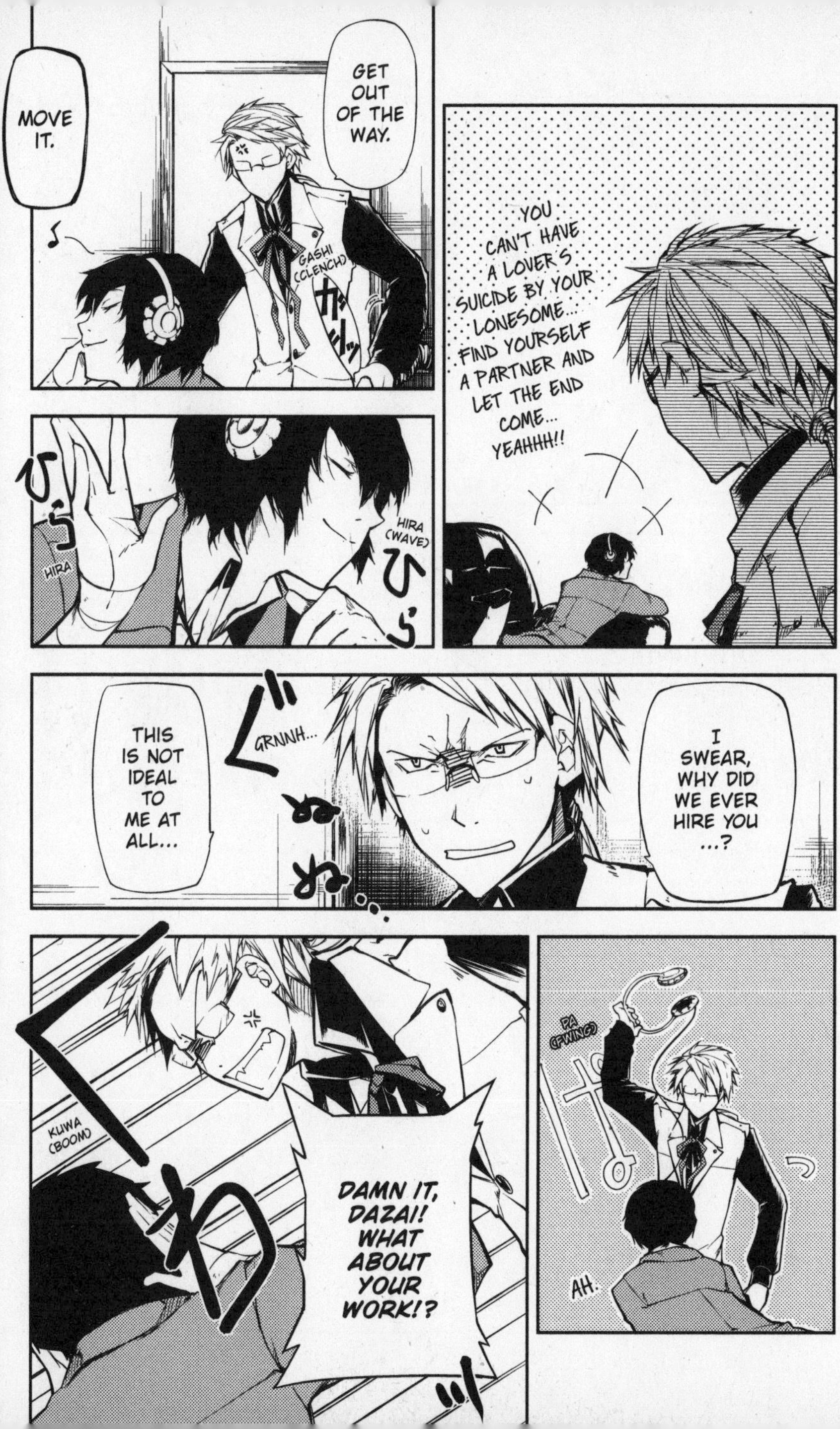
YOU CAN'T HAVE A LOVER'S SUICIDE BY YOUR LONESOME... FIND YOURSELF A PARTNER AND LET THE END COME... YEAHHH!!
GET OUT OF THE WAY.
MOVE IT.
GASHI (CLENCH)
HIRA (WAVE)
HIRA
I SWEAR, WHY DID WE EVER HIRE YOU ...?
GRNNH...
THIS IS NOT IDEAL TO ME AT ALL...
PA (FWING)
AH.
KUWA (BOOM)
DAMN IT, DAZAI! WHAT ABOUT YOUR WORK!?

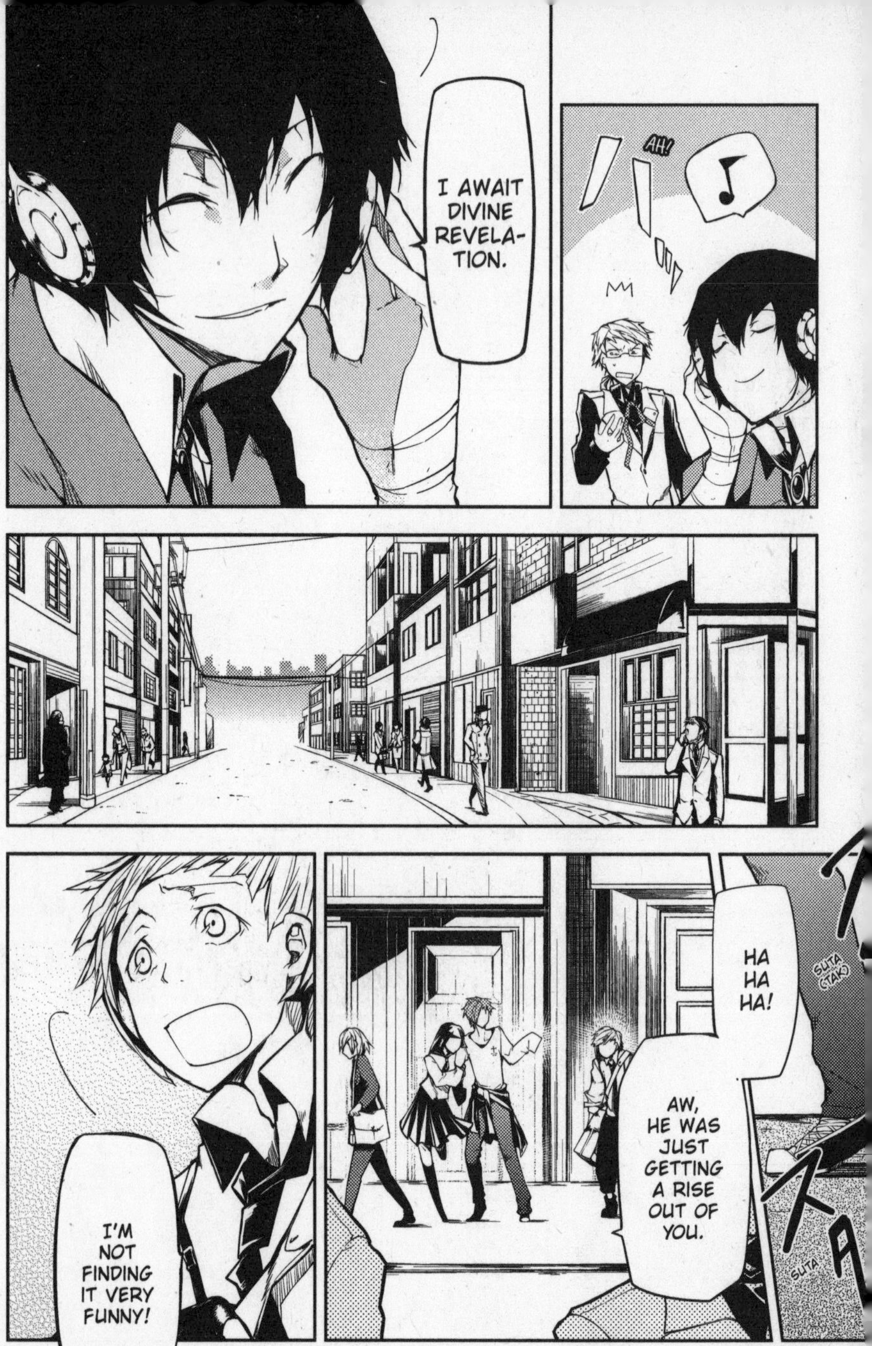
AH!
♪
I AWAIT DIVINE REVELATION.
SUTA (TAK)
SUTA
HA HA HA!
AW, HE WAS JUST GETTING A RISE OUT OF YOU.
I'M NOT FINDING IT VERY FUNNY!

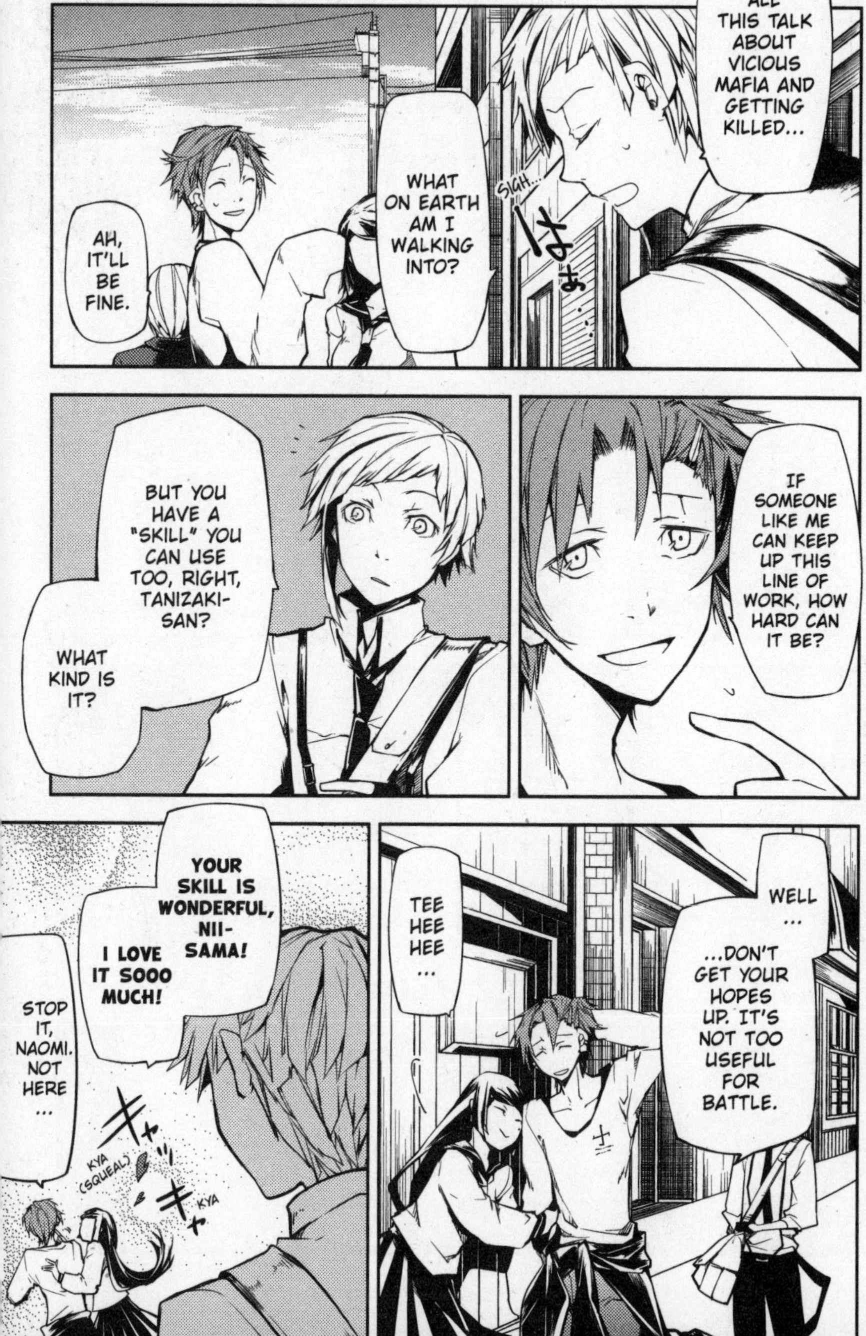
ALL THIS TALK ABOUT VICIOUS MAFIA AND GETTING KILLED...
SIGH...
WHAT ON EARTH AM I WALKING INTO?
AH, IT'LL BE FINE.
IF SOMEONE LIKE ME CAN KEEP UP THIS LINE OF WORK, HOW HARD CAN IT BE?
BUT YOU HAVE A "SKILL" YOU CAN USE TOO, RIGHT, TANIZAKI-SAN?
WHAT KIND IS IT?
WELL...
...DON'T GET YOUR HOPES UP. IT'S NOT TOO USEFUL FOR BATTLE.
TEE HEE HEE...
YOUR SKILL IS WONDERFUL, NII-SAMA!
I LOVE IT SOOO MUCH!
STOP IT, NAOMI. NOT HERE...
KYA (SQUEAL)
KYA

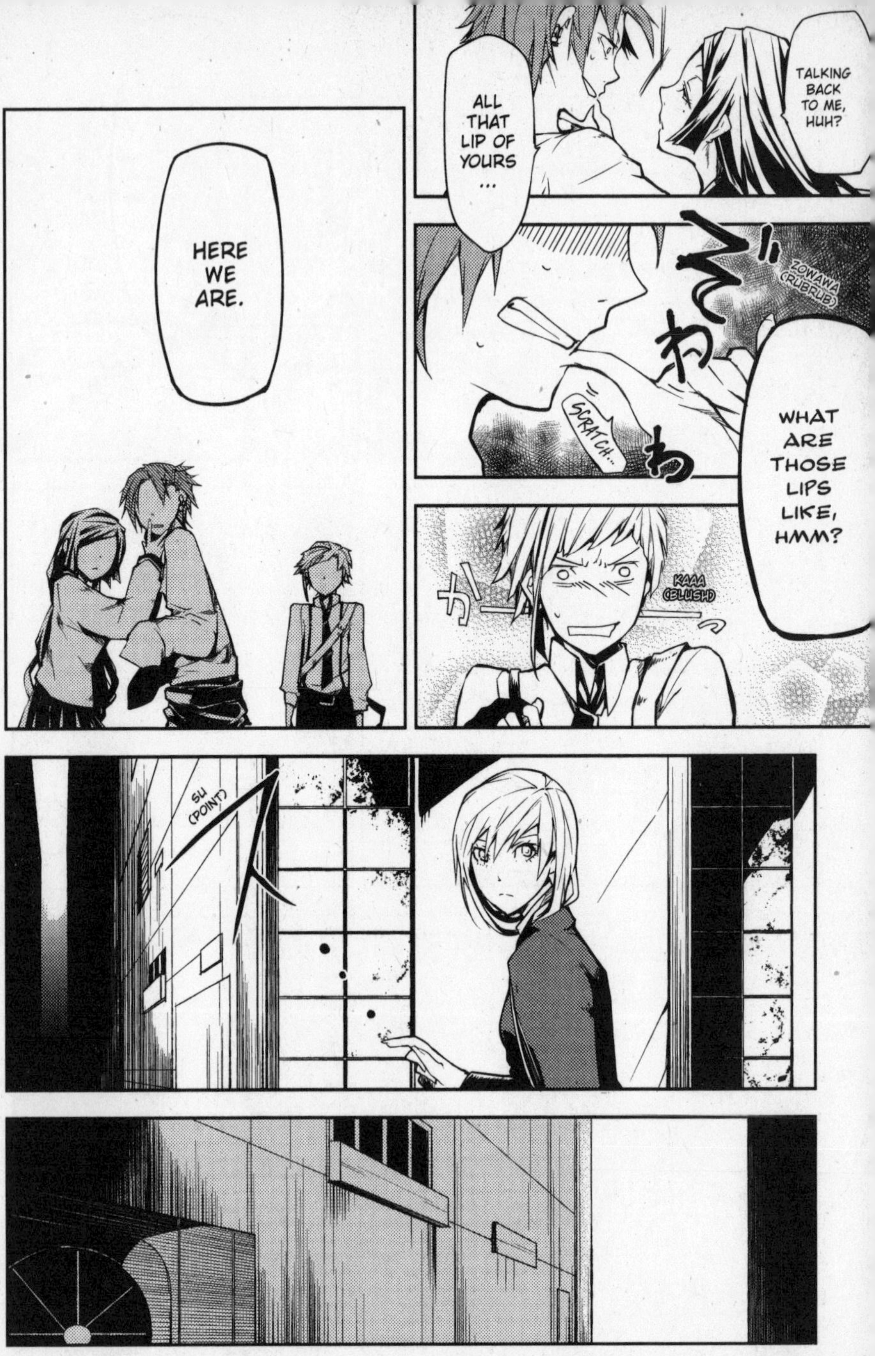
TALKING BACK TO ME, HUH?
ALL THAT LIP OF YOURS...
ZOWAWA (RUBRUB)
WHAT ARE THOSE LIPS LIKE, HMM?
SCRATCH...
KAAA (BLUSH)
HERE WE ARE.
SU (POINT)

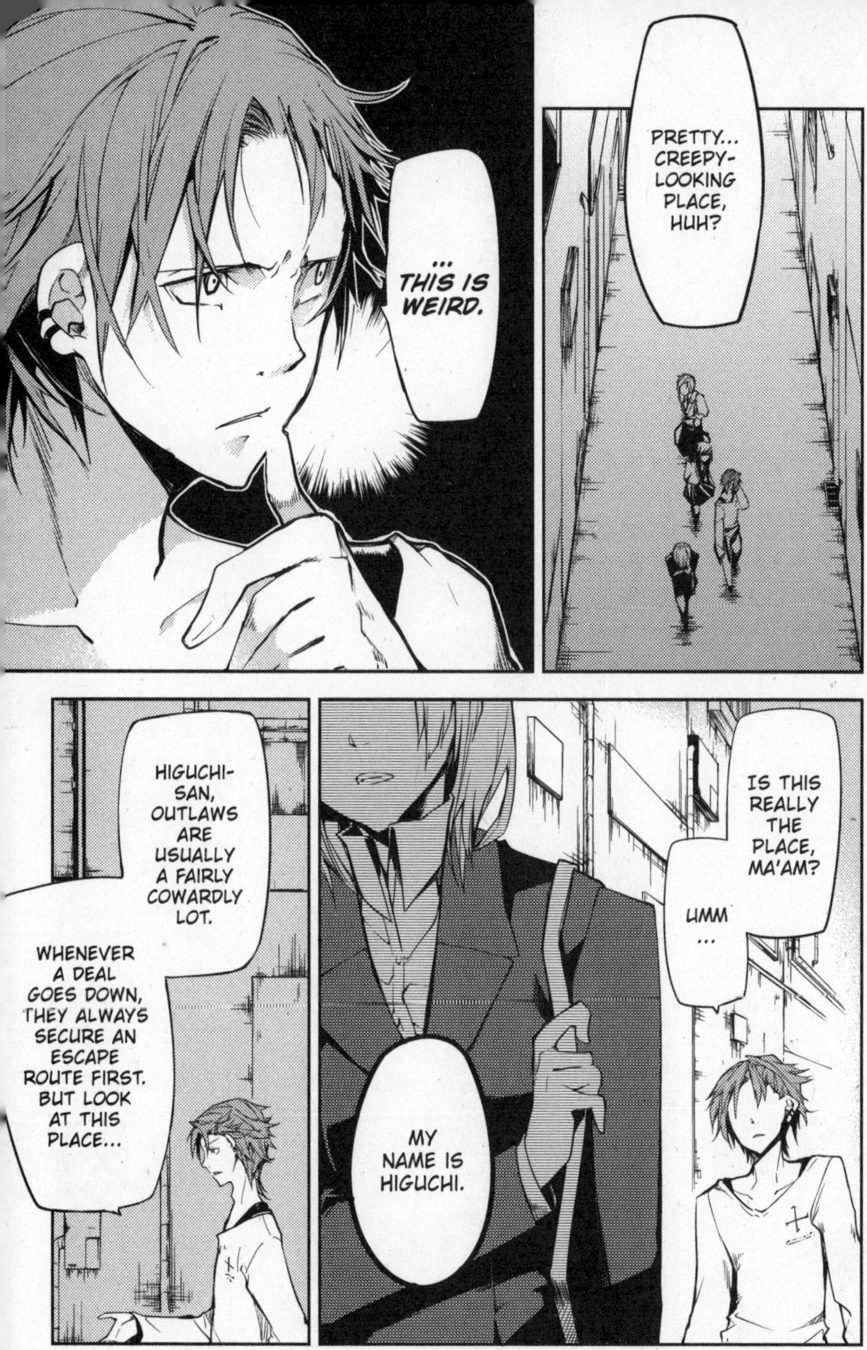
PRETTY... CREEPY-LOOKING PLACE, HUH?
... THIS IS WEIRD.
IS THIS REALLY THE PLACE, MA'AM?
UMM ...
MY NAME IS HIGUCHI.
HIGUCHI-SAN, OUTLAWS ARE USUALLY A FAIRLY COWARDLY LOT.
WHENEVER A DEAL GOES DOWN, THEY ALWAYS SECURE AN ESCAPE ROUTE FIRST. BUT LOOK AT THIS PLACE...

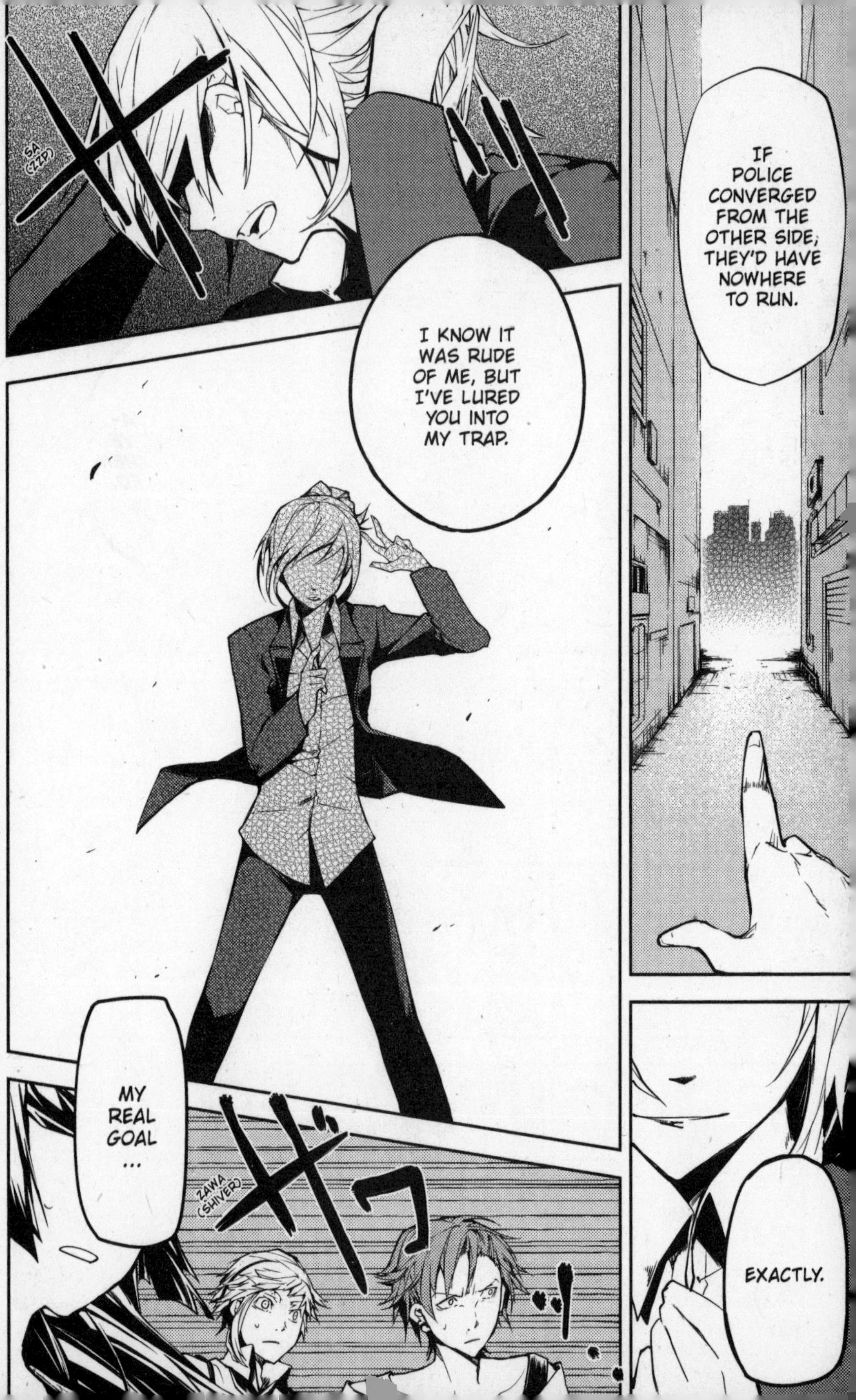
IF POLICE CONVERGED FROM THE OTHER SIDE, THEY'D HAVE NOWHERE TO RUN.
SA (ZZIP)
I KNOW IT WAS RUDE OF ME, BUT I'VE LURED YOU INTO MY TRAP.
EXACTLY.
MY REAL GOAL ...
ZAWA (SHIVER)

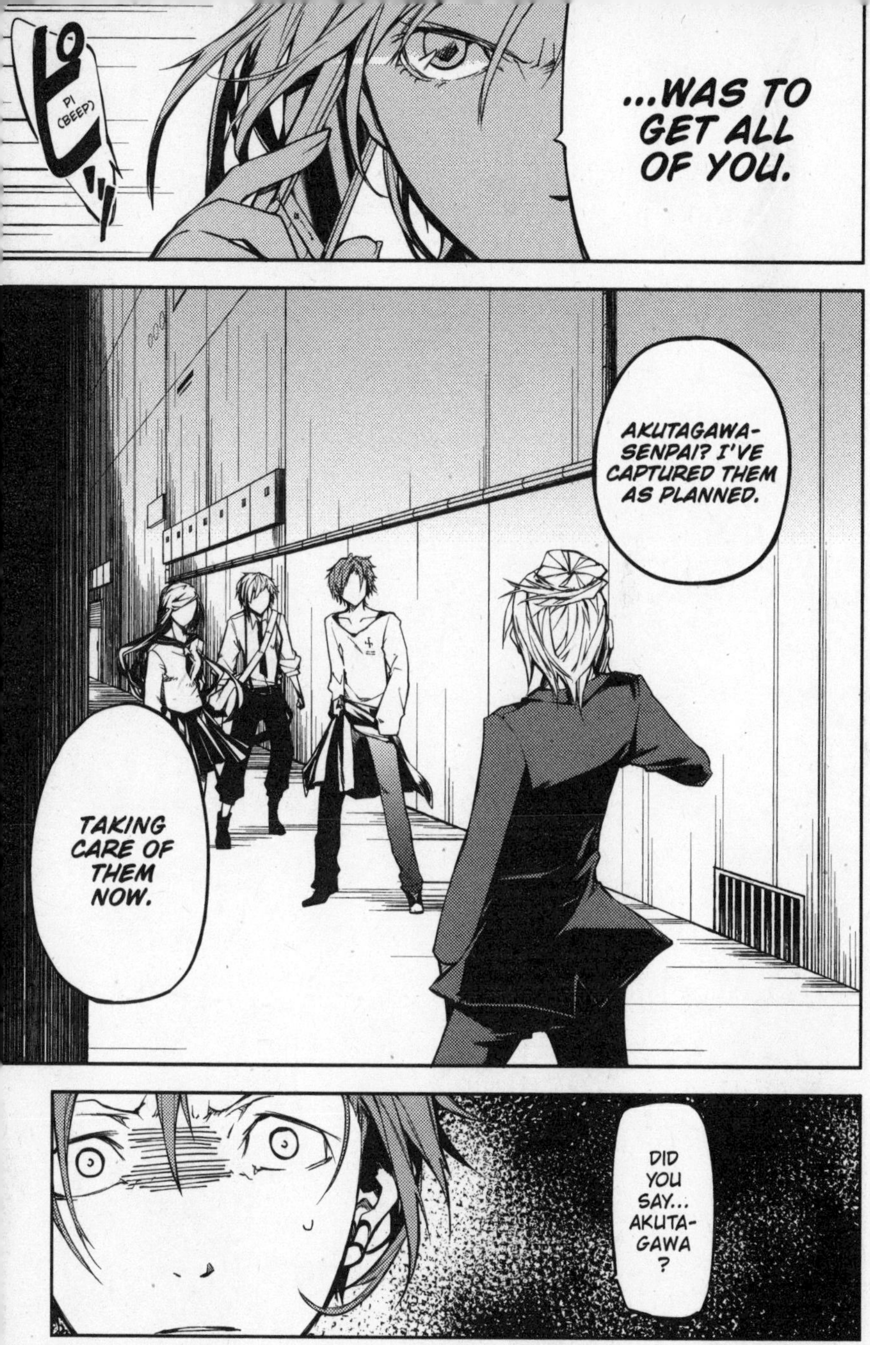
...WAS TO GET ALL OF YOU.
PI (BEEP)
AKUTAGAWA-SENPAI? I'VE CAPTURED THEM AS PLANNED.
TAKING CARE OF THEM NOW.
DID YOU SAY... AKUTAGAWA?

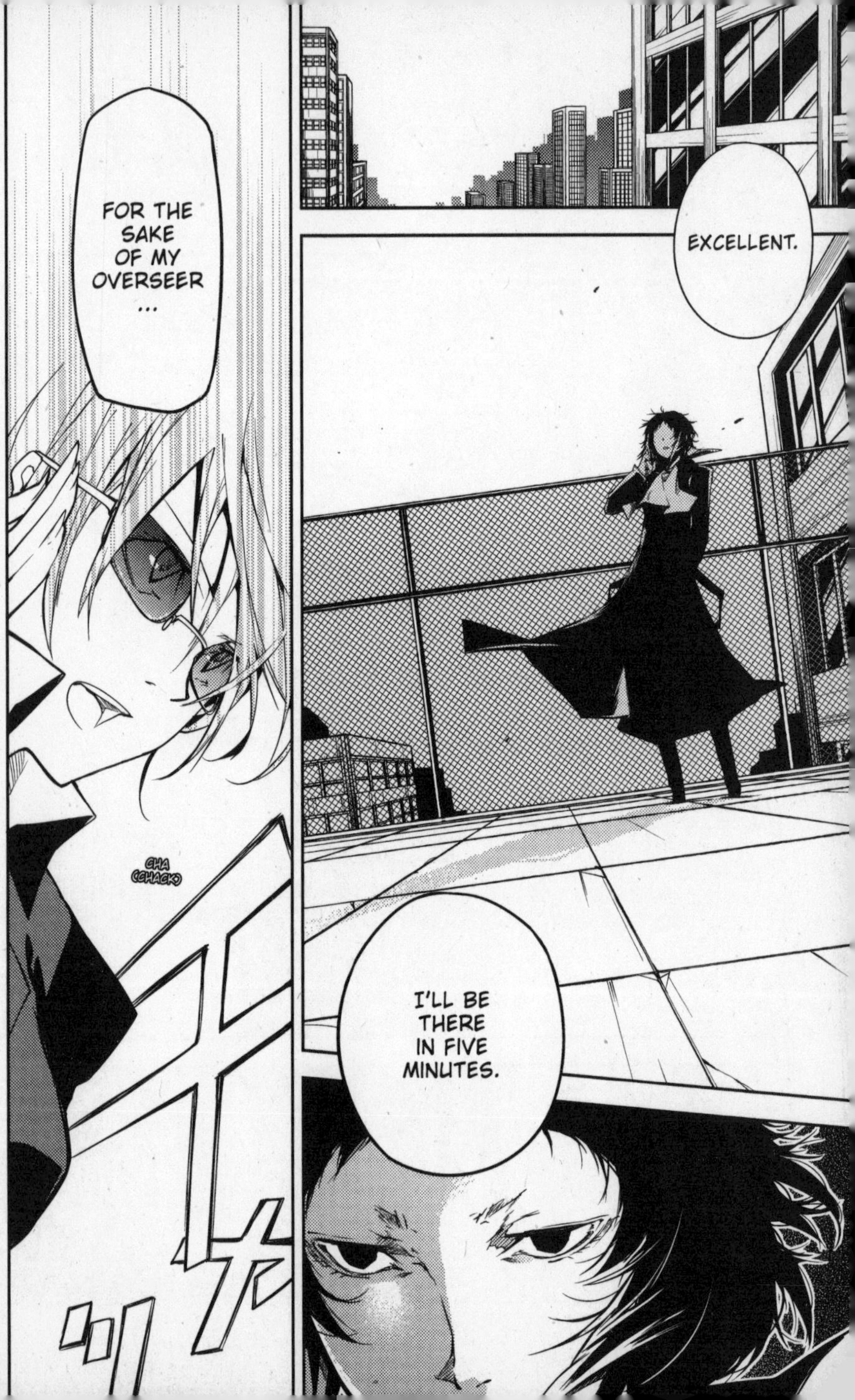
EXCELLENT.
I'LL BE THERE IN FIVE MINUTES.
FOR THE SAKE OF MY OVERSEER ...
CHA (CHACK)

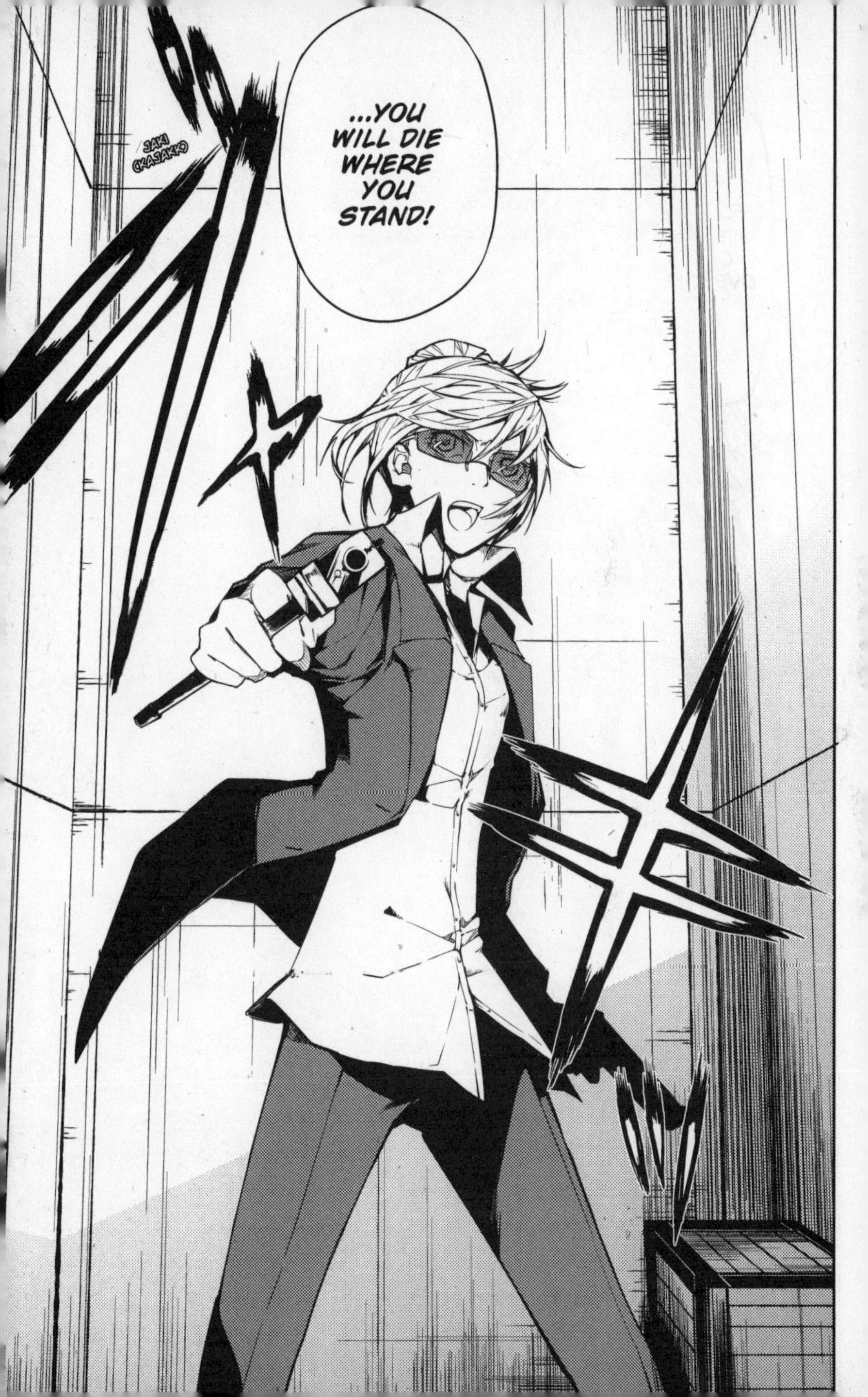
...YOU WILL DIE WHERE YOU STAND!
JAKI (KASAKK)

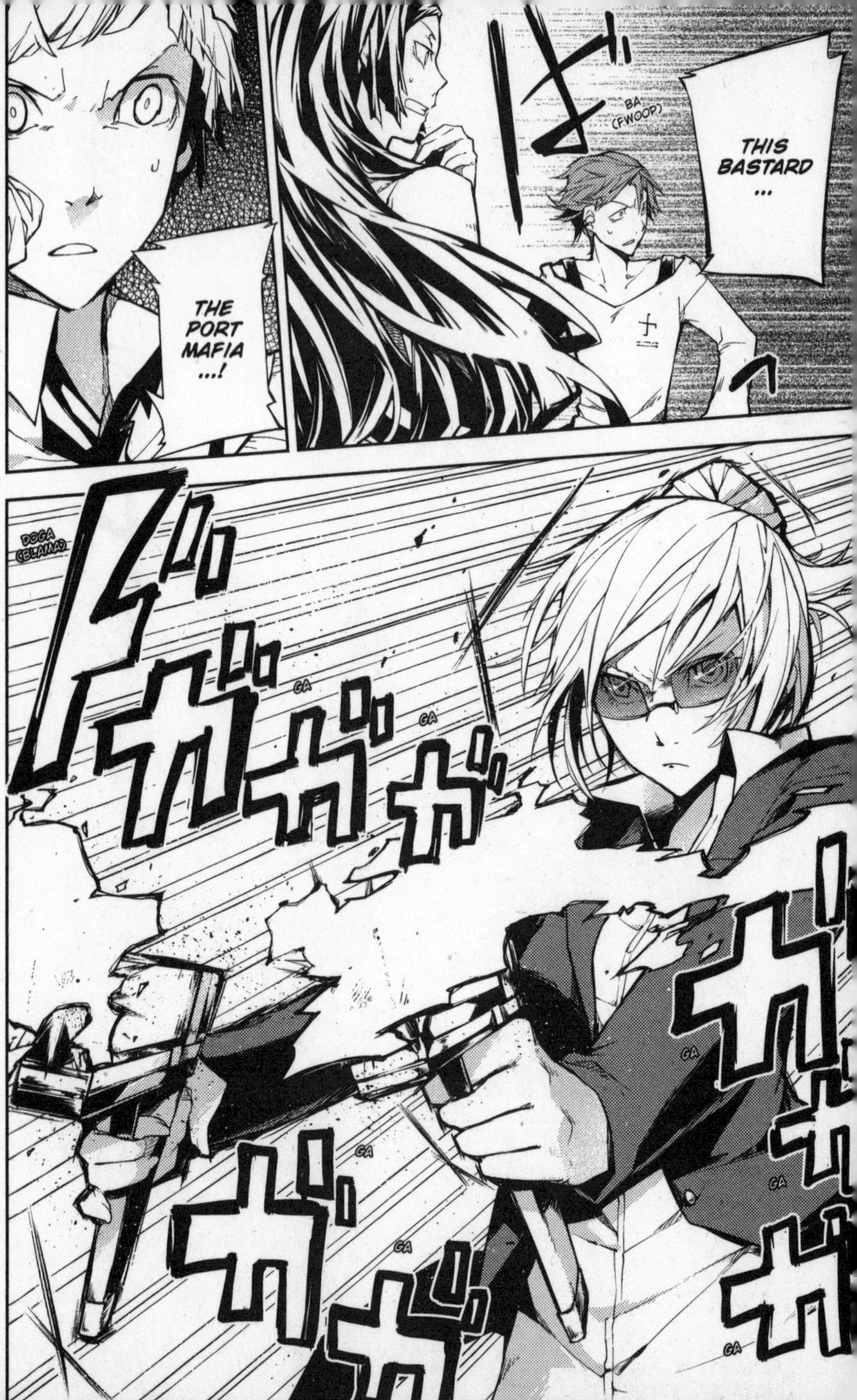
THIS BASTARD ...
BA (FWOOP)
THE PORT MAFIA ...!
GA
GA
GA
DOGA (BLAMA)
GA
GA
GA
GA

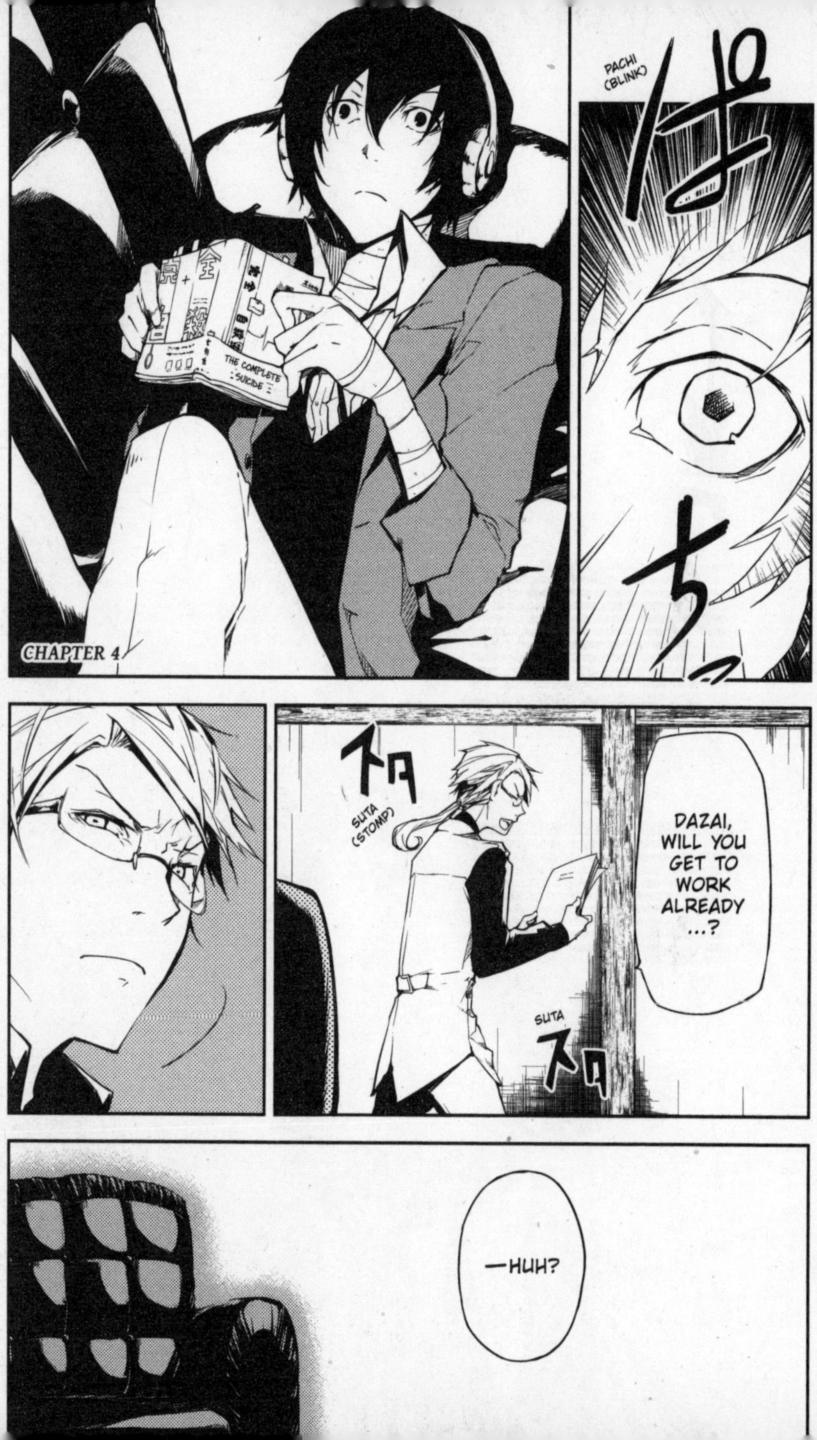

PACHI (BLINK)
THE COMPLETE SUICIDE
CHAPTER 4
DAZAI, WILL YOU GET TO WORK ALREADY ...?
SUTA (STOMP)
SUTA
—HUH?

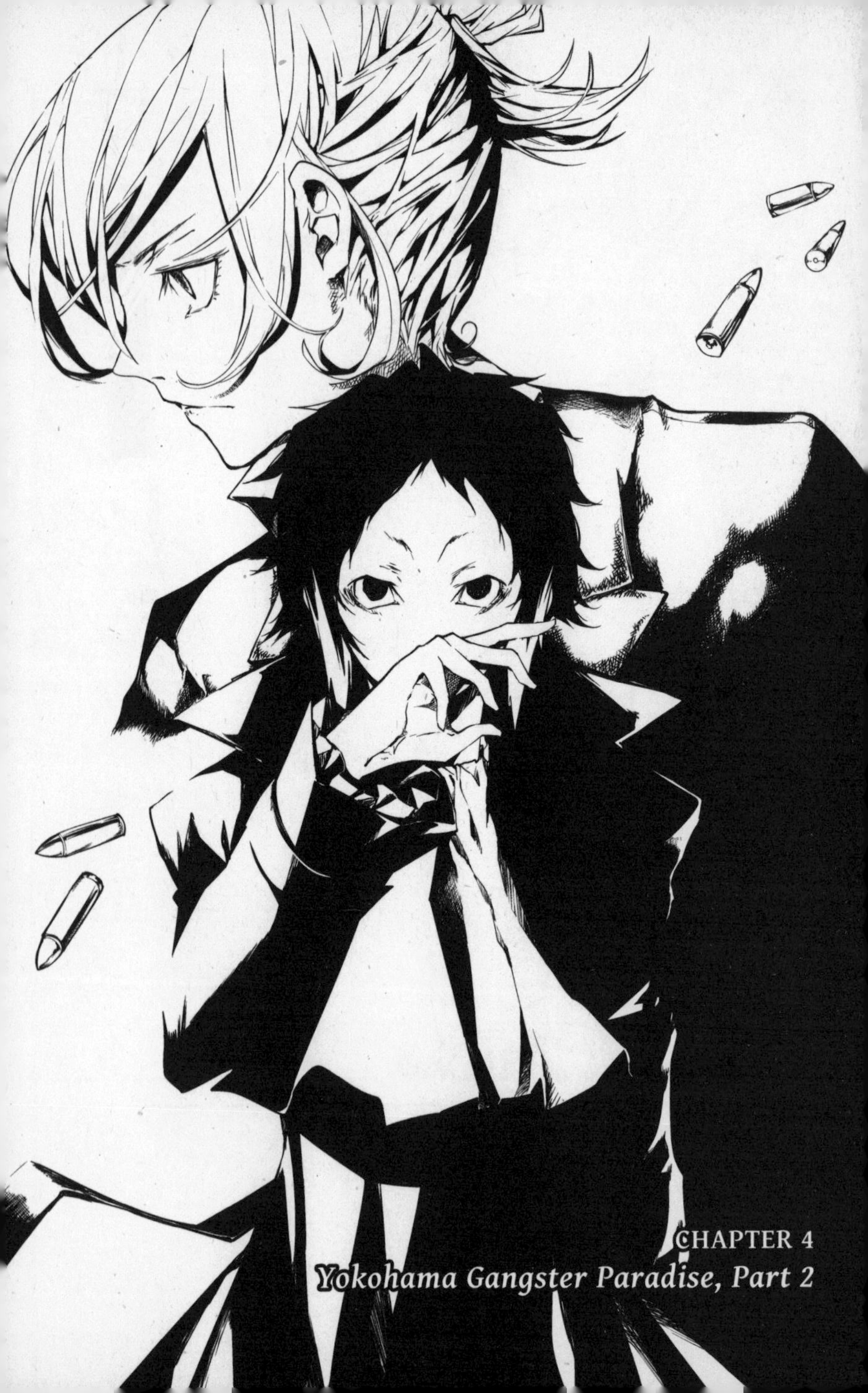

CHAPTER 4
Yokohama Gangster Paradise, Part 2

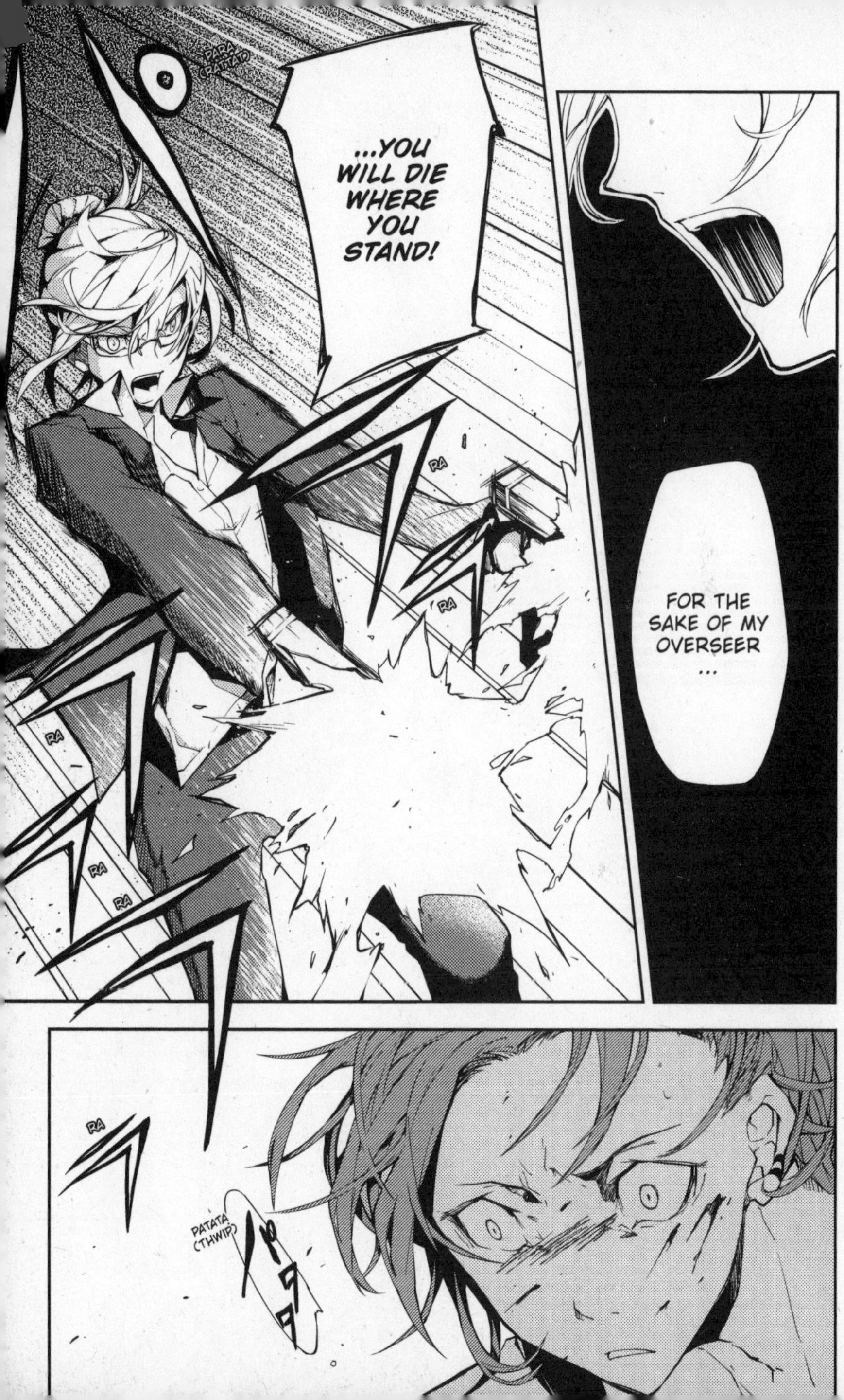
FOR THE SAKE OF MY OVERSEER ...
PARA (RATTAT)
...YOU WILL DIE WHERE YOU STAND!
RA
RA
RA
RA
RA
RA
PATATA (THWIP)

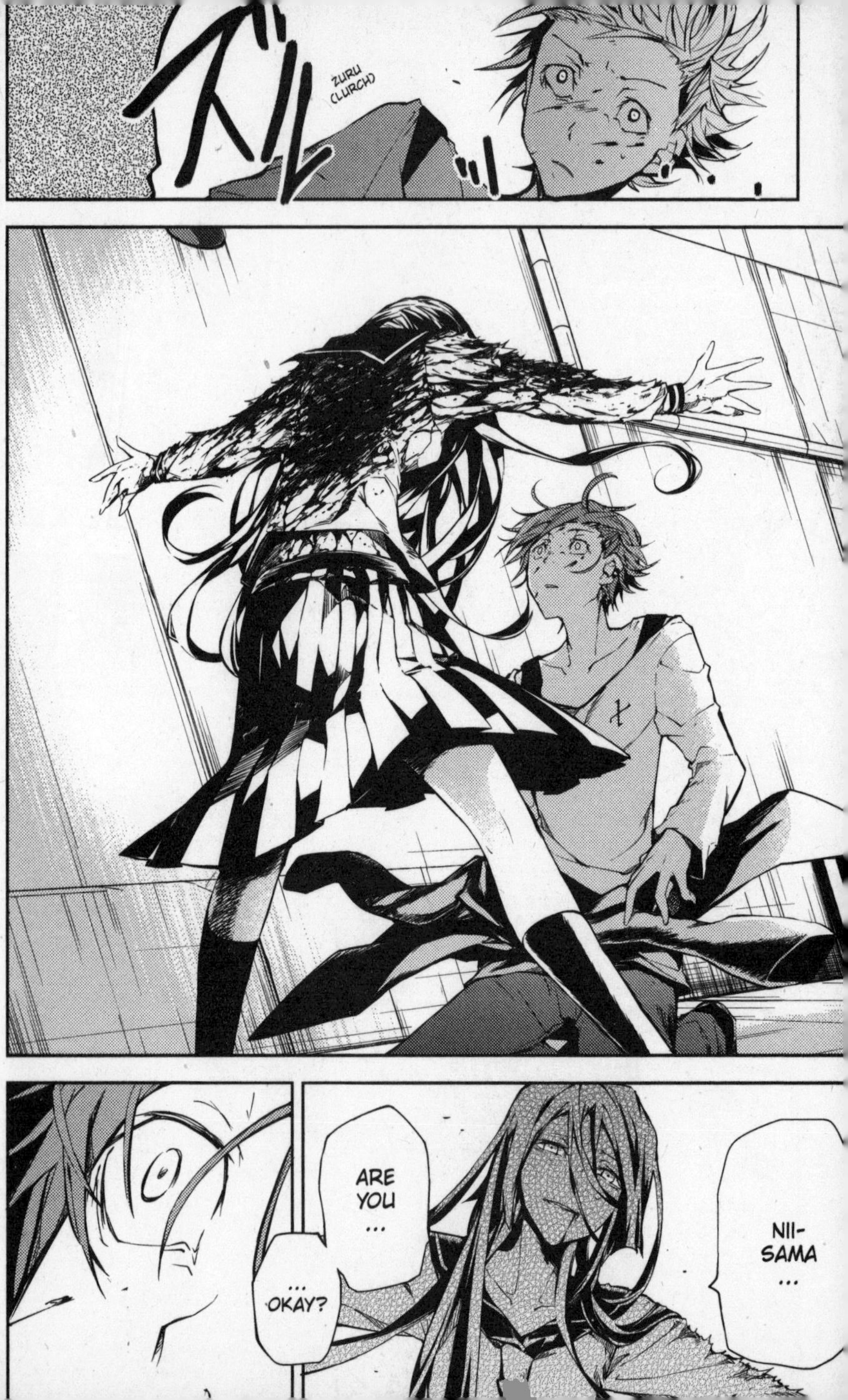
ZURU (LURCH)
NII-SAMA ...
ARE YOU ...
... OKAY?

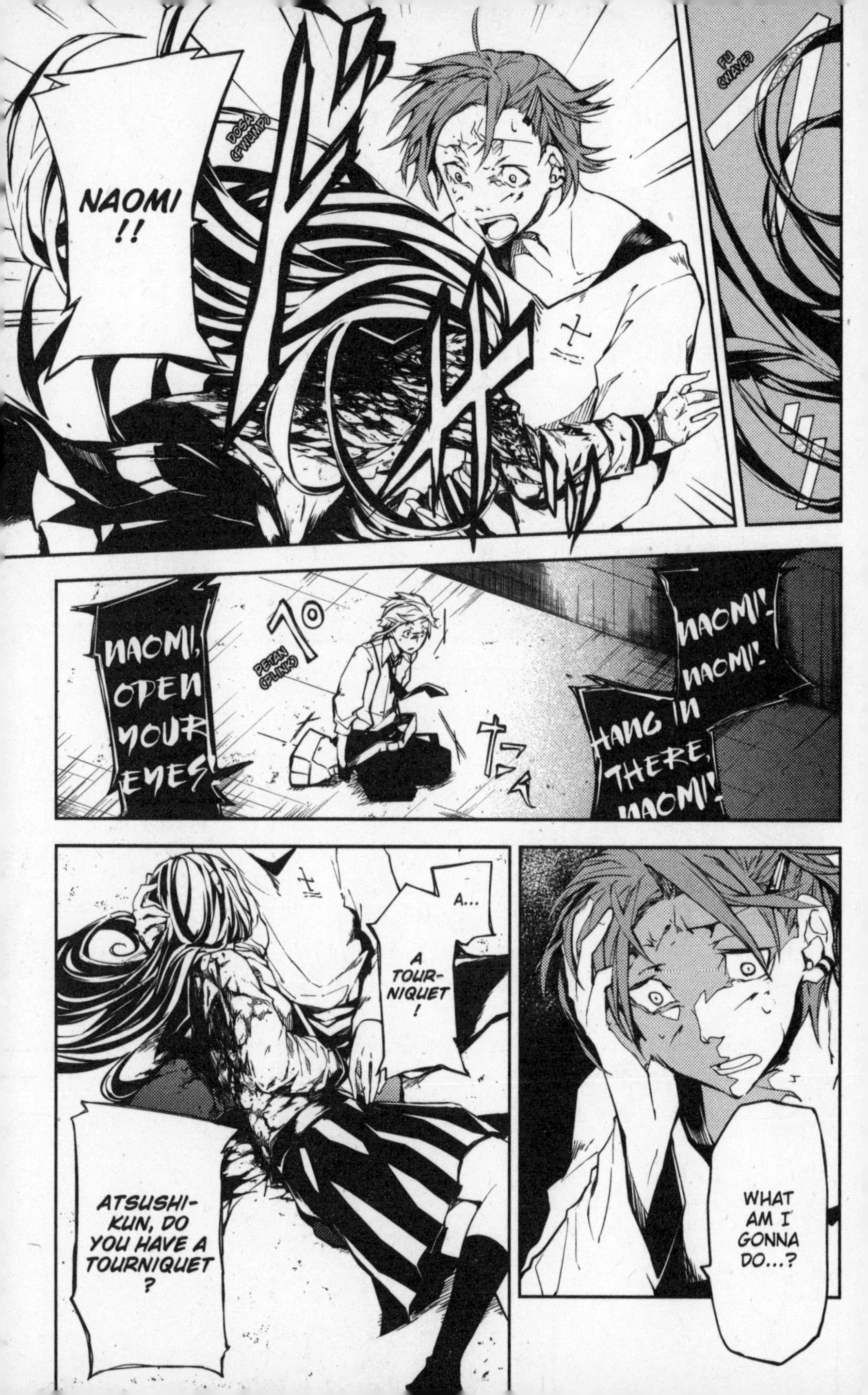
FU (WAVE)
DOSA (FWUMP)
NAOMI!!
NAOMI! NAOMI!
HANG IN THERE, NAOMI!
PETAN (PLINK)
NAOMI, OPEN YOUR EYES!
WHAT AM I GONNA DO...?
A...
A TOURNIQUET!
ATSUSHI-KUN, DO YOU HAVE A TOURNIQUET?

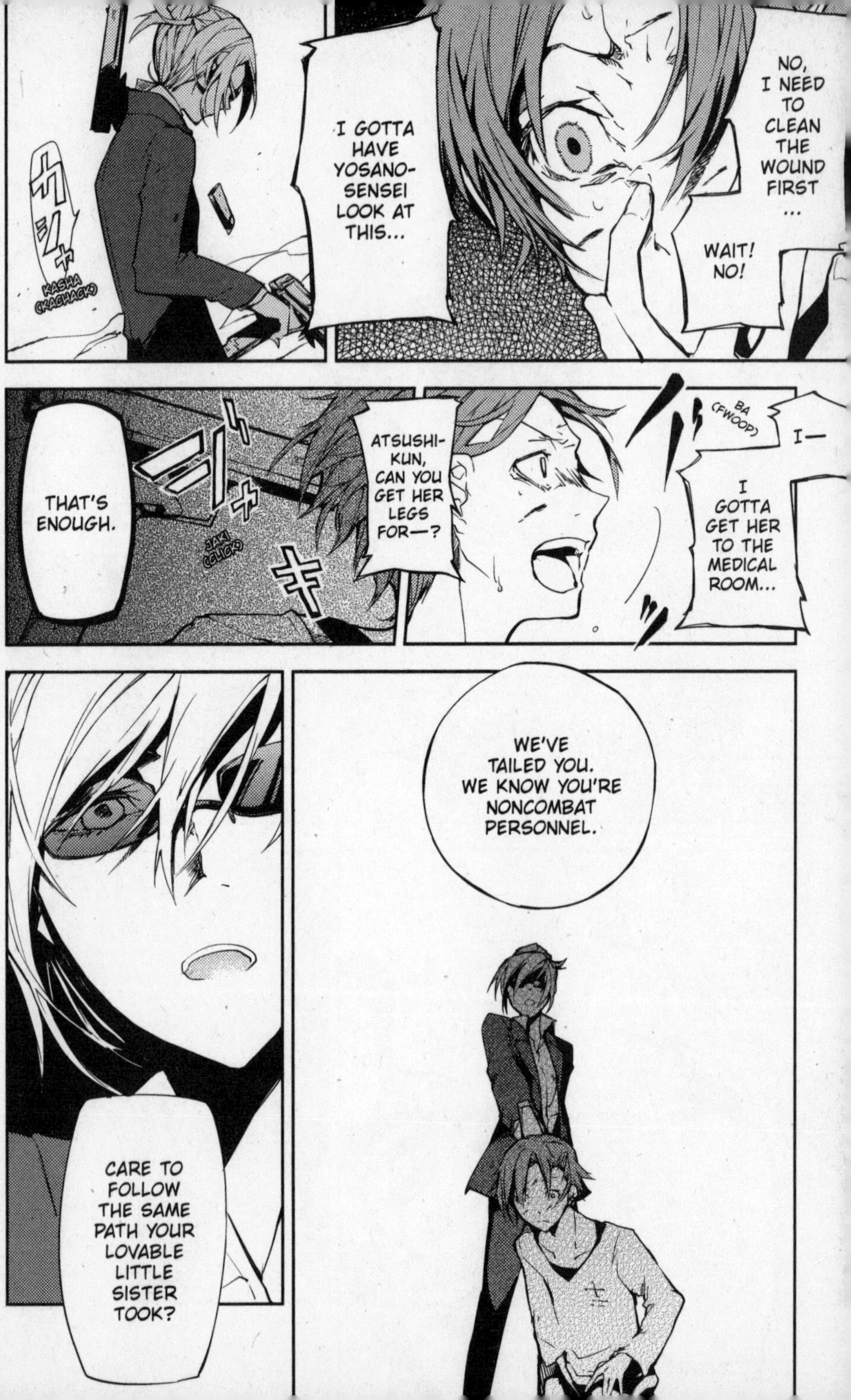

NO, I NEED TO CLEAN THE WOUND FIRST...
I GOTTA HAVE YOSANO-SENSEI LOOK AT THIS...
WAIT! NO!
KASHA (KACHACK)
BA (FWOOP)
I—
I GOTTA GET HER TO THE MEDICAL ROOM...
ATSUSHI-KUN, CAN YOU GET HER LEGS FOR—?
JAKI (CLICK)
THAT'S ENOUGH.
WE'VE TAILED YOU. WE KNOW YOU'RE NONCOMBAT PERSONNEL.
CARE TO FOLLOW THE SAME PATH YOUR LOVABLE LITTLE SISTER TOOK?

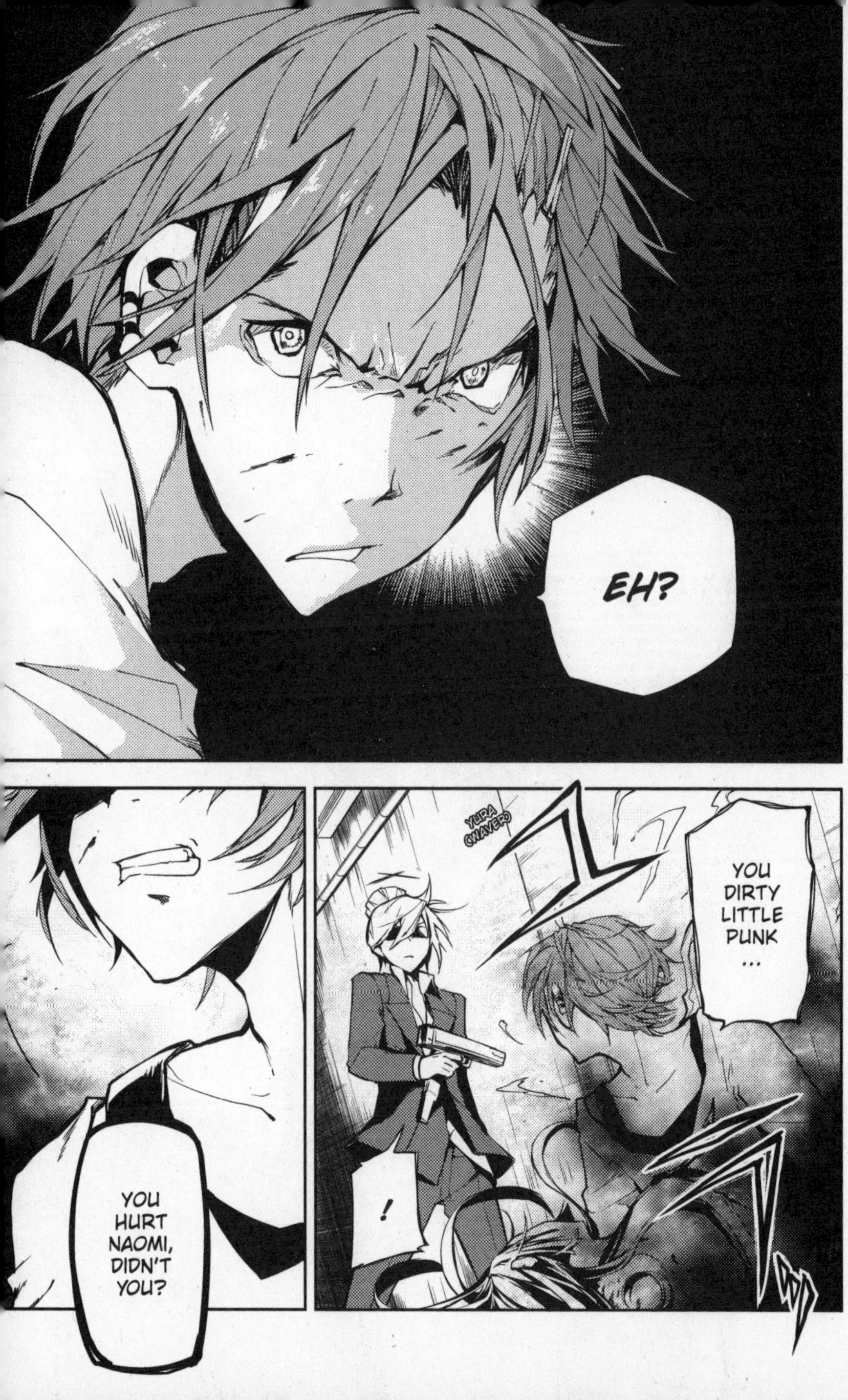
EH?
YURA (WAVER)
YOU DIRTY LITTLE PUNK ...
!
YOU HURT NAOMI, DIDN'T YOU?

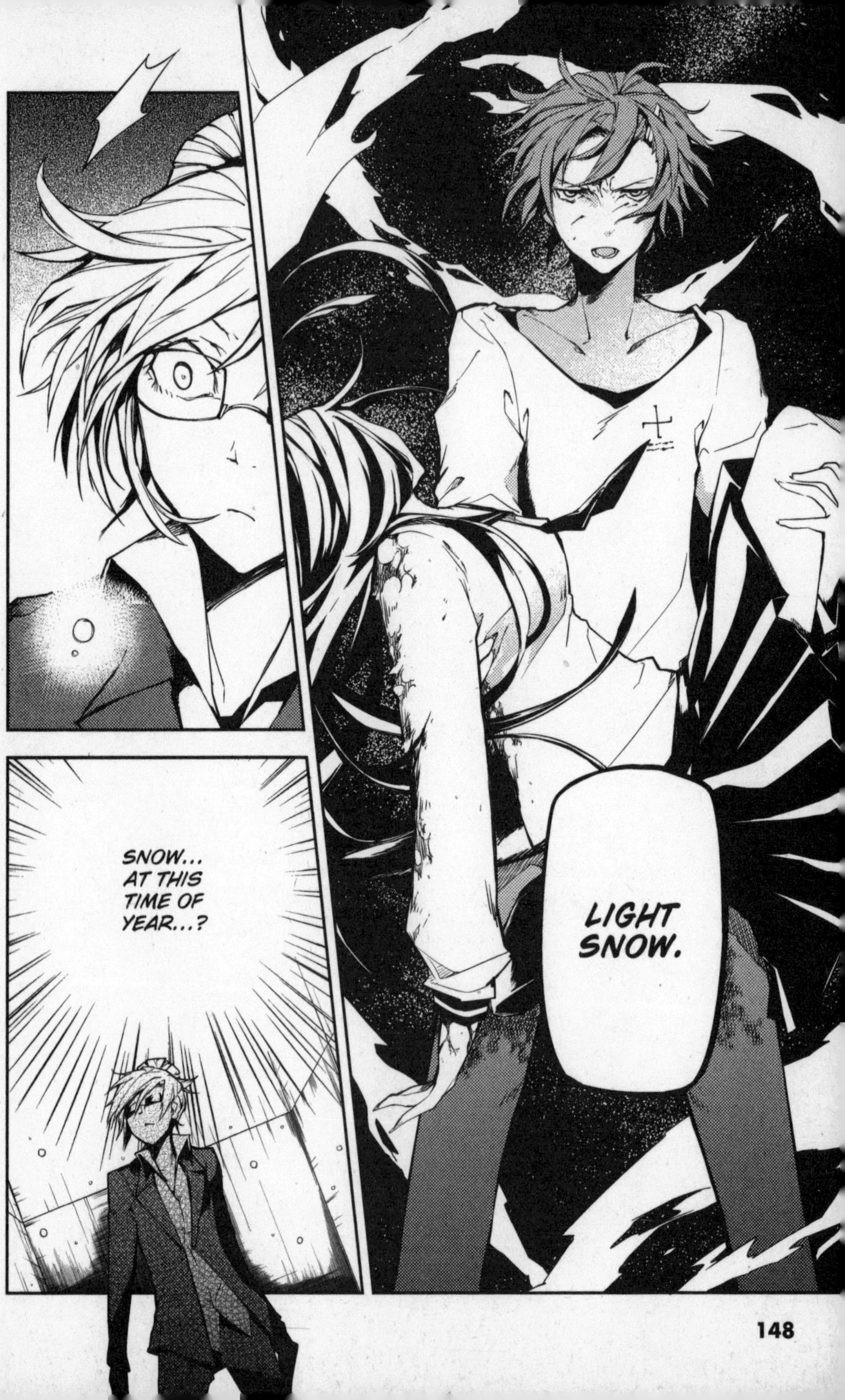
LIGHT SNOW.
SNOW... AT THIS TIME OF YEAR...?

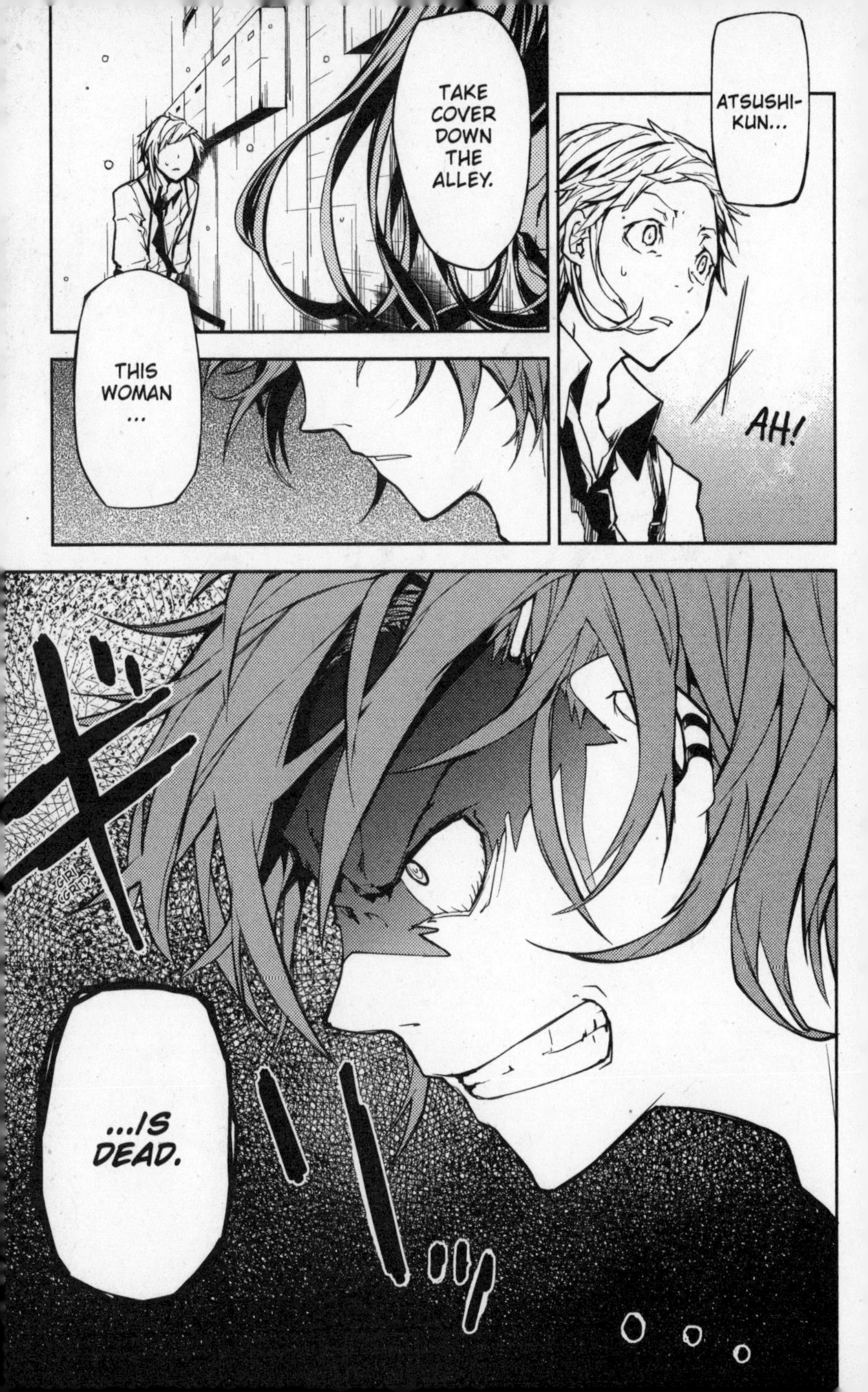
ATSUSHI-KUN...
AH!
TAKE COVER DOWN THE ALLEY.
THIS WOMAN ...
GIRI (GRIT)
...IS DEAD.

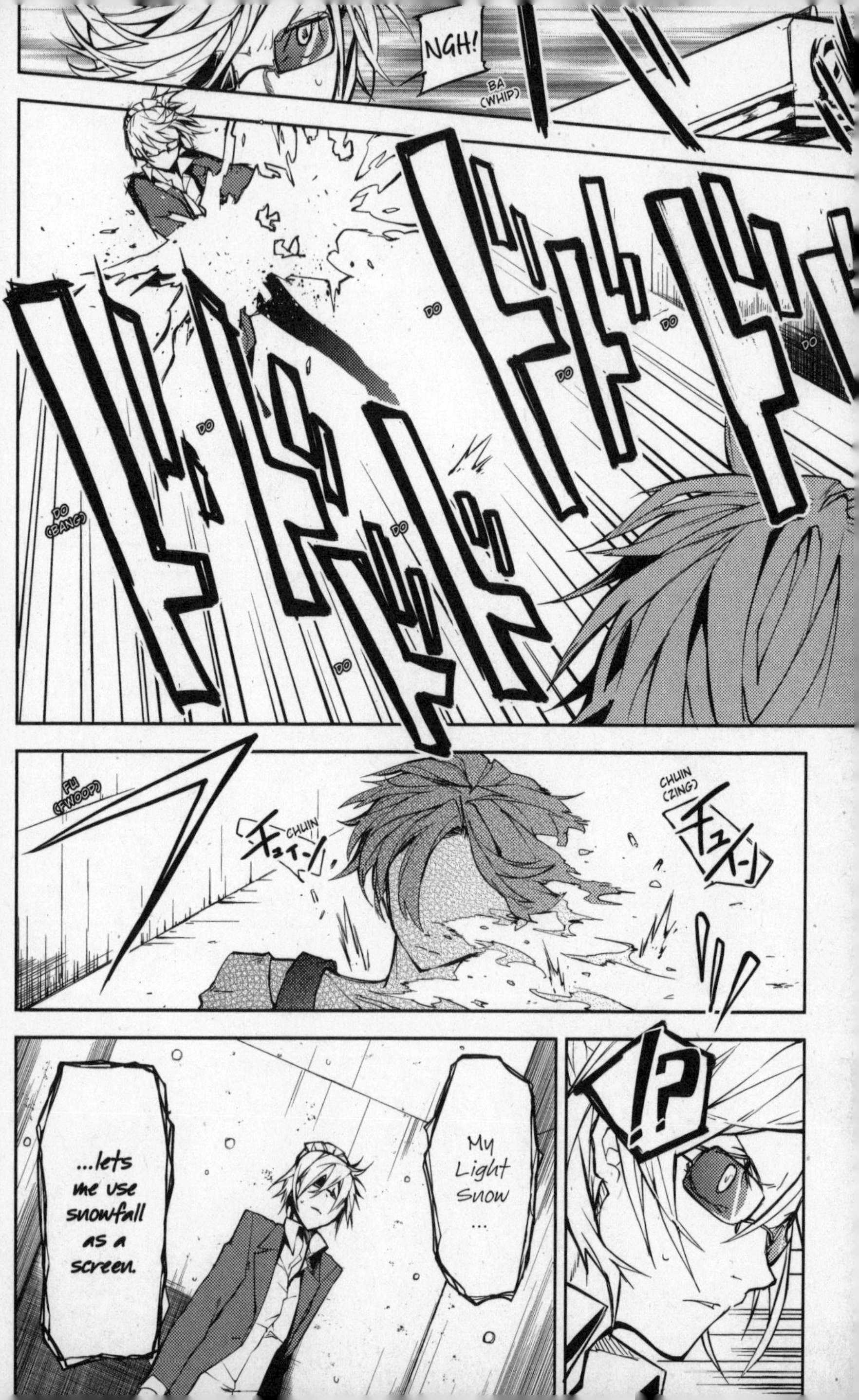
NGH!
BA (WHIP)
DO
DO
DO
DO
DO
DO
DO (BANG)
DO
CHUIN (ZING)
CHUIN
FU (FWOOP)
!?
My Light Snow ...
...lets me use snowfall as a screen.

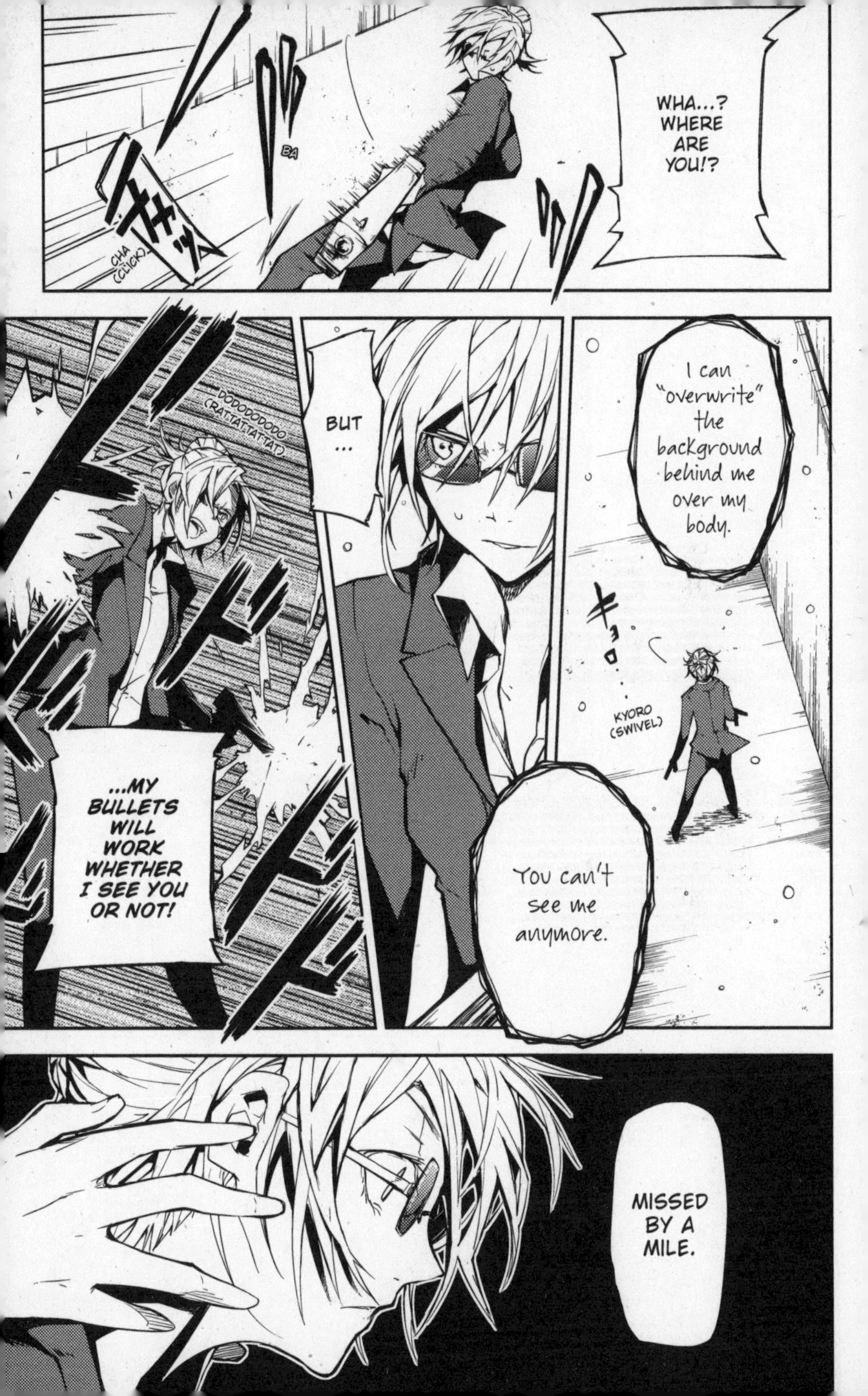
WHA...? WHERE ARE YOU!?
BA
CHA (CLICK)
I can "overwrite" the background behind me over my body.
KYORO (SWIVEL)
BUT ...
You can't see me anymore.
DODODODODO (RATTATTATTAT)
...MY BULLETS WILL WORK WHETHER I SEE YOU OR NOT!
MISSED BY A MILE.

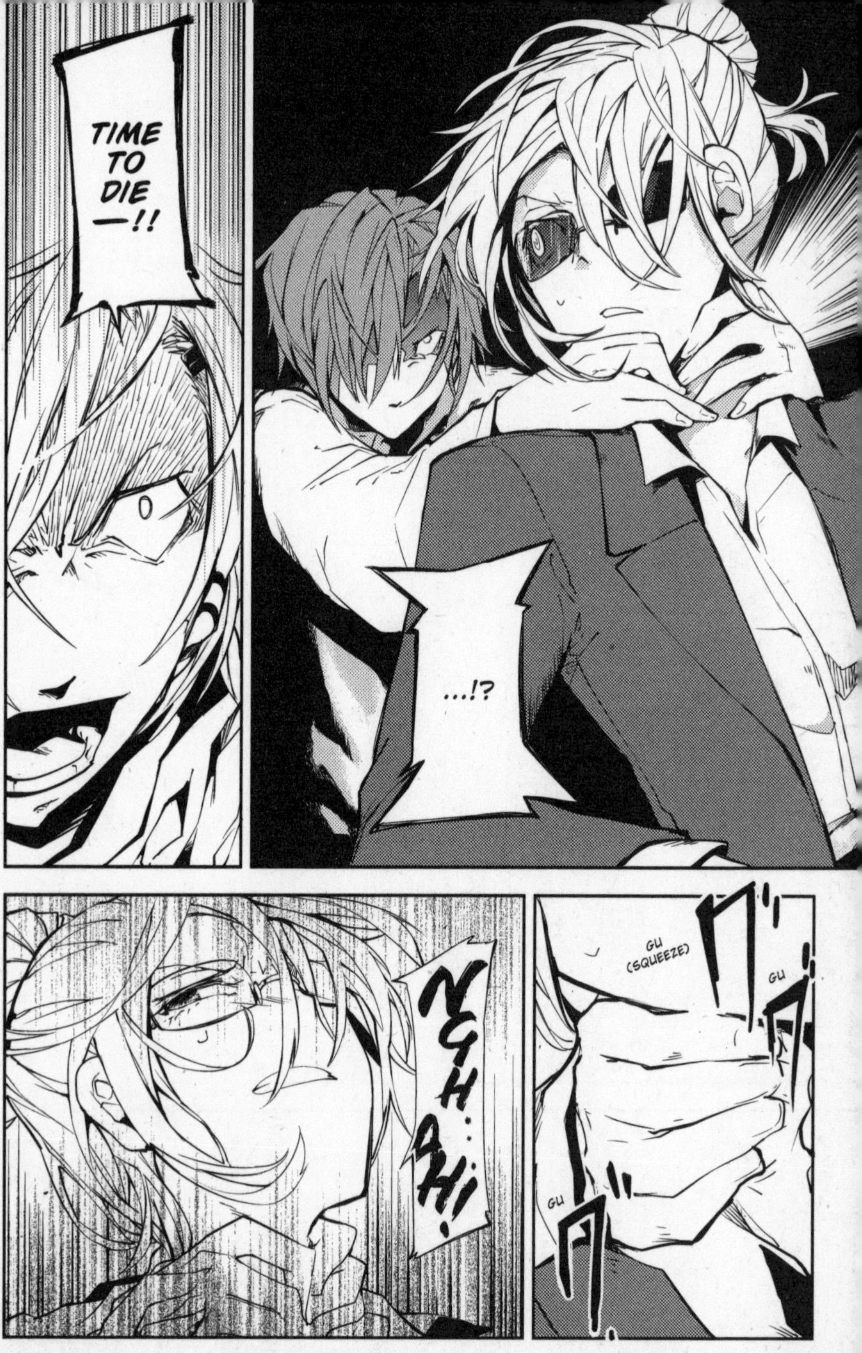
...!?
TIME TO DIE—!!
GU (SQUEEZE)
GU
GU
NGH...AH!

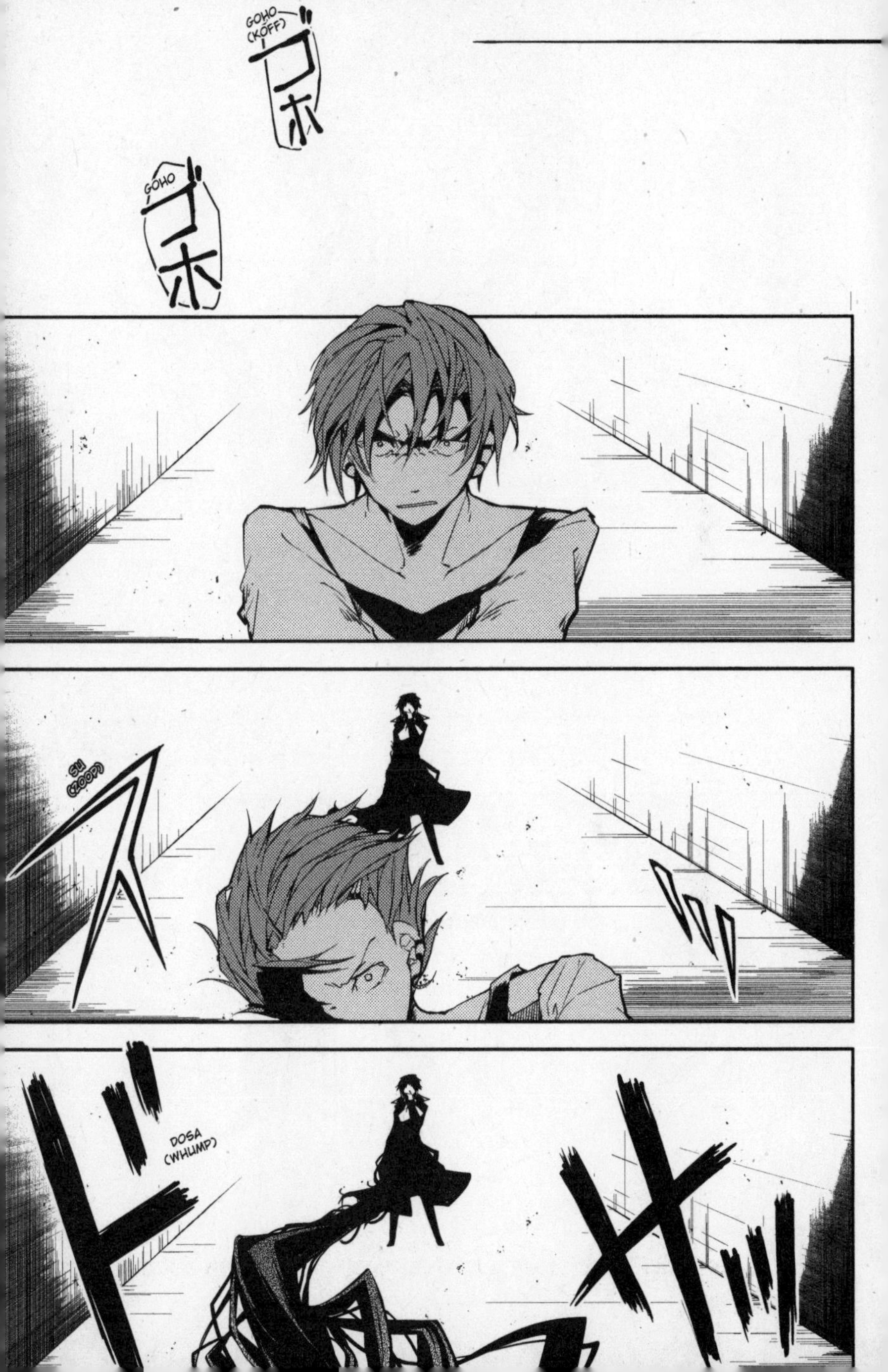
GOHO (KOFF)
ゴホ
GOHO
ゴホ
SU (ZOOP)
ス
DOSA (WHUMP)
ドサッ

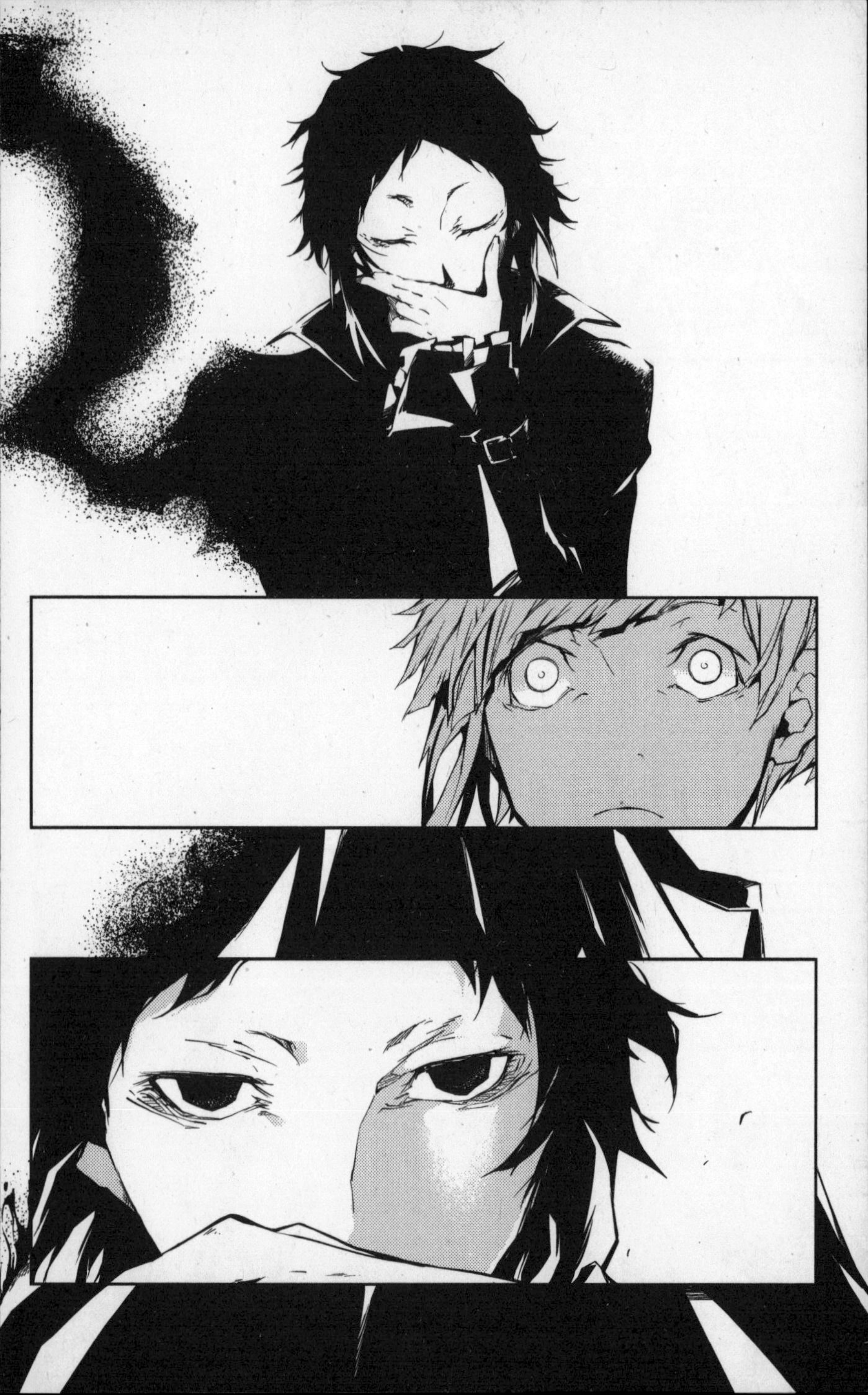

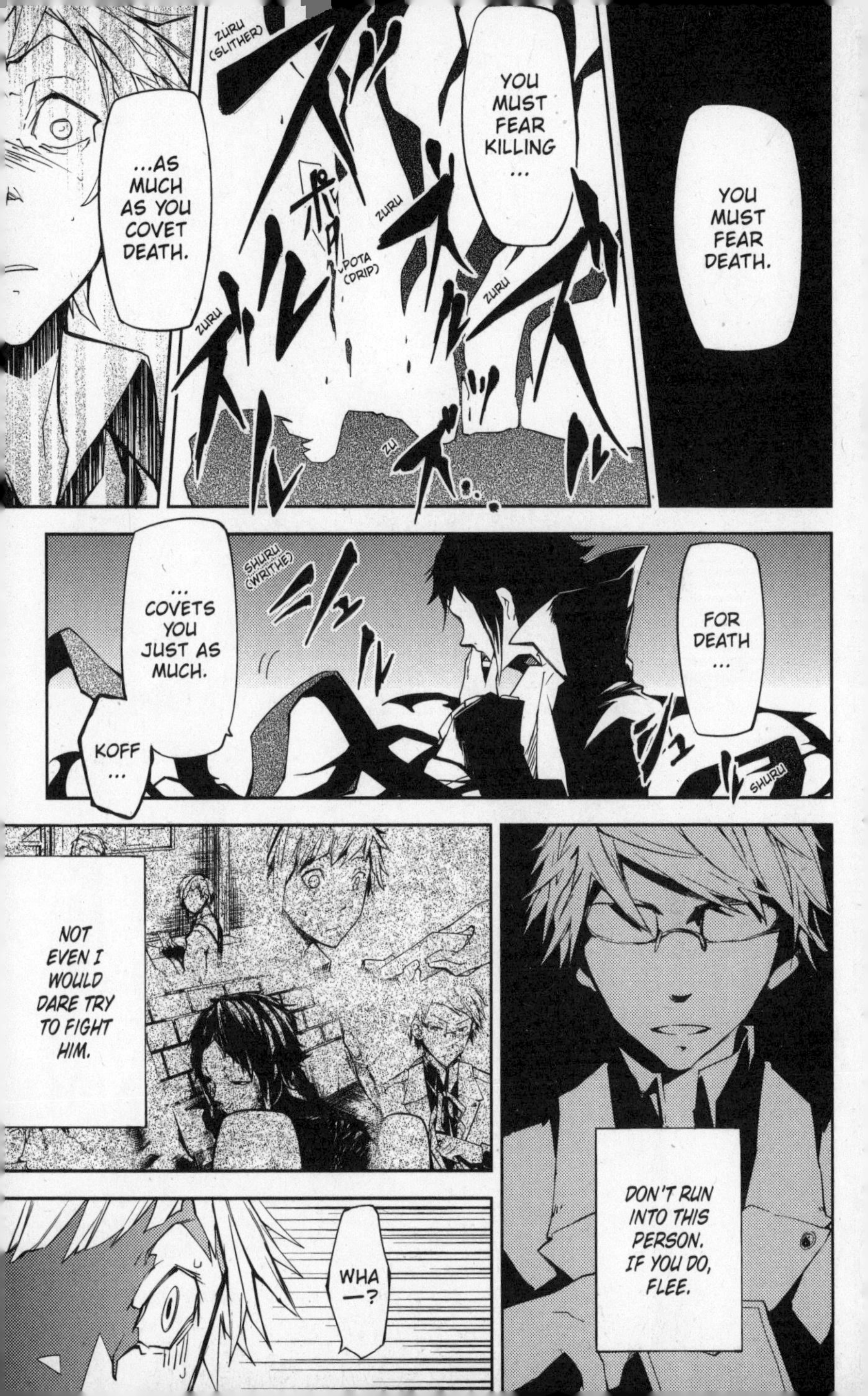
YOU MUST FEAR DEATH.
YOU MUST FEAR KILLING...
ZURU (SLITHER)
ZURU
POTA (DRIP)
ZURU
ZURU
ZU
...AS MUCH AS YOU COVET DEATH.
FOR DEATH...
SHURU
SHURU (WRITHE)
...COVETS YOU JUST AS MUCH.
KOFF...
DON'T RUN INTO THIS PERSON. IF YOU DO, FLEE.
NOT EVEN I WOULD DARE TRY TO FIGHT HIM.
WHA—?

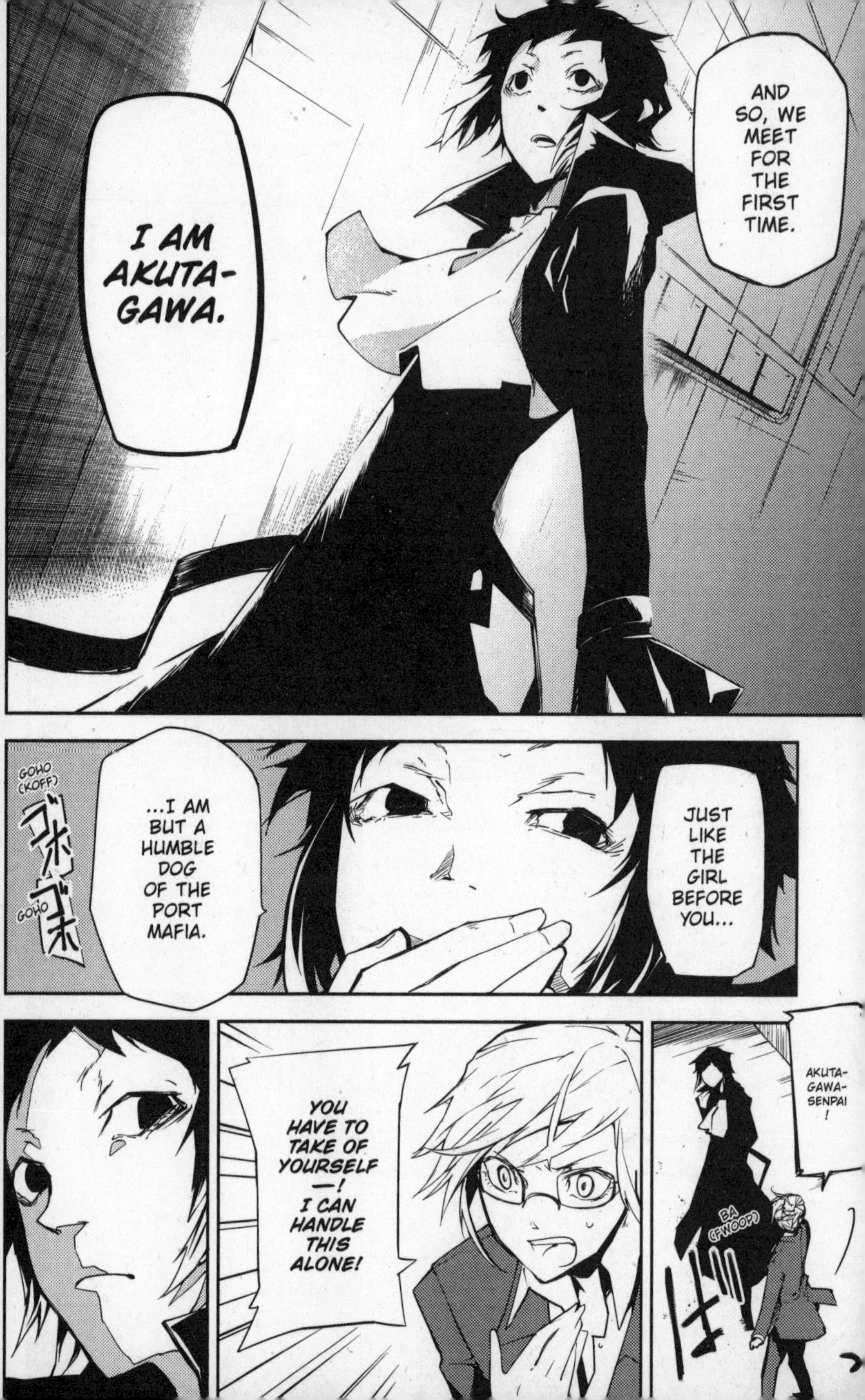
AND SO, WE MEET FOR THE FIRST TIME.
I AM AKUTA-GAWA.
JUST LIKE THE GIRL BEFORE YOU...
...I AM BUT A HUMBLE DOG OF THE PORT MAFIA.
GOHO (KOFF) GOHO
AKUTA-GAWA-SENPAI!
BA (FWOOP)
YOU HAVE TO TAKE OF YOURSELF—! I CAN HANDLE THIS ALONE!

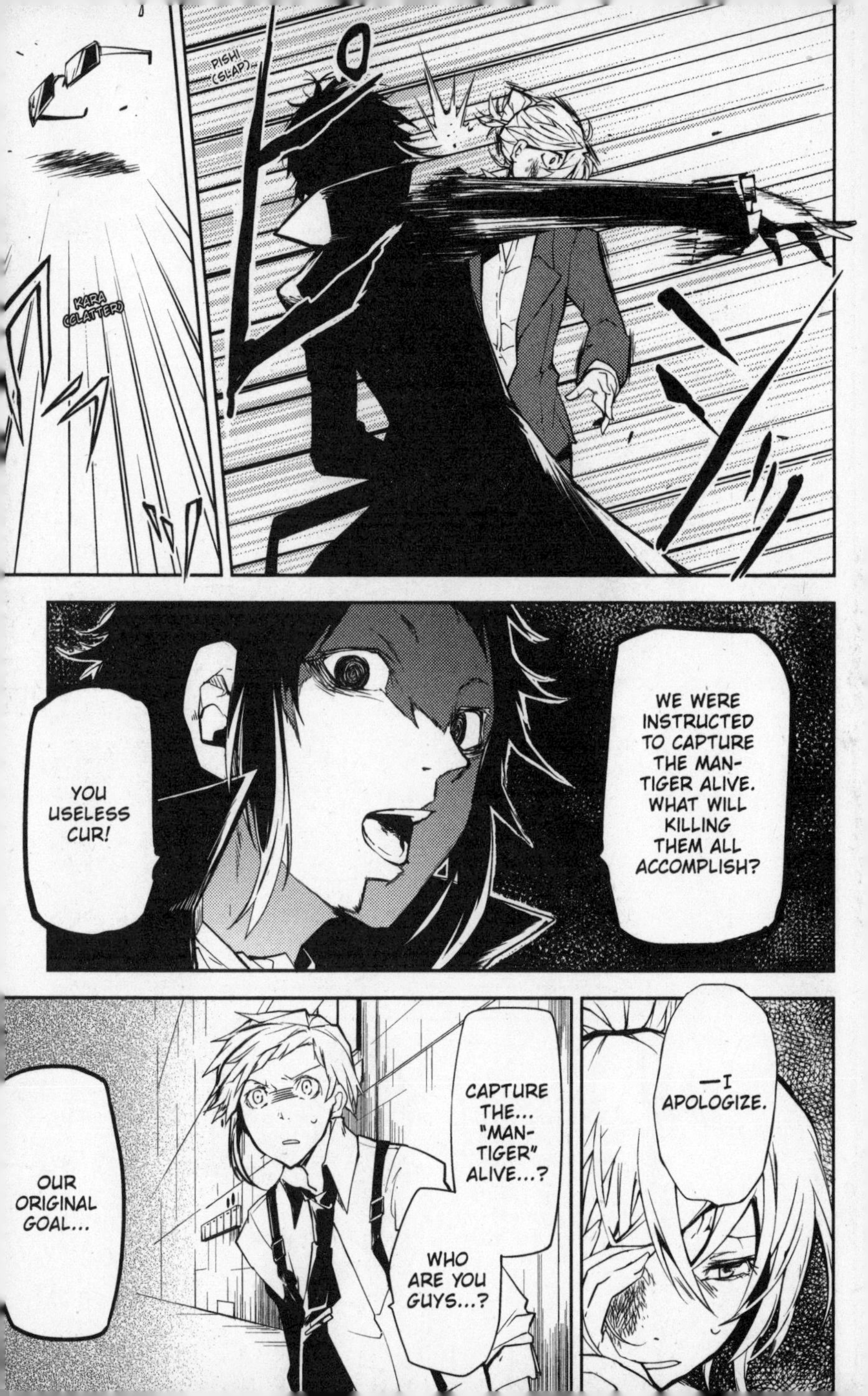
PISHI (SLAP)
KARA (CLATTER)
WE WERE INSTRUCTED TO CAPTURE THE MAN-TIGER ALIVE. WHAT WILL KILLING THEM ALL ACCOMPLISH?
YOU USELESS CUR!
—I APOLOGIZE.
CAPTURE THE... "MAN-TIGER" ALIVE...?
OUR ORIGINAL GOAL...
WHO ARE YOU GUYS...?

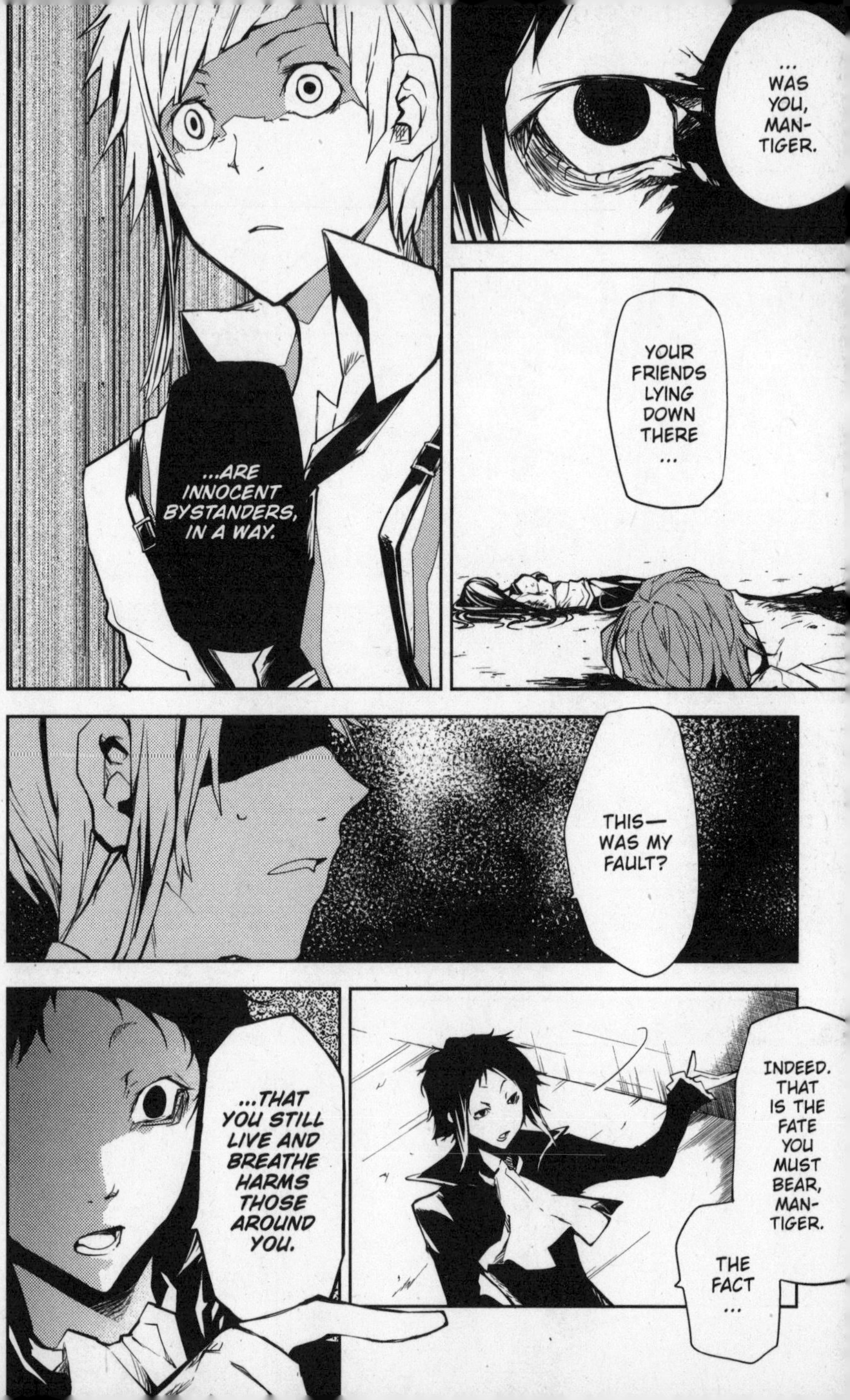
...WAS YOU, MAN-TIGER.
YOUR FRIENDS LYING DOWN THERE...
...ARE INNOCENT BYSTANDERS, IN A WAY.
THIS— WAS MY FAULT?
INDEED. THAT IS THE FATE YOU MUST BEAR, MAN-TIGER.
THE FACT...
...THAT YOU STILL LIVE AND BREATHE HARMS THOSE AROUND YOU.

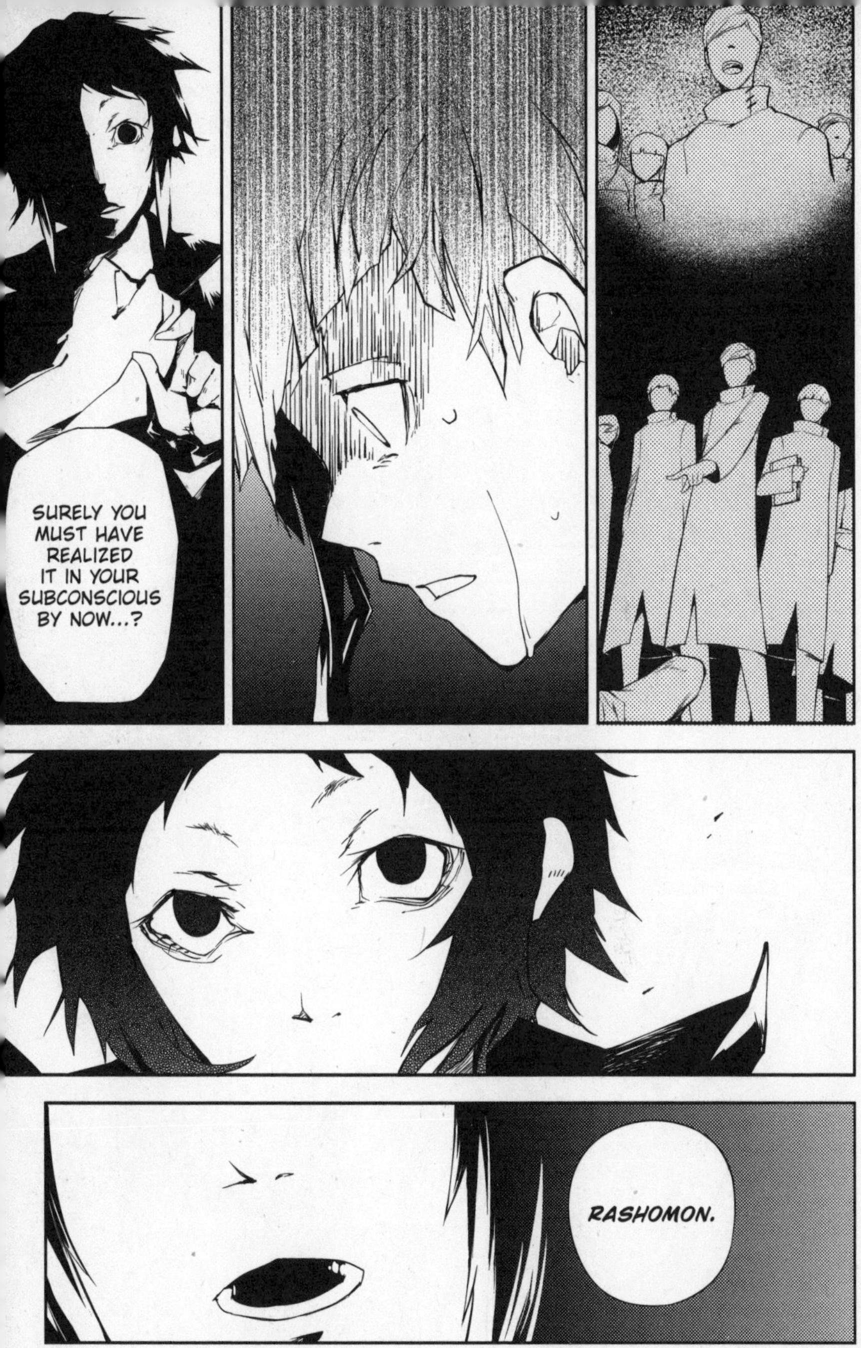
SURELY YOU MUST HAVE REALIZED IT IN YOUR SUBCONSCIOUS BY NOW...?
RASHOMON.

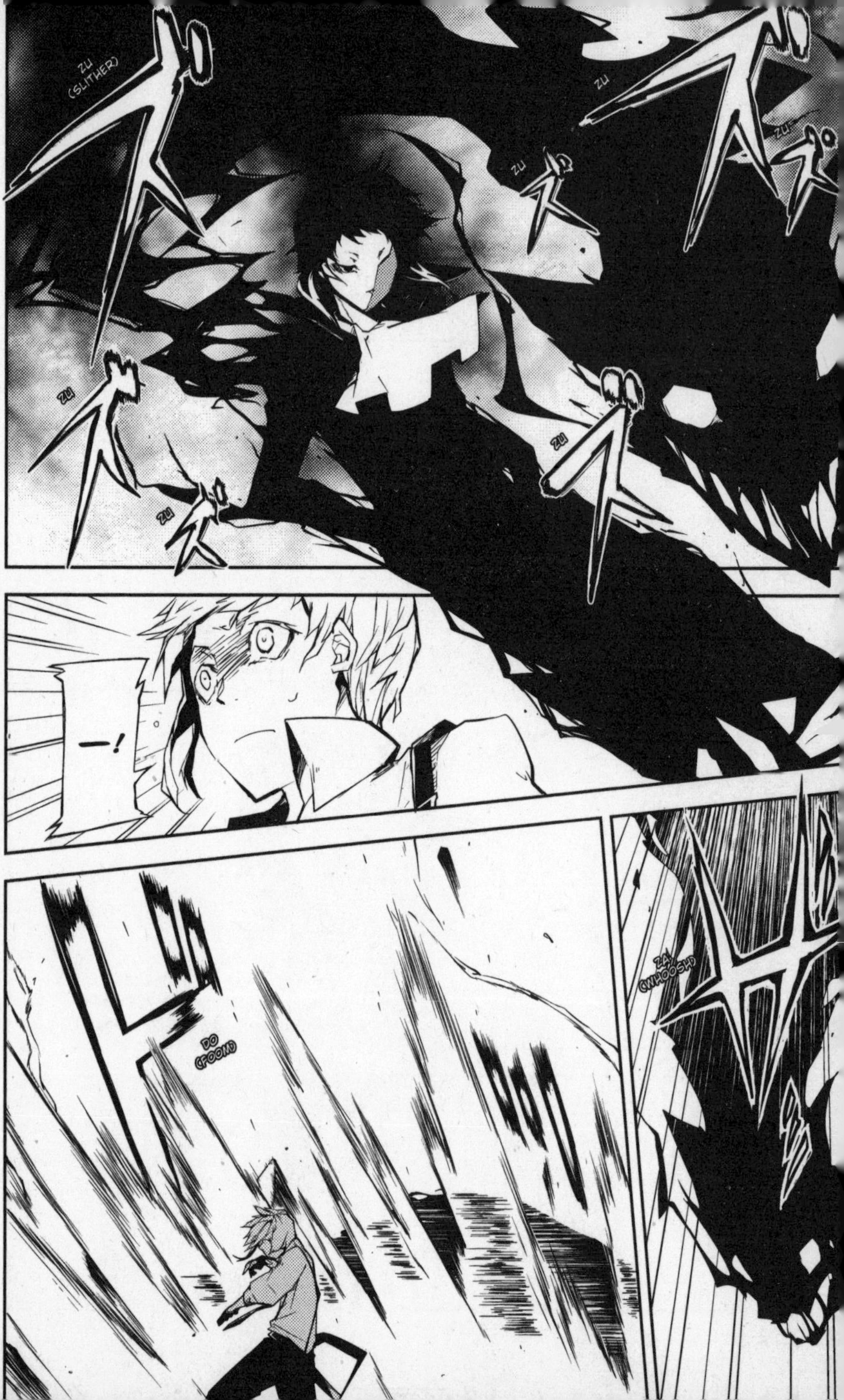
ZU
ZU
ZU
ZU
ZU
(SLITHER)
ZU
ZU
—!
ZA
(WHOOSH)
DO
(FOOM)

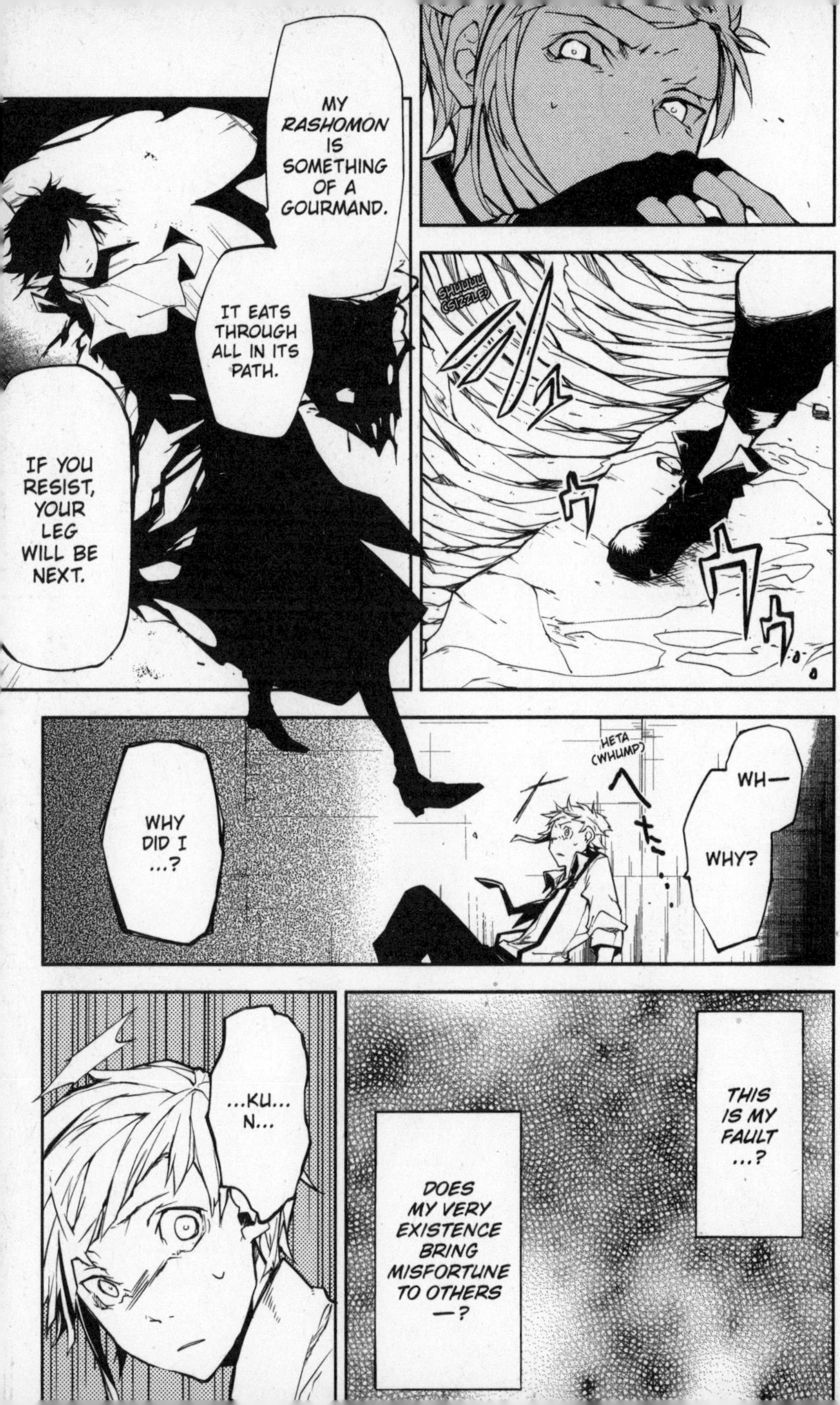
SHUUUU (SIZZLE)
MY RASHOMON IS SOMETHING OF A GOURMAND.
IT EATS THROUGH ALL IN ITS PATH.
IF YOU RESIST, YOUR LEG WILL BE NEXT.
WH— WHY?
HETA (WHUMP)
WHY DID I ...?
THIS IS MY FAULT ...?
DOES MY VERY EXISTENCE BRING MISFORTUNE TO OTHERS —?
...KU... N...

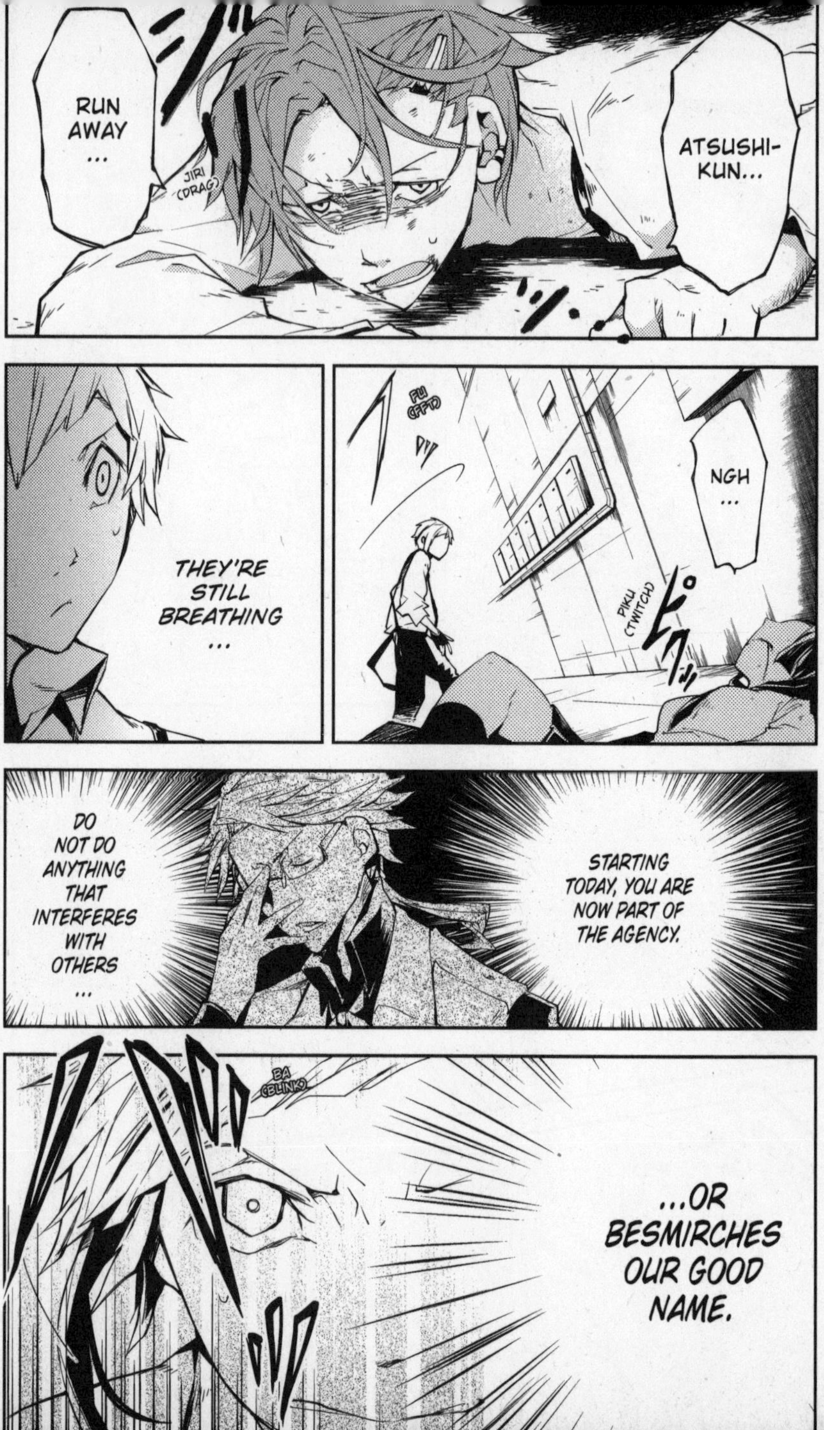
ATSUSHI-KUN...
JIRI (DRAG)
RUN AWAY ...
NGH ...
FU (FFT)
PIKU (TWITCH)
THEY'RE STILL BREATHING ...
STARTING TODAY, YOU ARE NOW PART OF THE AGENCY.
DO NOT DO ANYTHING THAT INTERFERES WITH OTHERS ...
BA (BLINK)
...OR BESMIRCHES OUR GOOD NAME.

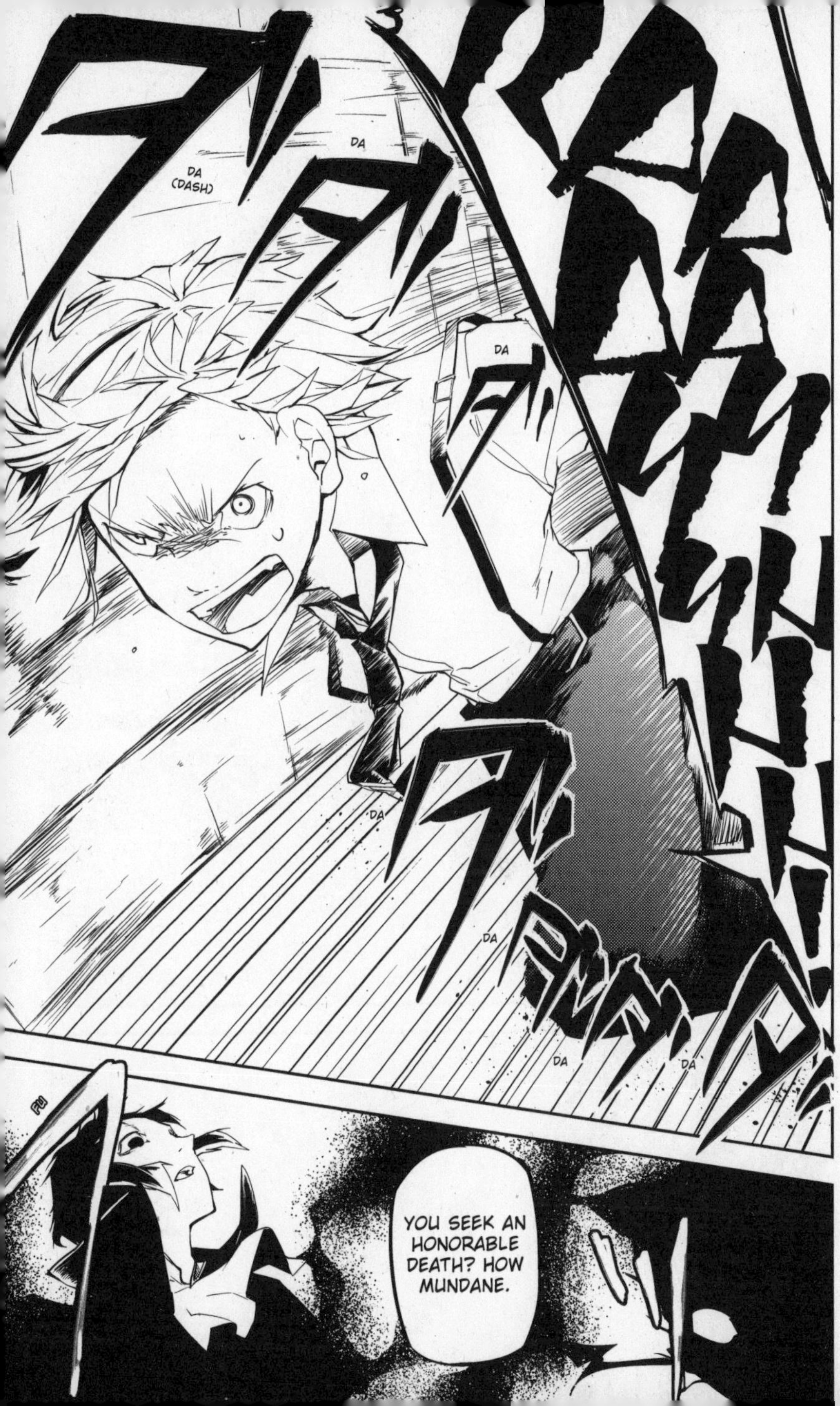
DA
DA
DA
(DASH)
DA
DA
DA
DA
FU
YOU SEEK AN HONORABLE DEATH? HOW MUNDANE.

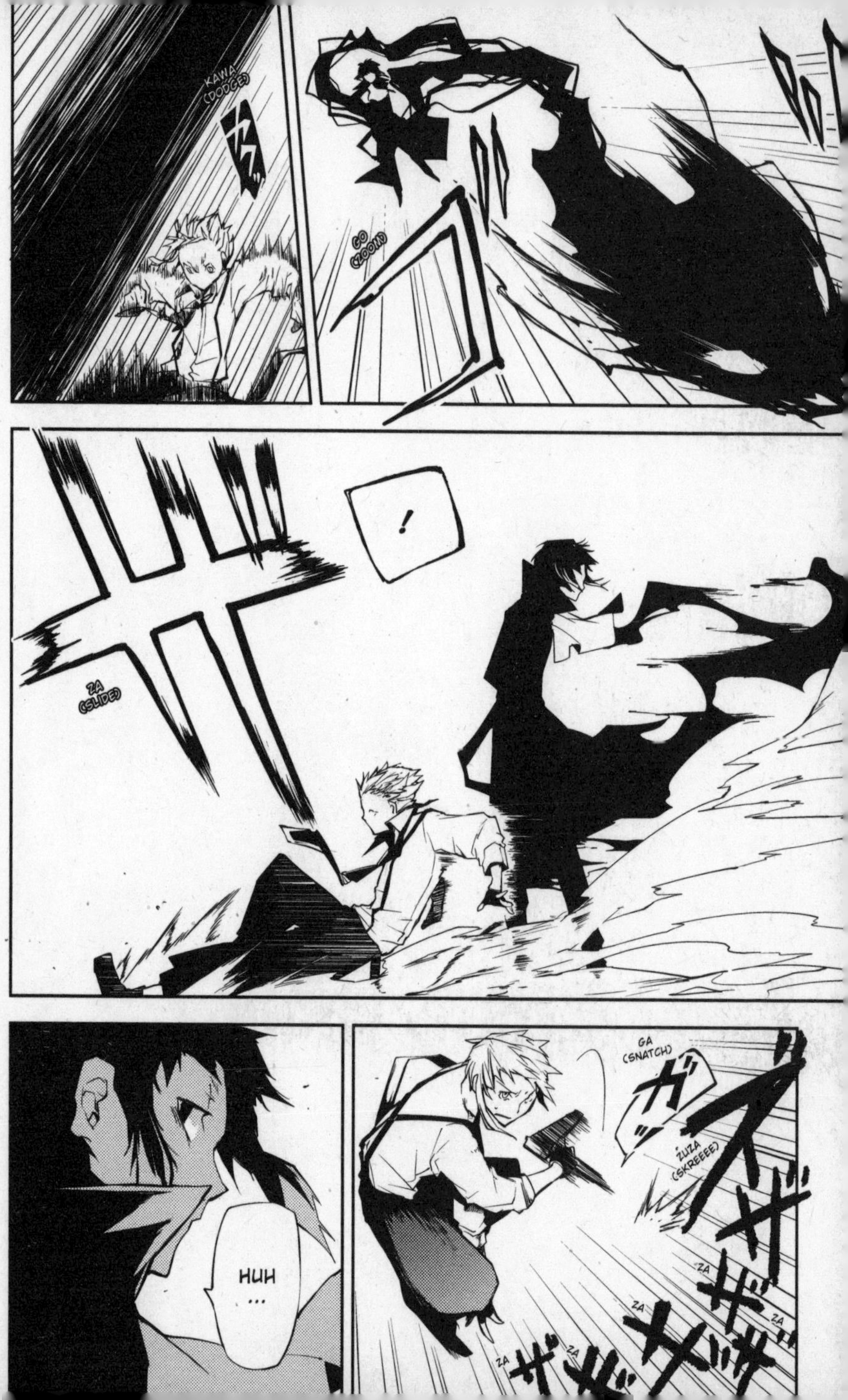
GO
(ZOOM)
KAWA
(DODGE)
!
ZA
(SLIDE)
GA
(SNATCH)
ZUZA
(SKREEEE)
ZA
ZA
ZA
ZA
ZA
HUH
...

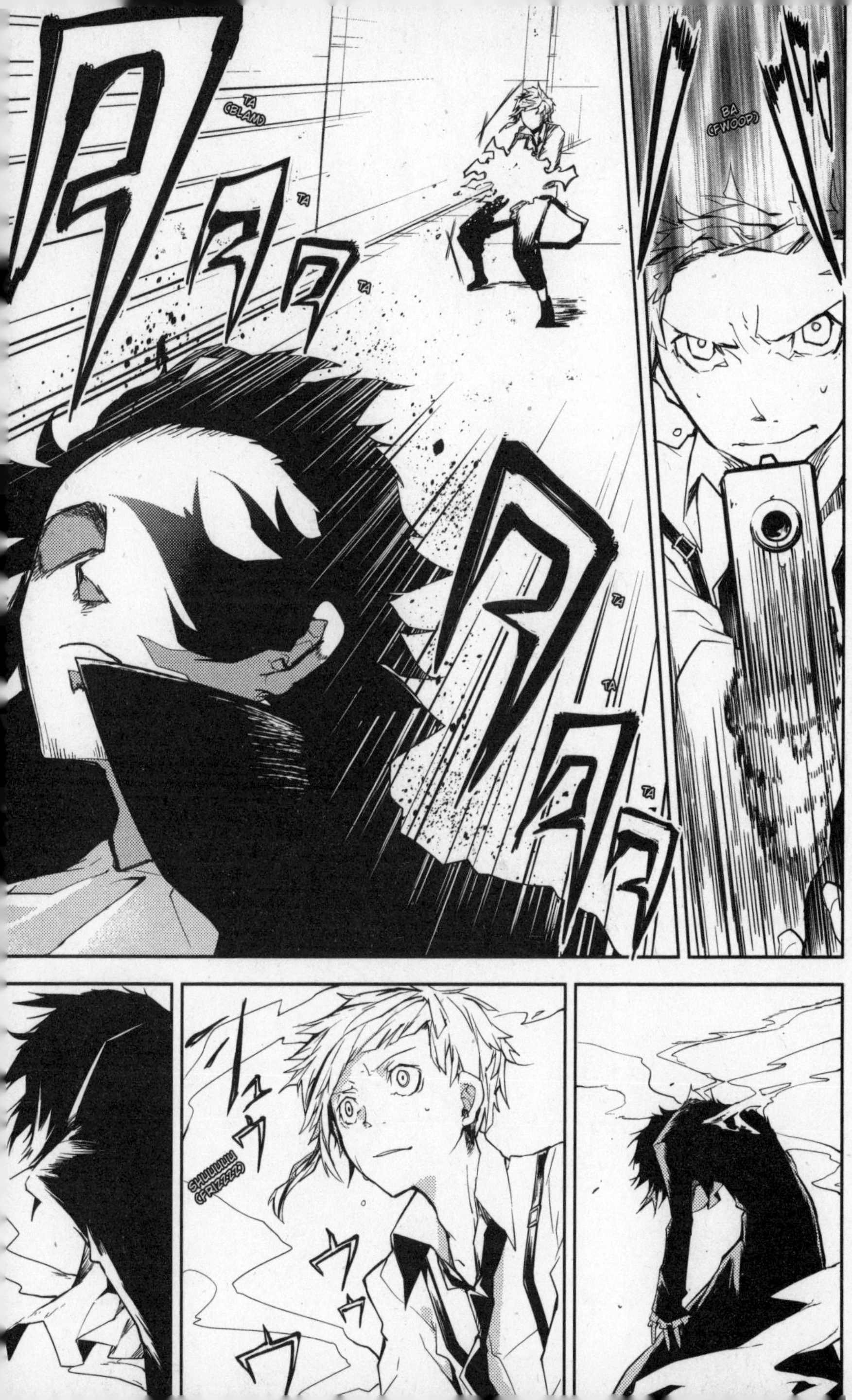
BA
(FWOOP)
TA
(BLAM)
TA
TA
TA
TA
TA
SHUUUUU
(FRIZZZZ)

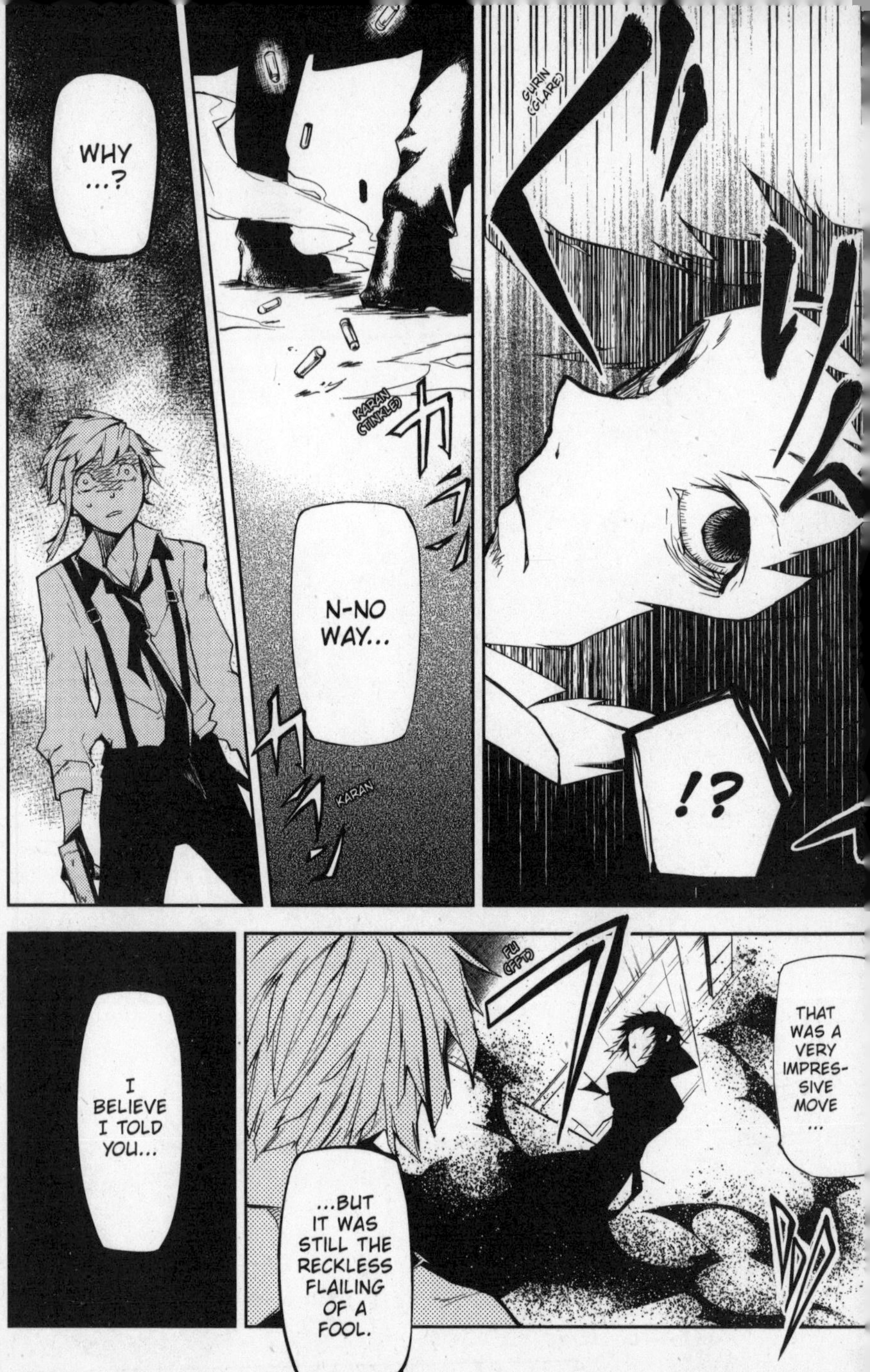
GURIN (GLARE)
!?
KARAN (TINKLE)
N-NO WAY...
KARAN
WHY ...?
FU (FFT)
THAT WAS A VERY IMPRESSIVE MOVE ...
...BUT IT WAS STILL THE RECKLESS FLAILING OF A FOOL.
I BELIEVE I TOLD YOU...

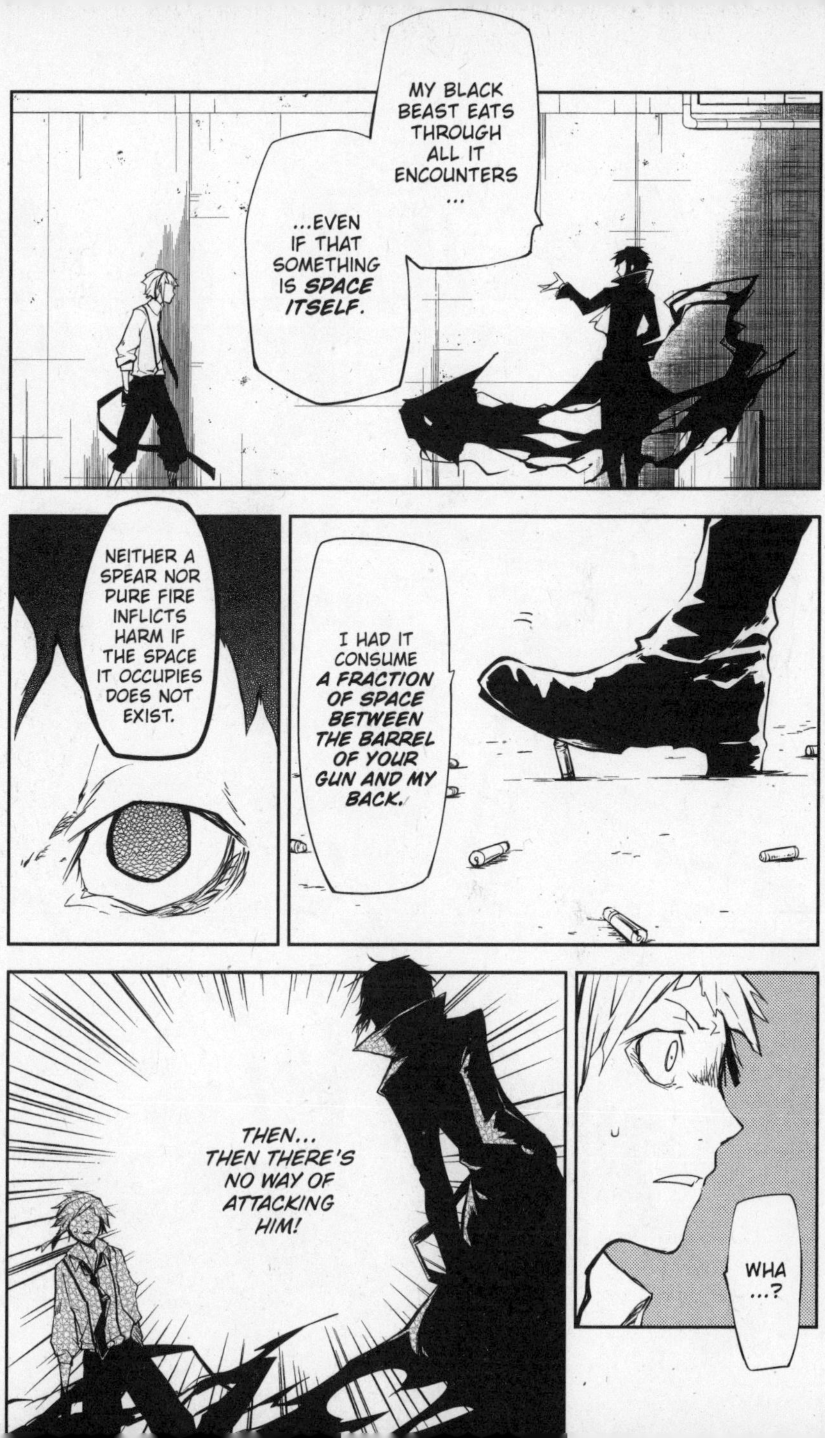
MY BLACK BEAST EATS THROUGH ALL IT ENCOUNTERS ...
...EVEN IF THAT SOMETHING IS *SPACE ITSELF*.
I HAD IT CONSUME *A FRACTION OF SPACE BETWEEN THE BARREL OF YOUR GUN AND MY BACK.*
NEITHER A SPEAR NOR PURE FIRE INFLICTS HARM IF THE SPACE IT OCCUPIES DOES NOT EXIST.
WHA ...?
THEN... THEN THERE'S NO WAY OF ATTACKING HIM!

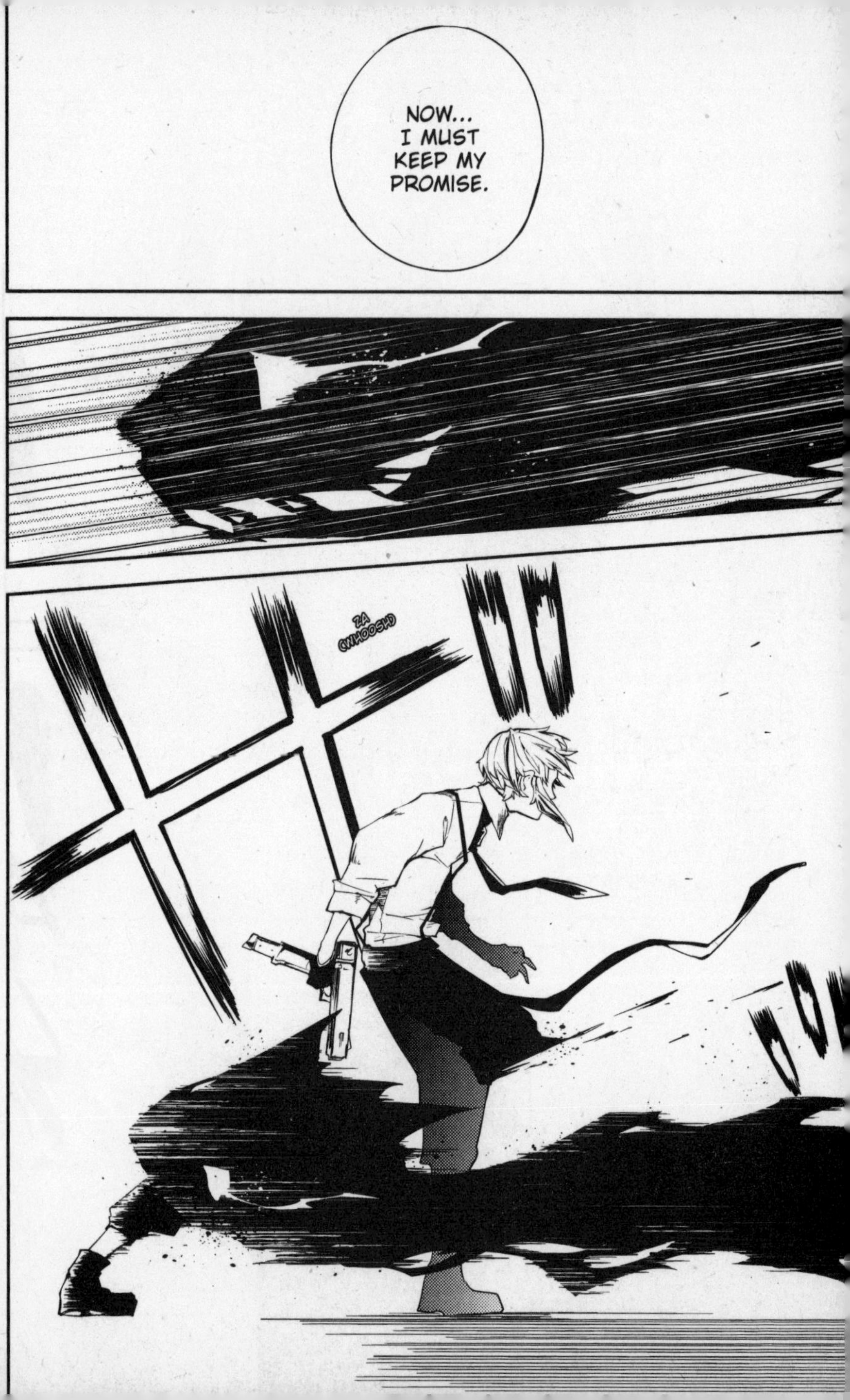
NOW... I MUST KEEP MY PROMISE.
ZA (WHOOSH)

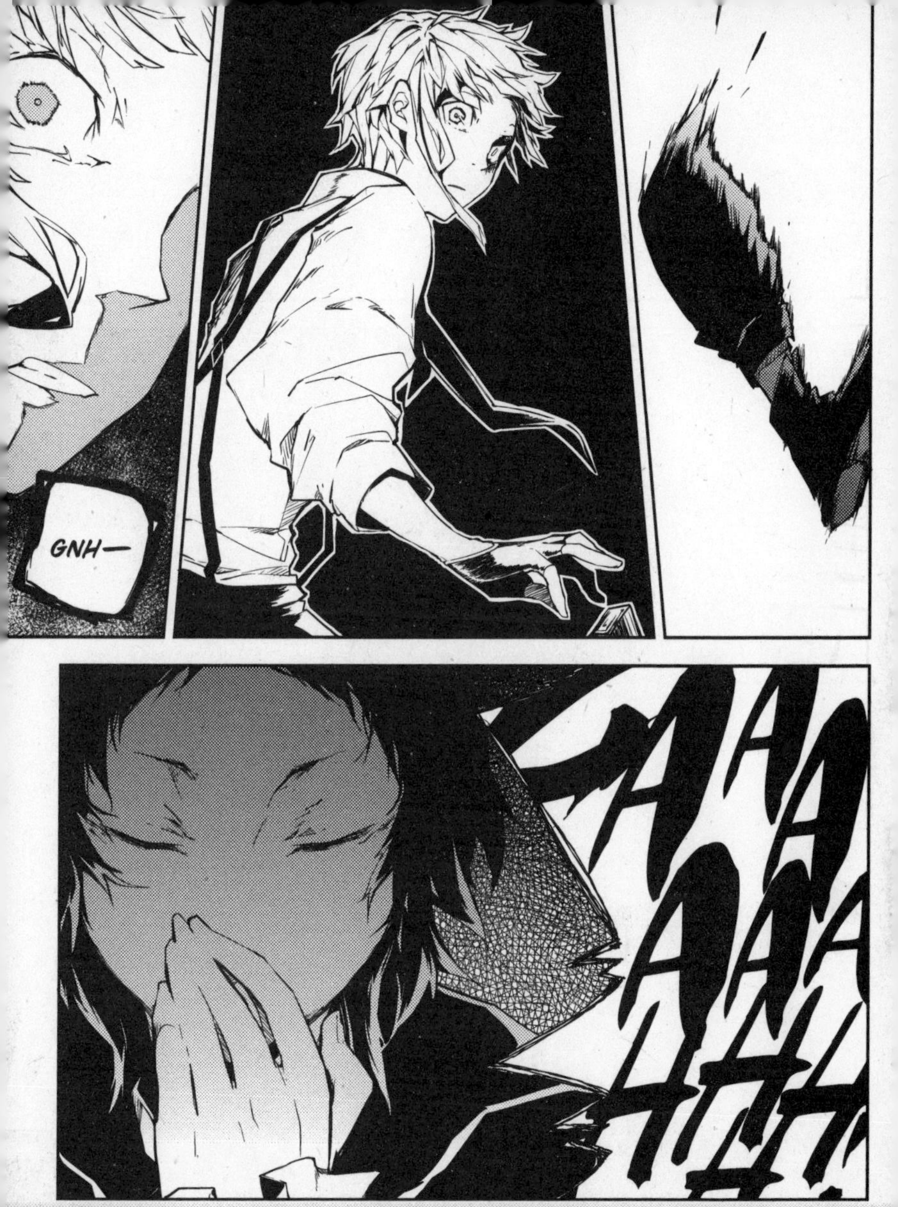
GNH—

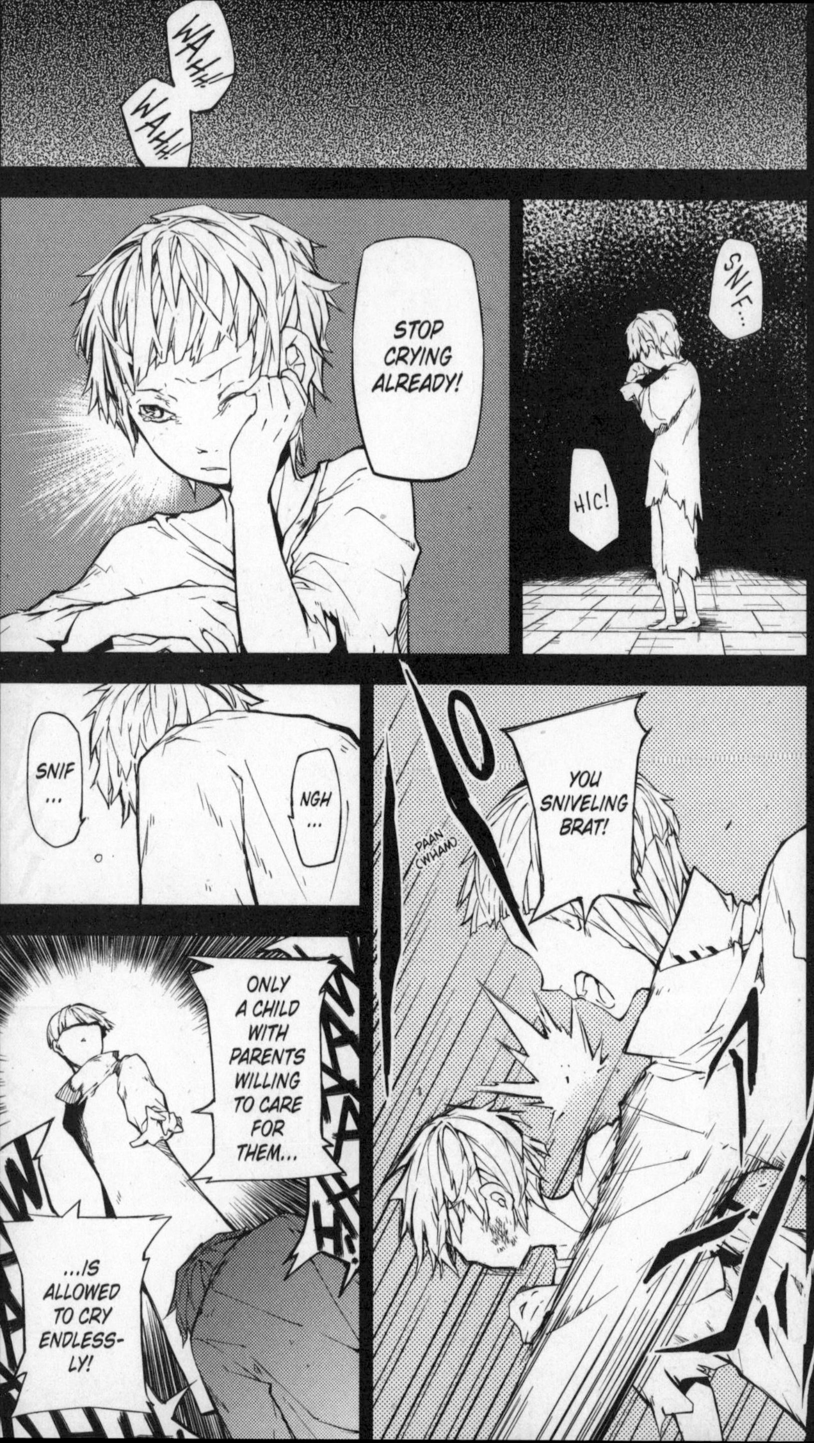
WAH!!
WAH!!
SNIF...
HIC!
STOP CRYING ALREADY!
YOU SNIVELING BRAT!
PAAN (WHAM)
NGH ...
SNIF ...
ONLY A CHILD WITH PARENTS WILLING TO CARE FOR THEM...
...IS ALLOWED TO CRY ENDLESS-LY!

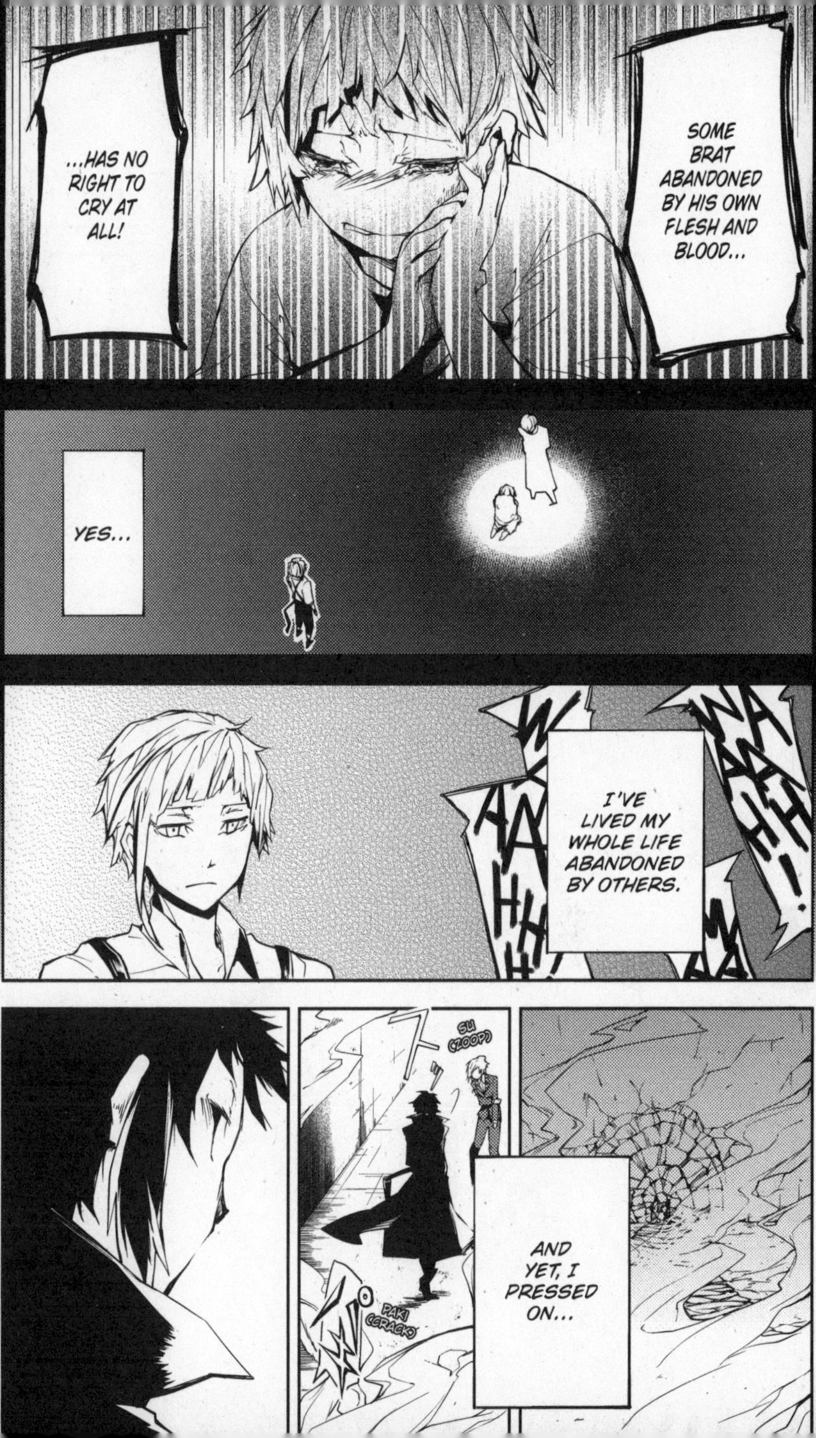
SOME BRAT ABANDONED BY HIS OWN FLESH AND BLOOD...
...HAS NO RIGHT TO CRY AT ALL!
YES...
I'VE LIVED MY WHOLE LIFE ABANDONED BY OTHERS.
AND YET, I PRESSED ON...
SU (ZOOP)
PAKI (CRACK)

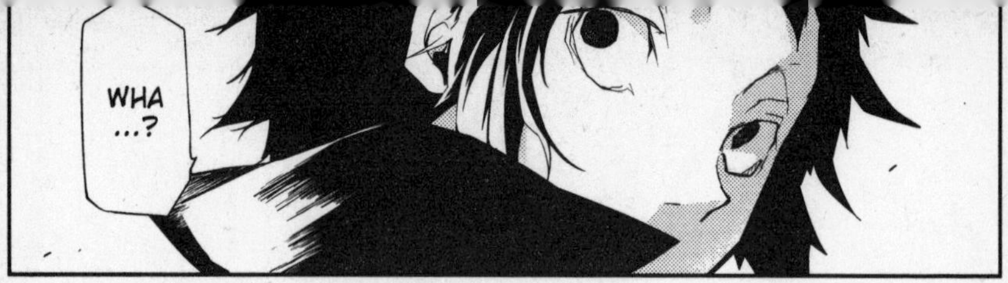
WHA ...?
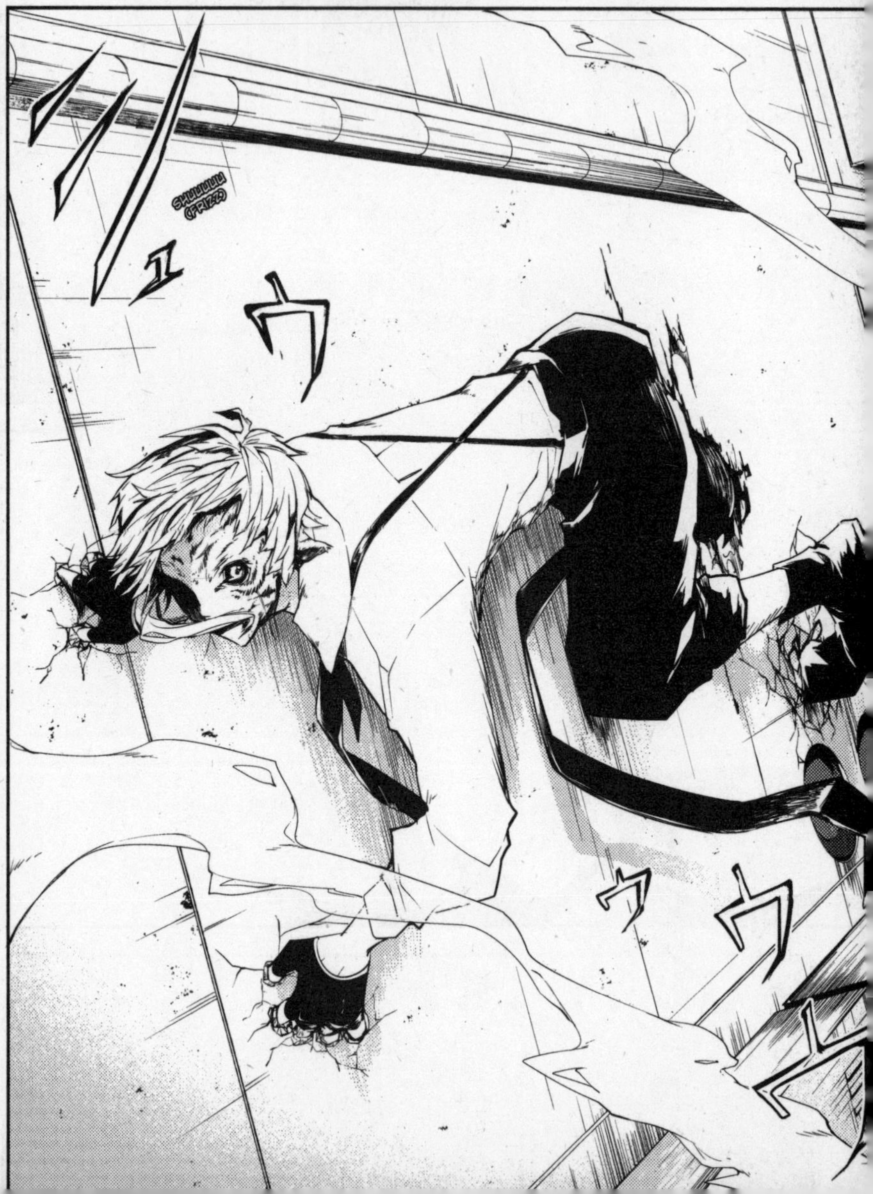
SHUUUUUU (FRIZZ)

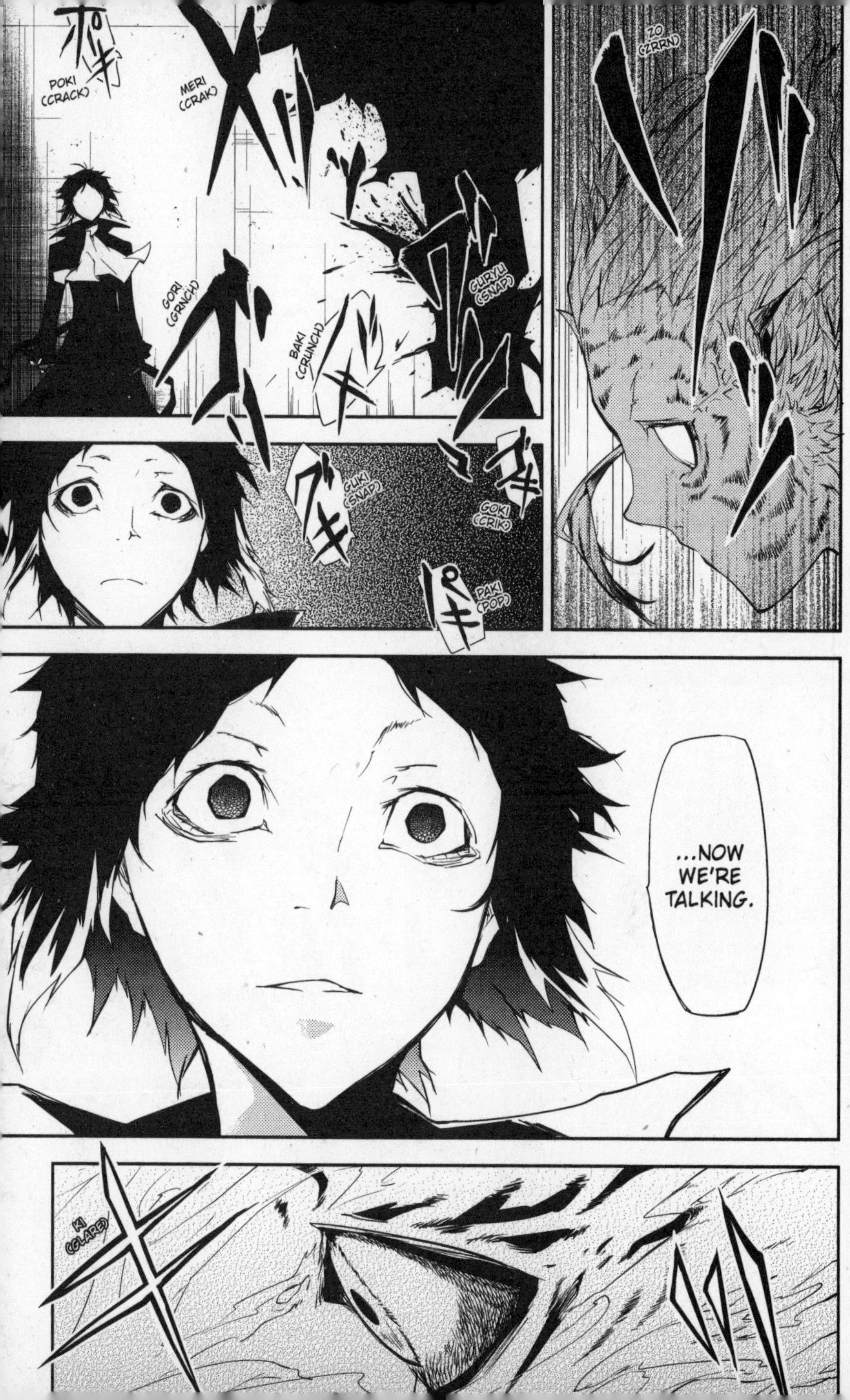
ZO (ZRRN)
GURYU (SNAP)
MERI (CRAK)
POKI (CRACK)
BAKI (CRUNCH)
GORI (GRNCH)
GOKI (CRIK)
GUKI (SNAP)
PAKI (POP)
...NOW WE'RE TALKING.
KI (GLARE)

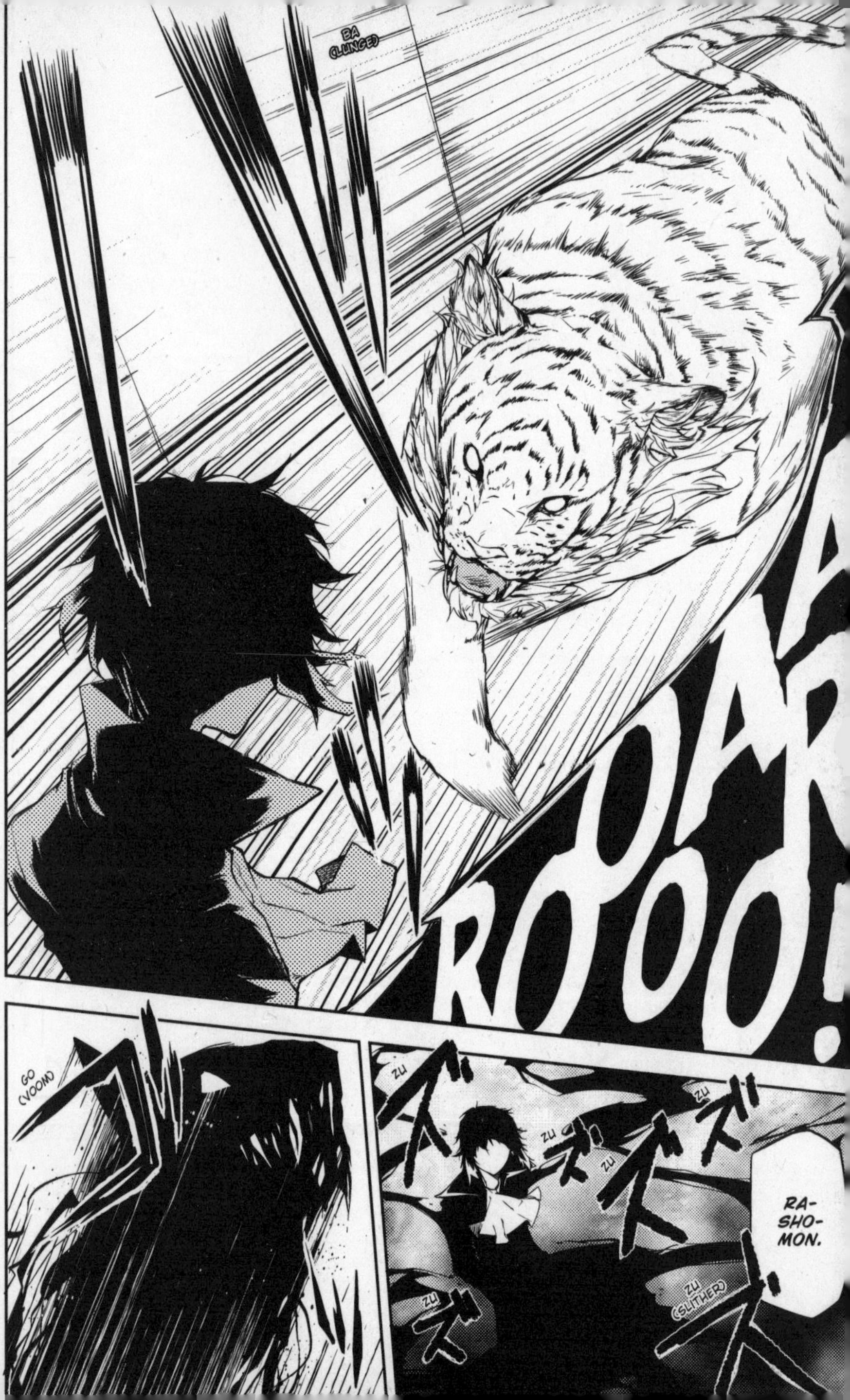
BA (LUNGE)
ROOOOAR!
ZU
ZU
ZU
ZU
RA-SHO-MON.
ZU (SLITHER)
ZU
GO (VOOM)

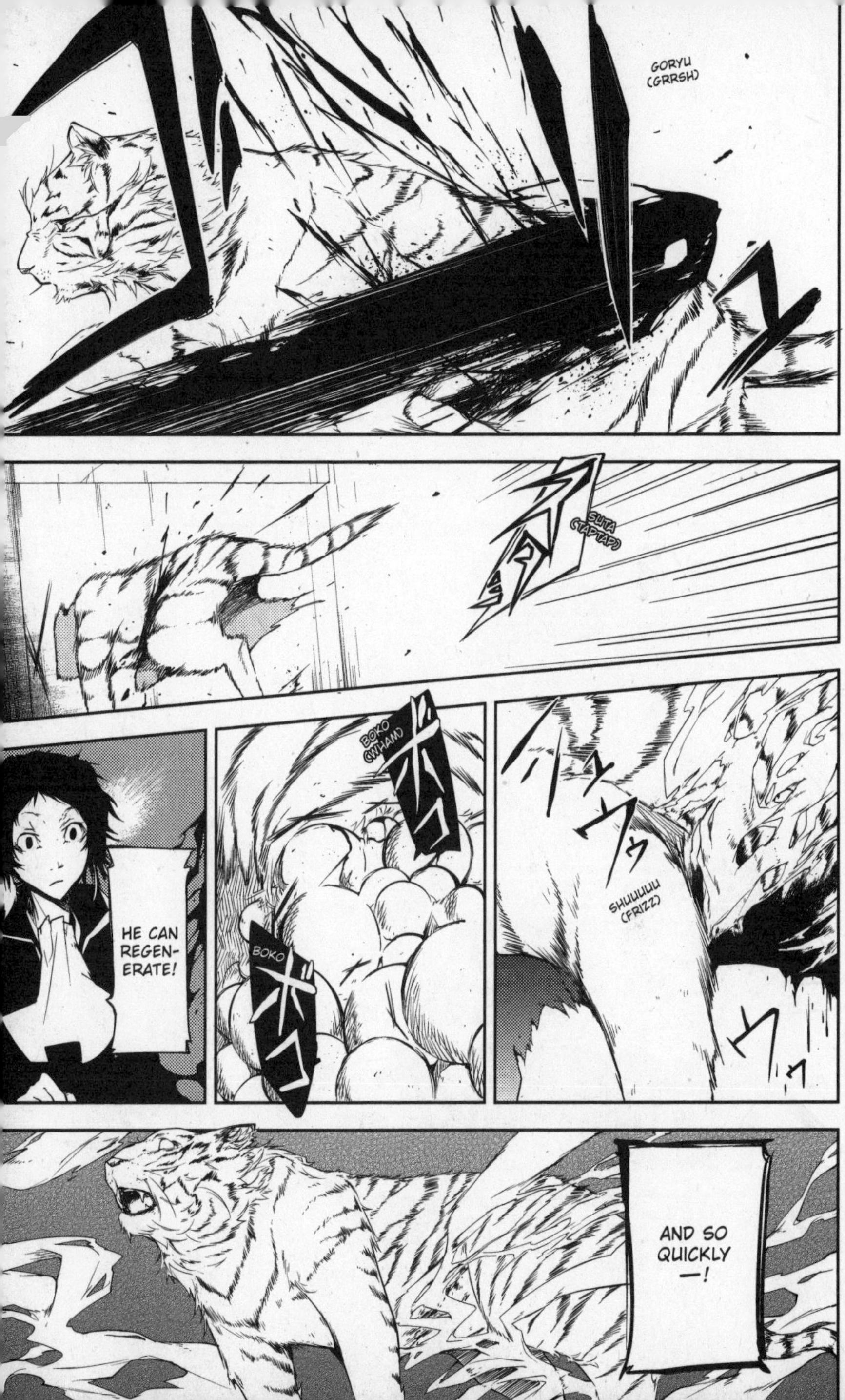
GORYU (GRRSH)
SUTA (TAPTAP)
SHUUUUU (FRIZZ)
BOKO (WHAM)
BOKO
HE CAN REGEN-ERATE!
AND SO QUICKLY—!

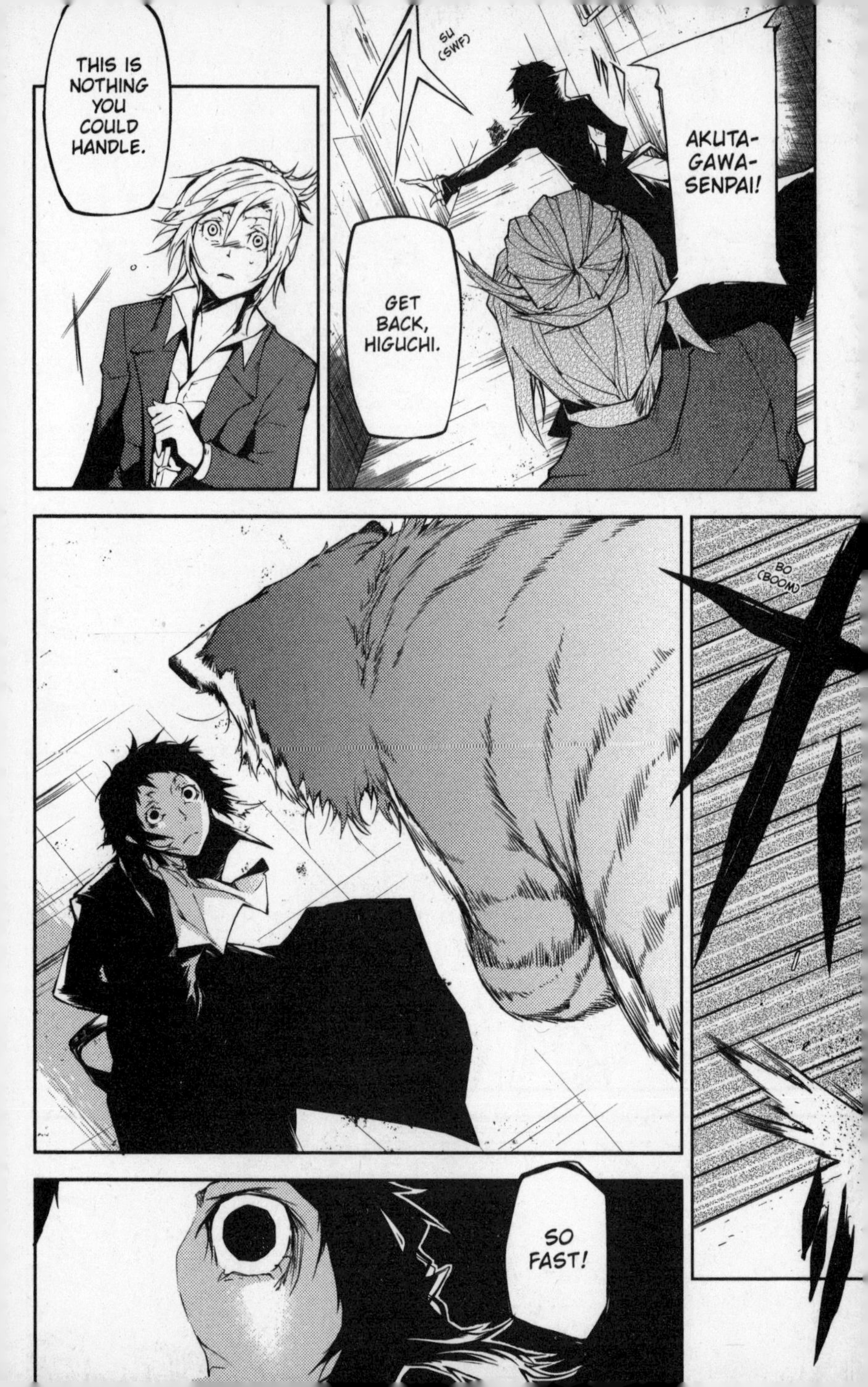
SU (SWF)
AKUTA-GAWA-SENPAI!
GET BACK, HIGUCHI.
THIS IS NOTHING YOU COULD HANDLE.
BO (BOOM)
SO FAST!

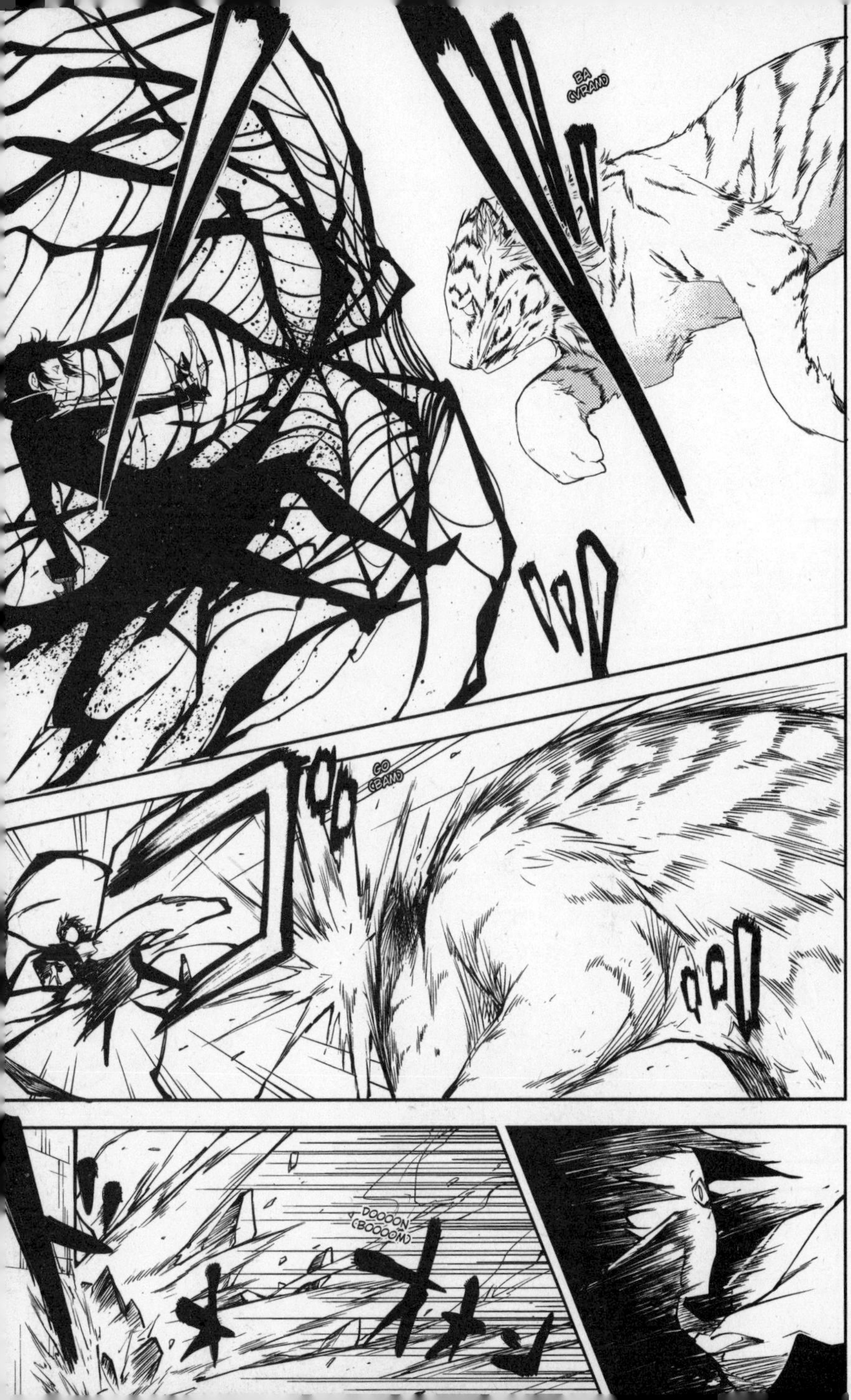
BA (VRAM)
GO (BAM)
DOOOON (BOOOOM)

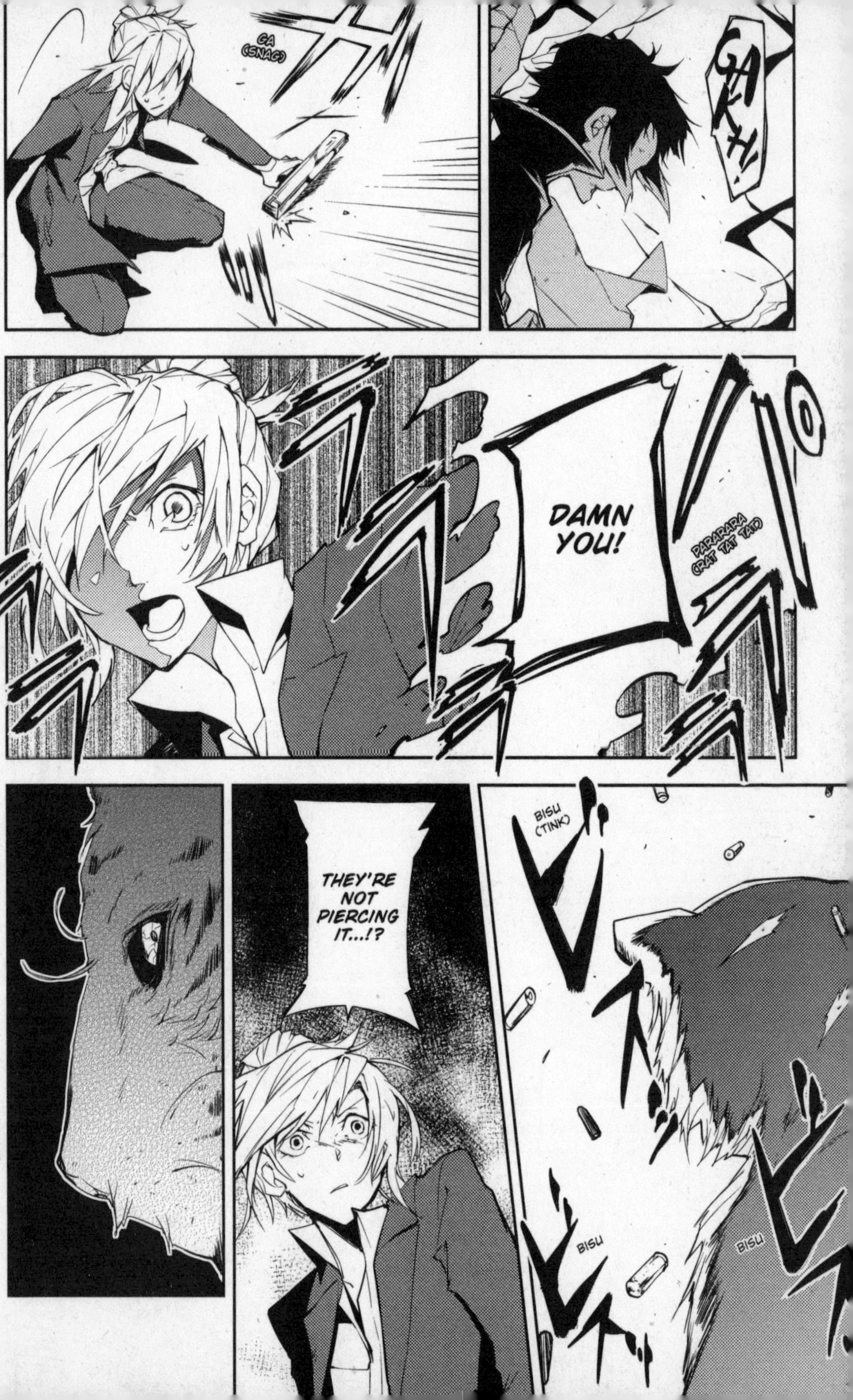
GAKH!
GA (SNAG)
DAMN YOU!
PARARARA (RAT TAT TAT)
BISU (TINK)
BISU
BISU
THEY'RE NOT PIERCING IT...!?

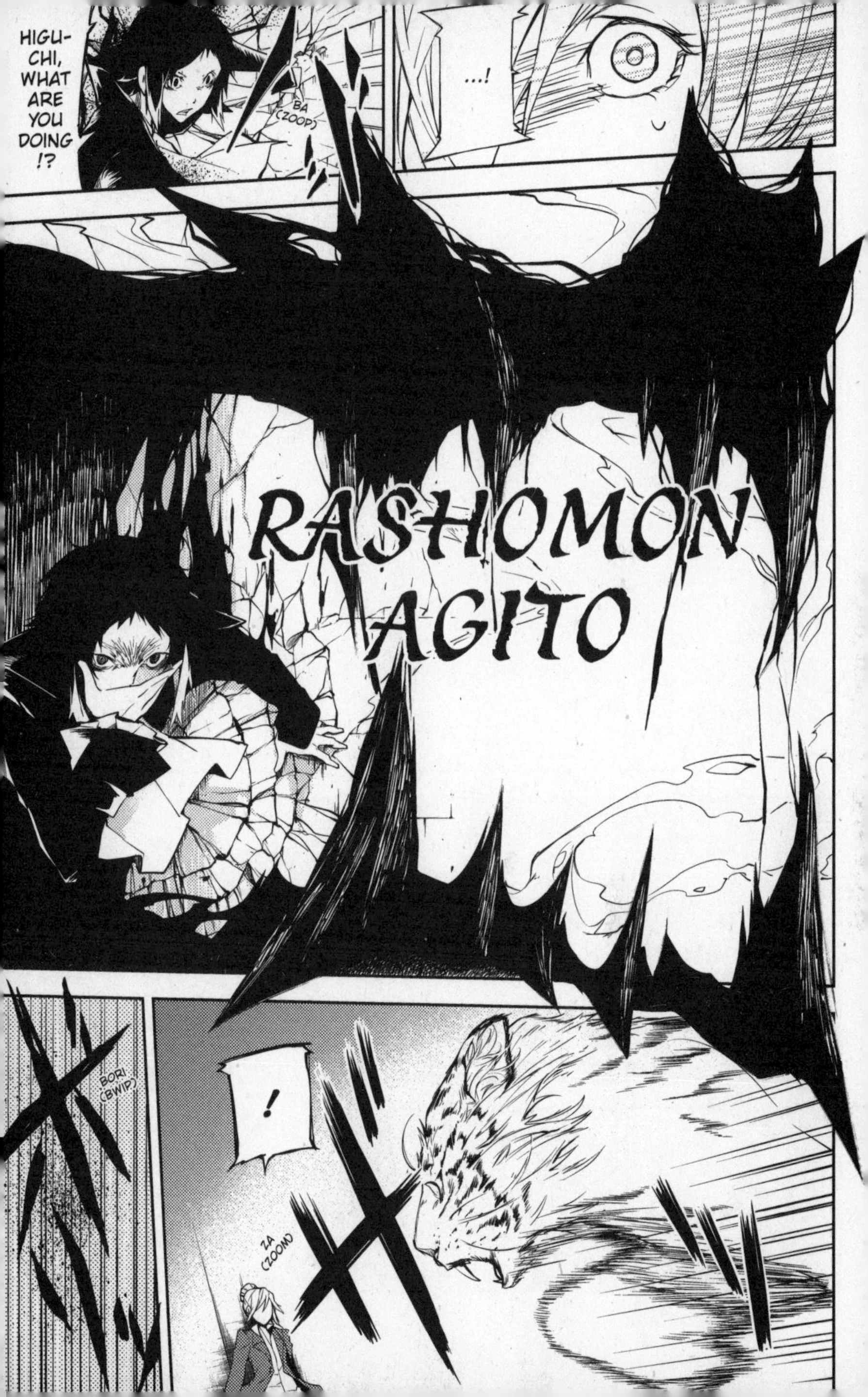
...!
HIGU-CHI, WHAT ARE YOU DOING !?
BA (ZOOP)
RASHOMON AGITO
!
ZA (ZOOM)
BORI (BWIP)

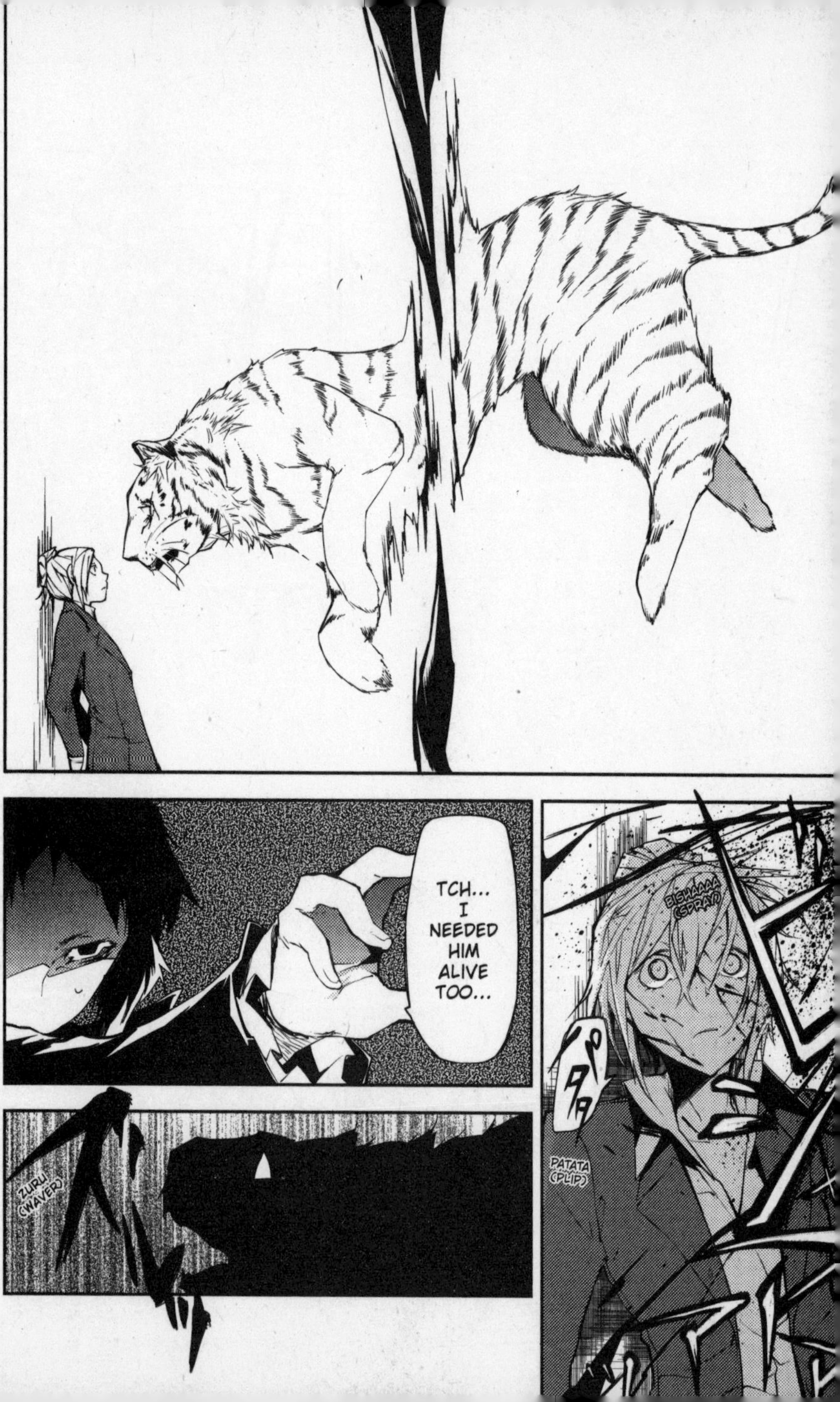
BISHAAAA (SPRAY)
PATATA (PLIP)
TCH... I NEEDED HIM ALIVE TOO...
ZURU (WAVER)

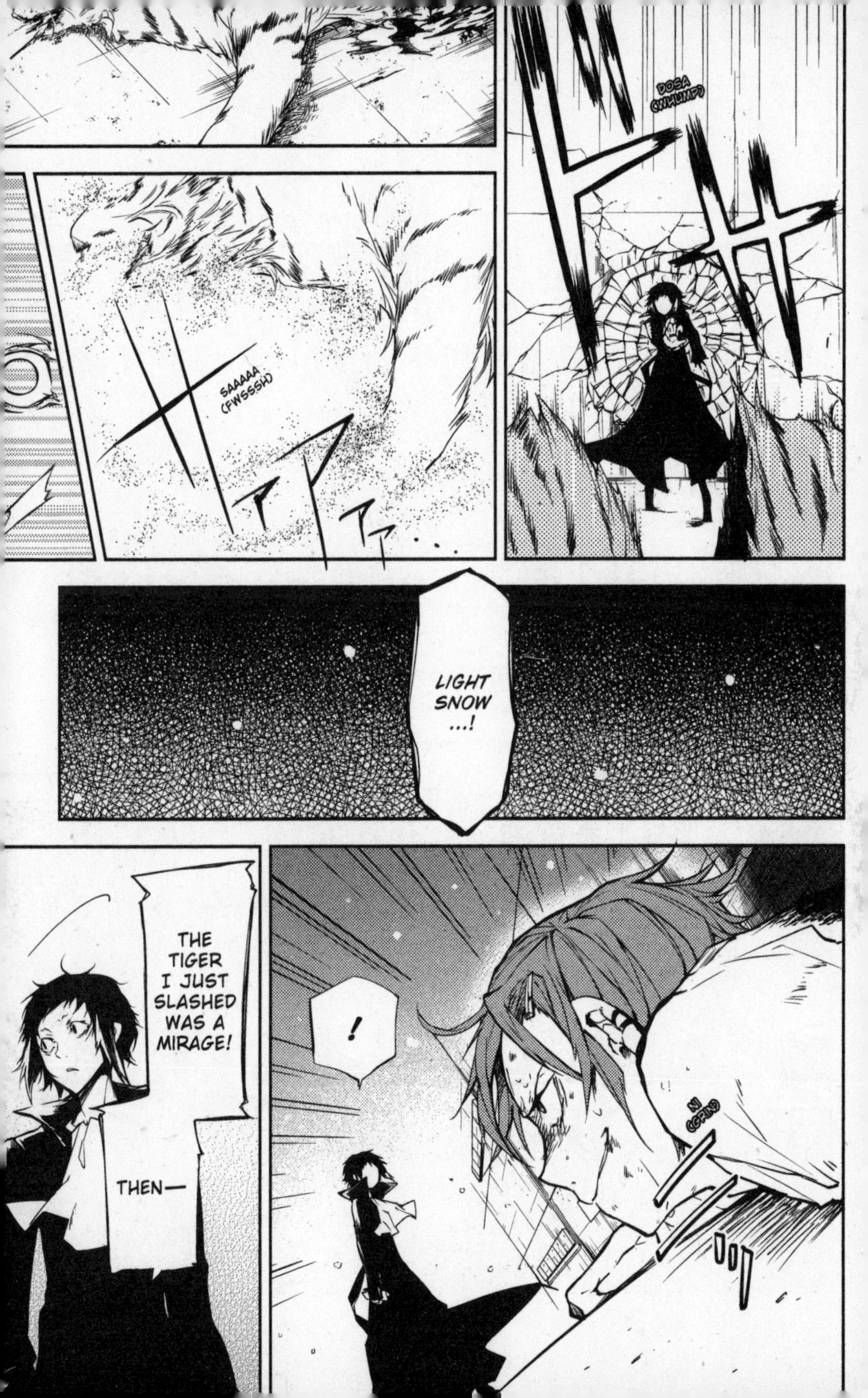
DOSA
(WHUMP)
SAAAAA
(FWSSSH)
LIGHT SNOW ...!
!
NI
(GRIND)
THE TIGER I JUST SLASHED WAS A MIRAGE!
THEN—

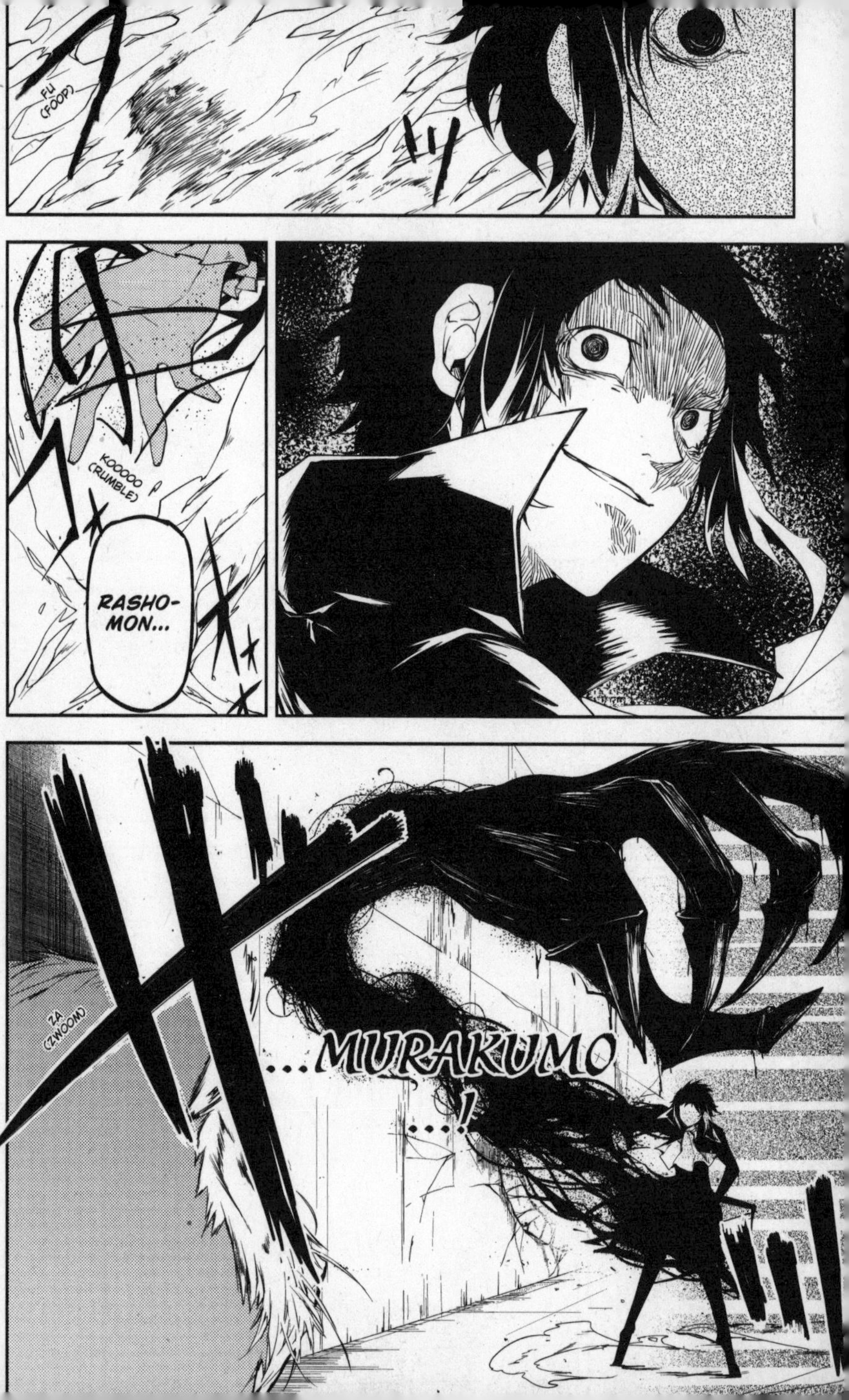
FU (FOOP)
KOOOOO (RUMBLE)
RASHO-MON...
...MURAKUMO
...!
ZA (ZWOOM)

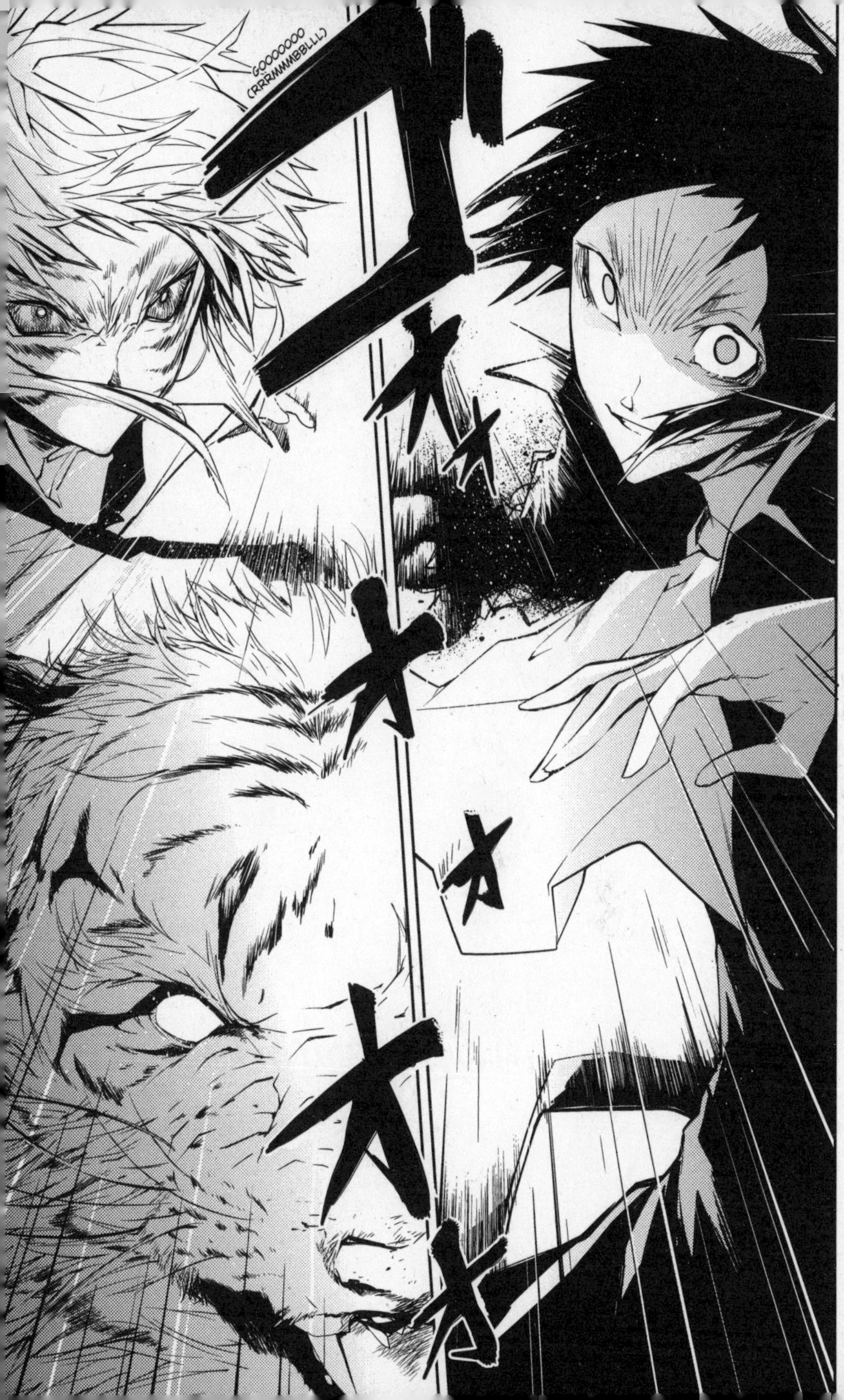
GOOOOOOO
(RRRMMMBBLLL)

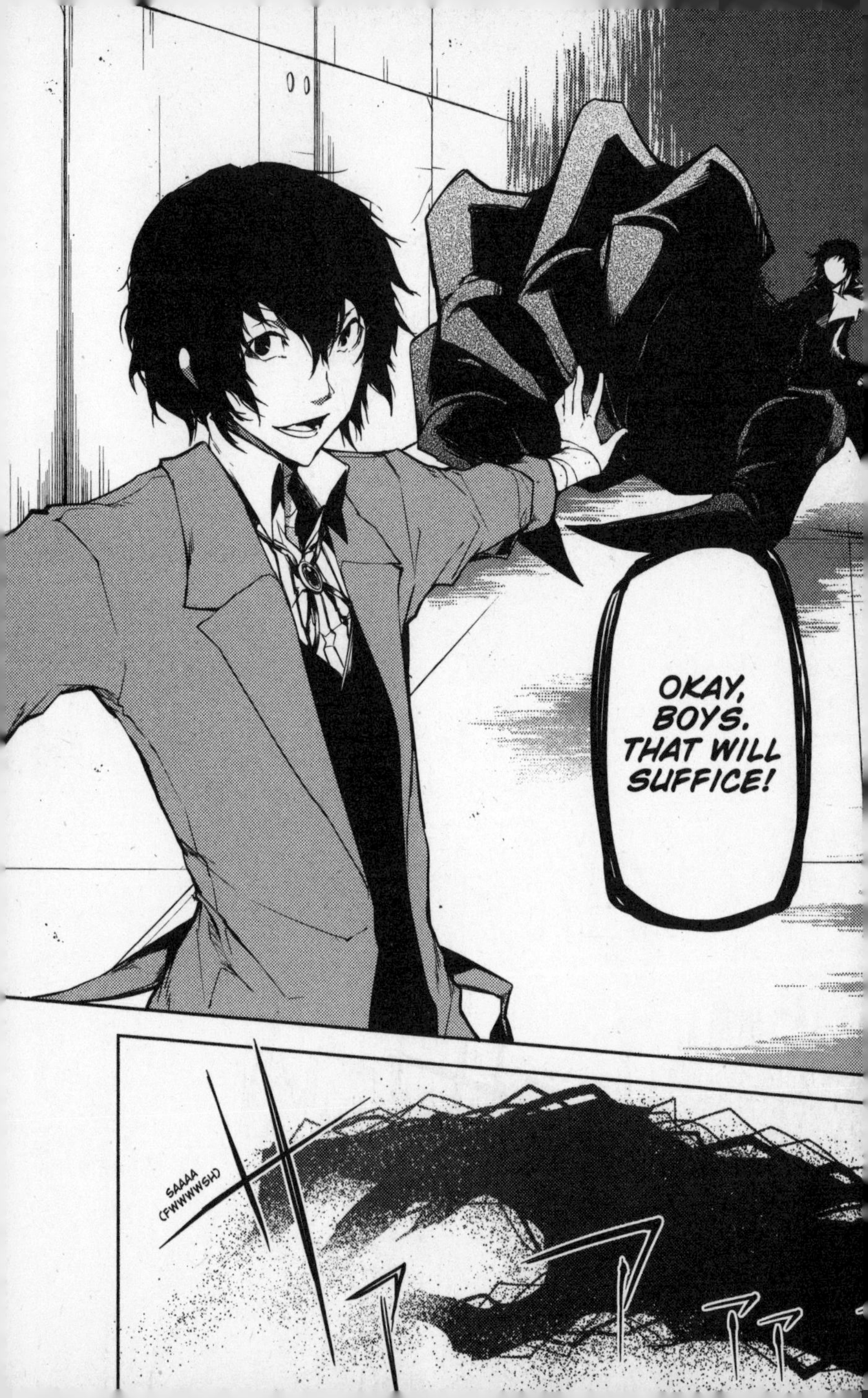
OKAY, BOYS. THAT WILL SUFFICE!
SAAAA (FWWWWSH)

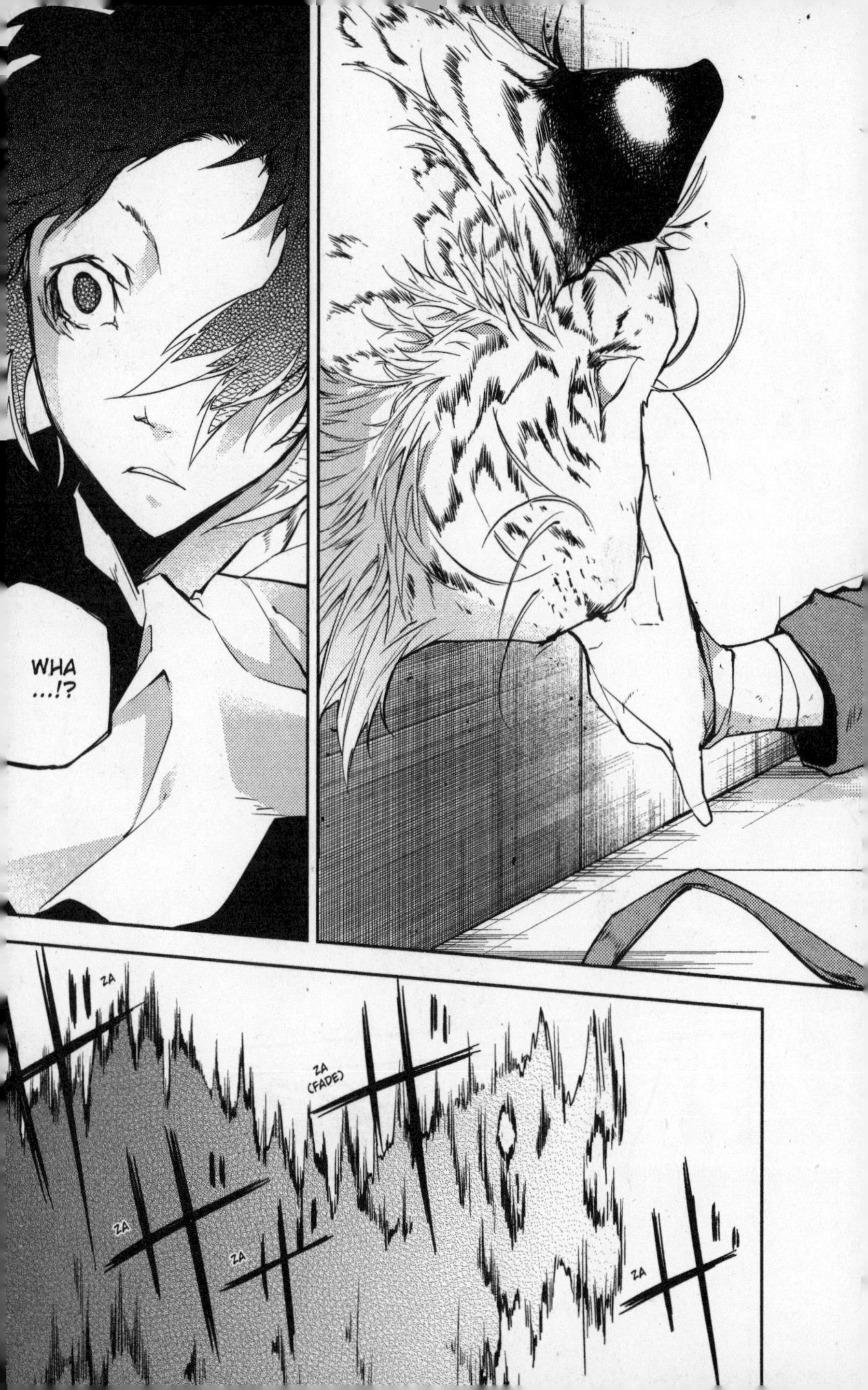
WHA ...!?
ZA (FADE)
ZA
ZA
ZA
ZA

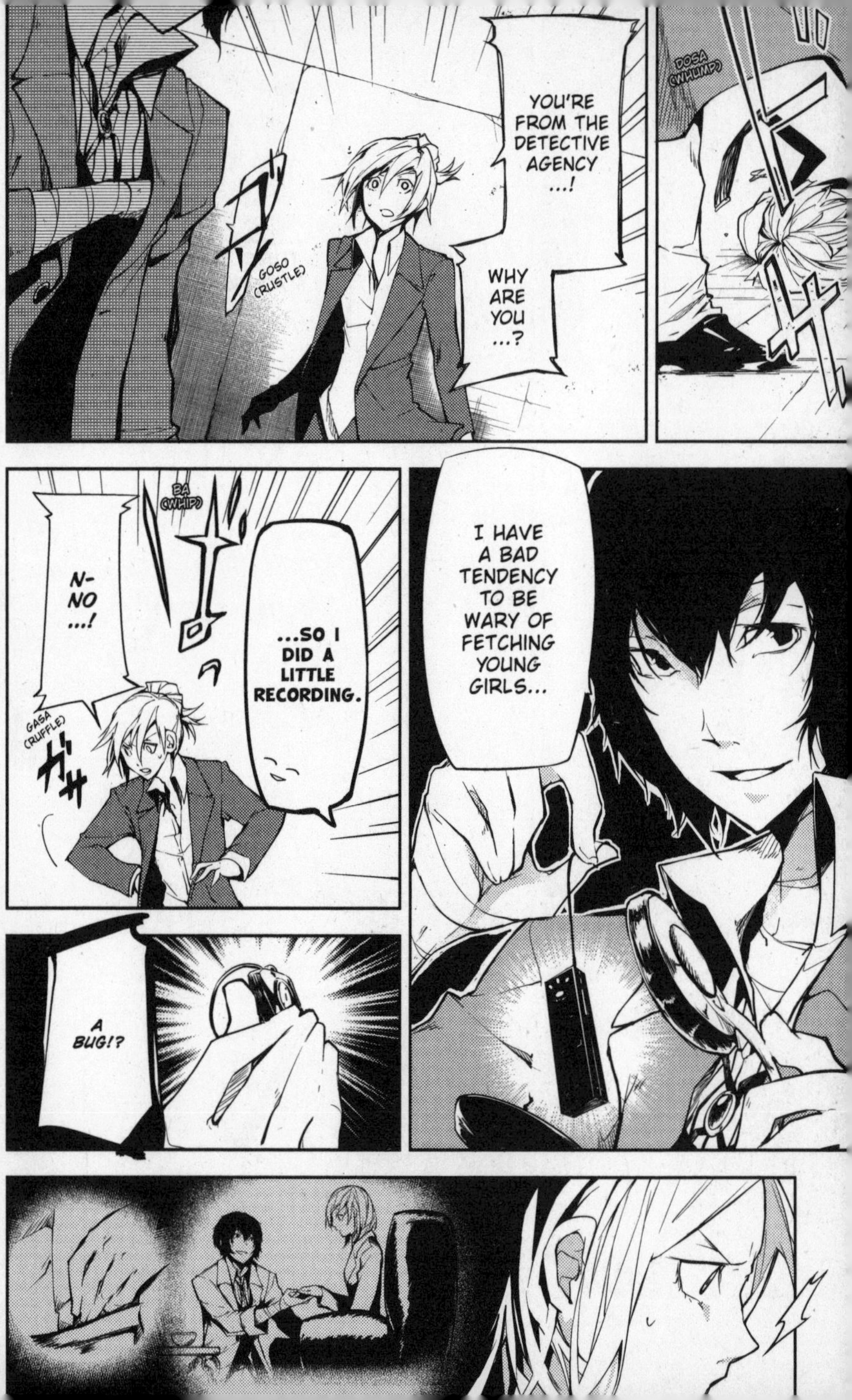
DOSA (WHUMP)
YOU'RE FROM THE DETECTIVE AGENCY ...!
WHY ARE YOU ...?
GOSO (RUSTLE)
I HAVE A BAD TENDENCY TO BE WARY OF FETCHING YOUNG GIRLS...
BA (WHIP)
...SO I DID A LITTLE RECORDING.
N-NO ...!
GASA (RUFFLE)
A BUG!?

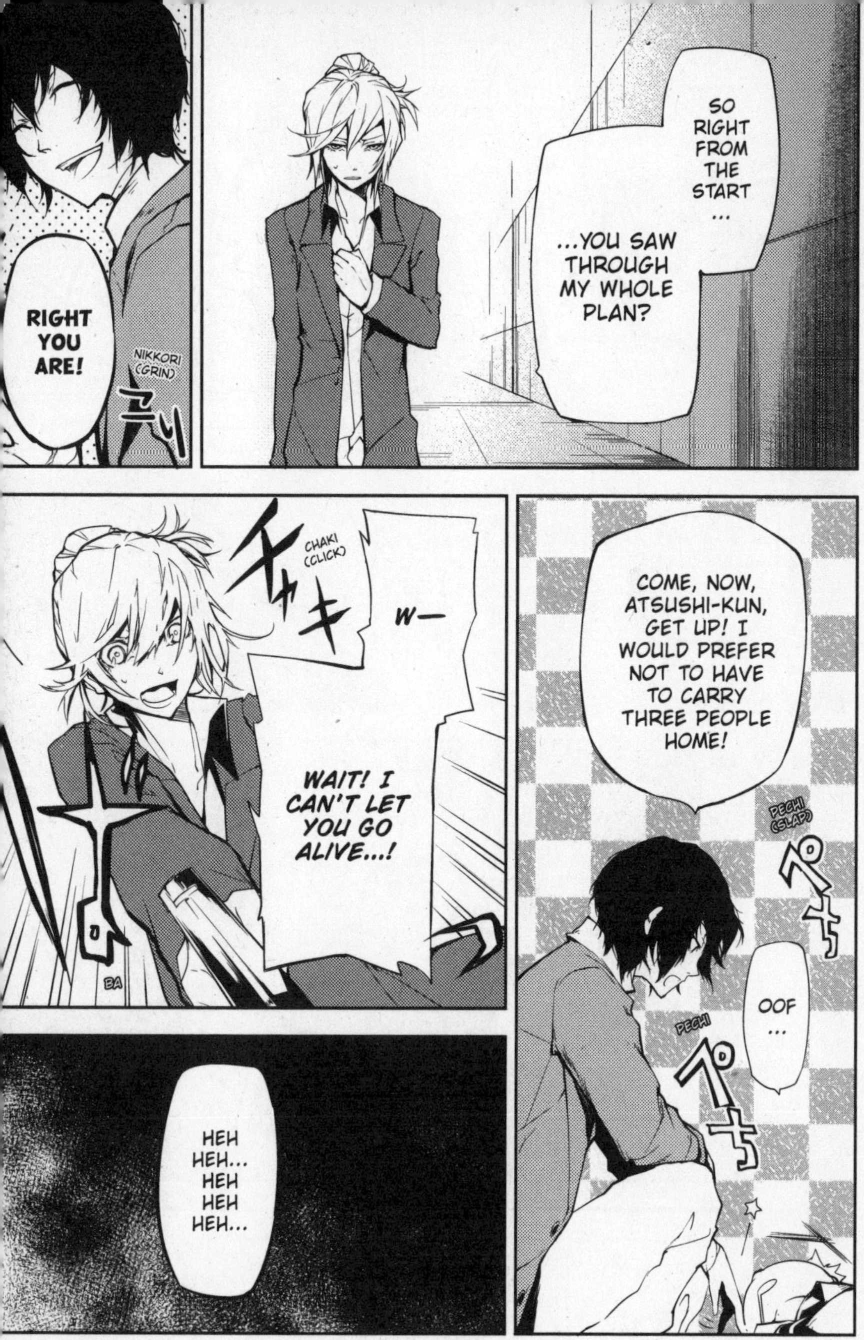

SO RIGHT FROM THE START...
...YOU SAW THROUGH MY WHOLE PLAN?
RIGHT YOU ARE!
NIKKORI (GRIN)
COME, NOW, ATSUSHI-KUN, GET UP! I WOULD PREFER NOT TO HAVE TO CARRY THREE PEOPLE HOME!
PECHI (SLAP)
OOF...
PECHI
CHAKI (CLICK)
W—
WAIT! I CAN'T LET YOU GO ALIVE...!
BA
HEH HEH... HEH HEH HEH...

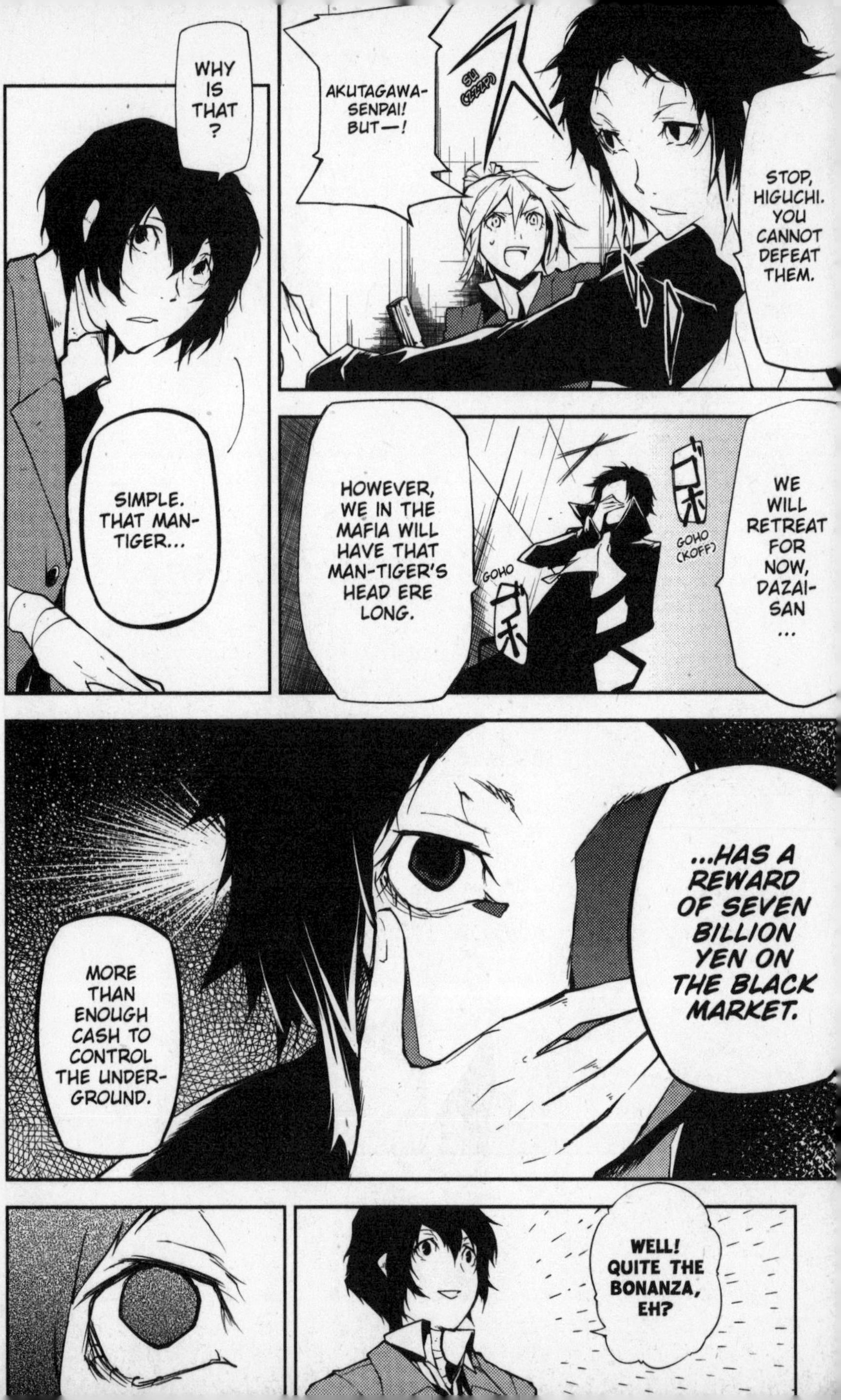
STOP, HIGUCHI. YOU CANNOT DEFEAT THEM.
AKUTAGAWA-SENPAI! BUT—!
WE WILL RETREAT FOR NOW, DAZAI-SAN...
GOHO (KOFF)
GOHO
HOWEVER, WE IN THE MAFIA WILL HAVE THAT MAN-TIGER'S HEAD ERE LONG.
WHY IS THAT?
SIMPLE. THAT MAN-TIGER...
...HAS A REWARD OF SEVEN BILLION YEN ON THE BLACK MARKET.
MORE THAN ENOUGH CASH TO CONTROL THE UNDER-GROUND.
WELL! QUITE THE BONANZA, EH?

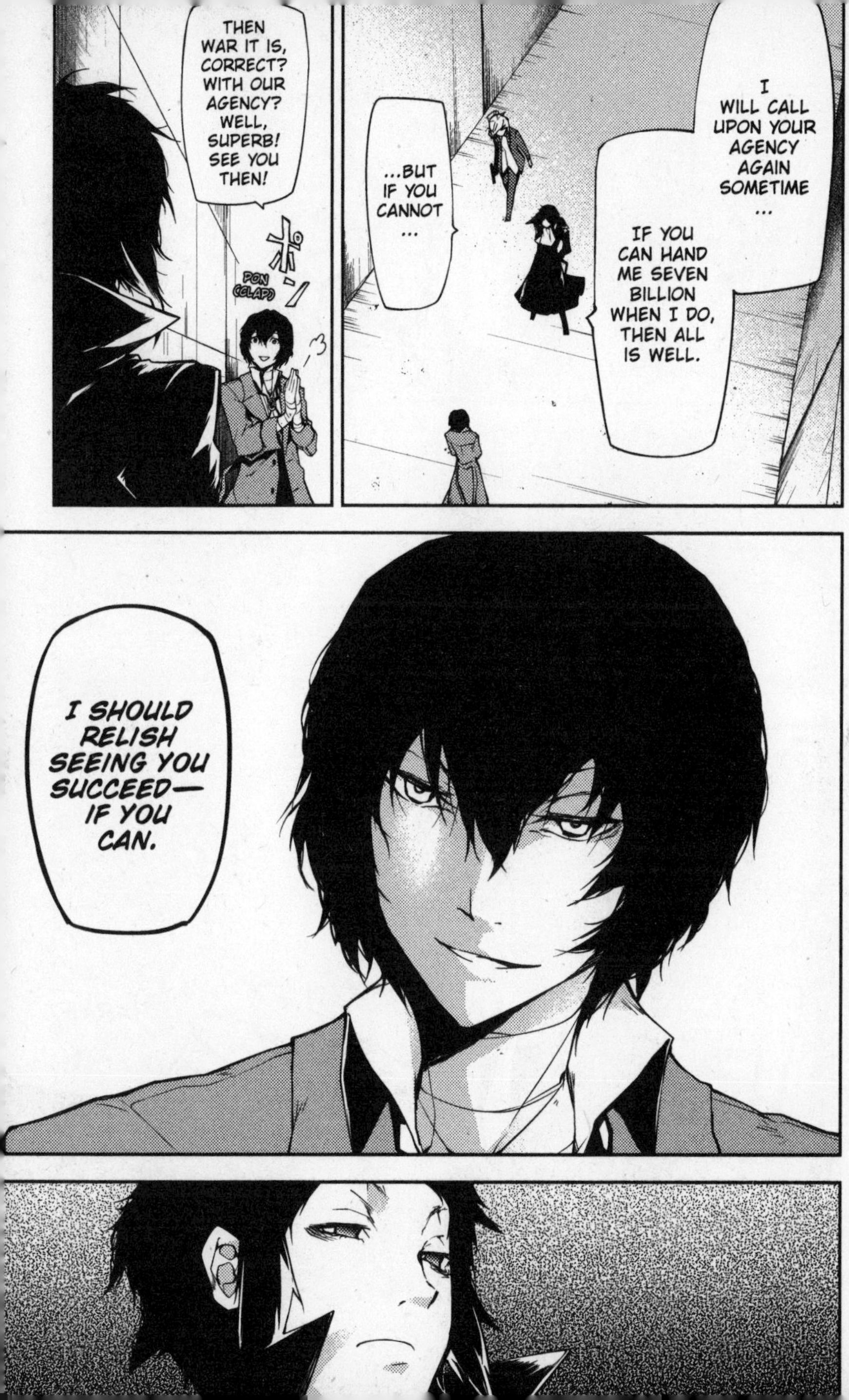
I WILL CALL UPON YOUR AGENCY AGAIN SOMETIME...
IF YOU CAN HAND ME SEVEN BILLION WHEN I DO, THEN ALL IS WELL.
...BUT IF YOU CANNOT...
THEN WAR IT IS, CORRECT? WITH OUR AGENCY? WELL, SUPERB! SEE YOU THEN!
ポン
PON (CLAP)
I SHOULD RELISH SEEING YOU SUCCEED—IF YOU CAN.

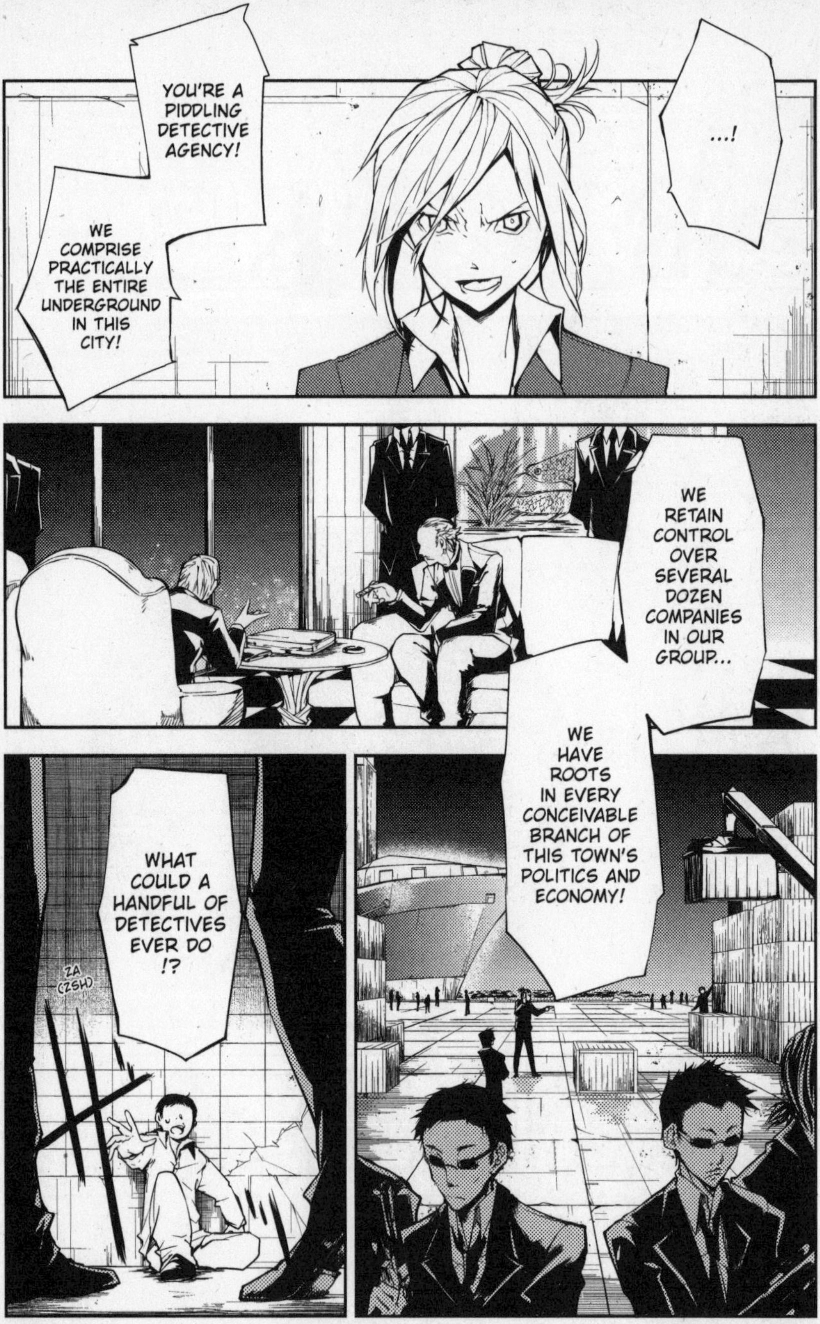
...!
YOU'RE A PIDDLING DETECTIVE AGENCY!
WE COMPRISE PRACTICALLY THE ENTIRE UNDERGROUND IN THIS CITY!
WE RETAIN CONTROL OVER SEVERAL DOZEN COMPANIES IN OUR GROUP...
WE HAVE ROOTS IN EVERY CONCEIVABLE BRANCH OF THIS TOWN'S POLITICS AND ECONOMY!
WHAT COULD A HANDFUL OF DETECTIVES EVER DO !?
ZA (ZSH)

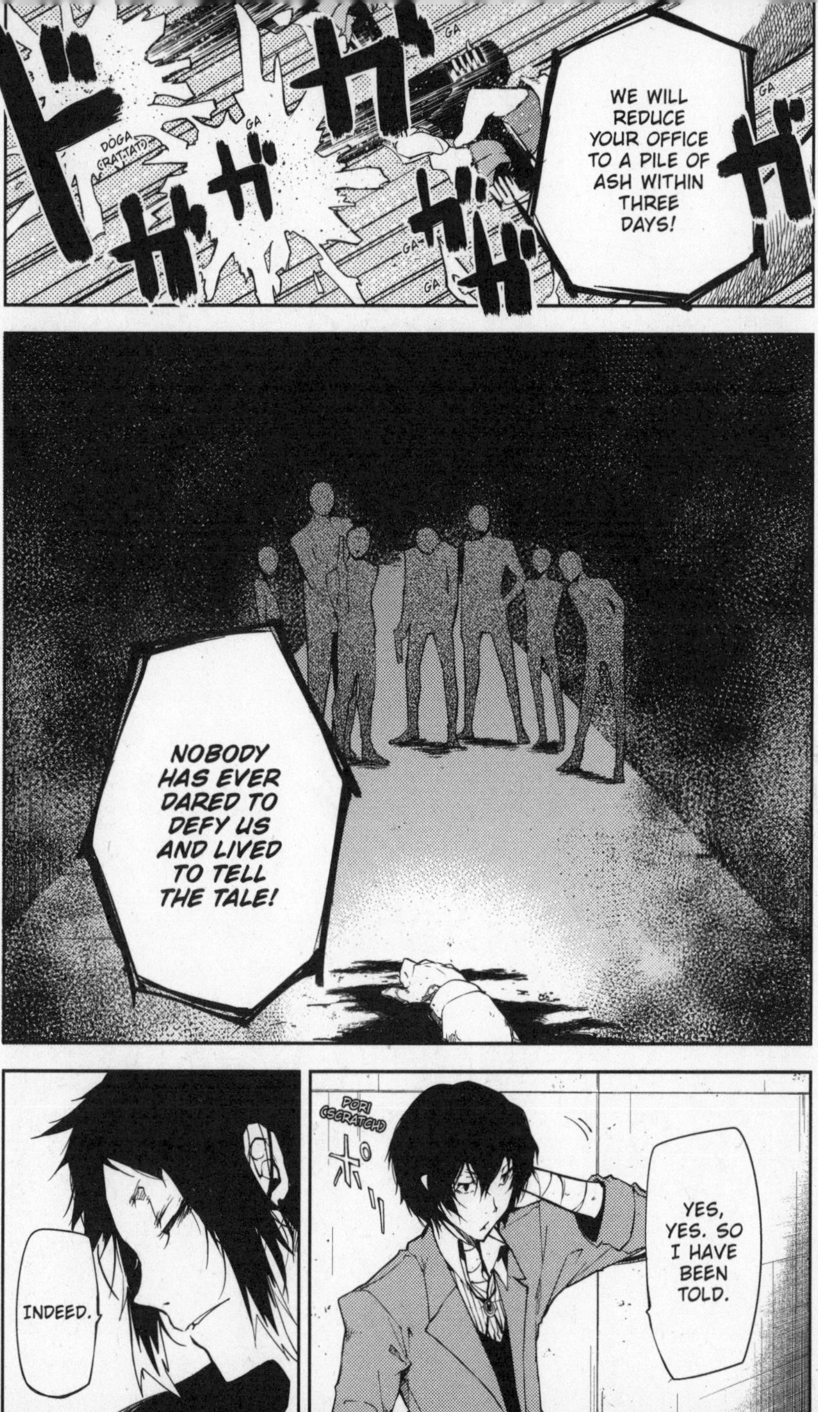
GA
GA
DOGA (RAT-TAT)
GA
GA
GA
WE WILL REDUCE YOUR OFFICE TO A PILE OF ASH WITHIN THREE DAYS!
NOBODY HAS EVER DARED TO DEFY US AND LIVED TO TELL THE TALE!
PORI (SCRATCH)
YES, YES. SO I HAVE BEEN TOLD.
INDEED.

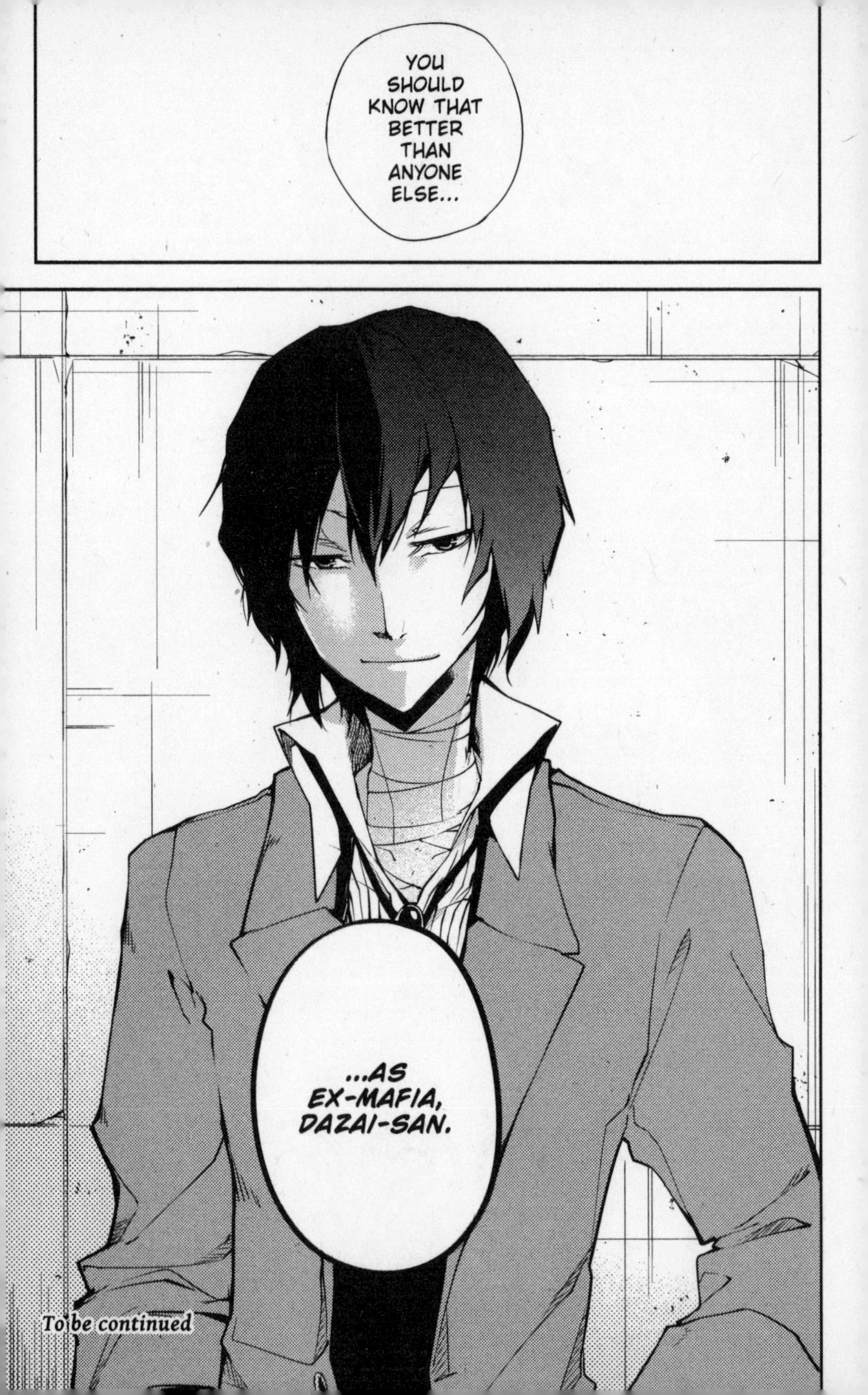
YOU SHOULD KNOW THAT BETTER THAN ANYONE ELSE...
...AS EX-MAFIA, DAZAI-SAN.
To be continued

BUNGO STRAY DOGS

DAZAI: So—! Here we are at the postscript, then.

ATSUSHI: Um...What? We're handling this? Isn't the author supposed to talk a bunch on this page?

DAZAI: The writer Asagiri, you mean? He ran off on us. I heard him shouting "The postscript would make me stand out too much! I'd be so embarrassed, I'd die on the spot!" He basically has the sense of presence of an inchworm, you see.

ATSUSHI: I'm impressed he could write anything at all...So what should we talk about?

DAZAI: Well, I have a rough draft on me, and I suppose we can make it a comedy-duo type of thing as we go. I'll be the straight man, so get going with the jokes, all right?

ATSUSHI: Huhh!? Me!? I really think you're more suited for that character-wise, Dazai-san.

DAZAI: ...Mm?

ATSUSHI: ...Right. Okay, then. Some jokes. Where should I start though?

DAZAI: Decide for yourself, Atsushi-kun.

ATSUSHI: Well, how about something about how this story got its start, then? That seems suitable for a postscript.

DAZAI: Umm...Oh, here's something from the draft. "I talked about how it'd be cool if the old guard of Japanese poets and novelists was remade into dashing young men with supernatural abilities, and the editorial room started going nuts for it."

ATSUSHI: That's certainly a...vivid word picture he's drawing there.

DAZAI: Yeah...You know, I don't think this approach is all that funny, is it?

ATSUSHI: Something brighter and happier might work, don't you think?

DAZAI: Nice. I like it. Brighter and happier. So what'll it be, Atsushi-kun?

ATSUSHI: Huh?

DAZAI: I still haven't heard any jokes from you.

ATSUSHI: ...Huh?

DAZAI: It's been about twenty lines of text since we assigned our roles for this postscript. Where's the comedy? I don't have anything to be "straight" about.

ATSUSHI: Huh!? Well, let's see...Umm...Oh, how about this? Look at my hand. I've got an apple perched on top of it.

DAZAI: Uh-huh...

ATSUSHI: ...Ha-ha! Just kidding! There's no apple at all! It's just a bunch of words!

DAZAI: Atsushi-kun...do you even know how to be a comedian?

ATSUSHI: I'm sorry...Maybe I don't, huh?

DAZAI: Okay, well, think of it this way. Just think about the stupidest person you've ever met in your life and imitate the guy. It's easy.

ATSUSHI: I see. Is that all there is to it?

DAZAI: More or less. Now give it a shot!

ATSUSHI: "Oooh, I wish there was a fast, non-painful suicide method anybody could pull off... preferably for free..."

DAZAI: ...

ATSUSHI: ...

DAZAI: Atsushi-kun...

ATSUSHI: Yeah...?

DAZAI: That was kinda funny.

ATSUSHI: Huh!?

To be continued (really?)

BUNGO
STRAY DOGS

Story: Kafka Asagiri   *Art: Sango Harukawa*

Translation: Kevin Gifford   †   Lettering: Bianca Pistillo

BUNGO STRAY DOGS Volume 1
©Kafka ASAGIRI 2013
©Sango HARUKAWA 2013
First published in Japan in 2013 by KADOKAWA CORPORATION, Tokyo.
English translation rights arranged with KADOKAWA CORPORATION, Tokyo through TUTTLE-MORI AGENCY, INC., Tokyo.

English translation © 2016 by Yen Press, LLC

Yen Press
1290 Avenue of the Americas
New York, NY 10104

Visit us at yenpress.com
facebook.com/yenpress
twitter.com/yenpress
yenpress.tumblr.com
instagram.com/yenpress

First Yen Press Edition: December 2016

Yen Press is an imprint of Yen Press, LLC.
The Yen Press name and logo are trademarks of Yen Press, LLC.

The publisher is not responsible for websites (or their content) that are not owned by the publisher.

Library of Congress Control Number: 2016956681

ISBNs: 978-0-316-55470-1 (paperback)
       978-0-316-46824-4 (ebook)

10 9 8 7 6 5

WOR

Printed in the United States of America

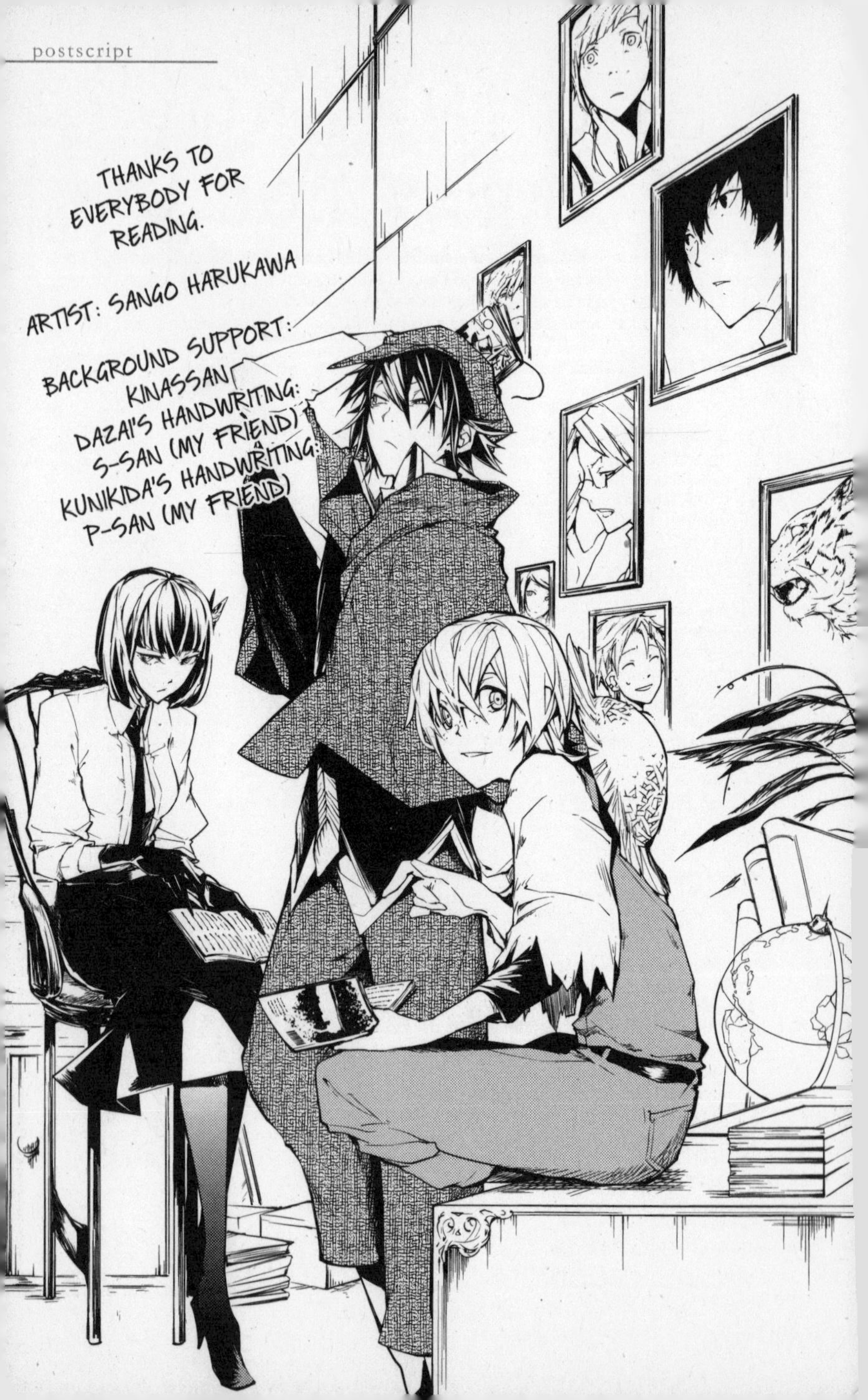
THANKS TO EVERYBODY FOR READING.
ARTIST: SANGO HARUKAWA
BACKGROUND SUPPORT: KINASSAN
DAZAI'S HANDWRITING: S-SAN (MY FRIEND)
KUNIKIDA'S HANDWRITING: P-SAN (MY FRIEND)